To Build a City in Africa

A History and a Manual

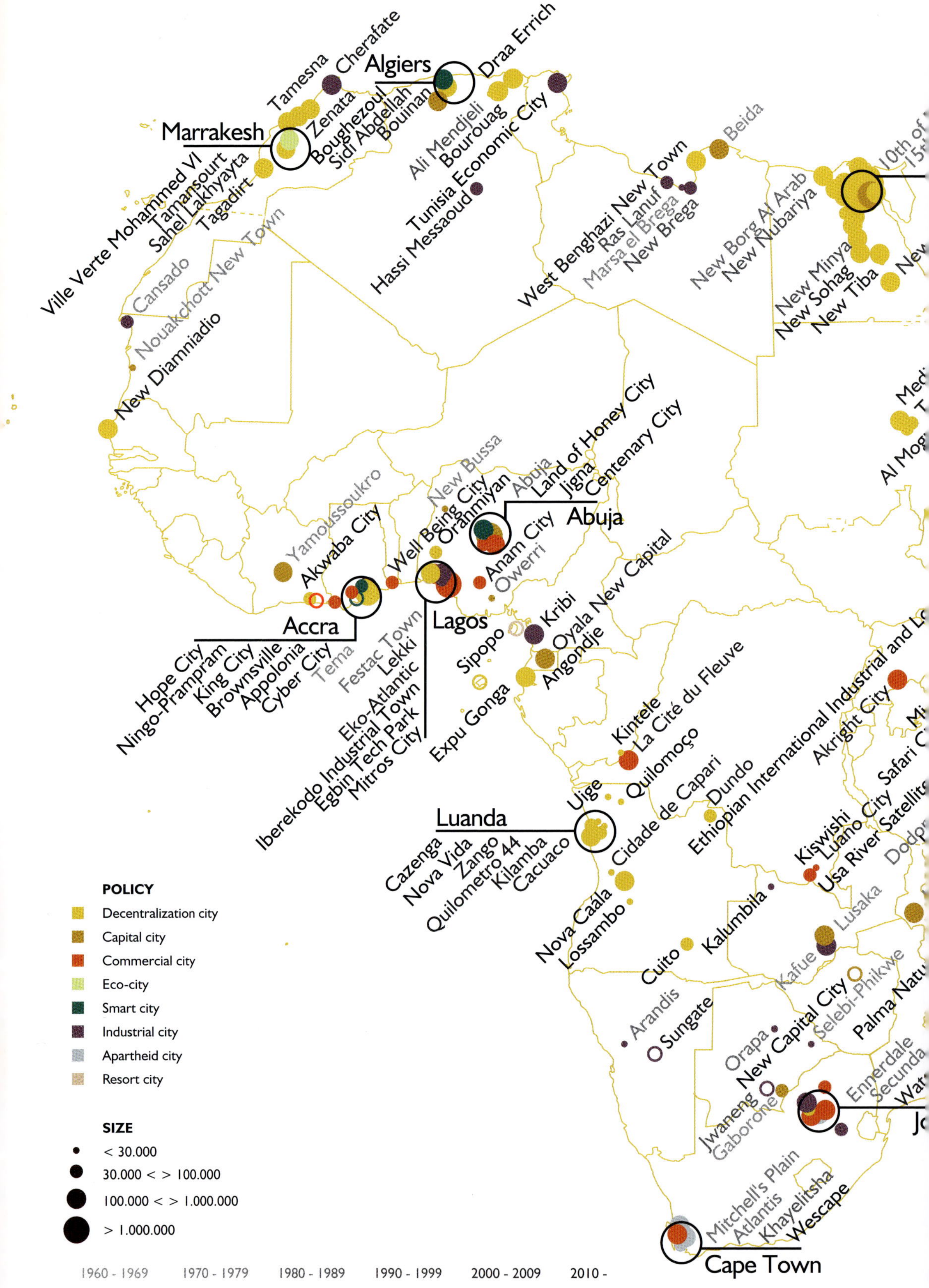

Marrakesh
Algiers
Tamesna
Cherafate
Zenata
Boughezoul
Sidi Abdellah
Bouinan
Draa Errich
Ali Mendjeli
Bourouag
Tunisia Economic City
Hassi Messaoud
Ville Verte Mohammed VI
Tamansourt
Sahel Lakhyayta
Tagadirt
Cansado
Nouakchott New Town
New Diamniadio
Beida
West Benghazi New Town
Ras Lanuf
Marsa el Brega
New Brega
New Borg Al Arab
New Nubariya
New Minya
New Sohag
New Tiba
10th of
15t
New
Medi
Al Mog
Yamoussoukro
Akwaba City
Well Being City
New Bussa
Oranmiyan
Abuja
Land of Honey City
Jigna
Centenary City
Abuja
Anam City
Owerri
Accra
Lagos
Hope City
Ningo-Prampram
King City
Brownsville
Appolonia
Cyber City
Tema
Festac Town
Lekki
Eko-Atlantic
Iberekodo Industrial Town
Egbin Tech Park
Mitros City
Sipopo
Kribi
Oyala New Capital
Angondje
Expu Gonga
Kintele
La Cité du Fleuve
Quilomoço
Uige
Cidade de Capari
Dundo
Ethiopian International Industrial and L
Akright City
Safari C
Luanda
Cazenga
Nova Vida
Zango
Quilometro 44
Kilamba
Cacuaco
Kiswishi
Luano City
Usa River Satellit
Dodo
Nova Caála
Lossambo
Kalumbila
Lusaka
Cuito
Kafue
Arandis
Sungate
Orapa
New Capital City
Selebi-Phikwe
Palma Natu
Jwaneng
Gaborone
Ennerdale
Secunda
Wat
Mitchell's Plain
Atlantis
Khayelitsha
Wescape
Cape Town
POLICY
Decentralization city
Capital city
Commercial city
Eco-city
Smart city
Industrial city
Apartheid city
Resort city
SIZE
< 30.000
30.000 < > 100.000
100.000 < > 1.000.000
> 1.000.000
1960 - 1969
1970 - 1979
1980 - 1989
1990 - 1999
2000 - 2009
2010 -

To Build a City in Africa

A HISTORY AND A MANUAL

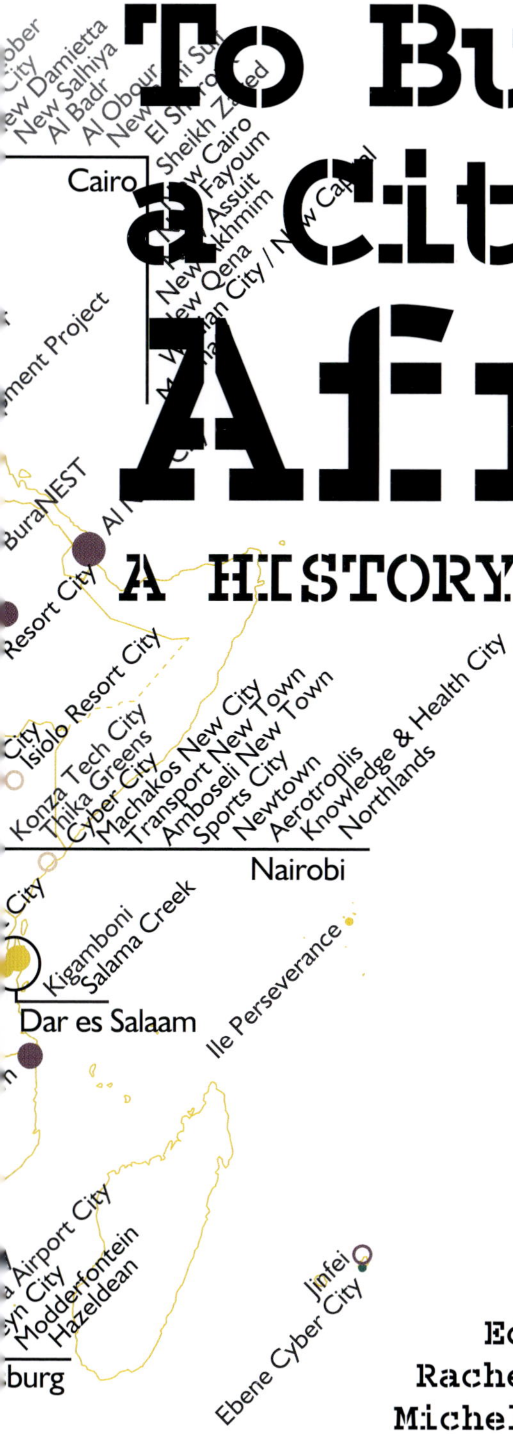

Edited by
Rachel Keeton &
Michelle Provoost

International New Town Institute

nai010 publishers

Editors: Rachel Keeton, Michelle Provoost
Copy editing: Gilles Provoost
Graphic design and cartography: Ewout Dorman
(Crimson Historians and Urbanists)
Printing: Wilco Art Books, Amersfoort
Paper: Condat Matt Perigord
Production: Milou van Lieshout, nai010 publishers
Publisher: nai010 publishers

This publication was made possible by financial support from the Creative Industries Fund NL, the EFL Foundation and UN-Habitat.

nai010 publishers is an internationally orientated publisher specialised in developing, producing and distributing books in the fields of architecture, urbanism, art and design.
www.nai010.com

nai010 books are available internationally at selected bookstores and from the following distribution partners:

North, Central and South America - Artbook | D.A.P., New York, USA, dap@dapinc.com

Rest of the world - Idea Books, Amsterdam, the Netherlands, idea@ideabooks.nl

For general questions, please contact nai010 publishers directly at sales@nai010.com or visit our website www.nai010.com for further information.

Printed and bound in the Netherlands

ISBN 978-94-6208-392-9

NUR 648
BISAC ARC010000, SOC026030, POL002000

Also available as:
To Build a City in Africa (e-book)
ISBN 978-94-6208-409-4

creative industries fund NL

EFL STICHTING

Introduction

PART I An Atlas

PART II A Manual

PART III A History

Tema (1960), Ghana (Photo: M. Provoost, 2007)

Dodoma (1973), Tanzania. (Photo: A. Pronkhorst, 2009)

12

Appolonia (2012), Ghana. (Photo: M. Provoost, 2018)

Sheikh Zayed (1995), Egypt. (Photo: R. Keeton, 2016)

6th of October (1979), Egypt. (Photo: R. Keeton, 2016)

New Towns in Africa 1960-2017

	year	target population
Algeria		
Ali Mendjeli	1988	335,000
Bouinan	2004	150,000
Sidi Abdallah	2004	500,000
Boughezoul	2004	350,000
Hassi Messaoud	2005	80,000
Bourouag	2009	18,000
Draa Errich	2012	250,000
Angola		
Cidade de Capari	2007	24,000
Zango	2007	254,000
Cacuaco / Dande	2008	60,000
Kilamba	2008	100,000
Quilometro 44	2008	13,000
Dundo	2009	90,000
Nova Vida	2012	46,000
Cuito	2013	30,000
Cazenga	2013	20,000
Uige	2013	22,500
Lossambo	2013	11,000
Quilomoço	2013	27,000
Nova Caála	2017	20,000
Botswana		
Gaborone	1963	88,000
Orapa	1971	10,000
Selebi Phikwe	1973	25,000
Jwaneng	1982	-
Cameroon		
Kribi Industrial Port Complex	2012	300,000
Congo DRC		
La Cité du Fleuve	2008	250,000
Luano City	2008	16,000
Kiswishi	2016	90,000
Congo Republic		
Kintele	2012	10,000
Côte d'Ivoire		
Yamoussoukro	1965	200,000
Akwaba City	2014	54,000
Brownsville	2017	-
Djibouti		
Al Noor City	2007	2,500,000
Egypt		
10th of Ramadan	1976	500,000
15th of May	1978	500,000
Sadat City	1978	1,000,000
6th of October	1979	6,000,000
New Borg Al Arab-New Ameriya	1979	570,000
New Damietta	1980	500,000
Al Badr	1982	840,000
Al Obour	1982	600,000
New Salhiya	1982	120,000
New Beni Suif	1986	268,000
New Minya	1986	638,000
New Nubariya	1987	80,000
El Shorouk	1995	500,000
Sheikh Zayed	1995	675,000
New Aswan	1999	850,000
New Akhmim	2000	120,000
New Assuit	2000	750,000
New Fayoum	2000	100,000
New Qena	2000	130,000
New Sohag	2000	820,000
New Tiba	2000	195,000
New Cairo	2009	200,000
Madinaty	2011	660,000
Wedian City New Capital City	2015	5,000,000
Equatorial Guinea		
Oyala New Capital Djibloho	2000	200,000
Sipopo	2011	-
Ethiopia		
BuraNEST	2010	40,000
Ethiopian International Industrial and Logistics City	2017	100,000
Gabon		
Angondje	2012	100,000
Ghana		
Tema	1960	250,000
King City	2011	90,000
Appolonia	2012	88,000
Hope City	2013	65,000
Ghana Cyber City	2015	-
Ningo-Prampram	2015	1,500,000
Kenya		
Konza Tech City	2008	250,000
Thika Greens	2009	17,000
Tatu City	2010	150,000
Northlands	2011	270,000
Migaa	2012	-
Aerotropolis	2013	100,000
Amboseli New Town	2013	100,000
Cyber city	2013	-
Knowledge/health city	2013	-
Sports city	2013	100,000
Transport city	2013	-
Isiolo Resort City	2016	-
Lamu Resort City	2016	476,000
Newtown	2016	40,000
Turkana Resort City	2016	-
Machakos New City	2017	-
Libya		
Marsa el Brega	1962	20,000
Beida (Al Bayda)	1966	100,000
Ras Lanuf	1981	40,000

	year	target population
New Brega	1984	45,000
West Benghazi New Town	2008	100,000

Malawi

	year	target population
Lilongwe	1965	500,000

Mauritania

	year	target population
Nouakchott New Town	1957	15,000
Cansado	1963	35,000

Mauritius

	year	target population
Ebene Cyber City	2001	25,000
Jinfei	2006	-

Morocco

	year	target population
Tamesna	2004	250,000
Tamansourt	2005	400,000
Sahel Lakhyayta	2006	300,000
Tagadirt	2006	200,000
Zenata	2006	300,000
Cherafate	2009	150,000
Ville Verte Mohammed VI	2010	130,000

Mozambique

	year	target population
Palma Natural Gas Town	2014	250,000

Namibia

	year	target population
Arandis	1978	10,000
Sungate	2009	-

Nigeria

	year	target population
New Bussa	1962	24,000
Abuja	1976	3,000,000
Festac Town	1976	45,000
Owerri	1976	1,400,000
Eko-Atlantic	2003	250,000
Lekki	2006	3.400,000
Anam City	2009	30,000
Land of Honey City	2010	100,000
Centenary City	2013	450,000
Egbin Tech Park	2013	250,000
Oranmiyan New Town	2013	80,000
Iberekodo Industrial Town	2015	60,000
Jigna	2015	30,000
Mitros City	2016	180,000

São Tome e Príncipé

	year	target population
Expu Gonga	2014	-

Senegal

	year	target population
New Diamniadio	2000	300,000

Seychelles

	year	target population
Ile Perseverance	2002	10,000

South Africa

	year	target population
Mitchell's Plain	1970	250,000
Atlantis	1972	500,000
Secunda	1974	40,000
Ennerdale	1976	300,000
Khayelitsha	1983	30,000
Waterfall City	2001	150,000
Cosmo City	2005	70,000
Lanseria Airport City	2008	150,000
Wescape	2012	800,000
Modderfontein	2013	100,000
Steyn City	2013	44,000
Hazeldean	2015	35,000

Sudan

	year	target population
Al Mogran Development Project	2004	58,000
Medinat Al-Nour	2009	-
Tuti Island	2009	40,000

Tanzania

	year	target population
Dodoma	1973	350,000
Kigamboni	2008	500,000
Safari City	2012	55,000
Usa River Satellite City	2012	-
Salama Creek	2014	50,000

Togo

	year	target population
Well Being City	2003	50,000

Tunisia

	year	target population
Tunisia Economic City	2014	500,000

Uganda

	year	target population
Akright City	2002	144,000

Zambia

	year	target population
Lusaka	1960	100,000
Kafue	1967	100,000
Kalumbila	2012	15,000

Zimbabwe

	year	target population
New Capital City (at Mt Hampden)	2012	-

total New Towns	total target population
148	47,508,500

Sometimes it was impossible to find the target populations of the New Towns in this inventory. In that case, we have stated the actual population using the most recent available figures (2018). Figures are based on multiple sources where possible, however, discrepancies and inconsistencies do appear. Especially in Egypt, figures from NUCA, the census and UN-Habitat differ widely. We have judged to the best of our ability what figures to choose and how to interpret them.

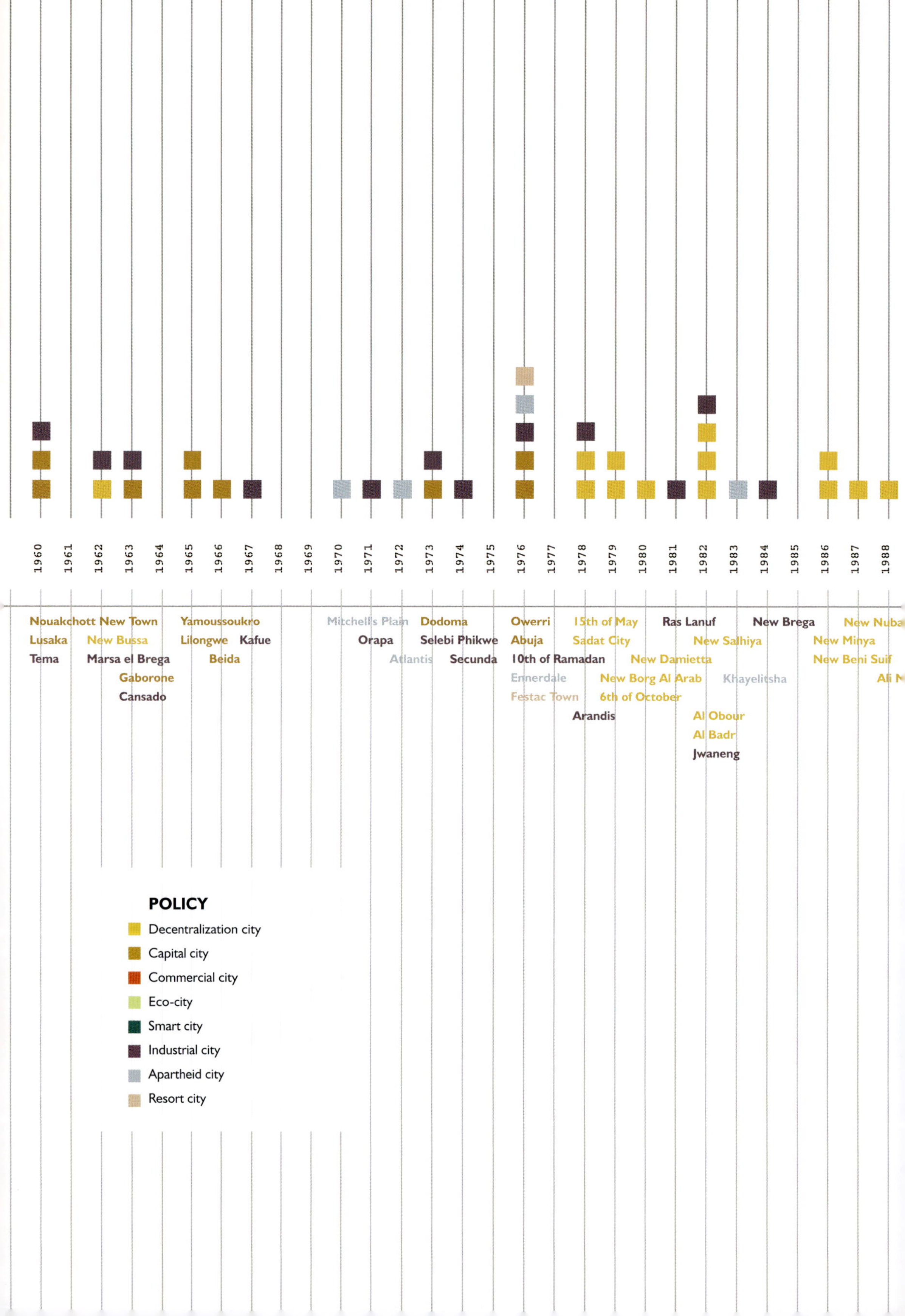
1960
1961
1962
1963
1964
1965
1966
1967
1968
1969
1970
1971
1972
1973
1974
1975
1976
1977
1978
1979
1980
1981
1982
1983
1984
1985
1986
1987
1988
Nouakchott New Town
Lusaka
Tema
New Bussa
Marsa el Brega
Gaborone
Cansado
Yamoussoukro
Lilongwe
Kafue
Beida
Mitchells Plain
Orapa
Atlantis
Dodoma
Selebi Phikwe
Secunda
Owerri
Abuja
10th of Ramadan
Ennerdale
Festac Town
15th of May
Sadat City
Arandis
New Damietta
New Borg Al Arab
6th of October
Ras Lanuf
New Salhiya
Al Obour
Al Badr
Jwaneng
Khayelitsha
New Brega
New Nuba
New Minya
New Beni Suif
POLICY
Decentralization city
Capital city
Commercial city
Eco-city
Smart city
Industrial city
Apartheid city
Resort city

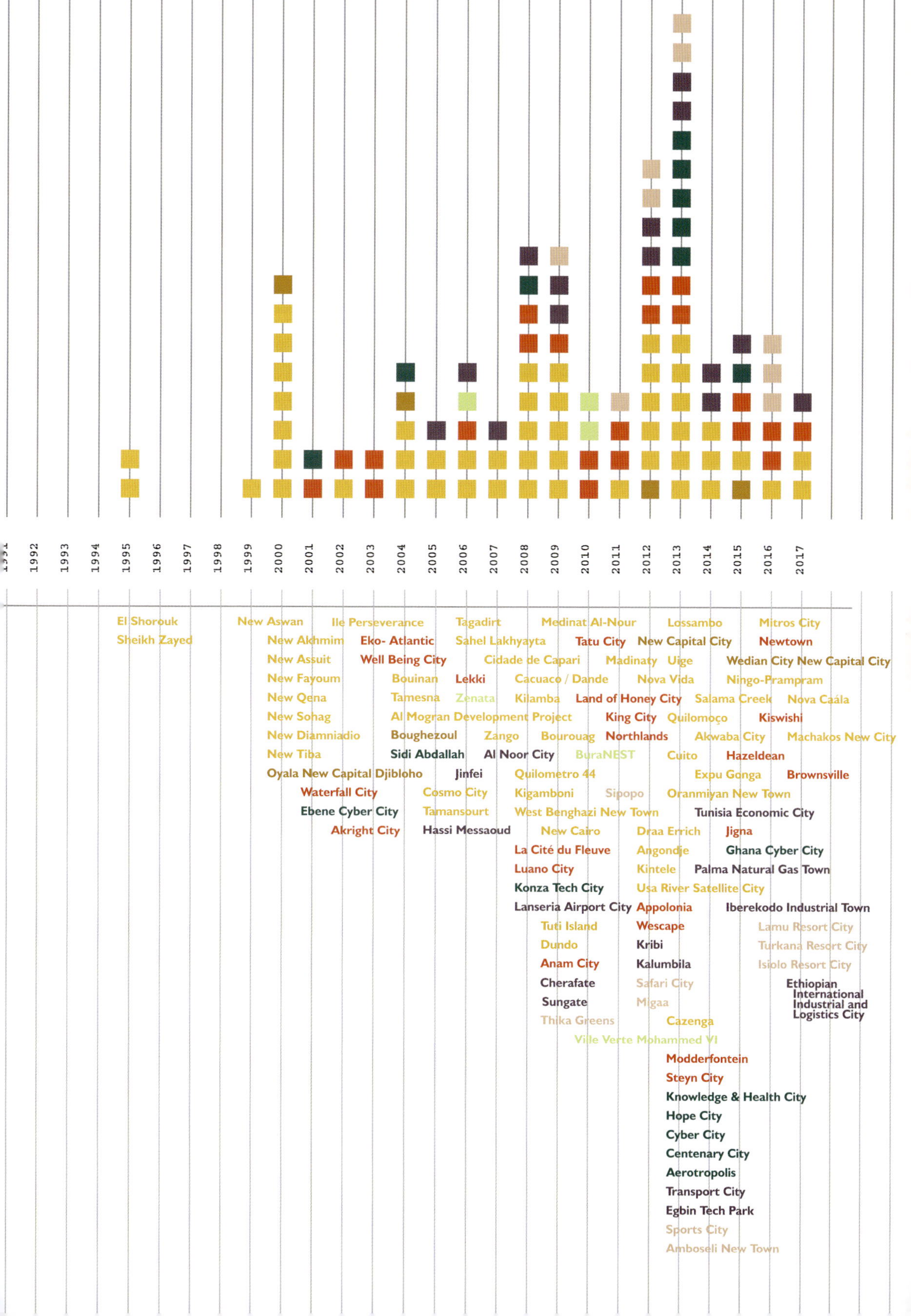
1992
1993
1994
1995
1996
1997
1998
1999
2000
2001
2002
2003
2004
2005
2006
2007
2008
2009
2010
2011
2012
2013
2014
2015
2016
2017
El Shorouk
Sheikh Zayed
New Aswan
New Akhmim
New Assuit
New Fayoum
New Qena
New Sohag
New Diamniadio
New Tiba
Oyala New Capital Djibloho
Ile Perseverance
Eko- Atlantic
Well Being City
Waterfall City
Ebene Cyber City
Akright City
Bouinan
Tamesna
Al Mogran Development Project
Boughezoul
Sidi Abdallah
Cosmo City
Tamansourt
Hassi Messaoud
Tagadirt
Sahel Lakhyayta
Lekki
Zenata
Jinfei
Al Noor City
Cidade de Capari
Cacuaco / Dande
Kilamba
Zango
Quilometro 44
Kigamboni
West Benghazi New Town
Medinat Al-Nour
Tatu City
Madinaty
Bourouag
New Cairo
La Cité du Fleuve
Luano City
Konza Tech City
Lanseria Airport City
Tuti Island
Dundo
Anam City
Cherafate
Sungate
Thika Greens
Land of Honey City
King City
Northlands
BuraNEST
Sipopo
Ville Verte Mohammed VI
New Capital City
Nova Vida
Draa Errich
Angondje
Kintele
Usa River Satellite City
Appolonia
Wescape
Kribi
Kalumbila
Safari City
Migaa
Lossambo
Uige
Salama Creek
Quilomoço
Akwaba City
Cuito
Expu Gonga
Oranmiyan New Town
Cazenga
Modderfontein
Steyn City
Knowledge & Health City
Hope City
Cyber City
Centenary City
Aerotropolis
Transport City
Egbin Tech Park
Sports City
Amboseli New Town
Wedian City New Capital City
Ningo-Prampram
Tunisia Economic City
Jigna
Ghana Cyber City
Palma Natural Gas Town
Iberekodo Industrial Town
Mitros City
Newtown
Nova Caála
Kiswishi
Machakos New City
Hazeldean
Brownsville
Lamu Resort City
Turkana Resort City
Isiolo Resort City
Ethiopian International Industrial and Logistics City

Ato Gebeyehu Endale, BuraNEST.
(Photo: R. Keeton, 2017)

To Build a City in Africa

"It will improve our lives."

About an hour north from Bahir Dar, Ethiopia, a New Town called BuraNEST is slowly taking shape.[1] The project promises to completely transform the lives of a local farming community that has practiced subsistence agriculture for centuries. Outside his wattle and daub house on a sunny day in November 2017, Ato Gebeyehu Endale, one of the community leaders, described his aspirations for the planned development: 'I want to live a modern way of life. [In the New Town] we will have basic infrastructure facilities like water, electricity, and education. We can also think about our private businesses, like trade. It will improve our lives.'[2] These modest dreams reflect the hopes of almost all the (future) residents of New Towns in the eight African countries we traversed over the course of four years while conducting research for this book.[3] It is a simple but powerful truth that people everywhere, despite their differences, seem to want the same thing: the tools to build a good life, a safe home for their family, and the support of a strong social network. In Sheikh Zayed City, Egypt, residents of the New Town repeatedly pointed to their quiet suburban lifestyle as the main motivation behind their choice to leave Cairo for an unfinished city in the desert.[4] Kilamba, Angola, a New Town an hour outside of Luanda, offers residents reliable electricity, potable tap water, high quality educational facilities, traffic lights, and personal parking spaces. It is the only place in the country that is able to offer that combination of urban services - a seductive cocktail that makes it one of the most sought after addresses in Angola.

1 BuraNEST is elaborated in a case study on page 363.

2 Interview with Ato Gebeyehu Endale at BuraNEST, Ethiopia on 15 November 2017. Interviewed by Rachel Keeton, simultaneously translated by Bizuayehu Jembere.

3 Fieldwork for this book was conducted during the period 2015-2018 and involved multiple site visits by the editors in Angola, Egypt, Ethiopia, Ghana, Kenya, Morocco, South Africa, and Tanzania, in addition to the research conducted by the contributing authors.

4 Interviews with female (24), male (32), male (37), and female (35) in Sheikh Zayed City, Egypt in January 2016. Interviewed by Rachel Keeton.

5 Email to authors from Tim Beighton, Rendeavour, April 2018.
6 Keeton, R. (2011) *Rising in the East. Contemporary New Towns in Asia*. Amsterdam: SUN/INTI.

The concepts of a 'good life', safety, and belonging clearly take different forms in different places, but they start with the benefits of planning: roads, electric and water networks, and adequate housing.

To be clear from the start: this book does not advocate for New Towns. In fact, our research points to such universal challenges arising from this type of development that one might easily question their validity as an urban solution. On the other hand, new cities have been planned and built in Africa for centuries, and are unlikely to stop any time soon. They are a complex, and as one developer put it, 'academia-defying' phenomenon.[5] Our aim with this book is to understand the challenges endemic to the vast majority of contemporary New Towns across Africa, and based on that understanding, to offer a manual for future developments that provides an alternative, inclusive, and adaptive planning approach.

Many decision-makers we spoke with were daunted by the prospect of designing a New Town 'from scratch'. Where to begin? We hope this book provides one answer to that most basic of questions. If New Towns are to remain an important part of the story of Africa's urbanising century, we want them to be better.

What this book is and what it is not

This is a book about the design of cities, not about the process of urbanisation or even about the economy, technology or governance of cities. It is about the role of urban planning and urban design in the genesis of an entirely new generation of new cities and New Towns that is being produced right now on the African continent.

A quick word on terminology seems to be in order here: what do we mean by New Towns? In this book, we have defined a New Town as a comprehensively planned, mixed-use urban development intended for more than 10,000 residents, and displaying some degree of political autonomy. These are not urban extensions, or redevelopments of existing urban areas. New Towns have always been a small niche of the total picture of urbanisation, but as complete urban projects they represent the ambitions and values of their creators perhaps more fully than any other form of city-making. Famous examples of New Towns include Brazilia, Brazil, Washington DC, USA, and Chandigarh, India.

In 2011 we published our research on Asian New Towns and their economic, financial and political backgrounds in *Rising in the East: Contemporary New Towns in Asia*.[6] The economic upsurge in China, India and other countries in South-East Asia was not only the cause of urbanisation but also actively used New Towns as an instrument for economic development from South Korea to Saudi Arabia. Since then, a whole new generation of New Towns with shared financial, spatial, and architectural characteristics has emerged. And although many of the elements of this new urban typology originally came from sources elsewhere, (usually from Europe or the USA), this urban type is not just a new international style, but can be labelled as a distinctly Asian type of 'skyline city', deeply concerned with slick modern architectural aesthetics, the latest technologies, and efficient housing systems, with the likes of Dubai and New Songdo as figureheads.

Proposed plan for the New Town Kigamboni, Tanzania. (source: www.ardhi.go.tz/kigamboni-new-city.html)

After *Rising in the East*, we continued to 'follow the money' and arrived very quickly in huge new cities like Kilamba in Angola (planned and constructed by the Chinese company CITIC) or Kigamboni in Tanzania (by the Korean developer Land & Housing Consortium). Now that the economic growth figures of Africa have been rising for a number of years, the continent appears to have been pinpointed as the next frontier for profitable urban development.

Just as with its prequel *Rising in the East*, this book is written with a full awareness of the distance between the Netherlands, where INTI is based, and the subject of study: the African continent.[7] The expectations we have, and the criteria we apply in analysing and criticising New Towns are rooted in our own planning history. Perhaps even more compelling is the fact that we in the West do not limit ourselves to analysis and criticism of the cities in Africa, in fact, we also play an important role in designing them. This book presents many projects by architects and urban designers from (or trained in) Europe and the United States whose professional, cultural and ethical baggage is steeped in the Western tradition, as can be seen in the many American suburban styled New Towns popping up in various African countries.

Still, the position of this book is more difficult than *Rising in the East* in the sense that Europe and Africa have a complex and disputed history. Centuries of colonial exploitation, abuse, and influence inevitably bear a mark. Our position as outsiders is therefore ambiguous. It is inevitable that we will bring to bear our own Western experiences with designing, building or restructuring New Towns. And yet despite numerous disadvantages, the position of outsider also has its advantages. One is sometimes able to see that which may remain invisible to locals, and draw conclusions based on different references. At the same time, postcolonial theory teaches us to question our roles and acknowledge the power, knowledge and representation differentials that have impacted any postcolonial state.

For that reason, this book is as much a history of New Towns in Africa and a manual for future New Towns, as an exploration of the attitude that foreign specialists in architecture and urban design should adopt with regard to the rapid and sometimes astonishing developments on the African continent. And yet, as any planner will tell you, there are no easy

7 We have chosen to address the entire continent of Africa in this analysis. This approach embraces Bill Freund's argument that discarding the traditional idea of sub-Saharan Africa and including all African countries in a single portrait 'may help in the task of deracializing the way readers look at this enormous continent and stress the human variety that can be found in... Africa.' See: Freund, W. (2007). *The African City: A History*. Cambridge: Cambridge University Press. P. ix.

answers. The complexity of seeing such large-scale projects brought to fruition among the procedural challenges of competing interests, disparate stakeholder groups, precarious institutional frameworks, and limited transparency is not to be underestimated. This is true of New Town planning projects across the world, to varying degrees.

It's also worth remembering that while planners and architects clearly play pivotal roles, their plans first and foremost reflect the goals and choices made by developers or governments, investors or other clients. Therefore, the quality of the resulting city is dependent on the quality of the client. Balancing 'good planning' with client demands is a difficult game, and sometimes, despite the best intentions, the implementation phase of a New Town may diverge greatly from the planners' intentions. Evaluating *why* a New Town faces specific spatial challenges then becomes a deep-dive into the muck of decision-making during the planning process; a futile quest, in many cases.

In contemporary African New Towns, we recognise not only European and American, but also Asian concepts as in the case of Kilamba, where accepted urban models are imported with only superficial contextualisation. In the larger, global picture, African New Towns are members of a growing family of cities, and their ubiquitous offspring is found all over the world. We have been startled again and again at the similarities of design concepts, financial constructions, programmatic themes, urban imagery and architecture related to contemporary New Towns in African countries, despite the massive cultural, historical, geographic and financial differences across fifty-four diverse countries. The common characteristics of these New Towns will be elaborated later in this introduction.

Finally, in this book we try to bridge the existing divide between academia and practice when it comes to opinions and debate on New Towns. The recent generation of New Town development has been the subject of a series of publications mostly coming from universities in South Africa and the USA, largely describing these cities as speculative developments. Most academics take a critical stance, denouncing the New Towns as profit-driven enclaves that employ inequitable infrastructural distribution to codify economic privilege. Vanessa Watson, Professor of City Planning at the University of Cape Town, was one of the first to bring contemporary African New Towns into the academic debate as a unique group, questioning whether the grand plans would ever be built, or whether they were merely 'urban fantasies' to fuel speculation.[8] Martin J. Murray, Professor of Urban Planning at the University of Michigan, has written repeatedly about 'fast-track urban enclaves' such as Waterfall City, South Africa, that indicate a global trend towards privatised urbanism.[9] Christopher Marcinkowski and Javier Arpa, both of the University of Pennsylvania, have documented privately-developed New Towns across the continent, and argue that urban planners are irresponsibly designing risky mega-developments that are likely to cause a real estate bubble with disastrous consequences.[10]

8 Watson, V. (2013) African urban fantasies: dreams or nightmares? *Environment and Urbanization* Vol 26(1): 215-231.

9 Murray, M. (2015) 'Waterfall City (Johannesburg): Privatized Urbanism in Extremis', *Environment & Planning*, Vol 47(3): 503-520. See also: Murray, M. (2015) 'City Doubles': Re-Urbanism in Africa. In: Miraftab, F., Wilson, D., and Salo, K. (Eds.) *Cities and Inequalities in a Global and Neoliberal World*. New York: Routledge.

10 C. Marcinkowski (n.d.) 'Africa's Speculative Urban Future', urbanNEXT. Available at: urbannext.net/africas-speculative-urban-future/.

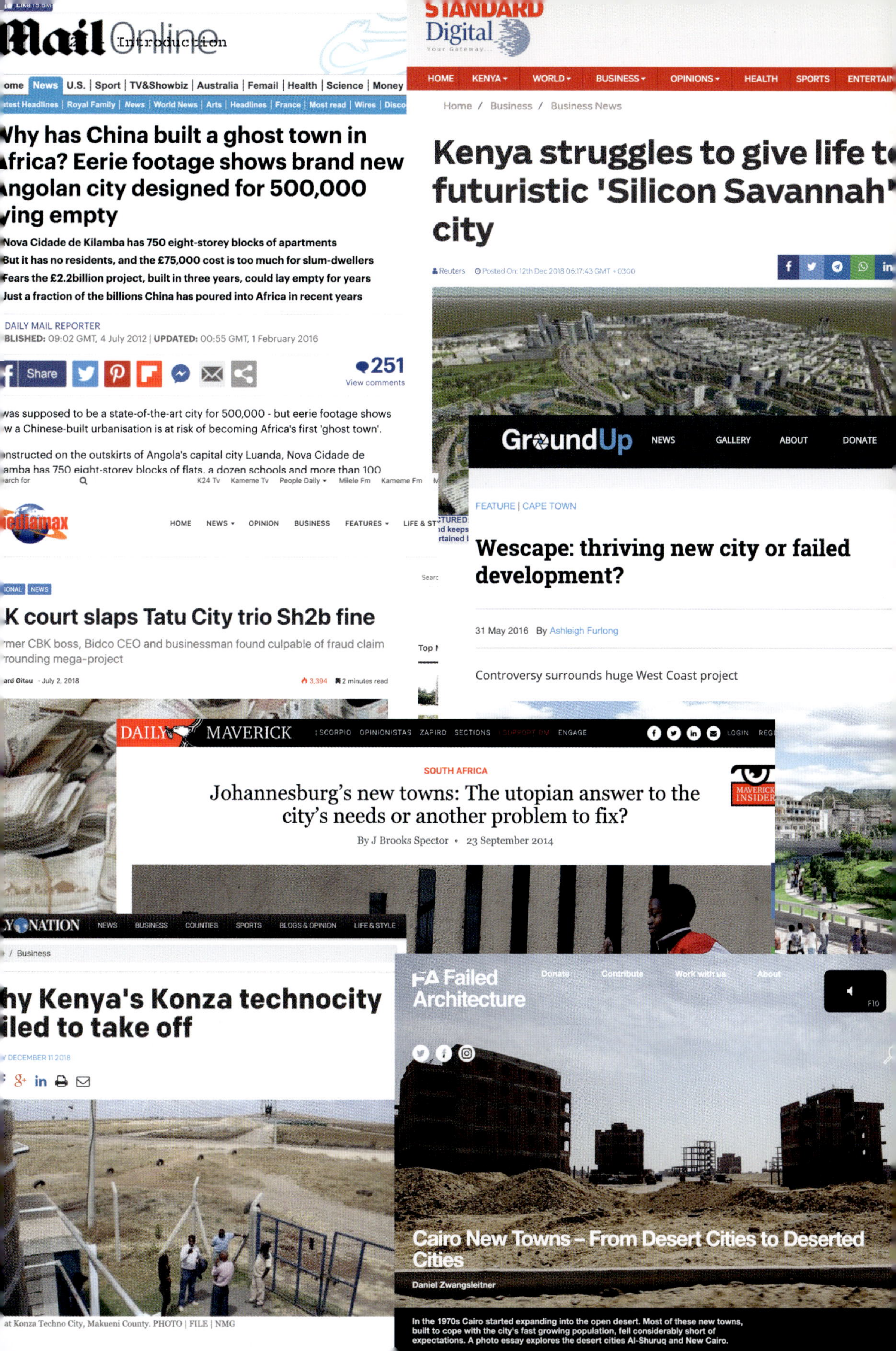

Mail Online

Why has China built a ghost town in Africa? Eerie footage shows brand new Angolan city designed for 500,000 lying empty

Nova Cidade de Kilamba has 750 eight-storey blocks of apartments

But it has no residents, and the £75,000 cost is too much for slum-dwellers

Fears the £2.2billion project, built in three years, could lay empty for years

Just a fraction of the billions China has poured into Africa in recent years

DAILY MAIL REPORTER

PUBLISHED: 09:02 GMT, 4 July 2012 | UPDATED: 00:55 GMT, 1 February 2016

It was supposed to be a state-of-the-art city for 500,000 - but eerie footage shows how a Chinese-built urbanisation is at risk of becoming Africa's first 'ghost town'.

Constructed on the outskirts of Angola's capital city Luanda, Nova Cidade de Kilamba has 750 eight-storey blocks of flats, a dozen schools and more than 100

Standard Digital

Kenya struggles to give life to futuristic 'Silicon Savannah' city

Reuters — Posted On: 12th Dec 2018 06:17:43 GMT +0300

GroundUp

FEATURE | CAPE TOWN

Wescape: thriving new city or failed development?

31 May 2016 By Ashleigh Furlong

Controversy surrounds huge West Coast project

Mediamax

K court slaps Tatu City trio Sh2b fine

Former CBK boss, Bidco CEO and businessman found culpable of fraud claim surrounding mega-project

July 2, 2018

Daily Maverick

SOUTH AFRICA

Johannesburg's new towns: The utopian answer to the city's needs or another problem to fix?

By J Brooks Spector • 23 September 2014

Daily Nation

Business

Why Kenya's Konza technocity failed to take off

DECEMBER 11 2018

at Konza Techno City, Makueni County. PHOTO | FILE | NMG

Failed Architecture

Cairo New Towns – From Desert Cities to Deserted Cities

Daniel Zwangsleitner

In the 1970s Cairo started expanding into the open desert. Most of these new towns, built to cope with the city's fast growing population, fell considerably short of expectations. A photo essay explores the desert cities Al-Shuruq and New Cairo.

Local and international media have also been quick to jump on the bandwagon, as evidenced by the BBC's early critique of Kilamba as a 'Chinese Ghost Town in Angola' (it is currently fully occupied with a long waiting list).[11] Or sensationalising scandals related to large scale land transfers, like those that plagued Tatu City's early days.

11 In 2012, the BBC reported on 'Angola's Chinese-built ghost town', see: Redvers, L. (2012) 'Angola's Chinese Built Ghost Town', BBC News. 3 July 2012. Available at: www.bbc.com/news/world-africa-18646243.

On the other hand, politicians and developers may take a purely propagandistic stance, using marketing lingo and conveniently avoiding social, cultural, political or environmental concerns. Practitioners on the ground claim that academics underestimate the complexities of large-scale development in low resource settings. They point to the double-bind of remaining blameless while operating among corrupt institutions. Planners scoff at the idea that a masterplan would ever be implemented as designed, indicating affordable housing on plans that never appears in reality and thus passing the buck to other decision-makers.

There is no discussion between these two groups, they are separate worlds. But their critiques of each other are broadly valid: Academics

resorting to armchair research often miss the nuance of individual situations, while developers too often focus on short term profits to the detriment of the New Town and surrounding communities.

In this book, we take the New Towns in Africa as a reality, not as something to condemn from the safety of our desks, but as a phenomenon that has always accompanied economic growth worldwide in a capitalistic system. To give both academics and practitioners a voice in this book, we have built it up by conducting in-depth interviews with parties from different backgrounds involved in New Town development. These include developers, construction workers, architects, planners, local academics, (future) residents, local and national politicians, activists, students, residents' associations, local community leaders and other stakeholders. Some of these interviews are presented in this book in condensed and edited formats. Others are quoted in the case studies. Still others inform the data used in the Atlas section of this book. We have also conducted workshops with stakeholders, individual expert reviews, and field interviews with residents to discuss the contents of the Manual and further refine them.

Our position is that lack of constructive debate, regulation, vision, and good governance facilitates the mushrooming commercial urbanism on the African continent. This threatens the long-term qualities of the urban environment by prioritising one socio-economic group while marginalising others. In these complex situations, it is useful to recall the different perspectives among actors, and especially the potential for mismatched priorities between planning bodies and (future or current) residents. Despite the temptation to move a project forward in a rigid, streamlined manner, 'on the ground' there is no single objective reality but rather, as political ecologist Piers Blaikie reminds us, many subjective realities perceived by different actors; all of which are equally valid.[12] Giving voice to these diverse perspectives can add richness and depth to New Town projects that often run a very real risk of becoming stifling, homogenous urban areas. Our ambition with this book is to provide an alternative way forward: one that raises expectations for urban planning and design, and demands the inclusion of voices and concerns generally seen as outside the scope of a New Town planning process.

12 Blaikie, P. (1995) 'Changing environments or changing views? A political ecology for developing countries.' Geography, 80 (3): 204.

13 United Nations (2014) World Urbanization Prospects. The 2014 Revision. New York: the UN Department of Economic and Social Affairs.

Unregulated urban development in the surroundings of Tatu City, Kenya. (Photo: M. Provoost, 2017)

The big picture: urbanisation in Africa

Back to the big picture and the context in which current New Town developments should be understood: rapid urbanisation across the African continent. For many people outside the continent, a romantic image of Africa as a rural arcadia dotted with villages persists despite the continent's incredible diversity of growing urban centres and densifying peri-urban areas. Africa is currently urbanising faster than anywhere else on the planet, and city-scale changes are happening in concert with that growth. Although projections for urban growth remain necessarily imprecise, they are stunning in scale: the United Nations estimates that the number of Africans living in cities will grow from 471 million in 2015 to 1.33 *billion* by 2050.[13] To put that into perspective, by 2050, African cities will need to accommodate three times as many people as today, whether through densification and regeneration, urban extensions or New Towns. Climate change threats may substantially shift these numbers, and we are already seeing record numbers of climate migrants and conflicts stemming from climate variability, which in turn triggers more migration to cities. Increasing precipitation extremes will drive more farmers to the urban centres, and food and water security threats may become more acute.

The unprecedented speed at which these changes are now occurring makes existing problems worse: uncontrolled growth leads to land mismanagement, a depletion of natural resources, increasing inequality, and related social issues such as crime, poor sanitation, and lack of access to services. Within this rapid urbanisation we can identify both universals among the specifics, and divergences within the group. The same diversity that characterises the inhabitants of this giant land mass can be seen in varying approaches to city building.[14] Among the different regions in Africa, geographically divided as Northern, Eastern, Western, Central, and Southern Africa, urbanisation is taking place at different rates and in different ways. Except for Central Africa, all the other regions have seen extensive urbanisation over the last two decades, particularly in coastal areas (see Atlas, page 66). While this urban growth takes various (mostly unregulated) forms, in countries with higher GDP rates it often includes the construction of New Towns.[15] This correlation is significant because it supports our findings that contemporary African New Towns, unlike immediate post-war European New Towns, are not built primarily to accommodate ever-increasing population growth, but rather for rising middle class markets and economic incentives.

New Towns are always a very small quantitative part of the larger story of urbanisation, whether in post-war Europe, present day Asia, or in Africa. Still, they are an important indicator of the contemporary planning paradigms and what are seen as contemporary best practices. It is surprising then, that the New Towns currently under construction across the continent do not offer many inventive urban solutions. Based on the analysis presented in the Atlas we can see that the majority of contemporary New Towns in Africa are intended for homogenous demographic groups (the upper 'middle class'[16]) and often fail to incorporate housing that would be accessible for lower income groups. They are almost uniformly designed around the expectation of personal car use, with inadequate or non-existent public transport systems. They are generally based on urban planning models that employ rigid zoning schemes and mono-functional blocks. Streetscapes and public spaces often lack the qualities, flexibility, and vibrancy of traditional city centres. Ecological and environmental concerns are largely ignored. Existing cultural and historical heritages are either erased or reinterpreted in commercial and superficial ways. The sometimes-violent relocation of indigenous farming communities or villagers is alarming and deserves more attention. The social segregation that develops as unregulated communities grow in tandem with, and adjacent to planned New Towns is equally worrying, as inequalities become more visible and social spheres become more strictly defined.

Africa will be the main stage for urbanisation in the twenty-first century, but the nature of that urban growth has yet to be determined. If things go on as they have, informal settlements will continue to proliferate

14 Heine. B. (ed.), (2000), African Languages: An Introduction. Cambridge: Cambridge University Press.
15 See maps on page 62 and page 80.
16 The meaning of the term 'Middle class' deserves some exploration, see page 30.

as most people continue to build in the only way available to them.[17] There is therefore a clear and urgent need for innovative urban planning, design, financial, and governance models tailored to the needs of African countries as they enter this phase of rapid urbanisation. This is formulated in a call to order by Edgar Pieterse, director of the African Centre for Cities, who states: 'As a continent that will be disproportionately shaped by the way in which society thinks about cities, Africa must assume an increasingly central position in the urban imaginary of theorists and practitioners'.[18] It is therefore mostly out of concern that this publication is undertaken. The aim of this book is to provide a critical view on the way African cities are developed and to contribute practical principles and new insights to improve their planning.

Why is the New Town construction boom happening now?

An avalanche of indignant academic literature has rightfully pointed to the cause of the recent boom in New Towns in Africa in recent years: It's the economy.[19] Today, New Towns are mainly built for economic and commercial reasons, and propelled by demographic and political urgencies. As these authors point out, Africa seems to have been chosen as the new frontier for urban development, mainly driven by economic growth on the continent and economic stagnation elsewhere.[20] Some cities are attractive for investors because the price per square meter is high, as is the case for Dar es Salaam and Nairobi, but the MasterCard Growth Index also points to factors like political stability and rule of law.[21] Considering these factors, Accra, Luanda, and Lusaka are the best performers. It is not without reason that we find most of the plans for New Towns in the countries and the big cities that are experiencing the greatest economic growth. As we alluded earlier, this indicates that the urban development projects are not so much related to demographic growth and a need for housing (as in Europe in the post-war period), but rather have to do with economic motives. There is indeed a huge need for housing in almost all large African cities, while New Towns only focus on a small segment of it and cater for the 'middle' or 'upper middle' classes.

The economic objective is reflected by the parties building the New Towns: it is not so much the governments that give the starting signal and take the initiative, but commercial parties. New Towns are seen as profitable. A series of companies that mostly originate outside of Africa have discovered urbanisation in Africa as a possible work field to make profit. They are not only private companies, but also state-owned companies in China, Korea and Singapore who, after having developed a standard urbanisation model in their own countries, aim to prolong their success in other parts of the world.

This influx of foreign parties also means the import of foreign urban concepts, often uncritically adopted by local governments. The role of the state in the creation of new cities diverges. Sometimes New Towns are part of a national policy, sometimes they are purely private, but most

17 Nnamdi Elleh points out that the slums, shantytowns, and *bidonvilles* stretched across much of Africa represent a reality that existed in much of Europe and North America less than two centuries ago. 'The visible infrastructure of housing stock on the ground, while unique within different African urban contexts in the manner of its construction, recalls the infrastructure and the social experience of the urban poor that a number of wealthy industrial nations underwent as they transformed from agrarian to industrial societies or post-industrial societies.' See: Ellah, N. (2013) 'Perspectives on the Architecture of Africa's Underprivileged Urban Dwellers'. In: Pieterse, E. and Simone, A. (eds.), Rogue Urbanism: Emergent African Cities. Sunnyside: Jacana Media, Ltd. P. 106.

18 Parnell, S. and Pieterse, E. (eds.), (2014) Africa's Urban Revolution. London/New York: Zed Books. P. 15.

19 Sheppard, E., Gidwani, V., Goldman, M., Leitner, H., Roy, A., and Maringanti, A. (2015) 'Introduction: Urban revolutions in the age of global urbanism', Urban Studies, Vol 52(11): 1947-1961. See also: Roy, A. and Ong, A. (eds.) (2011) Worlding Cities: Asian Experiments and the Art of Being Global. Malden: Wiley-Blackwell. And: Watson, V. (2013) 'African urban fantasies: dreams or nightmares?' Environment and Urbanization, Vol 26(1): 215-231. And: Murray, M. (2015) 'Waterfall City (Johannesburg): Privatized Urbanism in Extremis', Environment & Planning, Vol 47(3): 503-520.

20 Bafana, B. (2016) 'Africa's Cities of the Future. Proper planning key to sustainable cities', Africa Renewal. April 2016. Pp. 4-5.

21 Watson, V. (2013) 'African urban fantasies: dreams or nightmares?' Environment and Urbanization, Vol 26(1): 215-231. See also: Angelopulo, G. (2015) 2015 MasterCard African Cities

are in some way a public-private-partnership. As Femke van Noorloos writes, 'Some of the examples of the different modalities include strong centralised states (Rwanda, Ethiopia), more "enabling" or "rolled back" states competing over private investment (in some sense neoliberal: e.g. Kenya, Ghana, South Africa), to [...] states with isolated enclaves of privatised governance (Angola, DRC).'[22]

When national governments are involved in New Town construction, those projects are often conceived as economic catalysts for the national economy to provide a framework for further development and attract foreign direct investment.[23] To attract foreign capital is one of the main objectives of New Town developments and this is mirrored in their planning and design according to successful urban models from Singapore or Dubai. Such models use iconic architecture in high-rise CBDs to project an image of global modernisation and prestige.

This is the case with Kenya's Konza Techno City development, 'a sustainable, world-class technology hub and a major economic driver for the nation', as well as Nigeria's Eko-Atlantic development, 'the new economic capital of Africa' as these cities are characterised by their respective developers.[24] In these cases, the New Towns are part of national spatial planning policies, however, the private sector is leading their implementation and construction. As a result, the question of democratic legitimisation often remains unanswered: who will be responsible for public services, safety, governance? A New Town like Alphaville, Brazil (privately built 40 years ago as a large scale gated community), as well as recent private cities such as Lavasa, India, or New Songdo, South Korea, and many gated communities in Asia show the same issues, where governance is the remit of a private company.[25]

In addition to this, in the context of the 'Africa rising' narrative and the growth expectancy of the GDPs, developers have perceived a growing market for middle class housing. In Africa, there is a real and rising middle class, although the substance of this group varies from country to country and includes a much smaller percentage of the population than many news outlets would have us believe. As Henning Melber writes, the optimism of the African 'middle class' rhetoric sometimes gets in the way of a real discussion of development challenges and increasing inequality.[26] It also perpetuates a false image of western middle-class lifestyles (broadly characterised by car and home ownership, health and retirement security) in an African context where this remains the exception to the rule.

The myth of the African middle class does, however, have its roots in reality. While most Africans are either very rich or very poor, a small group of Africans have enough spending power to support the new wave of air-conditioned shopping malls and supermarkets. However, the African middle class is something very different from its European or North American incarnation, and shouldn't lead to the same imagery. Economists at the World Bank, OECD Development Centre, African Development Bank and Centre for Global Development define the

Growth Index. Crosscurrents of Growth, MasterCard.

22 Van Noorloos, F. (2017) 'Africa's new cities: The contested future of urbanization', Urban Studies, Vol 55(6): 1223-1241.

23 On the need for African cities to combine FDI attraction to sustainable urbanisation and urban policy development, see: Wall, R.S., Maseland, J., Rochelle, K. and Spaliviero, M. (2018) The State of African Cities 2018. The Geography of African Investment. Nairobi: UN-Habitat and Erasmus University Rotterdam.

24 See project websites for Konza City and Eco-Atlantic: www.konzacity.go.ke/the-vision/ and www.ekoatlantic.com.

25 For analysis of Alphaville see: Gotsch, P. (2010) 'AlphaVille-Tamboré: a NeoTown Between Planning and Self-Organisation', in: Provoost, M. (ed.) New Towns for the 21st Century. The Planned vs. the Unplanned City. Amsterdam: SUN/INTI. Pp. 58-71. For New Songdo see: Keeton, R. (2011) Rising in the East. Contemporary New Towns in Asia. Amsterdam: SUN/INTI. P.p. 306-331.

26 Melber, H. (ed.), (2016) The Rise of Africa's Middle Class. Myths, Realities and Critical Engagements. London: Zed Books.

Housing in Appolonia City, Ghana. (Photo: M. Provoost, 2018)

African middle class as earning or spending between 2 - 10 USD per day.[27] That definition includes a huge number of Africans, and thus supports the narrative of a continent with growing economic prowess. However, the group that can actually afford to buy real estate in the new developments is generally estimated to be only a small percentage of the continent's population, partly because of the lack of access to financing options. As the Worldbank states: '85 percent of Africa's urban population lacks access to formal housing loans and only three percent of the population is eligible for a conventional mortgage.'[28] Mortgages with interest rates up to 30 percent (see Atlas, page 85) are relatively expensive compared to other continents and people often rely instead on family loans or personal savings. But even though the number of people with access to the formal housing market is only a small percentage, in absolute numbers this is still a huge market for private developers. These are the clients snapping up homes in New Towns as diverse as Appolonia City (Ghana), Kilamba (Angola) and Sheikh Zayed City (Egypt).

Looking at the growing middle class, Africa is seen by some developers as a business opportunity and a huge future market. One of the most visible of those is the international developer Rendeavour, who is specifically targeting this market and has developed an urban model and method to develop cities across the continent, based on the same concept. As of writing, Rendeavour projects are planned or underway in Kenya (Tatu

27 For more elaboration on the debate around the African middle class see: van Blerk, H. (2018) 'Africa's Lions: Who are Africa's rising middle class?', Johannesburg: IPSOS. Available at: www.ipsos.com/sites/default/files/2018-04/african_lions.pdf.

28 Stocktaking of the Housing Sector in Sub-Saharan Africa. Challenges and Opportunities, Worldbank 2015. P. 58

City), Ghana (Appolonia City and King City), DRC (Kiswishi), Nigeria (Lekki and Jigna) and Zambia (Roma Park).

Taking Appolonia City as a typical example of Rendeavour's method it shows that the core consists of providing secure land titles, a masterplan (usually by a multinational design firm), and the building of residential, commercial, retail, and industrial areas, with a 'standalone' mixed-use environment as a result.[29] Adding affordable housing and creating new loan systems in cooperation with the local government and banks, Rendeavour aims to broaden the scope and the accessibility of their housing stock. These New Towns not only 'meet the aspirations of the burgeoning middle classes' but also that of (local) governments to attract and improve opportunities for business and industry. Tatu City, for example, has therefore also been given the status of a Special Economic Zone. The multifunctional and complete urban programme of these cities ultimately aims to minimise the need for commuting; however it has also been stated that it 'reinforces their enclave character and gives the rationale for autonomous, privatised governance'.[30] How this will play out in the Rendeavour cities remains to be seen.

29 Vice President of Rendeavour Preston Mendenhall describes their approach in more detail in the interview on page 322. See also: www.rendeavour.com/wp-content/uploads/REN-brochure-2016_Digital-S.pdf. Finished houses in The Oxford (a gated community in Appolonia) start at USD 86,599 (see: www.appolonia.com.gh/now-selling/the-oxford/your-home/). When adjusted by purchasing power parity (PPP), the Gross Domestic Product per capita in Ghana was USD 4227.60 in 2017, a record high (tradingeconomics.com/ghana/gdp-per-capita-ppp).

Congested infrastructures in Cairo. (Photo: R. Keeton, 2016)

Urban sprawl in the outskirts of Accra, Ghana. (Photo: M. Provoost, 2018)

The problems with New Town development

The New Town construction wave in Africa calls for questions and critique on a number of issues. In the first place, one problem created by New Town development is that it redirects resources that could be used instead to upgrade or densify existing urban areas. When enough resources are routed out of the existing cities, they will become even more congested and stagnate. New Towns in Africa commonly direct finance away from existing cities that already lack adequate public services, transport facilities, and other urban amenities. Yet this is exactly the reason why New Towns are so popular: because they *can* deliver the necessary services: electricity, water, roads, and sewage.

Fear of the unpredictability, unreliability and insecurity of the African metropolis influences not only the future residents of these new cities or the administrators and developers who build them, but also the architects who design them. Greenfield sites are attractive because they avoid the messy business of urban regeneration and piecemeal planning. With heavily congested roads and a widespread lack of basic planning tools like land ownership information or utility infrastructure maps, upgrading or densifying existing urban fabric is difficult. Many older African cities simply do not have detailed records of how those cities function. What lies below the ground is often an even greater mystery. As both spending power and urban populations increase, however, the market for upscale housing, more comfort, and safety grows accordingly. As elsewhere in the world, everyone wants a safe place to raise their children, surrounded by their peers. In situations like this, politicians and planners find fertile ground for New Town development. Starting fresh and minimising dependence on existing congested infrastructure has obvious appeal: the satisfaction of good organisation, reliable services, quality housing, safety, and the possibility of foregoing the chaotic city for a clean, controlled urban environment.

Secondly, like many cities facing rising inequality, New Towns in Africa have a tendency towards spatial segregation and poor inclusivity. This is a tendency that prevailed in many Western European cities in the 1970s, where satellite cities were built for the middle class, leaving the inner cities inhabited by the urban poor and creating the need for huge investments from national and municipal governments to improve the inner cities. It is doubtful whether most African cities have the governance structure and the financial capacity to cope with the negative tendencies of the spatial segregation caused by New Towns. At this moment the percentage of New Towns is only a fraction of the total urbanisation in Africa, which is mostly unregulated. However, we predict that spatial segregation will continue to increase in the near future, and extensive urban sprawl will be driven by the construction of private homes in peri-urban locations.[31] Alternative strategies to counter this include (1) making New Towns accessible for all groups in society, including the poor, (2) immediately investing in the quality of the inner cities, and (3) stimulating the redevelopment of brownfield sites and limiting the possibilities for extensions and New Towns. It is difficult to be optimistic about the viability of these options: There appears to be a growing inclination to leave urban upgrading and development of the cities to the private sector, which limits the possibilities of long-term urban development for the common good.

One of the dangers in this approach is that enclave developments exacerbate spatial segregation not only in the form of gated communities but also at the urban scale. New Towns are becoming islands with high quality services (their strongest selling points), while many existing African cities continue to suffer from unreliable electricity provision, limited access to clean water, and other ineffectual municipal services (trash collection, security, etc.). Because of limited access to mortgages and other home financing models, the *real* African middle class cannot afford to live in these New Towns (see Atlas, page 85).[32]

Thirdly, there are also serious ecological considerations. Many New Towns currently do nothing to acknowledge environmental vulnerabilities and future threats. While many African countries have a wealth of natural beauty and resources, most New Town designs simply ignore this bounty, and tend to avoid dealing with questions related to climate change issues (flooding or severe droughts), environmental degradation, or biodiversity

30 Van Noorloos, F. (2017) 'Africa's new cities: The contested future of urbanisation', Urban Studies Vol 55, (6): 1223-1241.

31 In the Accra region this is already happening; the sprawl is targeted by the national government in their spatial policies. See: Ghana National Spatial Development Framework (2015-2035), Government of Ghana, February 2015.

32 In Ghana, the Bank of Ghana and Worldbank estimate that 60 percent of the population could possibly afford to buy a home with some form of financial assistance. However, housing finance is notoriously hard to come by. According to the Bank of Ghana's Annual Percentage Rate (APR) and Average Interest (AI) report (2018), interest rates for mortgage loans among commercial banks in Ghana average 28.7 percent. Alternative home financing solutions are needed to allow wider access to the housing market. See: bog.gov.gh/privatecontent/Public_Notices/Banks%20APRs%20and%20Average%20Interest%20on%20Deposits%20as%20at%20February%202018.pdf. See also: World Bank (2015) Stocktaking of the Housing Sector in Sub-Saharan Africa. Challenges and Opportunities. Washington DC: World Bank.

loss. Urbanisation will increase water consumption and bring issues of water quality and water security to the fore. Projected sea level rise, an increasingly urgent issue for New Towns in coastal plains, is often not taken into account. Recent research shows the urgency of planning with and for water, if only because the most urbanised regions with the highest demographic predictions are along rivers, in deltas or in coastal areas: 'Concentrations of population and economic value in coastal zones and deltas increase not only the short-term flood risks, but also the long-term vulnerability with respect to sea level rise and storm surges. This will require continued protection efforts. The required protection will depend on population and economic developments in flood-prone areas, and developments in peak river flows, sea level rise and storm surge patterns.'[33]

33 Ligtvoet, W., et al. (2018) The Geography of Future Water Challenges. The Hague: PBL Netherlands Environmental Assessment Agency. P.p. 48-49.

34 Desertification also threatens the Sahel region as the Sahara slowly expands southward: according to a recent study by scientists at the University of Maryland, the Sahara has expanded by 10% since 1920. With a different mindset, these risks can also be observed as opportunities for radical change. New Towns are an ideal testing-bed for ambitious experiments with new ways of living with nature. See: Thomas, N. and Nigam, S. (2018) 'Twentieth-Century Climate Change over Africa: Seasonal Hydroclimate Trends and Sahara Desert Expansion,' Journal of Climate, Vol 31 (19): 3349–3370

These cities are at serious risk for flooding as a result of sea level changes, and some may disappear completely within the next fifty years. For example, much of Nouakchott, capital of Mauritania, is located at or below sea level, and the New Town now sees significant flooding *even during the dry season*. Heavy rainfall may exacerbate flooding and in addition to the immediate threats posed by a flood, longer-term effects such as the risk of disease outbreaks and poisoned groundwater can result from standing bodies of water. In peri-urban or rural areas, farmers may experience climate variability that threatens crops, whether in the form of too much rainfall, too little, or simply at the wrong time for carefully planned crops.[34] There is no city in Africa that doesn't experience a growing vulnerability towards climate and environment change and this urgent issue needs to be confronted.[35]

Flooded streets in Accra, Ghana. (source: africapro24.com)

Another overarching problem is that most urban planners and designers come from abroad and there are still very few African architects and design offices responsible for conceptualising and planning New Towns. The foreign architects and planners that are responsible, are often unfamiliar with the scale of urbanisation and connected challenges, nor are they intimately familiar with local contexts. Architecture and planning universities in the West tend to focus on popular small-scale projects in unregulated settlements. Few programmes ask students to consider the size and scale of urbanisation in the global south and equip students with instruments to think and conceptualise on this large scale. What we wrote in Rising in the East has only become more true over time:

35 UN-Habitat (2014) The State of African Cities 2014, Re-imagining Sustainable Urban Transitions. Nairobi: UN-Habitat. P. 17.

> 'The designing of New Towns, the construction of entirely new, integral urban systems, the writing of technocratic and ideological books on how to build new cities, has all but disappeared from architectural education and publications in Western architecture and planning schools. We might even go so far as to say that the architectural and planning elites, the ones who dominate the design debates, are in general not very interested in New

Towns. In the twenty-first century, building the New City is no longer the ultimate horizon, the climax of architectural thinking and urban ideology. Architectural debate, when applied to urban matters, is much more animated by the massive, unplanned migration to cities, by terrifying statistics and fascinating images coming from the megalopolises of the developing world than by any new version of Ekistics.[36] While architects and planners are designing entire cities and constructing architectural icons *ex nihilo* in green fields, "their" schools theorise mostly about the inability to plan urbanisation, architectural acupuncture and bottom-up urban politics.'[37]

This conceptual void on the part of architecture and planning, and the lack of education, debate and theory on large-scale planning leaves big engineering firms to dominate the field of New Town building. Many of them come from countries like China or South Korea, where a quantitative and functionalist approach to large-scale urbanisation has been common in recent decades. Those engineering firms are, in general, less interested in site specificity and more interested in solving problems pragmatically and efficiently. The problem with this, of course, is that a city is much more than a technical construct.

As a result of the foreign dominance of developers and urban planners, we also see a dominance of foreign urban models, flowing from one economic high-pressure area to another. Urban concepts from Asia and promises of economic growth are being imported in Africa and adopted like ready-made packages (see Manual, page 157). These New Towns are no longer places of experimentation for the common good (as in the early independence period), but rather cut-and-paste operations introducing existing urban concepts in vastly different contexts, reflecting, 'an inexcusable abdication of responsibility by the urban design disciplines'.[38] Again and again, we see the American model for suburban enclave cities and gated communities rolled out and snapped up for the aspirational lifestyle it espouses; Chinese grid cities designed for housing masses based on demographic data and a hyper-functionalist approach; Singaporean and Korean models for CBDs and economic districts introduced in places with much lower densities and different concepts of urban life.

While many African countries look to the similarities in (economic and demographic) growth patterns between China and Africa and regard this as positive and promising, China's interest in Africa has provoked an army of critics arguing that Africa is being 'colonised' by China, 'exploited', etc. The New Town of Kilamba, financed, designed, and built by the Chinese CITIC semi-governmental developer in exchange for Angola's oil, is one of the examples usually given to underline this argument.

Administration of the CITIC vocational school in Kilamba, Angola. (Photo: R. Keeton, 2016)

However much attention China is attracting with its conspicuous infrastructure and construction projects in exchange for land or natural resources, it is still Western countries leading in the 'scramble for Africa'.

36 Ekistics is the name of the comprehensive urban theory developed by the Greek planner Constantinos Doxiadis in the 1950s-1960s, which he applied in many cities in the Global South, amongst them Tema (Ghana), Islamabad (Pakistan) and Khartoum (Sudan).

37 Provoost, M., and Vanstiphout, W. (2011) 'Introduction', in: Keeton, R., Rising in the East: Contemporary New Towns in Asia. Amsterdam: SUN/INTI. P.p. 9-42.

38 Marcinkowski, C. (n.d.) 'Africa's Speculative Urban Future', urbanNEXT. Available at: urbannext.net/africas-speculative-urban-future/.

39 Curtis, M. (2016) 'Britain's New African Empire', Huffington Post. Available at: www.huffingtonpost.co.uk/mark-curtis/britain-africa-development_b_11191728.html?guccounter=1.

40 The fact that such a thing as a purely greenfield site hardly exists in Africa is obviously one of the problems in New Town planning, since almost always the displacement of smaller local communities or agricultural use is involved. See essay by Femke van Noorloos and Diky Avianto, page 410.

As recent research by the NGO War on Want has suggested, 'China's resources grabs have been widely vilified but the major foreign takeover of Africa's natural riches springs from a lot closer to home.'[39] Perhaps unsurprisingly, the UK owns a staggering amount of concessions for Africa's resources in five commodities - oil, gold, diamonds, coal and platinum. In urban planning projects, European developers, Dutch and Danish engineering firms, and American architecture firms are just as present as Chinese firms.

What is the structure of this book?

An Atlas

The Atlas consists of various elements. First, a series of maps depicts relevant data for African urbanisation per country, such as the (future) population living in cities or in slums, demographic developments, fertility rates, and the New Towns built over the period of this book (from 1960 to 2016); figures on the immaterial quality of life as measured in the Freedom index and the GINI index; the economic conditions of African countries, depicted through the amount of Foreign Direct Investment and the GDP per capita in every country, compared to the economic levels in other countries outside Africa; as well as the number of cars and mobile phones; the share of migrant's remittances in the country's economy; the accessibility of the housing market expressed in the levels of interest on mortgages and loans; and finally, the ecological conditions for African urbanisation on a map showing current and projected climate and water challenges.

Secondly, the Atlas contains an inventory of 148 New Towns. This longlist is published on page 16 and lists the names, countries, and target population size of all discoverable New Towns planned and/or built from 1960-2017. Commonly called 'The Year of Africa', 1960 was chosen because it marks the building of the first New Town (Tema) to be constructed after the first African country gained independence (Ghana in 1957). The longlist can be understood as a snapshot of a moment in time, since new plans and images of new urban developments are published of shinier, bigger urban developments, almost every day, while other New Town plans are temporarily or indefinitely delayed.

The inventory is based on our definition of New Towns as cities built from scratch according to a comprehensively planned masterplan on a greenfield site (no previous urban development), backed by a political decision, with a target population of at least 10,000 residents, mixed-use, and with some degree of political autonomy.[40] All the same, there are fluid boundaries within that definition: there are small and large New Towns, and the degree of autonomy varies. The ambition to become a complete city and include a mix of programmes and functions separates New Towns from mono-functional business parks or large residential communities. Many of these developments are commonly referred to in articles on New Towns, such as Ouaga 2000 (Burkina Faso) Airport City (Ghana) or Century City (Cape Town), but do not fit our definition of New Towns because they are too small in size or population, are commercial and mono-functional developments only, or are extensions, urban renewal projects, or inner city developments.[41] They lie outside the scope of this book.

The total target population of all New Towns from the period 1960-2016 together is approximately 47 million inhabitants. Recently the Egyptian government announced the building of 20 extra New Towns for 30 million inhabitants, which will raise the total inhabitants of New Towns in Africa to 77 million. In 2030 it is estimated that the urban population of Africa will be 791 million people.[42] If only the New Towns presently planned and built meet their targets and no other New Towns will be added (which is highly unlikely) almost 10 percent of the urban population will live in a New Town. Our hunch would be that the New Towns produce even more than 10 percent of the GDP, since they usually attract FDI, huge industrial terrains and are connected to Special Economic Zones.

Thirdly, the Atlas includes 'City Passports' that elaborate the characters of 30 different New Towns. To be able to draw useful conclusions from the inventory, we selected a representative sample of 30 New Towns with the most available data, to add depth to our analysis. We asked: which concepts drive these New Towns forward? What parties are involved and from what part of the world? How many cities are built, how many only planned, never to be built? Who will live there? Whose ideas and whose money are involved? How does the New Town function in relation to existing cities and settlements, and what is its projected programme? The 30 City Passports offer quantitative data on size, density, projected population, real population, location and dates of development, urban morphology, and also (if known) information on the housing types, infrastructures, and urban amenities. We have also looked at the roles of commercial and governmental parties involved in the initiation, financing, design, and development of these New Towns. We visualised our findings in ways that also point to the relationships between different aspects of city building. Finally, we have included a short description of each New Town, its development, and its challenges.

Based on the inventory and the city passports, we combined, compared, and visualised the data in a series of diagrams. By analysing different variables over time, we are also able to identify trends at the continental scale.

We counted the cities being planned and built from 1960-2016 to indicate the extent of the present building boom and saw a strong acceleration in the numbers of New Towns being initiated. In the period of early independence (1960-1990) 39 cities were built, from 1990-2000 only 3, while in the last two decades since 2000 this number rose to 109 cities. This increase is mainly happening in countries with the highest GDPs. In Sub-Saharan Africa those are: Kenya (16), Nigeria (10), Ghana (5), South

41 Watson, V. (2013) African urban fantasies: dreams or nightmares? Environment and Urbanization Vol 26(1): 215-231; C. Marcinkowski (n.d.) 'Africa's Speculative Urban Future', urbanNEXT. Available at: urbannext.net/africas-speculative-urban-future/; Van Noorloos, F. (2017) 'Africa's new cities: The contested future of urbanization', Urban Studies, Vol 55(6): 1223-1241.

42 IRIN www.irinnews.org/news/2007/06/27/urban-population-double-unfpa

Africa (8) and Angola (13). In Northern Africa they are: Egypt (9), Algeria (6) and Morocco (7).

To clarify the *raison d'être* for the New Towns in the Atlas, we have made a categorisation according to the main motives for their initiation. This results in eight categories: Decentralisation Cities (to decongest overcrowded metropolises), Capital Cities (to represent government), Commercial Cities (to attract investment or provide profit for developers), Eco-Cities (to achieve the best environmentally friendly performance), Smart Cities (to offer state-of-the-art technology and use this as an attraction), Industrial Cities (to support industry hubs, sometimes related to a port), Apartheid Cities (to spatially segregate ethnic groups), and Resort Cities (dedicated to tourism and leisure facilities). These categories build on the distinctions made in Rising in the East, but are modified to fit the conditions on the African continent. In the period 1960-2016 we can discern a shift from the building of Capital Cities and Industrial Cities in the first decades of independence, to a growing number of Decentralisation Cities, Commercial Cities and Smart Cities. The category of Resort Cities is the most recent: Resort Cities large enough to be included in our definition of New Towns have only been introduced since the beginning of the twenty-first century, mainly in Kenya (5), Tanzania, Nigeria and Equatorial Guinea (1 each).

We have explored the 30 New Towns in the city passports by looking at their masterplans, housing plans, descriptions, and terms of reference to determine resident target groups. In this analysis, we see a shift from New Towns built for local inhabitants and lower middle class in the twentieth century to upper middle class and an international clientele in recent decades. None of these New Towns was ever able to provide housing for the urban poor or the lowest paid workers. Contemporary New Towns are not even trying to cater for these groups. Our conclusion is that New Towns have become less inclusive in the period 1960-2016.
We looked at the way in which the growing globalisation of urban development manifests itself by trying to define what parties initiated, built, and financed the New Towns. These data are hard to collect because so many parties and companies are temporarily involved in constructing a city, and in every phase the team is different. Moreover, companies are not always transparent about who does what, when, and how; after all, they are mostly private projects. As a consequence, these New Towns are hardly ever discussed in public, they are just presented.

One conclusion from our inventory is that among the abundance of foreign parties connected to New Town planning in Africa, four countries stand out: China, the United Kingdom, South Africa, and the United States (in that order). European countries are also very much present, from Portugal to Finland, and from the Netherlands to Greece. Additionally, there is growing influence from Singapore and South Korea, however, much like the Chinese companies they are not (yet) necessarily focused on New Town development, but rather involved in large-scale construction and engineering projects in general.

When looking at the responsibilities and the democratic legitimisation of New Town planning, we can clearly see a shift from state-driven development in the mid-twentieth century to a majority of private developments in the twenty-first century. The role of governments in the planning of New Towns greatly diminished during this period. While in the 1960s and 1970s national governments initiated cities, this role was taken over by commercial and private parties, sometimes working in PPPs with governments. Only a few countries have a national policy steering New Town development, such as Egypt, Ethiopia, and Morocco, and to a certain extent, Ghana and Kenya as well.

Chinese contractors building the new highrises in Tema, Ghana. (Photo: M. Provoost, 2015)

We also looked into the urban morphology of these New Towns. To be able to discern trends in the urban design and character of the cities we have categorised their urban models and fabric, using typological characterisations of street patterns (such as 'warped grid', 'orthogonal grid', 'composite' and 'loops and lollipops'), and urban forms (such as 'grid', 'polycentric', 'radial', 'linear', 'township', and 'skyline'). In recent decades, we see an abundance of the 'skyline' model among the recent New Towns, even in cities such as Eko-Atlantic City, Nigeria, or Newtown, Kenya, that are being developed by local or Western parties. This ubiquity is proof of the increasing popularity of this model worldwide and shows it is steadily becoming the global standard. Most of these cities can be considered commercial cities and have business parks at the heart of the project. Shiny architecture and generic renderings play a significant role in selling the plans. Often, urban planning is reduced to land use schemes, without an integral design approach or urbanist vision. Many of these New Towns are plagued by legal issues or land ownership complexities, and take a long time to start construction. However, compared to processes of urban development in other parts of the world, this does not seem to be significantly longer in Africa.

A History

Next to the quantitative research in the Atlas, we have collected qualitative data on New Towns that have actually been built and inhabited, so as to be able to evaluate their merits. We describe and analyse the origins and design concepts of postcolonial New Towns from the period 1960-2016, keeping in mind that contemporary New Towns in Africa are part of a long history of planning across the continent. Comprehensive urban planning, in fact, has been part of African urban development since long before colonial powers began importing European models. For millennia, African rulers have overseen the construction of planned cities across the continent, often as an expression of political and social power.

Among many other examples, archaeological evidence from ancient cities like El-Lahun, Egypt (1700 BCE), Timgad, Algeria (100), Kilwa Kisiwani, Tanzania (700), Edo, Nigeria (1100), and Loanga City, Angola (1500) indicate geometric order, clear spatial patterns, and monumentality in the urban plans. These highly specific urban forms were influenced by local religious and cosmological beliefs, intricate social organisations, and political hierarchies. Eleventh century Edo (Benin City), Nigeria, for example, was designed based on fractals, and included underground drainage as well as a centralised and sophisticated bureaucracy. Tragically, most of these ancient planned cities were destroyed by European colonising powers and have been all but forgotten. As a result, Africa is too often unjustly perceived as a continent with no indigenous urban tradition.

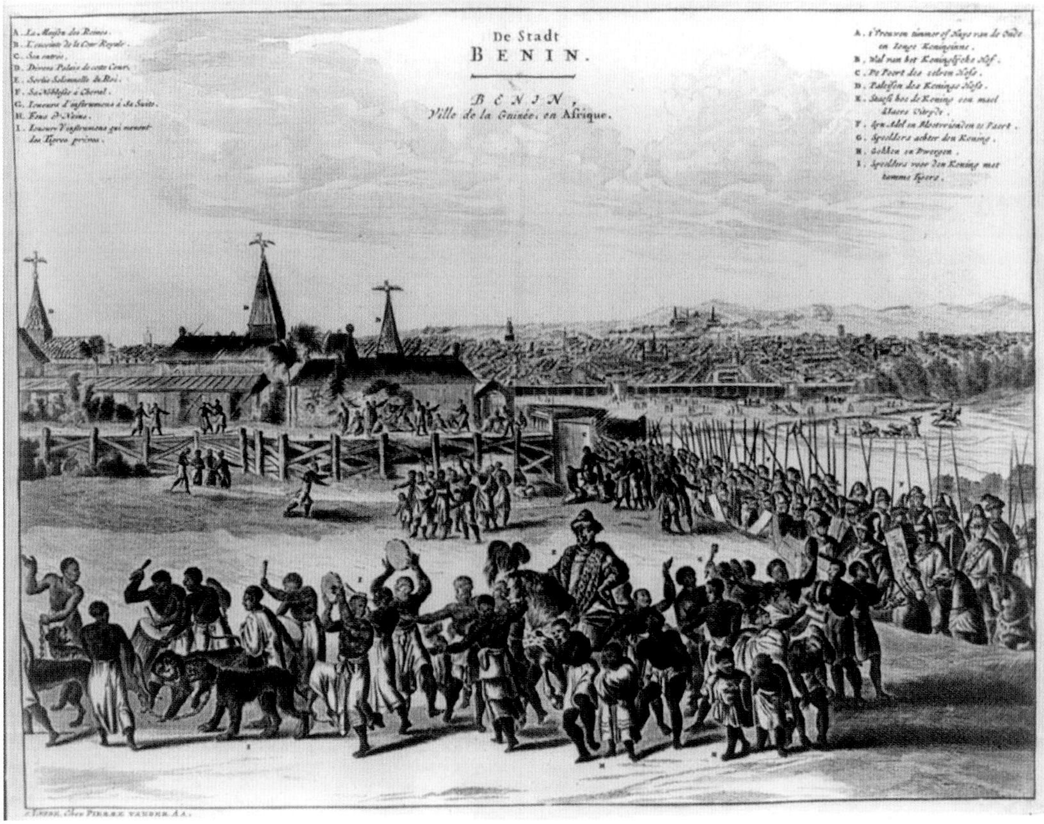

The ancient Nigerian city of Benin was recorded in Olfert Dapper's 1668 book "Description of Africa". It is one of the few etchings of ancient planned cities in Africa currently known. (Source: Wikimedia)

During the colonial era, European heads of state infamously regulated the 'Scramble for Africa' at the three-day Berlin Conference of 1887. From that moment on, openly racist urban planning was used to facilitate 'control' over native populations. Ideas regarding urban design differed from one colonising power to the next, and those ideas then had to be reconciled with the reactions of native people. Planning approaches and implementation also changed considerably over time in individual places, but segregation between European, African, and Asian residents was a constant factor in urban planning. Later, as the Garden City model gained popularity in Europe during the early twentieth century, it became one of the preferred urban models for African colonies. As preferences changed in Europe, that shift was also reflected in African colonies: following the Second World War, it was the Modern Movement and CIAM discourses that became most influential on urban planning practices.[43]

Kwame Nkrumah meets Constantinos Doxiadis, planner of Tema, Ghana, 1960. (Source: Constantinos A. Doxiadis Archives. © Constantinos and Emma Doxiadis Foundation)

In the first decades of independence, New Towns were often seen by national governments as a way of affirming national identities. Political ideology drove the construction of new capitals like Dodoma, Tanzania, and Abuja, Nigeria, among others. Ideas about equal representation and national unity were especially important in young countries where political allegiances roughly correlated to tribal identity. New economic policies led to the creation of New Towns such as Tema, an industrial port city in Ghana, and Julius Nyerere's African Socialist *Ujamaa* villages in Tanzania. Cities such as Tema and 10th of Ramadan, Egypt, were part of national spatial-economic policies that aimed for development at a national scale.

Julius Nyerere with the plan for Dodoma, 1976. (Source: unknown)

During the 1990s there were hardly any New Towns planned at all, while the 21st century began with a new generation of New Towns, reflecting the worldwide shift to neoliberalism. During this neoliberal era, which extends to the present day, economic motives dominate the construction landscape, and we see an increase in privatisation, a surge of gated communities, and a proliferation of 'Skyline Cities'. As we wrote seven years ago in Rising in the East: Contemporary New Towns in Asia:

> 'The uniformity of many of these cities is not so much the choice of the urban planners and designers as the consequence of a market orientation and the identical groups targeted by the investors. While in the 1960s the uniformity of cities was blamed on the dominant role of central government, it is now the market that is responsible for the uniformity of cities. James C. Scott, Professor of Political Science at Yale University, demonstrates in his well-known book, **Seeing like a State** (1998), that it is not just the (socialist) state or a national government that leads to large-scale, homogeneous, utopian plans because its power is not counterbalanced by lack of opposing forces: "[...] large-scale capitalism is just as much an agency of homogenisation, uniformity, grids, and heroic simplification as the state is, with the difference being that, for capitalists, simplification

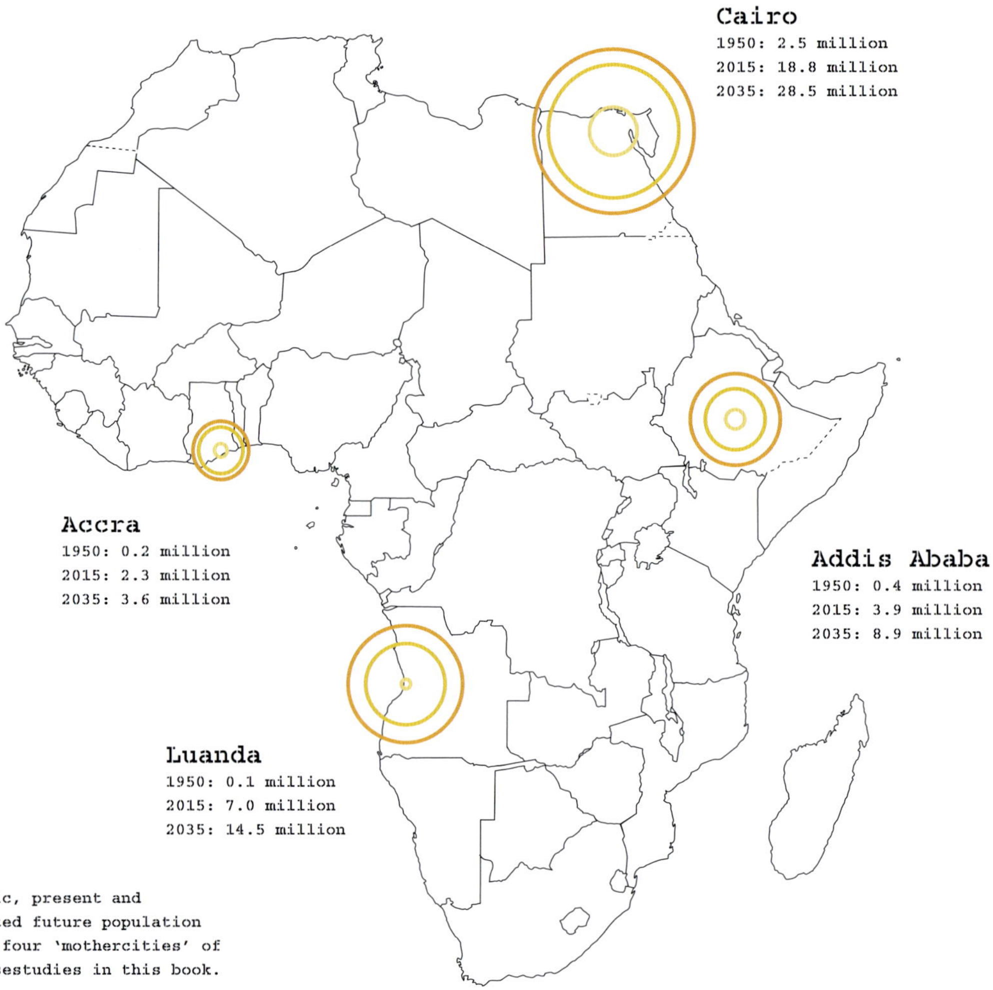

Historic, present and projected future population of the four 'mothercities' of the casestudies in this book.

must pay. A market necessarily reduces quality to quantity via the price mechanism and promotes standardisation; in markets, money talks, not people. Today, global capitalism is perhaps the most powerful force for homogenisation, whereas the state may in some instances be the defender of local difference and variety."[44]

This explains the sometimes stupefying uniformity of the African New Towns presented in this book, but also their strong similarities with New Towns in other parts of the world such as Asia, Latin America, or the Middle East.

This part of the book, *A History*, uses case studies, articles by experts, and interviews with professionals from different backgrounds to elaborate on the historical development of planning New Towns in Africa. The five case studies (Tema, Ghana; 10th of Ramadan, Egypt; Sheikh Zayed City, Egypt; Kilamba, Angola; BuraNEST, Ethiopia) were selected because they display the broad diversity within this single phenomenon. They are located at

43 Silva, C.N. (ed.), (2015) Urban Planning in Sub-Saharan Africa: Colonial and Post-Colonial Planning Cultures. New York: Routledge.

44 Provoost, M. and Vanstiphout, W. (2011) 'Introduction', in: Keeton, R., Rising in the East: Contemporary New Towns in Asia. Amsterdam: SUN/INTI. P. 35. Quote from: Scott, J.C. (1998) Seeing like a State. How Certain Schemes to Improve the Human Condition Have Failed. New York: Yale University Press. P. 8.

geographic extremes and characterised by different climates, cultures, histories, and purposes. At the same time, the analysis clearly indicates a number of recurrent issues that appear *despite* idiosyncratic geographic, cultural, and planning contexts because they are inherent to the building of a completely new city. In both sections, we evaluate the selected case study cities according to the principles formulated in the Manual, which is elaborated in the following section. Our intention is that the combination of in-depth case studies will allow for a greater understanding of the complexities of individual situations, while simultaneously providing a test for the validity of the conclusions drawn from the database results.

The articles provide a background by looking specifically into a number of issues at stake. In 'Debunking Myths about African Urbanisation', Edgar Pieterse (African Centre for Cities) cuts through four common myths in the discussion about African New Towns, namely that, 'urbanisation is out of control', 'rural-to-urban migration is the main driver of urbanisation', 'in time, informality will be replaced by formality', and 'the rapidly growing middle class will sustain the demand for New Towns'. He not only debunks these clichés but also replaces them with a nuanced vision on exactly the topics that drive this discourse.

The article by Anne Erdl ('Mitchell's Plain: The Translation of a British Urban Planning Model to South Africa's Apartheid New Town') analyses the complex way in which British New Town planning informed the urban design and thinking behind Mitchell's Plain, a township in Cape Town, South Africa. Using Konza City as an illustrative example, the essay by Femke van Noorloos and Diky Avianto (University of Utrecht) examines and analyses how history teaches us that New Towns not only attract those who can afford their relative luxuries, but also those who cannot: the poor who follow new developments looking for opportunities to improve their quality of life. This was the case with Tema, Ghana, and its neighbouring shantytown Ashaiman, with Konza Tech City, Kenya, and the adjacent villages that mushroomed with informal housing after the project was announced, with Kilamba and its bordering *musseque*, and nearly every other New Town around the continent. The reality of this twin phenomena of informal settlements and planned New Towns gives us an opportunity to reflect on the current approach to city-making in Africa. As African countries become increasingly unequal, and increasingly urbanised, informal settlements will continue to grow if governments fail to meet the demand for affordable housing. If urban development continues as it has, we might imagine a sort of nightmare

Two Appolonia's: the New Town Appolonia City (above) lies adjacent to the old village of Appolonia (below). (Photo: M. Provoost, 2018)

scenario: an endless sea of informal settlements, dotted with small islands of planned urbanisation—accessible only to the privileged few. Finally, the article by Alonso Ayala Aleman, Maartje van Eerd, and Ellen Geurts (Institute for Housing and Urban Development Studies, IHS) examines the conditions necessary for the provision of 'affordable, available, accessible and acceptable' housing in New Towns.

The interviews give voice to the perspectives of different stakeholders in the planning process and are loosely related to the case studies. The economist and urban planner David Sims sheds light on the political implications of the extensive New Town programme in Egypt; Mayor Israel Marques talks about the start-up problems and outlook for Kilamba; Vice President of Rendeavour Preston Mendenhall shares the lessons from the seven urban projects in Africa his company is involved in; Ethiopian architects and academics Fasil Giorghis and Zegeye Cherenet talk about the obstacles on the way to building BuraNEST, and urban planner Gareth Edwards talks about the ambitions of his firm SOM when designing Tatu City.

A Manual

While the Atlas points to general conclusions about the current state of New Towns in Africa, the Manual section presents a synthesis of the results of the database, our (historical) research into the case studies, contributions from authors included in this book and other experts, and our own research at the International New Town Institute and TU Delft.[45] The urgency of coming up with principles for New Town design became clear in the run-up to the conference Habitat III in Quito, Ecuador in 2016. The New Urban Agenda which was presented on that occasion talked about city transformation and city extensions but not about the specific issues of New Towns. For that reason, we distilled a set of ten principles specifically geared towards the design and planning of New Towns and presented them as an addition to the New Urban Agenda at Habitat III.[46]

The Manual is based on the premise that we can learn from history; that we can find successful examples as well as failed examples to study in order to avoid repeating mistakes in the future. The Manual gives positive advice on how to use these experiences. New Towns share a universal DNA, but must be customised to local contexts and local approaches. The guidelines therefore focus on the specific design decisions required in New Town planning that we find are often overlooked or not taken into account. They attempt to pre-empt the specific spatial challenges that New Towns often encounter.

The Manual was developed as a coherent set of planning principles, but we recognise that planning does not happen in a vacuum. Although it is beyond the scope of this book, we believe good governance is necessary to facilitate good planning. A strong institutional framework that can implement an adaptive strategy is a necessary underpinning for the deployment of these principles. Without a (private or public) body capable

45 We have conducted fieldwork for this book in eight African countries and twelve African New Towns. Our research methods include semi-structured interviews, expert group meetings, design workshops, site observation, photography, and literature review.

46 The first version of these principles was published in June 2016, see: Provoost, M, 'The New Urban Agenda: The Perspective of New Towns', www.newtowninstitute.org/spip.php?article1161.

of overseeing a massive management project and adapting its vision over time, no New Town can flourish.

The principles are:
1. Planning is an ongoing process
2. Plan for adaptivity
3. No New Town is an island
4. Use no cut and paste universal model
5. Embrace new ideas
6. Infrastructure and mobility for all, from the start
7. Use a blue-green infrastructure as the central framework
8. Incorporate local cultural heritage(s)
9. Combine top-down and bottom-up
10. New Towns need diversity

The principles are organised in a way that loosely follows the order from long-term and large-scale decisions and processes to smaller scale and urban design advice. The first three guidelines therefore address issues related to process and site selection such as the need for long-term planning and planning for adaptivity, affirming the need to view New Town planning as a process of evolution over time, rather than a product that is 'complete', as well as integration into large-scale spatial planning and existing networks at different scales. The fourth and fifth guidelines argue against the tendency to copy-paste urban models from elsewhere, plead for innovative, local designs, and recommend experimentation and exploration. The sixth and seventh address urban design issues and convey the lesson that successful New Towns include infrastructure for every modality right from the start, as well as the inclusion and integrated planning of green open spaces and water networks as the backbone of the urban plan. The final three guidelines deal with the need to embed the New Town in its local context, local culture, and heritage, and the needs for transparent public engagement in the planning process and inclusion of existing residents and communities.

Right to the planned city

This manual is intended to define underlying, often overlooked principles of urban planning that can be used to improve future New Towns. It aims to share good examples, innovative practices, and technologies. It also aims to extend the worldwide accepted principles of the New Urban Agenda, from which New Towns are excluded as an undesirable type of urbanisation. These principles should nonetheless extend to New Town planning.

Finally, this Manual wants to make a case for the 'right to the planned city'. If we accept the astonishing numbers connected to urbanisation in Africa and the projections about the size of future African cities, we should ask what percentage of urban dwellers will actually live in an environment that has been *planned and designed* as a city, a town, a neighbourhood. Most likely, the vast majority of people will live in an urban environment that has not been planned by professionals at all, but has been self-organised by its inhabitants. The unregulated settlement is a universal condition that has occupied different places at different times. Since the second half of the twentieth century, it has been spreading across the so-called 'global South'. One current estimate is that 200 million people in Sub-Saharan African cities are living in slums (or 61.7 percent of the region's urban population); far more than in planned cities.[47] The lack of access to clean drinking water and sanitation, the lack of accessibility of work and school opportunities, and the lack of safety and security are often directly connected to a lack of planning and management of the living environment. This is why the right to the planned city should be central, especially in developing countries, to guarantee a basic quality of life: *planning is essential in creating liveable cities*. As has become clear from our historical research, every New Town should expect an influx of low-income residents, and respond to this certainty in ways that accommodate, incorporate, and respect the needs of the urban poor. This assertion puts forward questions for the design, finance, and governance of future African New Towns. It also requires strong political commitments since there is currently no consensus on the necessity to build inclusive cities and no financial system to support it. With continued focus on neoliberal policies, it is hard to imagine that developers will be asked to provide for groups when they cannot make a profit.

Sites and services schemes exist in different shapes and sizes. Above: Tema, Ghana (1970s). Below: Dandora, Kenya (1970s). (Photos: M. Provoost, 2015 and 2017)

Chronic poverty must for now be accepted as a reality in many African cities. Until New Towns are planned with consideration for the majority, they will be seen and experienced as enclaves that perpetuate feelings of otherness, apartness—*apartheid*. A mentality change is needed. The top-down, hierarchical approach that is typical in African urban planning must learn to include the vitality and dynamics of the informal sector. In Africa, it is difficult to imagine an inclusive and fair urban model without including the informal economy and self-built tradition. Governments and the private sector must begin accepting the existence of the informal sector before real change can be made.

The inclusion of self-organised settlements in New Towns remains as yet untried. Worldwide experiences with 'sites and services' for the urban poor (dating back to the second half of the twentieth century), now seem to be forgotten. Flexible planning methods may be one solution. For example, combining commercial and informal housing development by

47 This percentage is the highest in the world. North Africa had another 12 million slum dwellers; that was just 13.3 percent of its urban residents, the lowest rate in the developing world. See: Racelma, K. (2012) 'Towards African Cities without Slums', www.un.org/africarenewal/magazine/april-2012/towards-african-cities-without-slums UN-Habitat estimates that in 2050 the majority of people in Africa will still live in slums, see: UN-Habitat (2014) The State of African Cities 2014, Re-imagining Sustainable Urban Transitions. Nairobi: UN-Habitat. P. 25.

leaving areas open to self-building, while still providing basic services like water, roads, sewage, and energy. By approaching planning as a tool to build social sustainability, one imagines different degrees of completion for different income groups within a single development. Combining self-building with well-designed infrastructures can decrease spatial segregation and give the urban poor access to the same urban amenities available to the wealthy.

Given the scale of African urbanisation, the question of what the next African cities will be needs to be paramount in the urban imaginations of planners and designers. The present New Towns don't yet offer an inspiring design vocabulary for a new African urbanity. Perhaps there is an opportunity for future New Towns and African cities to learn from the past, and incorporate those lessons in a new urbanism that is distinctly African and not copied from twentieth century European, Chinese, Middle Eastern or American models.

In the introduction to his book *Urban Environments in Africa*, urban scholar Garth Myers lays out a hard truth: 'any efforts to "improve" urban environments in Africa will fail without engagement with and (re)building from the reality of the diverse and complex perspectives on those urban environments'.[48] We see an opportunity and responsibility for future New Towns in Africa to take a more inclusive and adaptive approach to city-making. We believe they have the potential to reimagine the conceptual limits of urban environments and transform the lives of their residents. This book hopes to provide a roadmap for one way to do that.

48 Myers, G. (2016) *Urban Environments in Africa: A Critical Analysis of Environmental Politics*. Bristol: Policy Press. P. 9.

Debunking Myths about African Urbanisation

Edgar Pieterse

In the Introduction chapter the editors make a compelling case that we need to forego the easy options of either vilifying New Towns or simply embracing them as the answer to the intractable problems of 'dysfunctional' African cities. They position this book as a form of ground clearing in order to build a new, historicised, evidence-based debate in order to identify what 'innovative urban, design, financial, and governance models tailored to the needs of African countries' might involve. In supporting this goal, I want to address a number of surprisingly widespread myths about African urbanisation. This is imperative because it is impossible to spawn nuanced debate and effective action unless there is a commitment to fully understand the complex specificities of African urbanisation as it unfolds in variable geographies and political landscapes.

At the outset, it is important to acknowledge the dramatic reversal that has occurred in the formal political and policy arenas during the last eight years regarding the significance of urbanisation in Africa. A number of academic and policy reviews of policy responses from African governments towards urbanisation pointed out the widespread anti-urban bias that characterised dominant political attitudes since independence. UN-Habitat reflected with grave concern that the majority of African governments were more likely to install anti-migration policy reforms instead of pro-actively seeking to understand and harness urbanisation processes. This disposition was further reflected in large donor programmes focused on Africa[1 2]'s green revolution and improving the productivity of agriculture with the subtext that it would keep people in rural areas, and thus prevent the further 'slumification' of cities.

However, between 2010 and 2013, when the first draft of 'Agenda 2063'[3] was debated, a veritable sea change took place. Urbanisation came to be seen as essential to support economic diversification and more active participation in global value chains. It was also recognised that if the renewed investment interest in Africa was to be optimised, it was essential to address the profound infrastructural deficits in most parts of the

1 This is elaborated upon in: Pieterse, E. (2018) The Politics of Governing African Urban Spaces. In: Ammann, C. and Förster, T. (eds.) *African Cities and the Development Conundrum*. International Development Policy Series, No. 10. Geneva: Graduate Institute Publications and Boston: Brill-Nijhoff.

2 UN-Habitat (2014) *State of African Cities Report 2014. Re-imagining sustainable urban Transitions*. Nairobi: UN-Habitat.

3 *Agenda 2063* is both a manifesto and strategic agenda for African countries to guide policy priorities for the long-term. It was produced to mark the 50th anniversary of the establishment of the Organisation for African Unity and project how Africa could fulfil her potential over the next fifty years. It also serves as a policy touchstone for the region when it engages with global development policy processes related to sustainable development, climate change, trade, and multilaterialism.

African continent. This suggests the need for connectivity infrastructure to get resources and commodities out of Africa into the world, and the expansion of meagre network infrastructures for energy, water, transport and other systems in major cities because this was where international investors wanted to be based. Put differently, the larger perception shift that took root in the 2000s[4]—i.e. 'Africa rising'—which redefined Africa as a continent of economic opportunity, provided the impetus for political elites to pay attention to the urban question in a novel way.

This proved fortuitous for the urban policy communities because they could now draw a connection between governance reform (decentralization), territorial planning, infrastructure investment, and improving economic performance. Tellingly, in 2010, the African Development Bank (AfDB) quietly published 'The Bank Group's Urban Development Strategy: Transforming Africa's Cities and Towns into Engines of Economic Growth and Social Development.'[5] Thereafter, it was the first draft of *Agenda 2063* that added momentum to this shift:

> We aspire that by 2063, Africa shall be a prosperous continent, with the means and resources to drive its own development, with sustainable and long-term stewardship of its resources and where: [...] Cities and other settlements are hubs of cultural and economic activities, with modernized infrastructure, and people have access to affordable and decent housing including housing finance together with all the basic necessities of life such as, water, sanitation, energy, public transport and ICT.

This is from the final version adopted in 2015, but the tenor of Agenda 2063 must be read in the context of the broader political momentum that was being built through a variety of inter-locked UN summits: the Sendai Framework for Disaster Risk Conference (March 2015); the Financing for Development Conference in Addis Ababa (June 2015); the Sustainable Development Goals Summit (September 2015); the Paris Climate Change Conference (December 2015); and then Habitat III (October 2016) where the 'New Urban Agenda' was adopted. It is important to keep in mind that each African government and the African Union must formulate official responses to be tabled at each of these events, which all contributes to forging a new 'common sense' in terms of macro and micro development policies related to urbanisation.

In parallel, a number of private sector think tanks were making very similar arguments as part of that larger discursive machinery that shapes investor perceptions of risk and opportunity. It took no time at all for these 'messages' to find their way into political speeches and policy pronouncement. A third track of ideas came from the African academic and NGO sector. They equally sensed there was a real opportunity to make a case for more rigorous research and the establishment of scientific databases to underpin the newfound appetite for urban policy reform. The collective and individual contributions of the members of the African Urban Research Initiative (AURI) and Association of African Planning Schools (AAPS) are good examples of this.[6]

4 Parnell, S., Pieterse, E. and Haysom, G. (2018) African Dreams: locating urban infrastructure in the 2030 sustainable developmental agenda. Area Development & Policy. doi: 10.1080/23792949.2018.1428111

5 AfDB (2010). The Bank Group's Urban Development Strategy: Transforming Africa's Cities and Towns into Engines of Economic Growth and Social Development. Tunis: African Development Bank.

6 In the past, African scholars would only be engaged by UN-Habitat and other policy agencies as experts to perform consultancy services. There were hardly any opportunities for academic critique and engagement. With the establishment of AURI and AAPS, organised local government, UN agencies, development banks, and pan-African institutions had counterparts from the academy to engage and these organisations established an advocacy platform.

Paradoxically, the upshot of all this discursive swirl was often a dumbing down of the debate and issues. Politicians and investors are naturally drawn to assuring narratives, and such storylines find traction because they operate through simplistic myths. If INTI and other actors are to succeed in bringing more thought, evidence, and care to the debate on what role New Towns can play in the larger story of Africa's development trajectories, we need to upend these myths. This chapter will illustrate the potential of this line of research, but much more empirically grounded work is required, and this is exactly what African knowledge institutions should be doing.

Myth 1: Urbanisation is out of control

> Kinshasa had just 20,000 people in 1920. By 1940 it was home to about 450,000 people. Today it has possibly 12 million and is predicted to be Africa's second largest city with 75 million people inside 50 years. By western standards it is a dysfunctional, sprawling megalopolis, ringed by vast shantytowns of informal settlements, their infrastructure non-existent or collapsing.[7]

7 Vidal, J. (2018) 'The 100 million city: is 21st century urbanisation out of control?' The Guardian, March 19. www.theguardian.com/cities/2018/mar/19/urban-explosion-kinshasa-el-alto-growth-mexico-city-bangalore-lagos

This quote is drawn from an article that rings the alarm siren about the unfathomable consequences of unmanaged urbanisation. This kind of discourse operates on the assumption that if you scare decision-makers enough they will see the light and start acting proactively to manage urbanisation. A lot of popular reporting is based on this kind of extrapolation with no qualifiers that the specific dynamics and trajectories in various regions of the continent, and within countries, are extremely variable.

	Diversifiers	Early urbanisers	Late urbanisers	Agrarians	Natural resource-based
Ubn rate	40-60%	35-50%	18-30%	<30%	30-70%
Fertility	<3 children	5 children ave	>5 children	high	high
GNI p/c (USD)	<$10000k	$1-4000	$1-2.200	<$1600	$500-20000
HDI	Above 0.60	0.40-0.57	0.38-0.51	0.34-0.48	Wide range
	5 countries	9 countries, mainly West African	11 countries, a number in East Africa	11 countries, many landlocked	13 countries

Table 1: African countries by economic category, urbanisation rate and other variables. (Source: OECD, AfDB and UNDP (2016) *African Economic Outlook 2016. Sustainable Cities and Structural Transformation.* Paris: OECD)

A useful corrective was put forward by the Organisation for Economic Co-operation and Development (OECD) and partners in 2016 when they published the 'Africa Economic Outlook 2016'. This document suggests that it is crucial to keep in mind the economic structure of each African country, its socio-economic indicators and the kind of exogenous forces that impact demographic dynamics. Thus, they provide the following typology (Table 1) to demonstrate the links between economic structure (top row), variable rate of urbanisation, average fertility rates, gross national income per capita and the average human development index for each group of countries. The last row shows the variety across Africa and the obvious implication is that the urbanisation dynamic in these diverse countries cannot be spoken about as if it is one trajectory. Moreover, local and regional geopolitical dynamics can also distort conventional projects. We know that both conflict-related pressures and extreme climate events can trigger accelerated displacement and bolster urbanisation patterns.[8]

8 OECD, AfDB and UNDP (2016) African Economic Outlook 2016. Sustainable Cities and Structural Transformation. Paris: OECD.

9 "Rural migration puts African cities under strain", verbal news reporting by Ntokozo Khumalo for ECNA. Online: youtu.be/9Lcn5BnPoJM

Myth 2: Rural-to-urban migration is the primary driver of African urbanisation

> In many cities, overpopulation due to rural migration has seen infrastructure collapse, potholed streets, traffic jams, frequent power outages and poor sanitation are the result.[9]

This is the taken-for-granted assumption about the primary driver of urbanisation among the lay population, political parties and politicians. In countries where the rural population continue to be the majority and where urban dwellers regard rural areas as an important part of their collective identity, it is understandable that this is the perception. However, the report cited above paints a much more variegated picture. In the first decade of the postcolonial era, migration from rural areas accounted for more than 50% of urban growth but during the 1980-1990 decade, it was already down to 25%. Moreover, due to the different economic structure and demographic dynamics we still see tremendous variation. For example, 'Rural-urban migration accounts for less than a third of urban population growth in 22 African countries. It accounts for

Figure 1: Urban growth rates in selected African countries, 1960-2010. (Source: OECD, AfDB and UNDP (2016) *African Economic Outlook 2016. Sustainable Cities and Structural Transformation*. Paris: OECD)

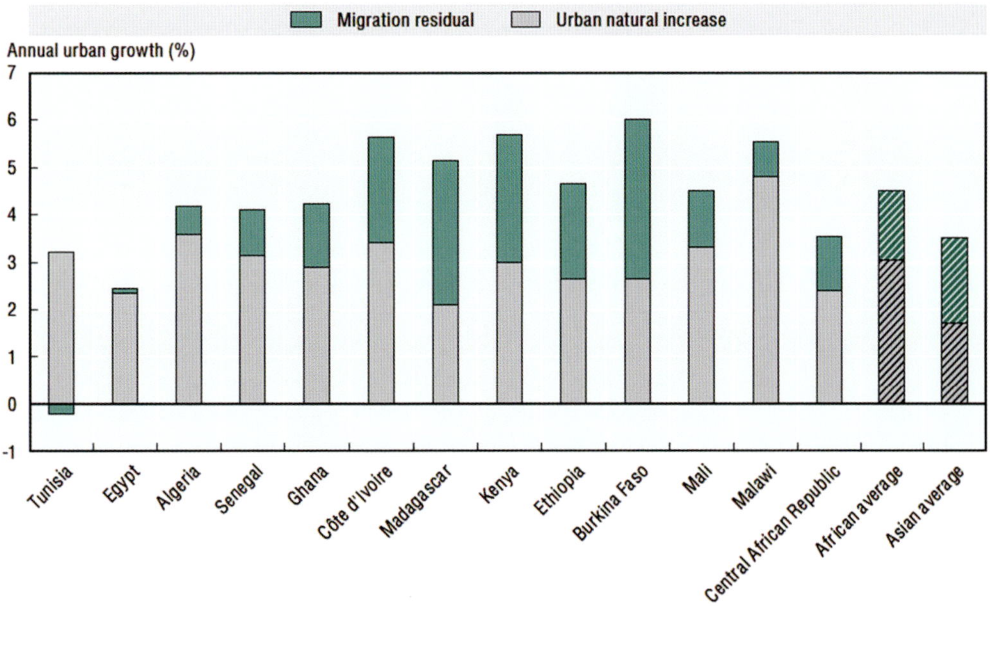

over 50% in only 7 African countries (Burkina Faso, Cabo Verde, Lesotho, Namibia, Rwanda, Seychelles and South Africa).'[10] This variation across countries over a forty-year period is illustrated in Figure 1, drawn from the same study.

Even though it is clear that urbanisation is not primarily driven by rural-to-urban migration, it is crucial to keep in mind that rural areas also continue to grow and agriculture will remain a significant share of GDP. In fact, since most (three quarters) urban Africans live in relatively small urban settlements with populations well below the 300,000 threshold, the OECD and partners urge us to think of 'a rural-urban interface' zone as the variable landscape where people are compelled to engage in livelihood strategies that are effectively both rural and urban. The pervasive rural vs. urban mentality has little practical or analytical value. These territories need to be understood in concrete terms as African economies evolve and improve productivity across value-chains.

Myth 3: In time, informality will be replaced with formality

In mainstream policy responses there is a powerful modernist confidence about the inevitable causal connections between: planning for urbanisation, installing the necessary infrastructure to buttress economic development, and as growth takes off, finding suitable revenue sources for the (local) state to continue with further infrastructure investments making firms, labour and households more productive. This is the assumed pathway that will ineluctably lead to an expansion of formal jobs, raising household incomes which in turn will allow people to leave their shacks and enter the housing mortgage market, or at least be provided with some form of public housing. For the politicians this represents the sure signs that they are making the journey from being classified 'low-income' to 'middle-income' status. I understand and appreciate why this policy recipe is so appealing. However, the evidence suggests it will be more complicated.

The main issue is that very few African economies are sufficiently diversified to ensure an underlying robustness of the economy. A durable economy is more likely to navigate risks and shocks—which is a precondition in an increasingly globally connected and volatile economy—and therefore more likely to generate sustainable jobs across a wider spectrum. However, there is a deeper structural economic problem that mitigates against the generation of large-scale formal jobs. One powerful illustration of this is the postcolonial record, which shows that since 1960 there has effectively been a decline of manufacturing jobs from an already low base (see Figure 2).

10 OECD, AfDB and UNDP (2016) African Economic Outlook 2016. Sustainable Cities and Structural Transformation. Paris: OECD. P. 154.

11 According to the International Labour Organisation, 'stable employment' includes wage and salaried employees and business owners. 'Vulnerable employment' includes subsistence farming, informal self-employment and work for family members and is characterised by low and erratic incomes.

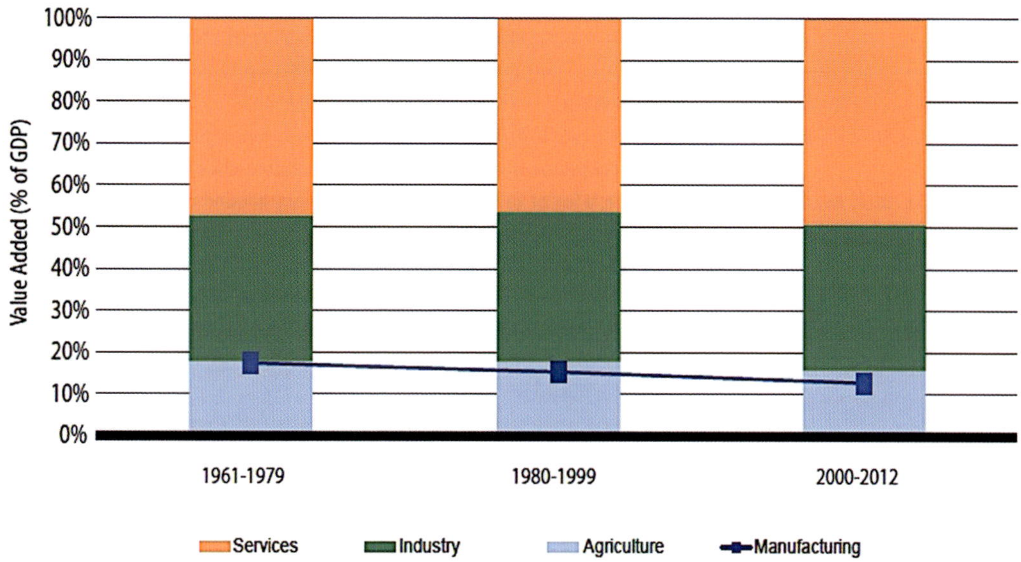

Figure 2: GDP Composition by sector, Africa, 1961-2012. (Source: UNECA [United Nations Economic Commission for Africa] (2015) *Economic Report on Africa 2015: Industrializing Through Trade*. Addis Ababa: UNECA. P.47)

Furthermore, a recent AfDB and OECD report reflects that since 2000 when the economic upturn set in across most of the continent, there has hardly been any decline in the proportion of workers—the vast majority—trapped in vulnerable employment. Figure 3 demonstrates this clearly. The conclusion that one has to draw is that for the foreseeable future, if current conditions remain equal, most African households will not be able to access formal jobs at a large scale, nor will they be able to find formal accommodation. Given the business models that underpin New Town proposals, I cannot think of a more pertinent trend to be addressed by the debates on the appropriateness and viability of New Towns.[11]

Figure 3: Employment status for Africans, 2000-2022, and the 2023 targets of Agenda 2063. (Source: AUC/OECD (2018) *Africa's Development Dynamics 2018: Growth, Jobs and Inequalities*. Paris: OECD Publishing. P.42. DOI: 10.1787/888933782525)

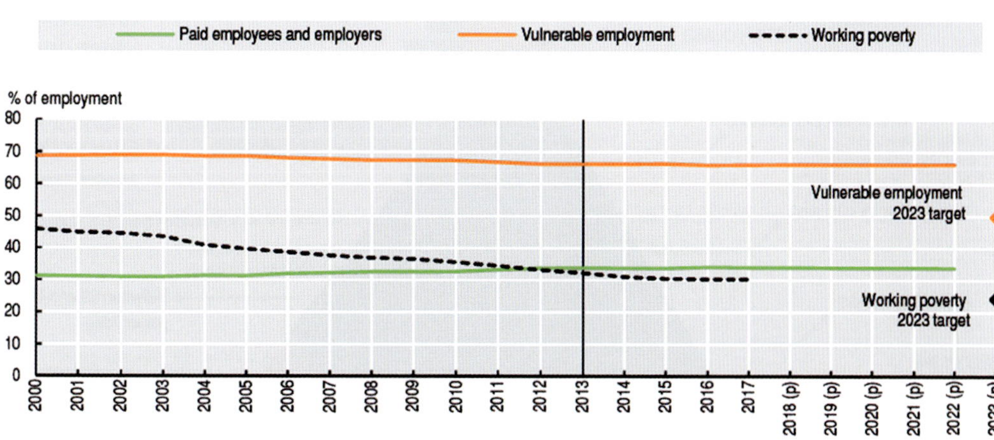

Note: (p) : projections.
Source: Authors' calculations based on the ILO (2017), *ILOSTAT*.

Conclusion

It is clear that there is a massive gap between the picture afforded us by available data/evidence and the popular myths about African urbanisation. Innovation will not be possible unless the basis for engagement about appropriate and viable responses to unjust urbanisation is underpinned with an informed account of what is actually happening on the ground. In this spirit, I want to suggest a few requirements for genuine innovation to emerge. First, and predictably, there has to be a shared commitment or fealty to the collection and analysis of available data. This should spur on investments in improving these collective resources. African universities, science councils, statistical bureaus and multilateral development institutions should work together to achieve this.

Second, policy makers and activists should adopt a holistic systems perspective on the urban to allow us to move beyond formal-informal dichotomies in order to better understand the hybrid nature of all aspects of contemporary life. Land markets, housing markets, labour markets, and infrastructure networks are amalgams of institutional practices that contravene binaries all the time. Our policy frameworks and planning tools need to come to terms with this and work with the grain of complex, adaptive urban dynamics. There is increasingly a recognition of this requirement but it is hard to find examples where it is being implemented.

Third, we need to appreciate that politics matter and are inescapable if we want to improve the substance and efficacy of urban policies. Productive politics demand networked leaders from across society that are able to sustain collaborative decision-making forums and timeously address inevitable conflicts and trade-offs. This is only possible if there is some kind of shared vision and vocabulary nurtured across institutional and cultural divides. Productive politics is further dependent on effective accountability mechanisms. Reforms in planning and budgetary processes of the state and corporatized Public Private Partnerships to enable participatory democracy are essential to achieve substantive accountability. Given the interdependent nature of urban challenges, effective solutions can only be co-produced. This is not about achieving so-called win-win solutions but achieving democratic agreements on how trade-offs are being managed through sequenced and articulated investments.[15]

Finally, this conceptualisation of responsive, democratic, evidence-based urban politics is not something that can be engineered through top-down edicts or reforms. It demands spaces with a culture that nurtures vibrant feedback loops between planning, experimentation, action, learning, and so forth. The kind of innovation that the editors envisage for the future of New Towns and holistic urban development cannot arise without an appetite to consciously foster a different culture of politics, collaboration, decision-making, and deep reflection.

15 This is elaborated upon in: Simone, A. and Pieterse, E. (2017) New Urban Worlds. Inhabiting Dissonant Times. Cambridge: Polity.

PART 1. ATLAS

Introduction

These maps are intended to add context to the essays and case studies. They illustrate the diversity of conditions across the African continent, and indicate trends over time. We have selected the maps presented here to give more background to the complex issues related to urbanism and urban growth. Issues depicted in these maps, such as fertility rates, average incomes, and home financing rates, are deeply connected to these processes.

The short texts added to the maps are sourced from the essays in this book, and point to both extreme conditions as well as anecdotes that build a fuller picture of the data quantified in the maps. The maps themselves are drawn based on data in the sources listed at the bottom of the page.

Following the maps, the Atlas provides an overview of the 148 New Towns from 1960-2017 that meet the criteria set out in the introduction to this book. As stated, there are likely more examples that we were unable to identify. We have done our best to present verified data, but New Towns, like other cities, are in a constant state of flux and numbers may have changed since the time of writing.

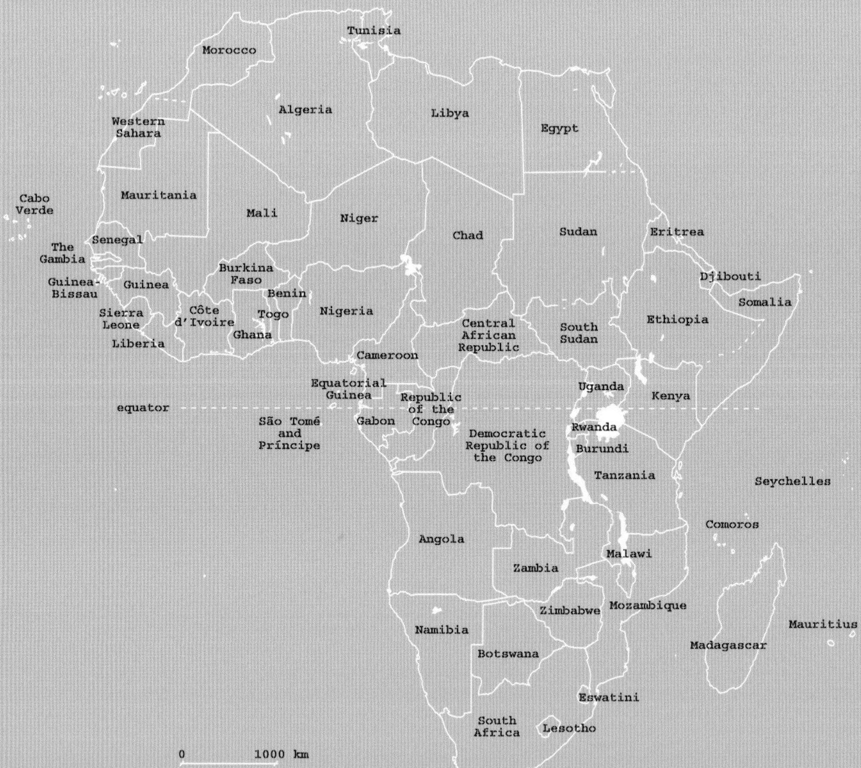

1960 - 1969

1970 - 1979

POLICY

- Decentralization city
- Capital city
- Private city
- Eco-city
- Smart city
- Industrial city
- Apartheid city
- Resort city

SIZE

- < 30.000
- 30.000 < > 100.000
- 100.000 < > 1.000.000
- > 1.000.000

1980 - 1989

1990 - 1999

POLICY

- Decentralization city
- Capital city
- Private city
- Eco-city
- Smart city
- Industrial city
- Apartheid city
- Resort city

SIZE

- < 30.000
- 30.000 < > 100.000
- 100.000 < > 1.000.000
- > 1.000.000

2000 - 2009

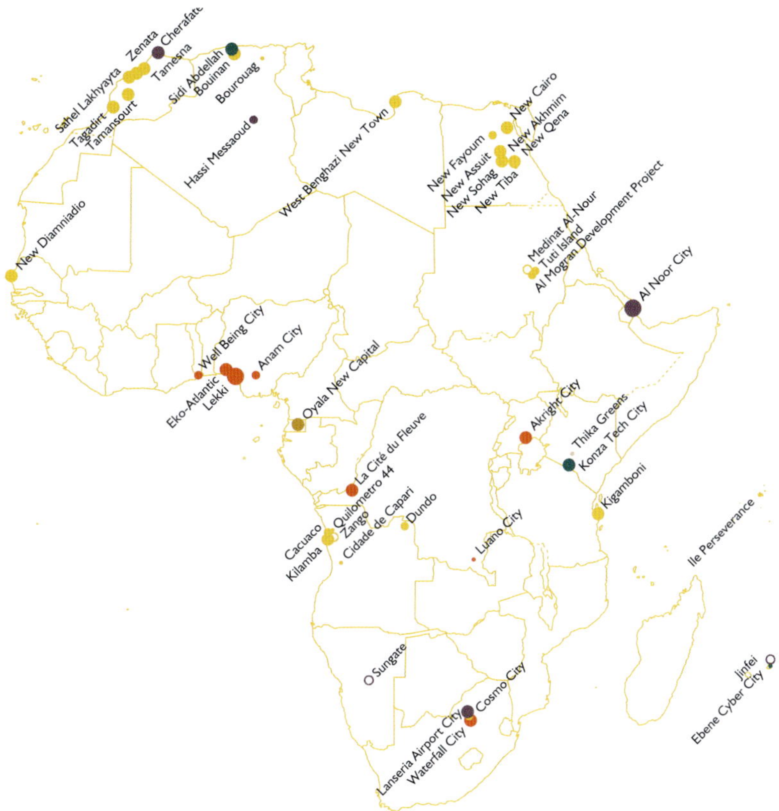

2010 -

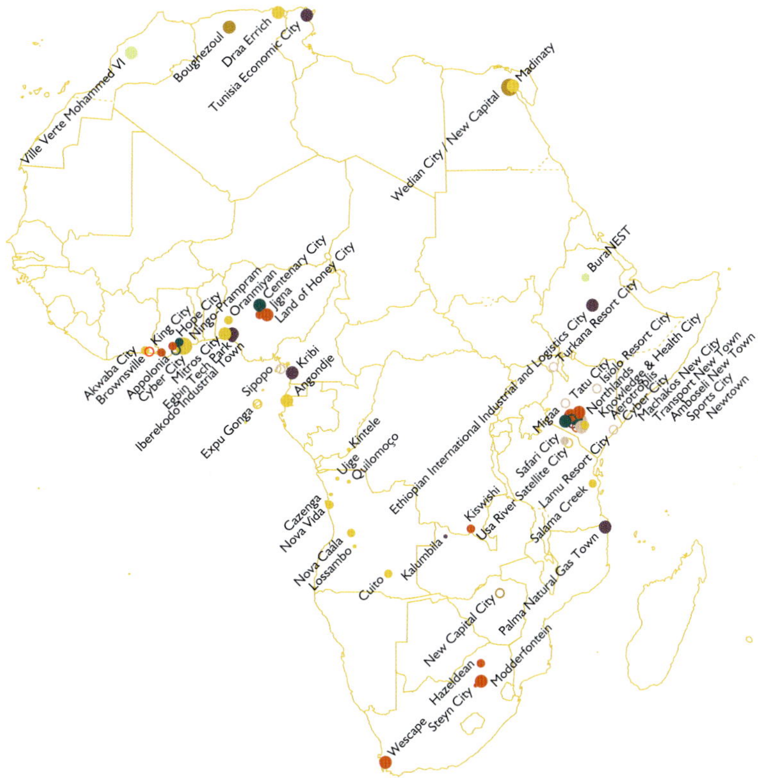

POLICY

- Decentralization city
- Capital city
- Private city
- Eco-city
- Smart city
- Industrial city
- Apartheid city
- Resort city

SIZE

- < 30.000
- 30.000 < > 100.000
- 100.000 < > 1.000.000
- > 1.000.000

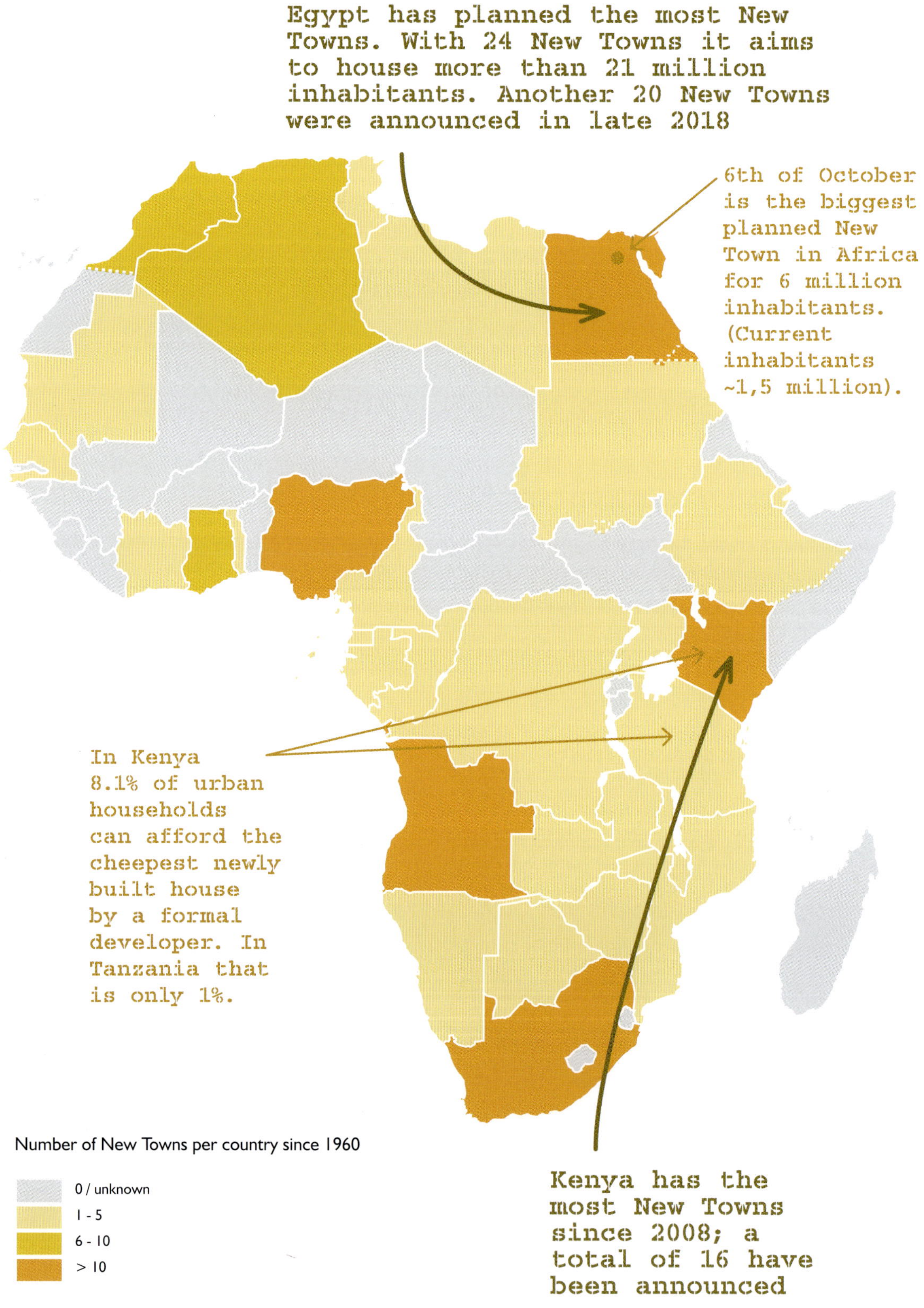
Egypt has planned the most New Towns. With 24 New Towns it aims to house more than 21 million inhabitants. Another 20 New Towns were announced in late 2018
6th of October is the biggest planned New Town in Africa for 6 million inhabitants. (Current inhabitants ~1,5 million).
In Kenya 8.1% of urban households can afford the cheepest newly built house by a formal developer. In Tanzania that is only 1%.
Kenya has the most New Towns since 2008; a total of 16 have been announced
Number of New Towns per country since 1960
0 / unknown
1 - 5
6 - 10
> 10

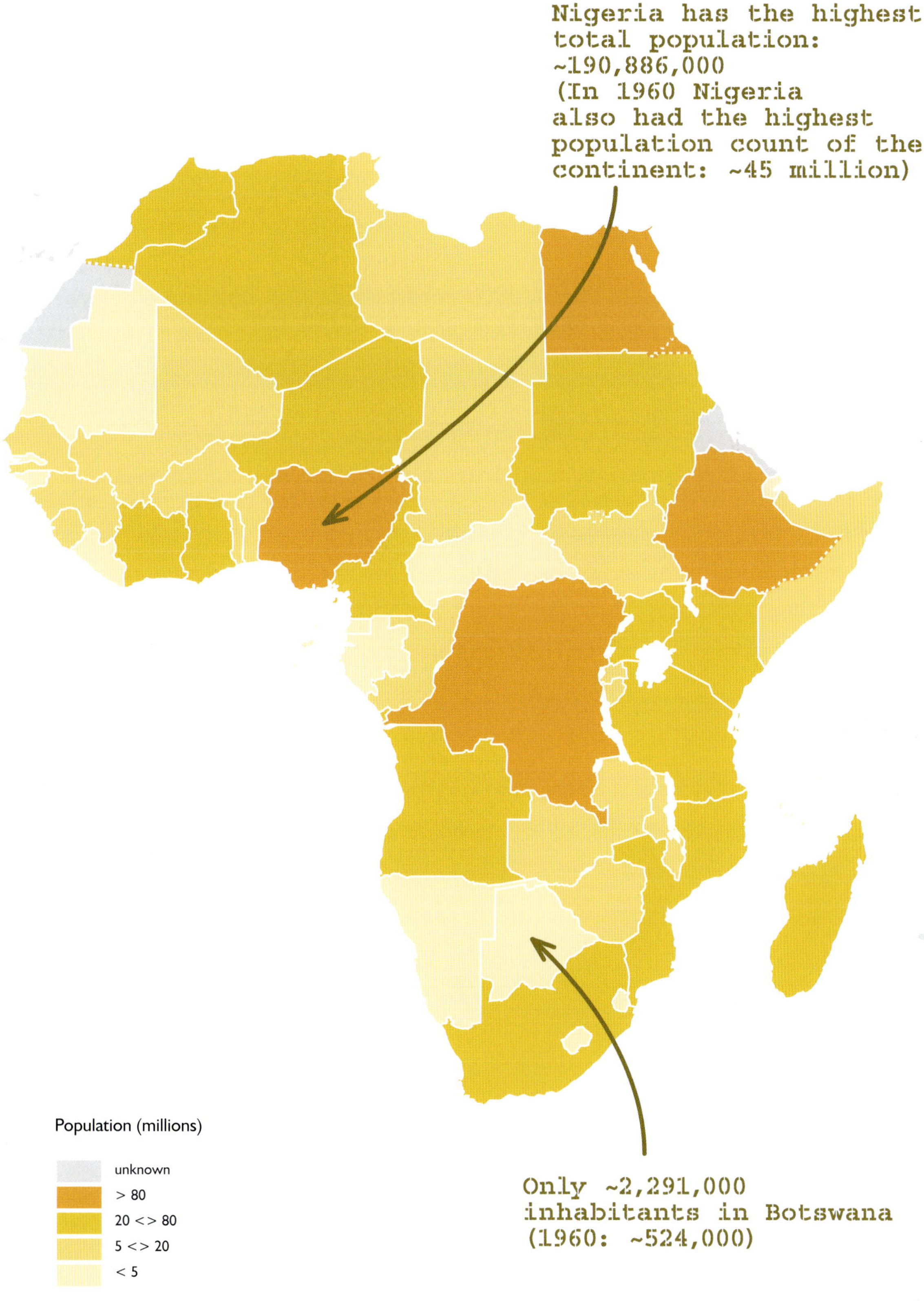

data.worldbank.org (2017)

The biggest change of average births per woman is in Libya. It went from an average of 7.2 in 1960 to 2.3 in 2016

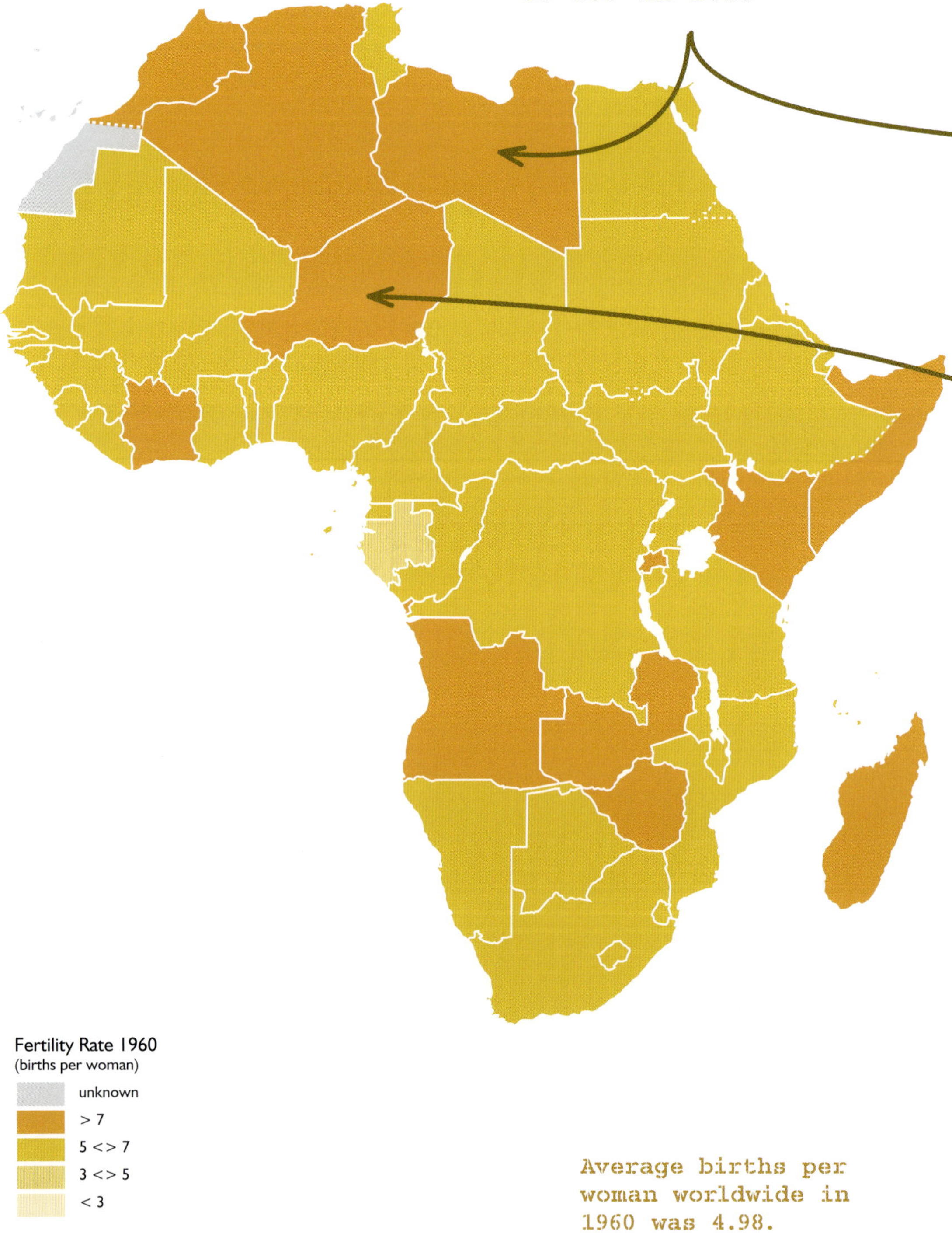

Average births per woman worldwide in 1960 was 4.98.

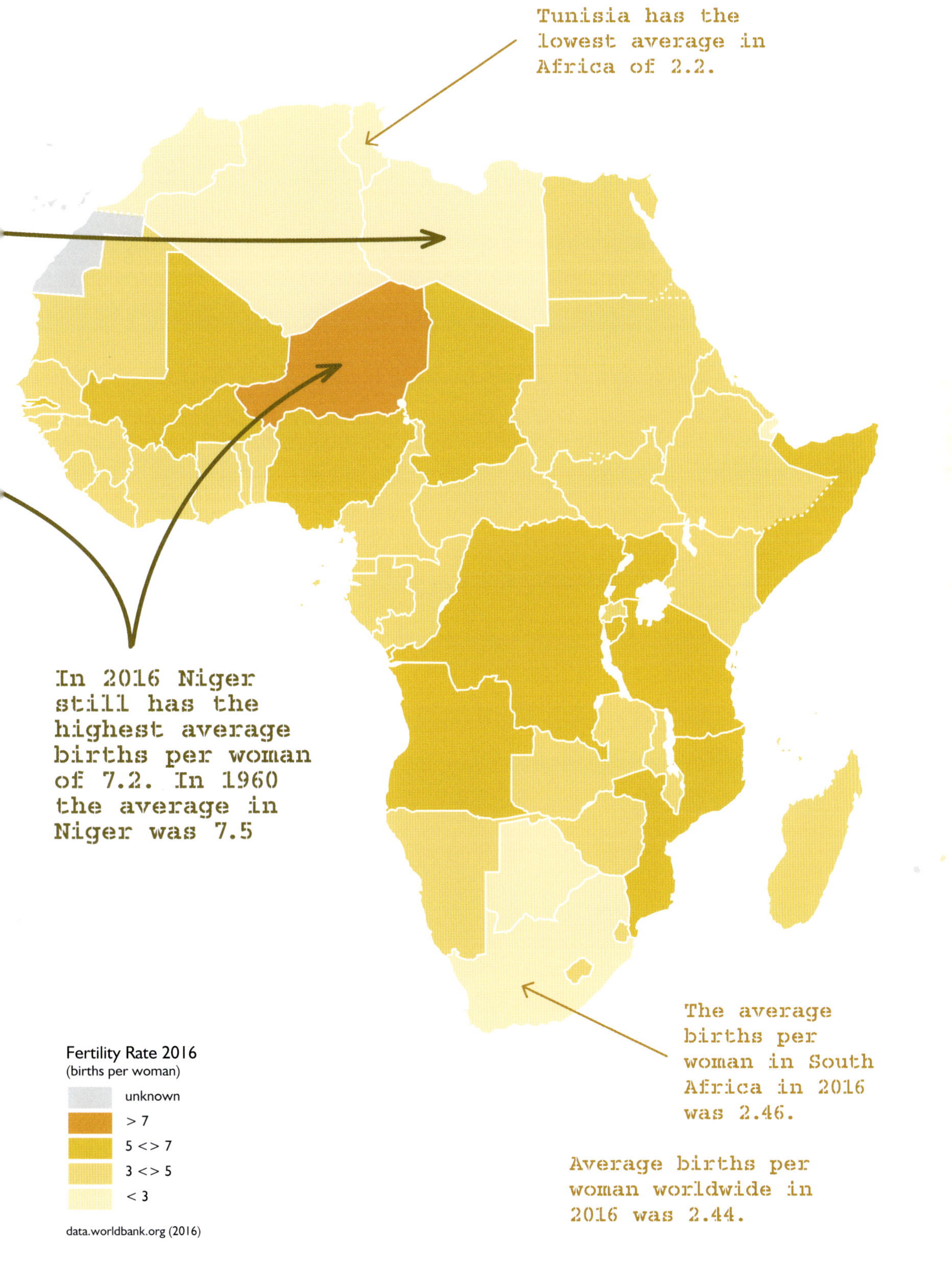
Tunisia has the lowest average in Africa of 2.2.
In 2016 Niger still has the highest average births per woman of 7.2. In 1960 the average in Niger was 7.5
The average births per woman in South Africa in 2016 was 2.46.
Average births per woman worldwide in 2016 was 2.44.
Fertility Rate 2016
(births per woman)
unknown
> 7
5 <> 7
3 <> 5
< 3
data.worldbank.org (2016)

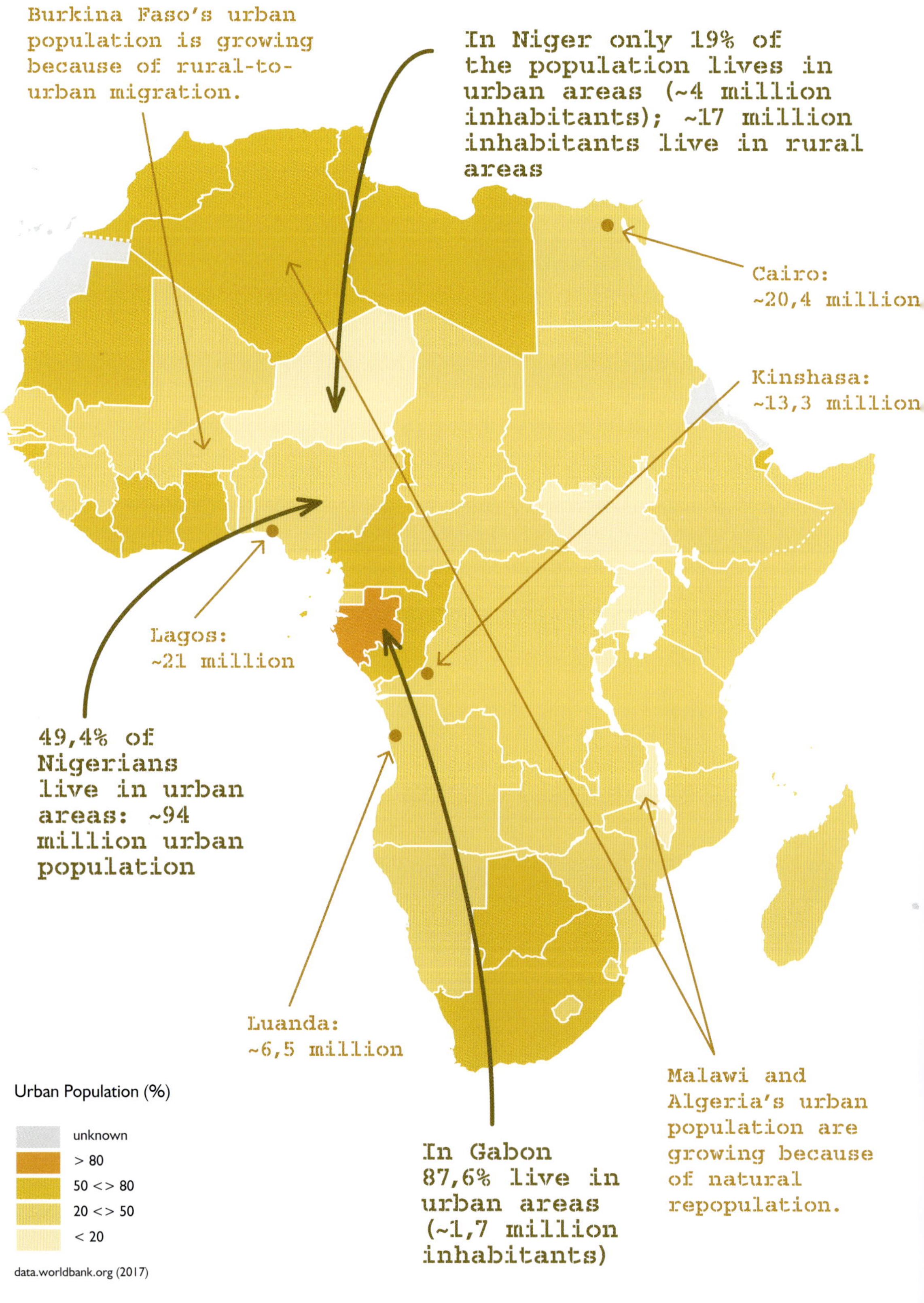

Burkina Faso's urban population is growing because of rural-to-urban migration.
In Niger only 19% of the population lives in urban areas (~4 million inhabitants); ~17 million inhabitants live in rural areas
Cairo: ~20,4 million
Kinshasa: ~13,3 million
Lagos: ~21 million
49,4% of Nigerians live in urban areas: ~94 million urban population
Luanda: ~6,5 million
Malawi and Algeria's urban population are growing because of natural repopulation.
In Gabon 87,6% live in urban areas (~1,7 million inhabitants)
Urban Population (%)
unknown
> 80
50 <> 80
20 <> 50
< 20
data.worldbank.org (2017)

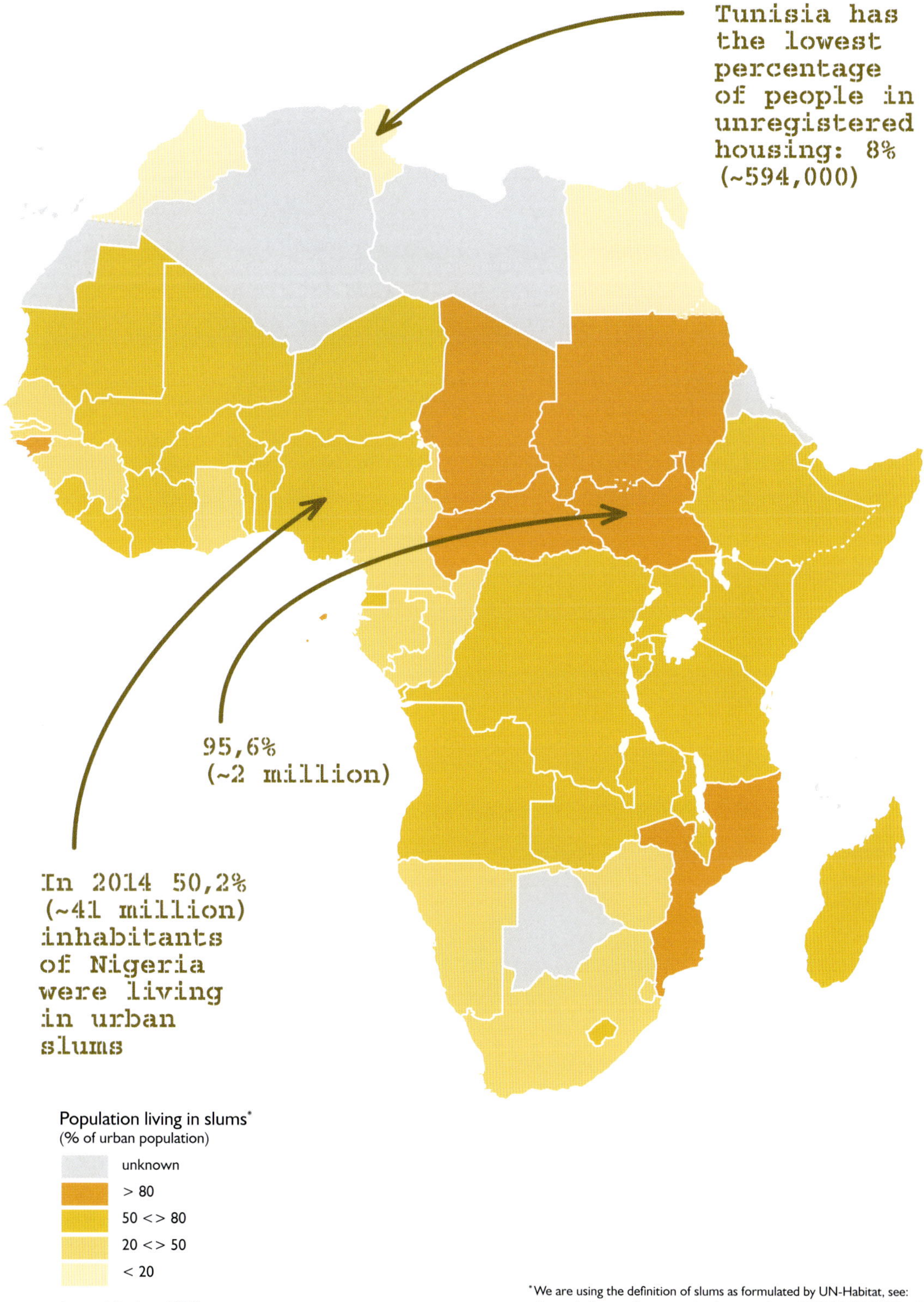

data.worldbank.org (2014)

*We are using the definition of slums as formulated by UN-Habitat, see: mirror.unhabitat.org/documents/media_centre/sowcr2006/SOWCR%205.pdf

Climate map 1980-2016

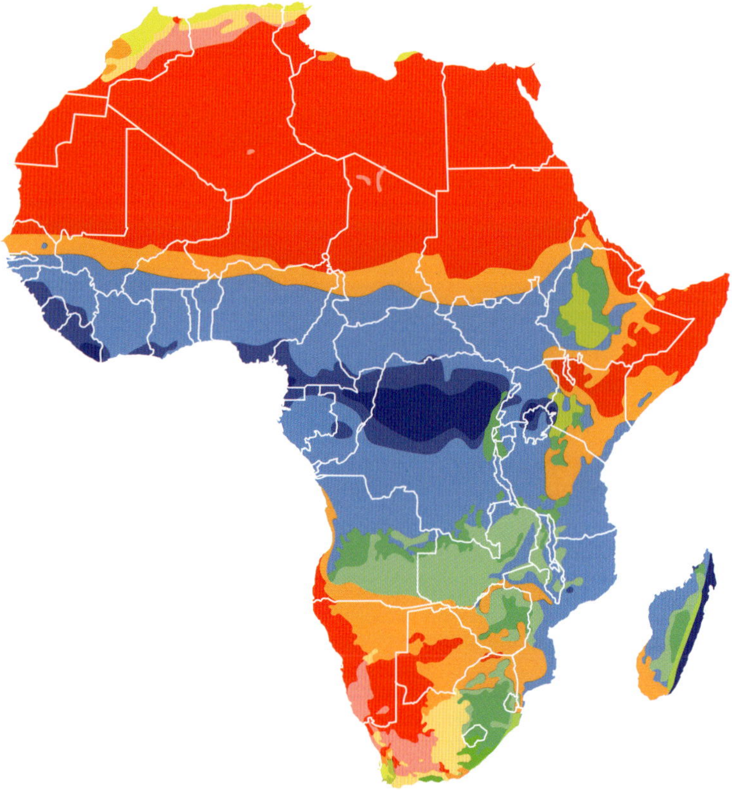

Climate map 2071-2100

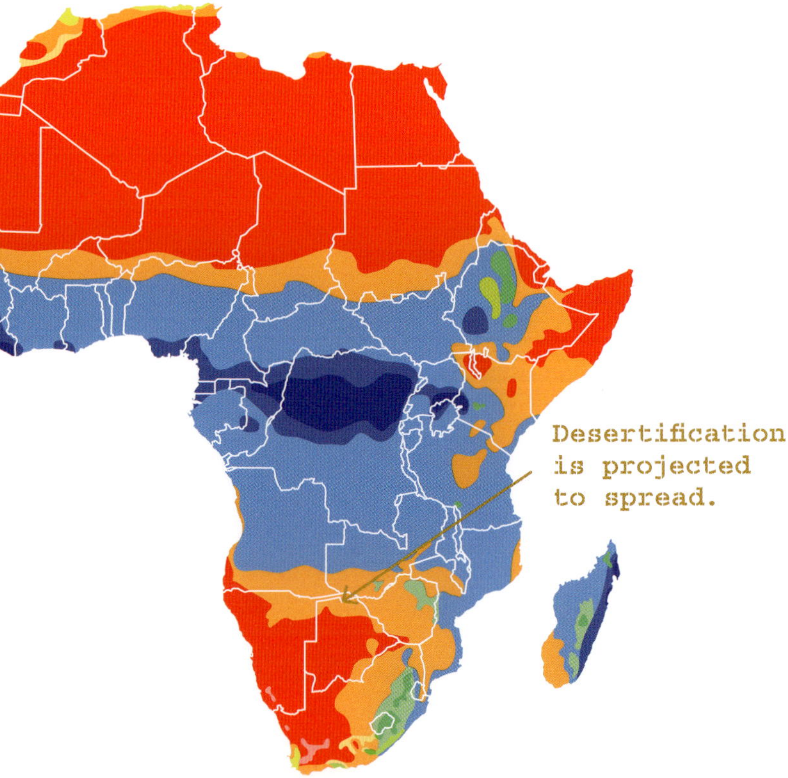

Köppen-Geiger
climate classification

- Equatorial (Af)
- Monsoon (Am)
- Tropical Savanna (Aw)
- Warm Desert (BWh)
- Cold Desert (BWk)
- Warm Semi-Arid (BSh)
- Cold Semi-Arid (BSk)
- Warm Mediterranean (Csa)
- Temparate Mediterranean (Csb)
- Humid Subtropical (Cwa)
- Subtropical Oceanic Highland (Cwb)
- Warm Oceanic (Cfa)
- Temperate Oceanic (Cfb)

Beck, H.E., N.E. Zimmermann, T.R. McVicar, N. Vergopolan, A. Berg, E.F. Wood: Present and future Köppen-Geiger climate classification maps at 1-km resolution, Nature Scientific Data, 2018.

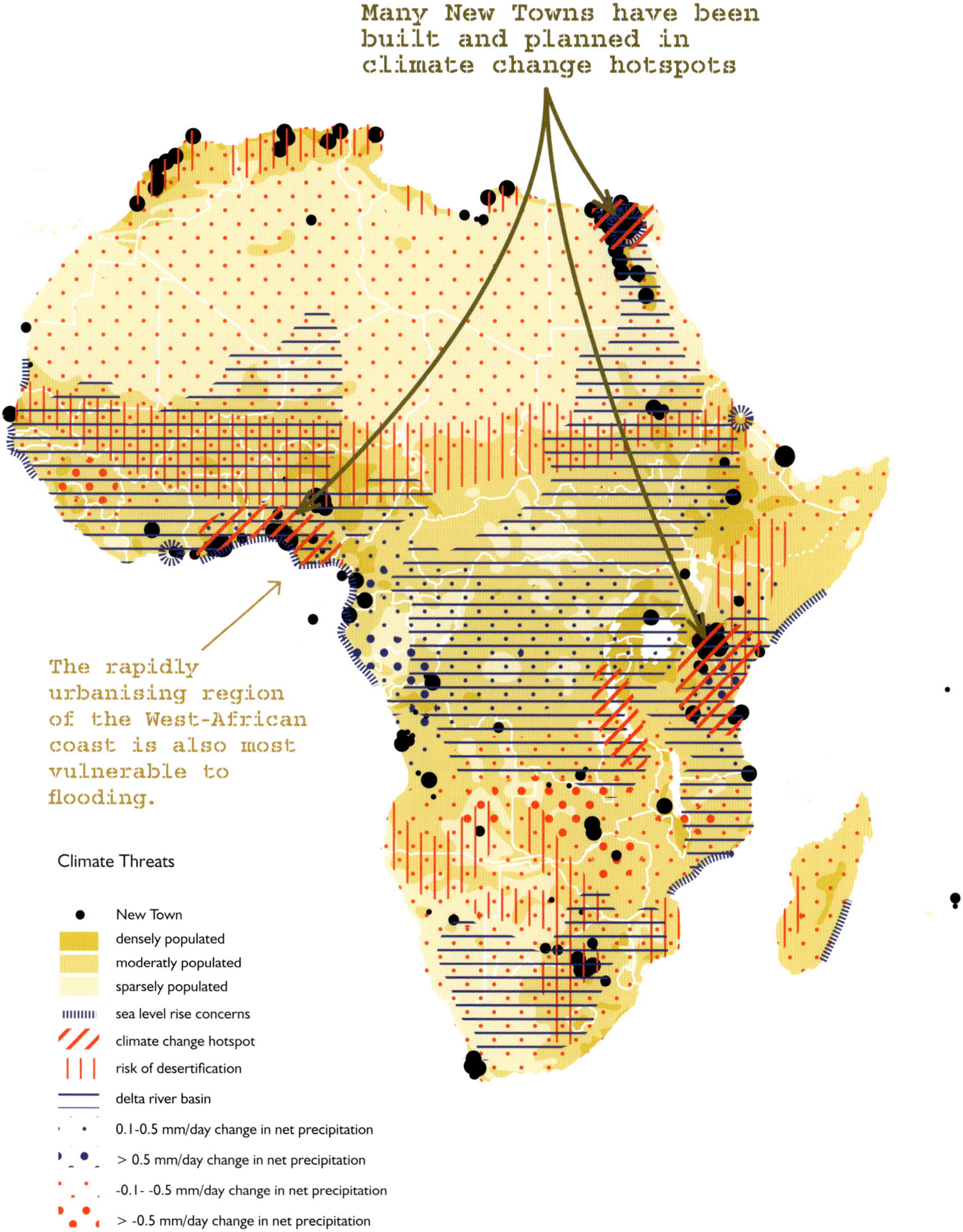

The Geography of Future Water Challenges, PBL (2018) / Migration, Environment and Climate Change: Evidence for Policy (MECLEP) in collaboration with IOM (2015)

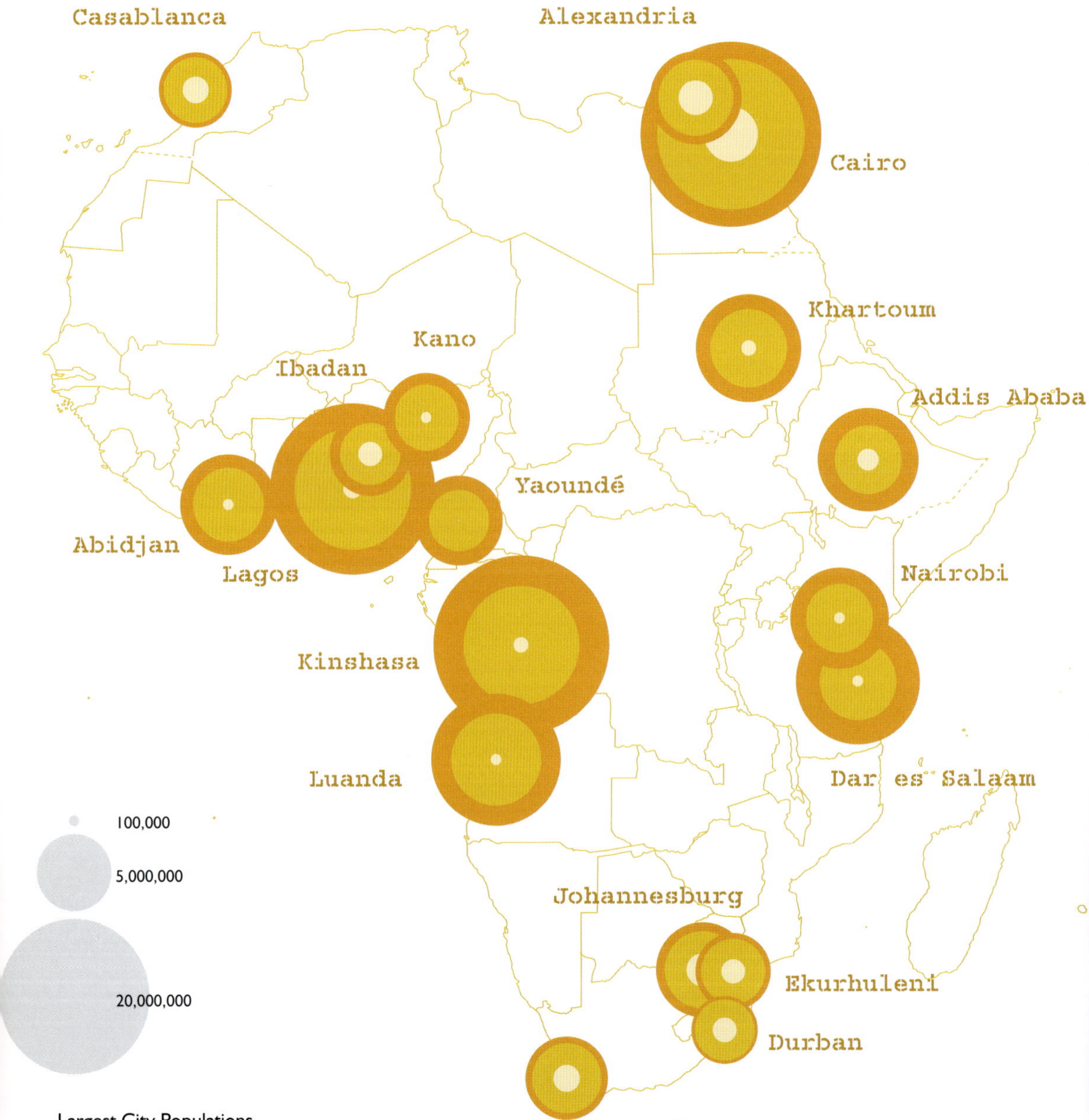

Largest City Populations
Cities with a total population of more than 3 million in 2015

1950

2015

2035

United Nations (2018)

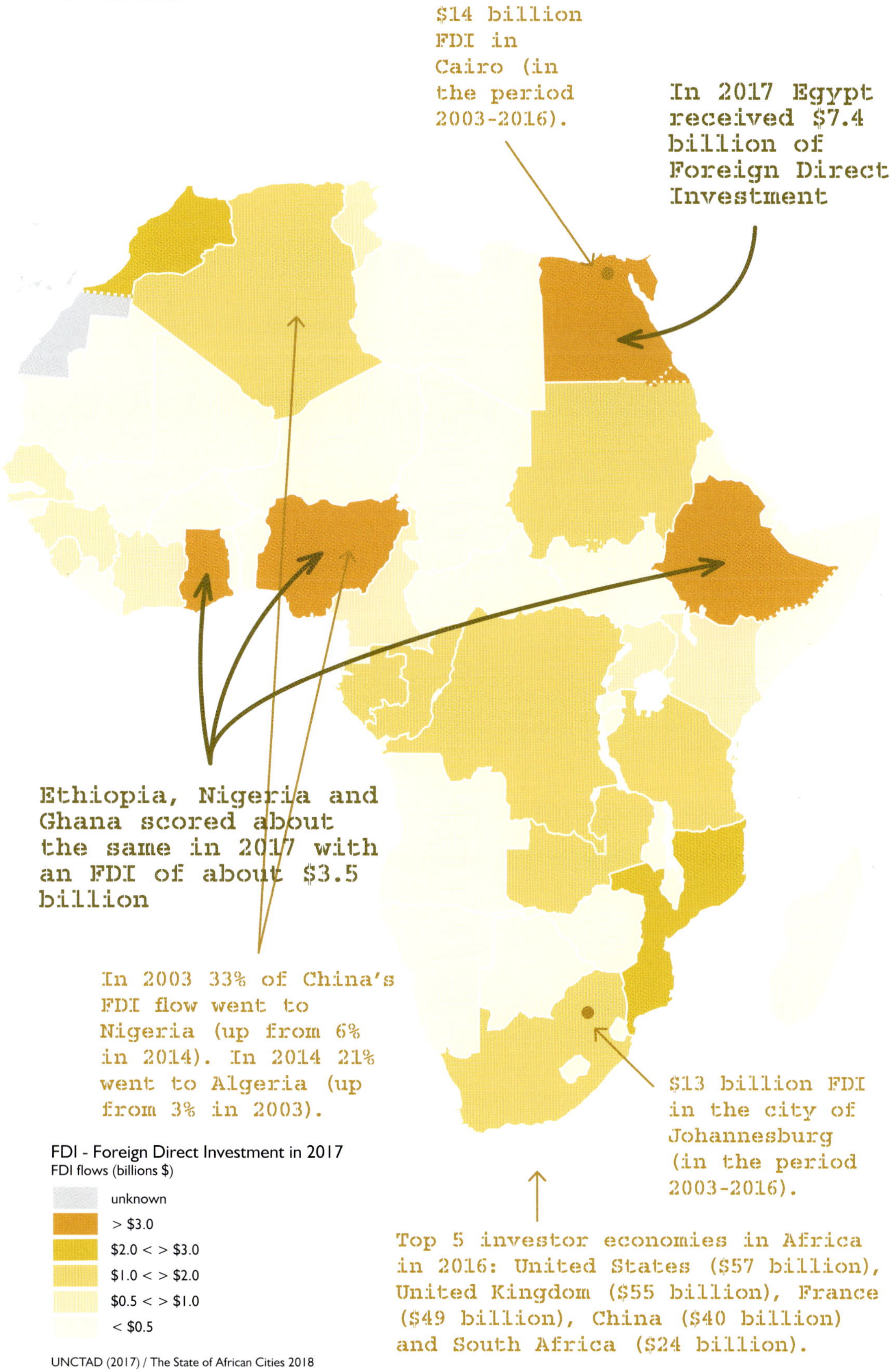

UNCTAD (2017) / The State of African Cities 2018

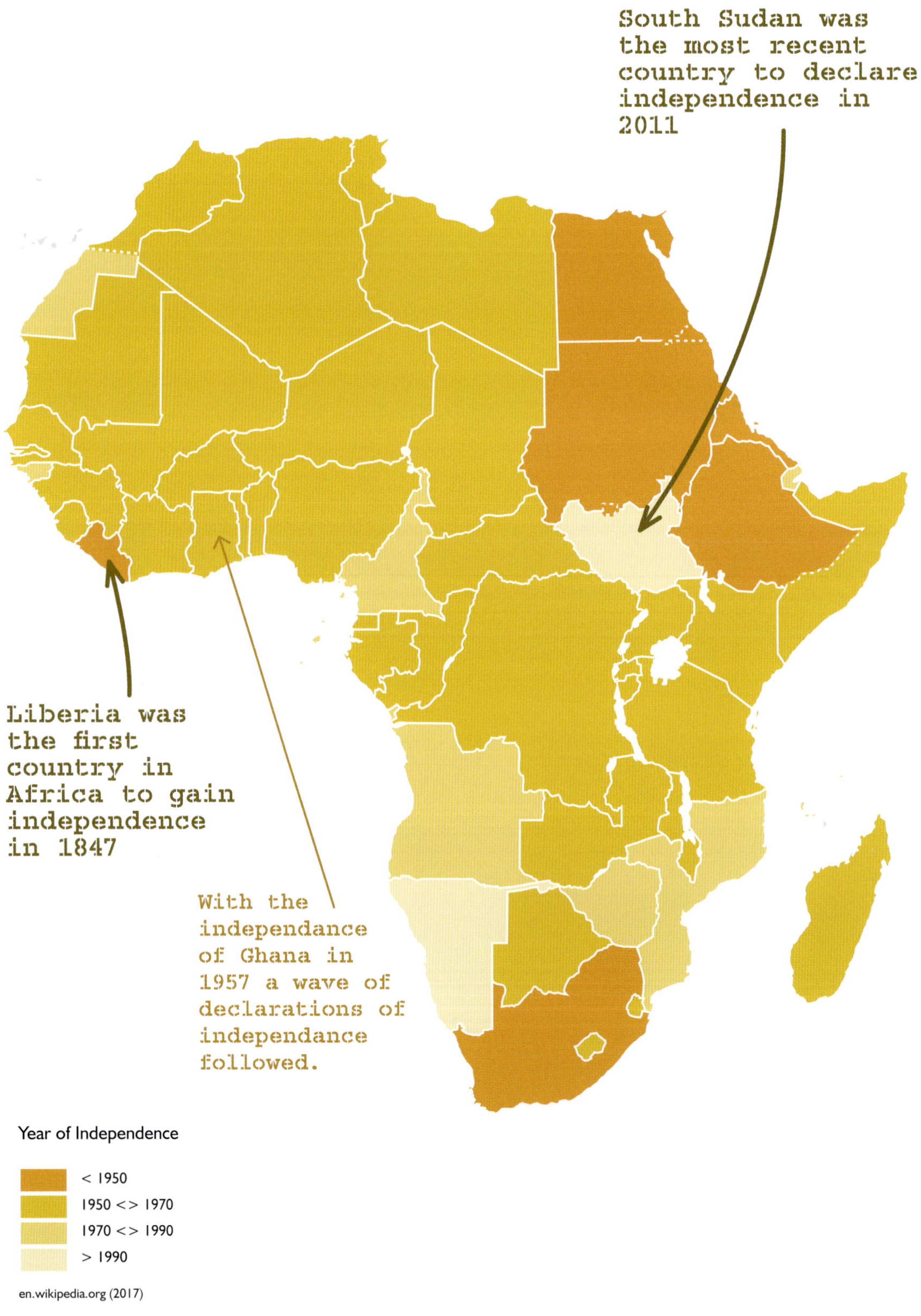

en.wikipedia.org (2017)

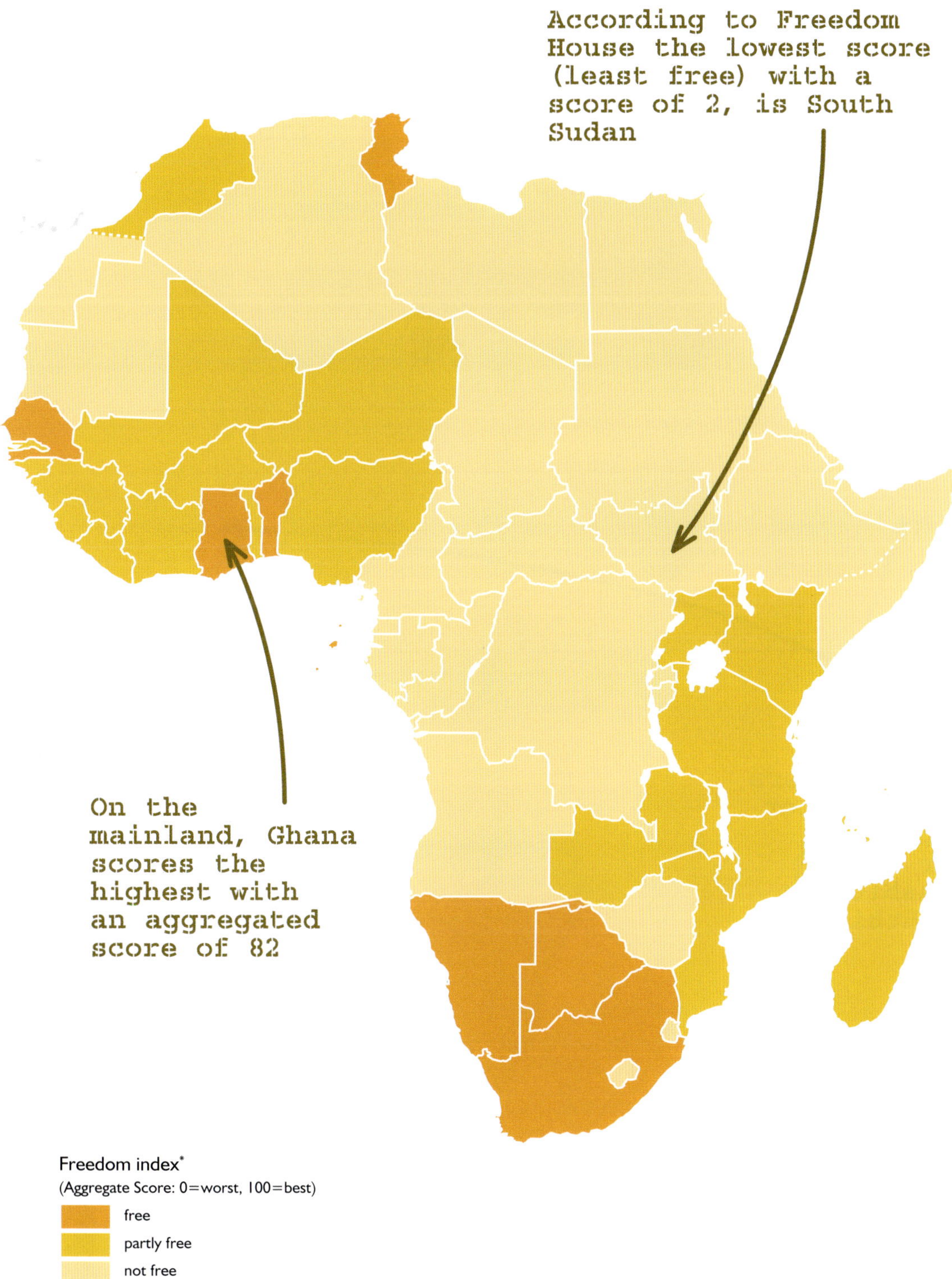

freedomhouse.org (2018)

*The Freedom Index indicates the degree of democratic freedoms and civil and political rights. For the full methodology and rating see: freedomhouse.org/report/freedom-world-2016/methodology

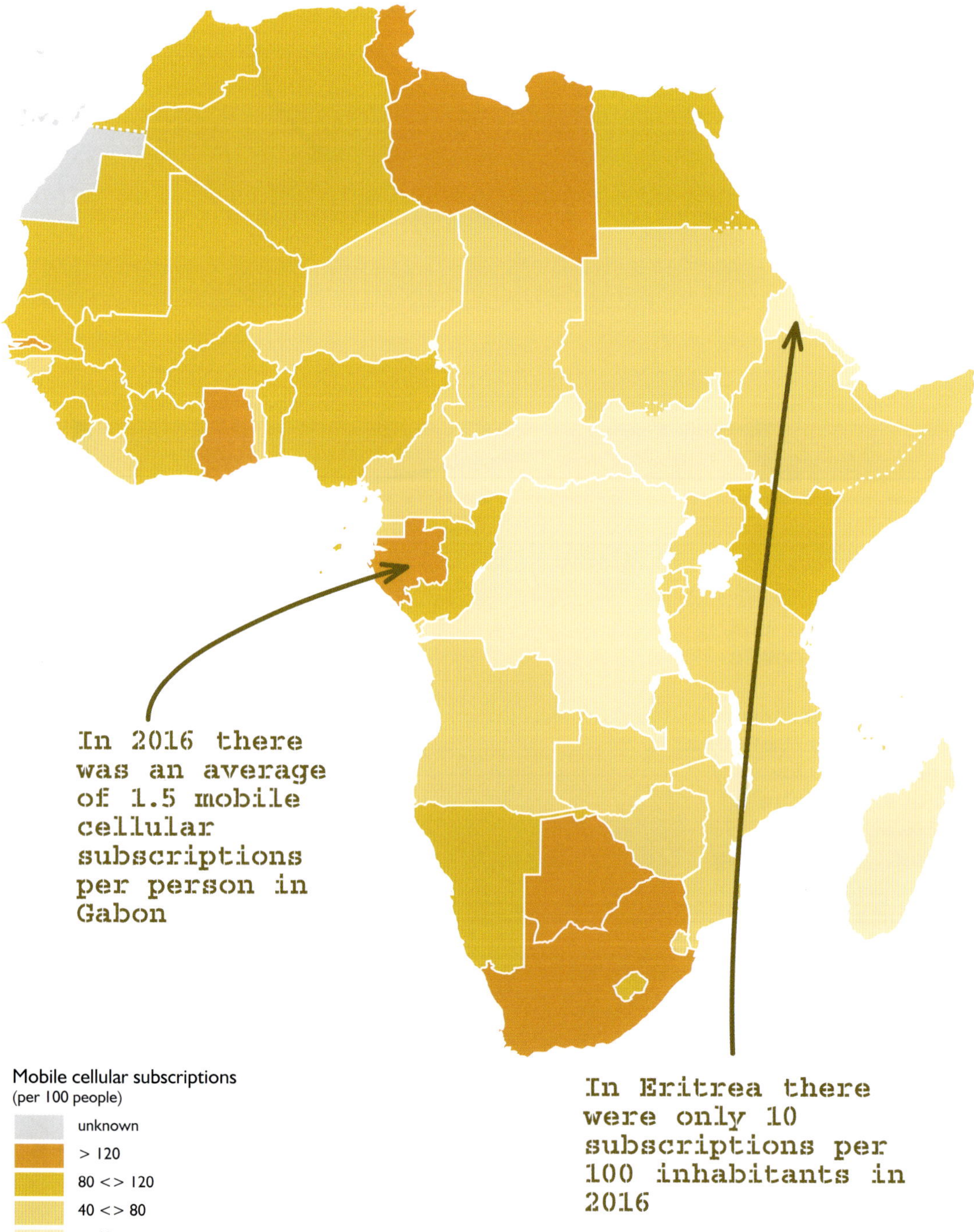

databank.worldbank.org (2016)

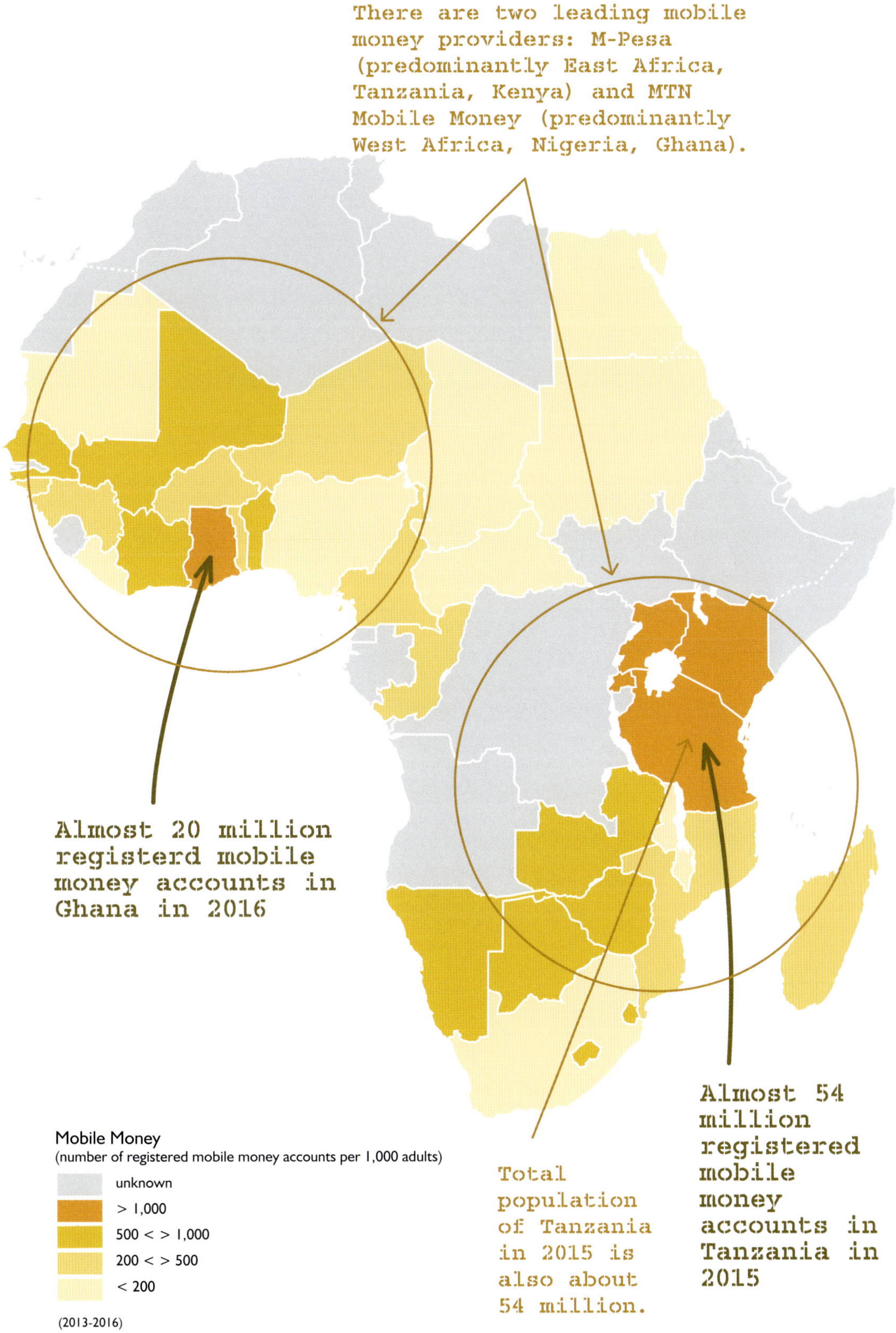
There are two leading mobile money providers: M-Pesa (predominantly East Africa, Tanzania, Kenya) and MTN Mobile Money (predominantly West Africa, Nigeria, Ghana).
Almost 20 million registerd mobile money accounts in Ghana in 2016
Total population of Tanzania in 2015 is also about 54 million.
Almost 54 million registered mobile money accounts in Tanzania in 2015
Mobile Money
(number of registered mobile money accounts per 1,000 adults)
unknown
> 1,000
500 < > 1,000
200 < > 500
< 200
(2013-2016)

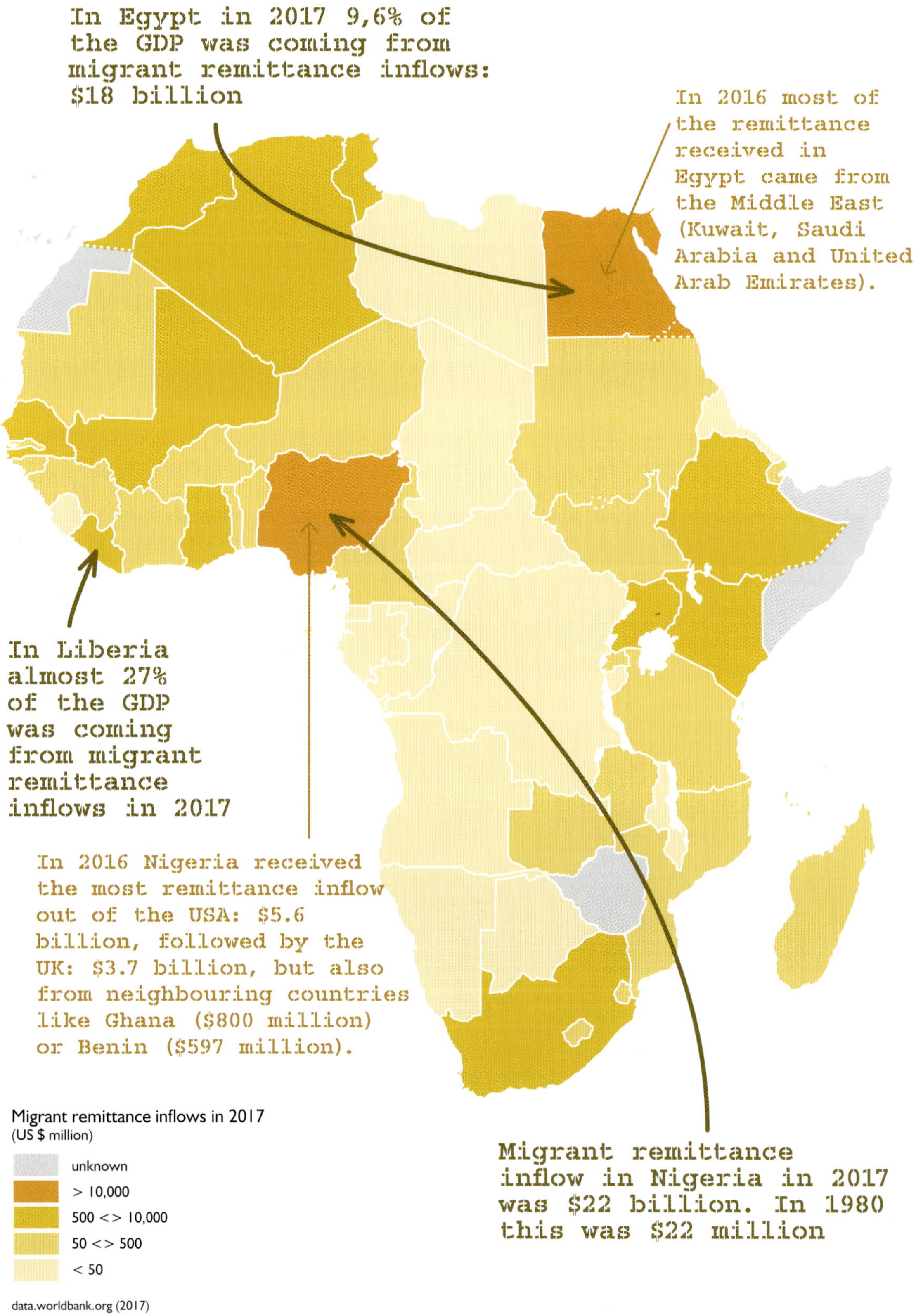
In Egypt in 2017 9,6% of the GDP was coming from migrant remittance inflows: $18 billion
In 2016 most of the remittance received in Egypt came from the Middle East (Kuwait, Saudi Arabia and United Arab Emirates).
In Liberia almost 27% of the GDP was coming from migrant remittance inflows in 2017
In 2016 Nigeria received the most remittance inflow out of the USA: $5.6 billion, followed by the UK: $3.7 billion, but also from neighbouring countries like Ghana ($800 million) or Benin ($597 million).
Migrant remittance inflow in Nigeria in 2017 was $22 billion. In 1980 this was $22 million
Migrant remittance inflows in 2017
(US $ million)
unknown
> 10,000
500 <> 10,000
50 <> 500
< 50
data.worldbank.org (2017)

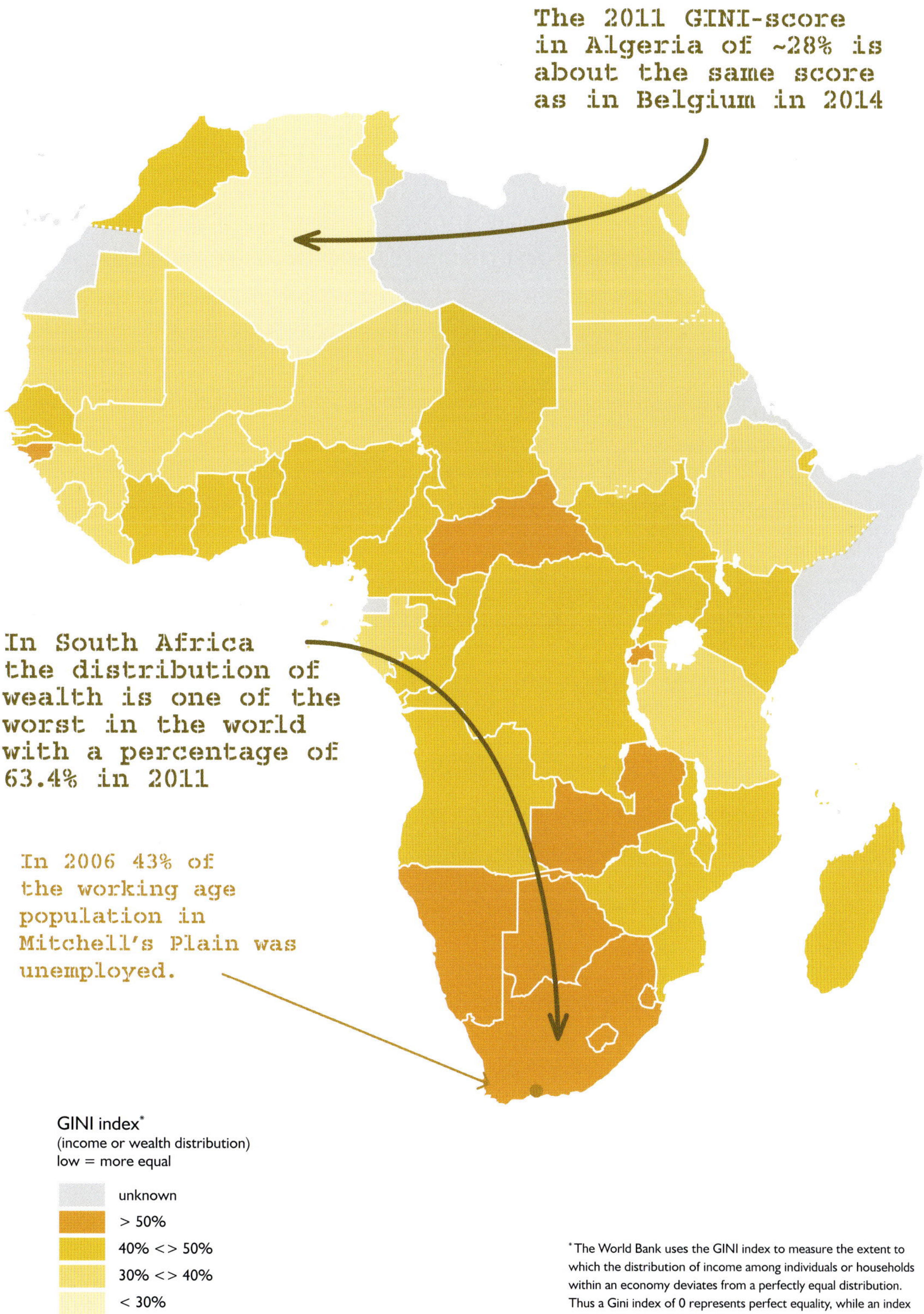

data.worldbank.org (2003-2016)

*The World Bank uses the GINI index to measure the extent to which the distribution of income among individuals or households within an economy deviates from a perfectly equal distribution. Thus a Gini index of 0 represents perfect equality, while an index of 100 implies perfect inequality.

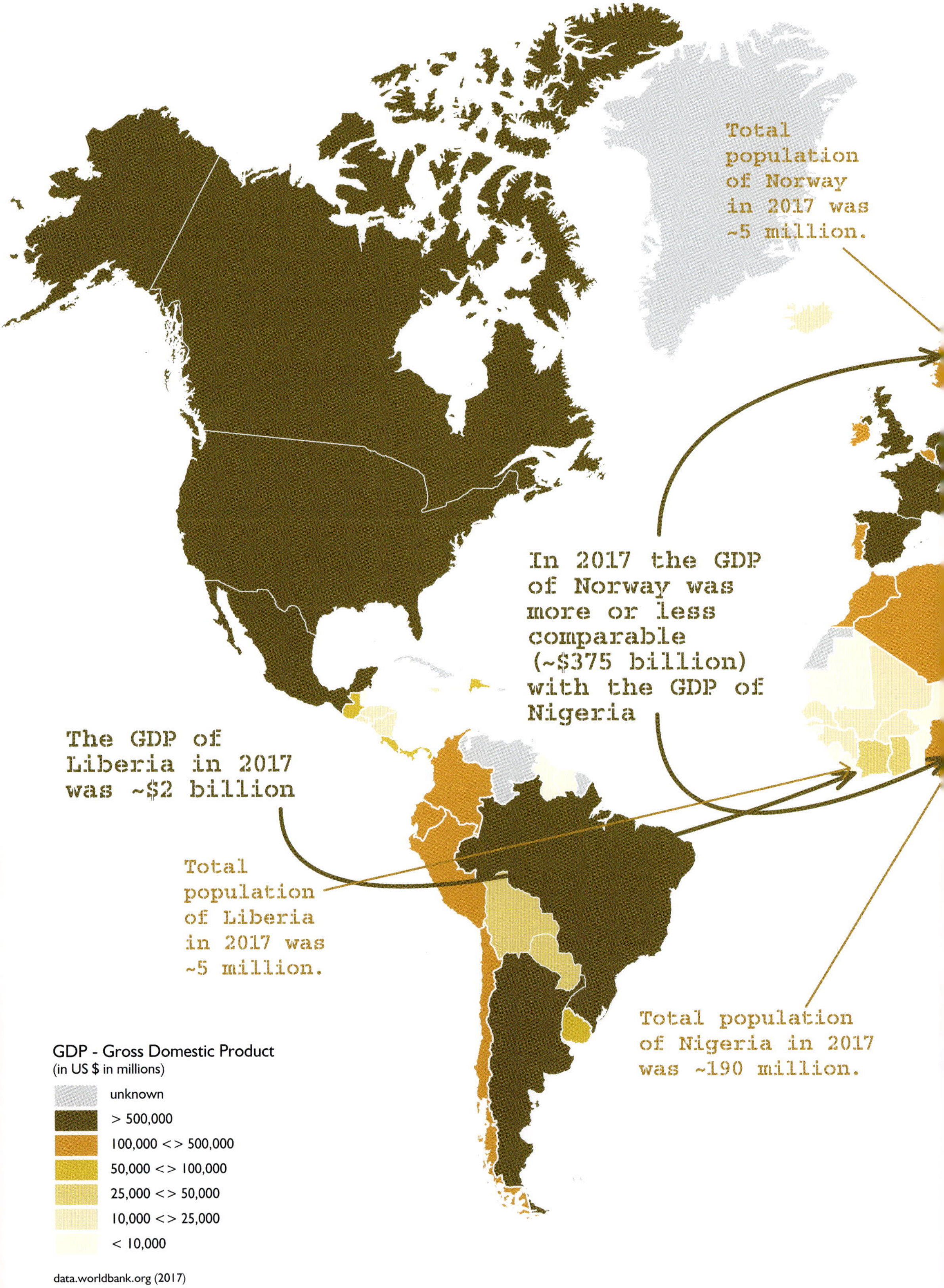
Total population of Norway in 2017 was ~5 million.
In 2017 the GDP of Norway was more or less comparable (~$375 billion) with the GDP of Nigeria
The GDP of Liberia in 2017 was ~$2 billion
Total population of Liberia in 2017 was ~5 million.
Total population of Nigeria in 2017 was ~190 million.
GDP - Gross Domestic Product
(in US $ in millions)
unknown
> 500,000
100,000 <> 500,000
50,000 <> 100,000
25,000 <> 50,000
10,000 <> 25,000
< 10,000
data.worldbank.org (2017)

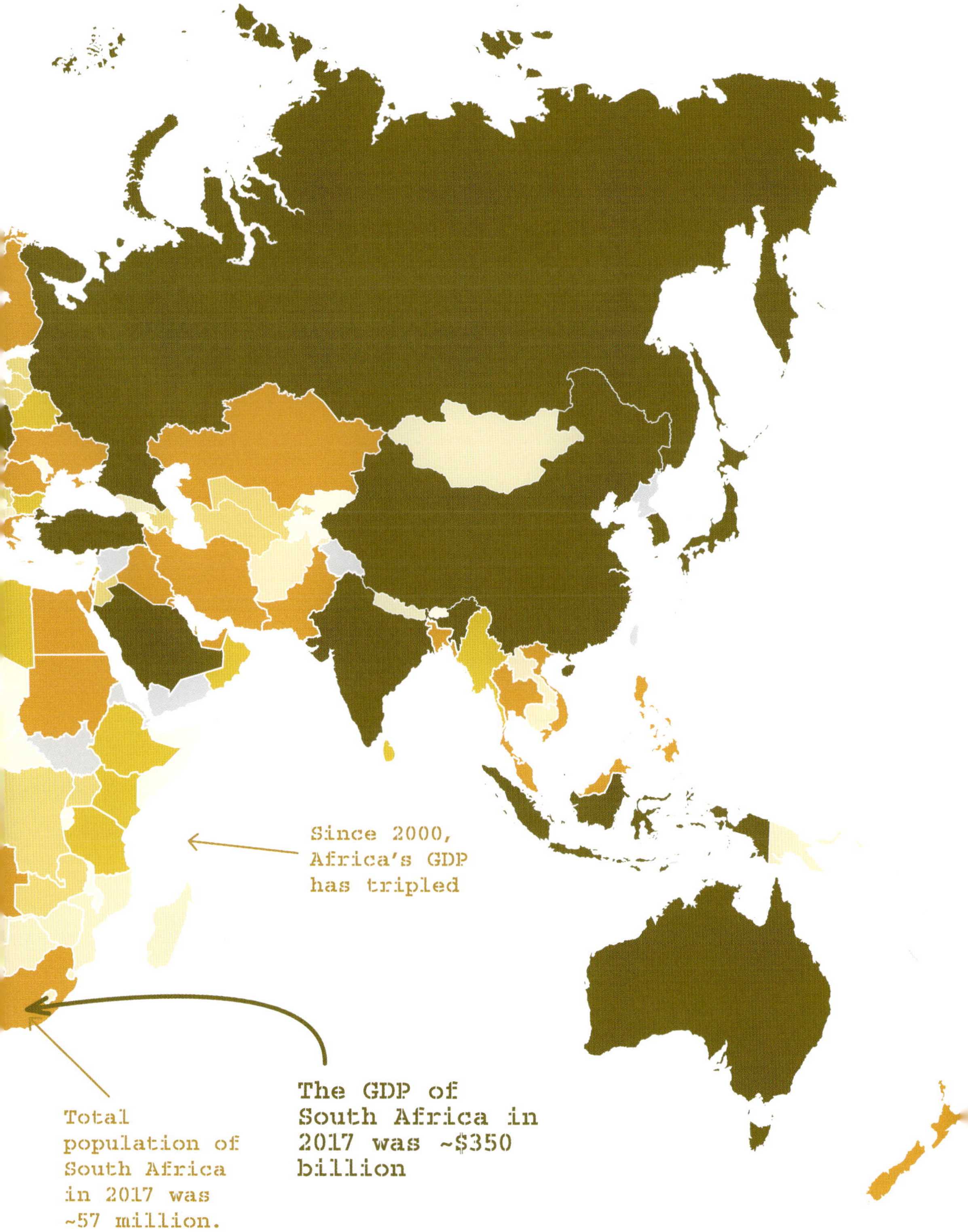
Since 2000, Africa's GDP has tripled
Total population of South Africa in 2017 was ~57 million.
The GDP of South Africa in 2017 was ~$350 billion

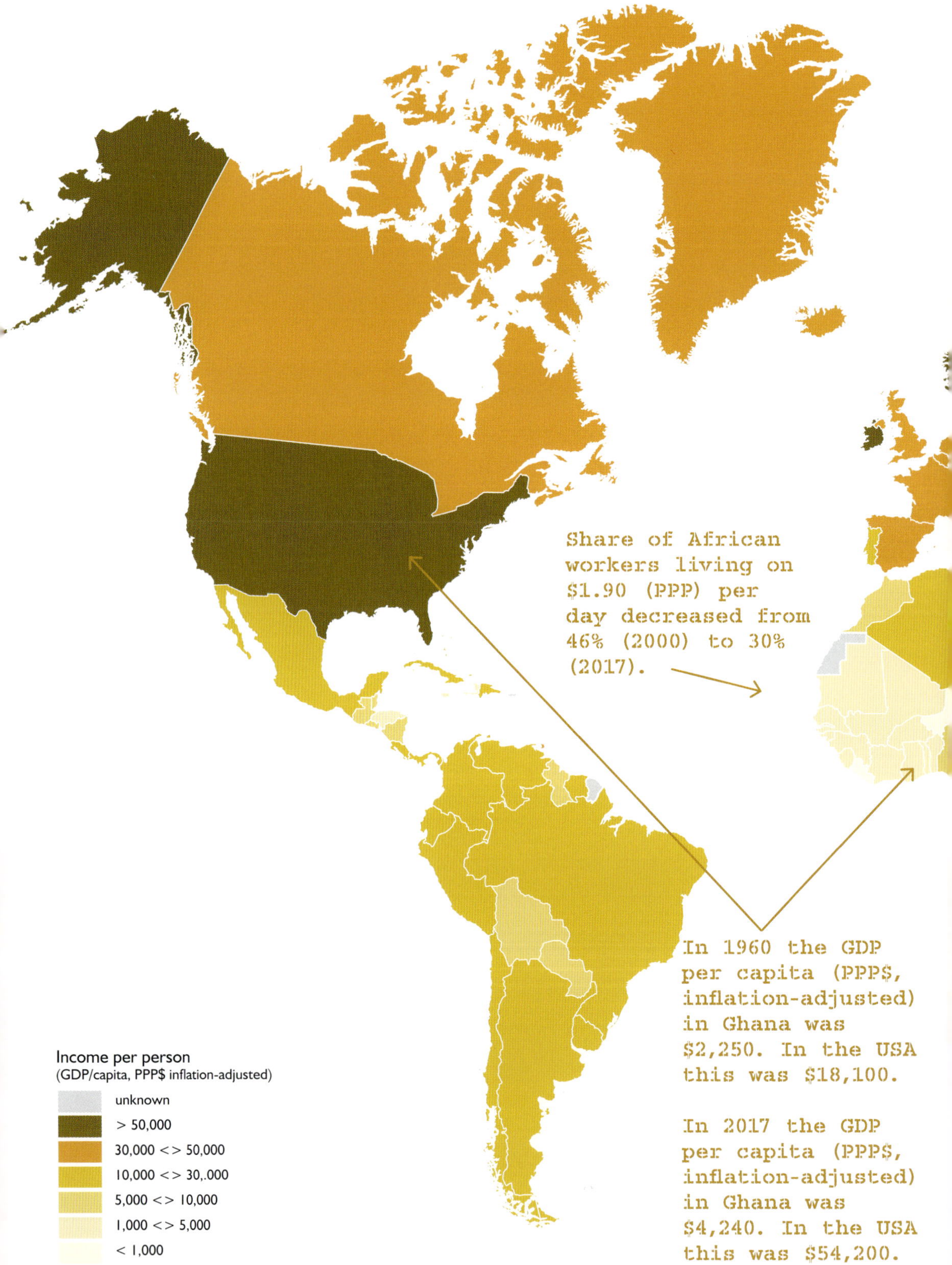

Gapminder / World Bank (2018)

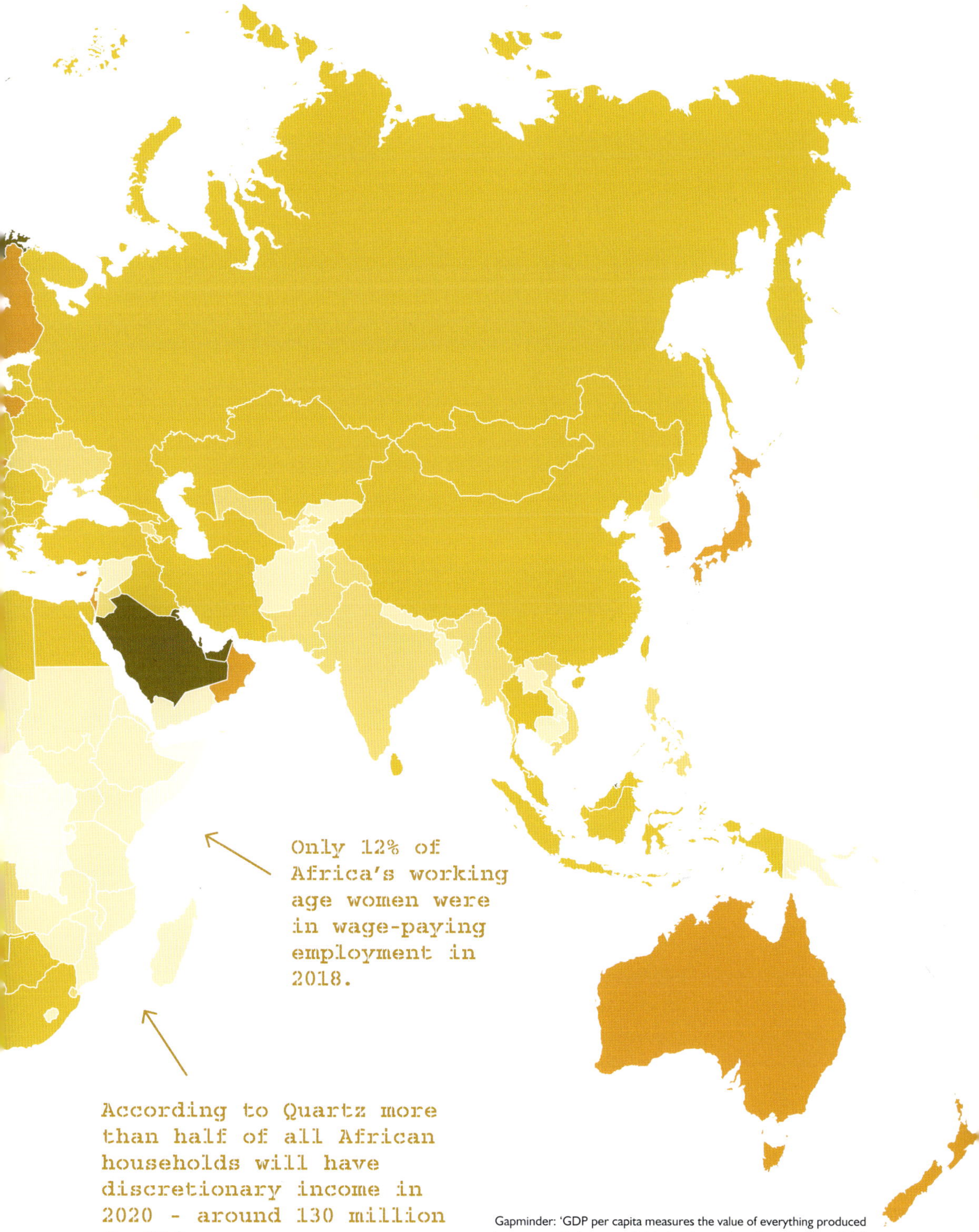

Only 12% of Africa's working age women were in wage-paying employment in 2018.

According to Quartz more than half of all African households will have discretionary income in 2020 - around 130 million families.

Gapminder: 'GDP per capita measures the value of everything produced in a country during a year, divided by the number of people. The unit is in international dollars, fixed 2011 prices. The data is adjusted for inflation and differences in the cost of living between countries, so-called PPP dollars.' see: www.gapminder.org/data/documentation/gd001/

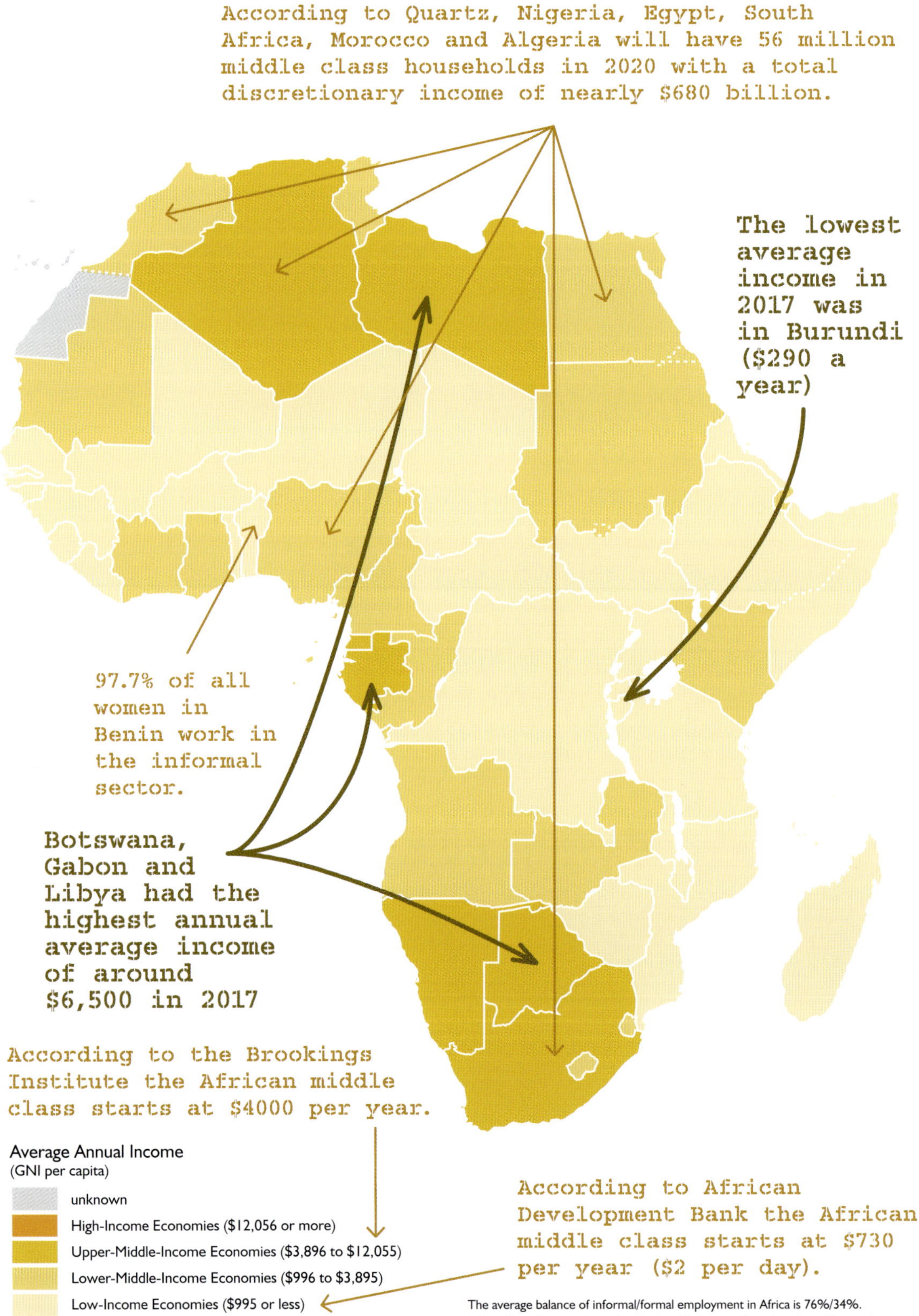

datahelpdesk.worldbank.org (2018)

The average balance of informal/formal employment in Africa is 76%/34%. Informal employment is rarely calculated in income data, therefore this map is limited in scope to income from formalised employment.

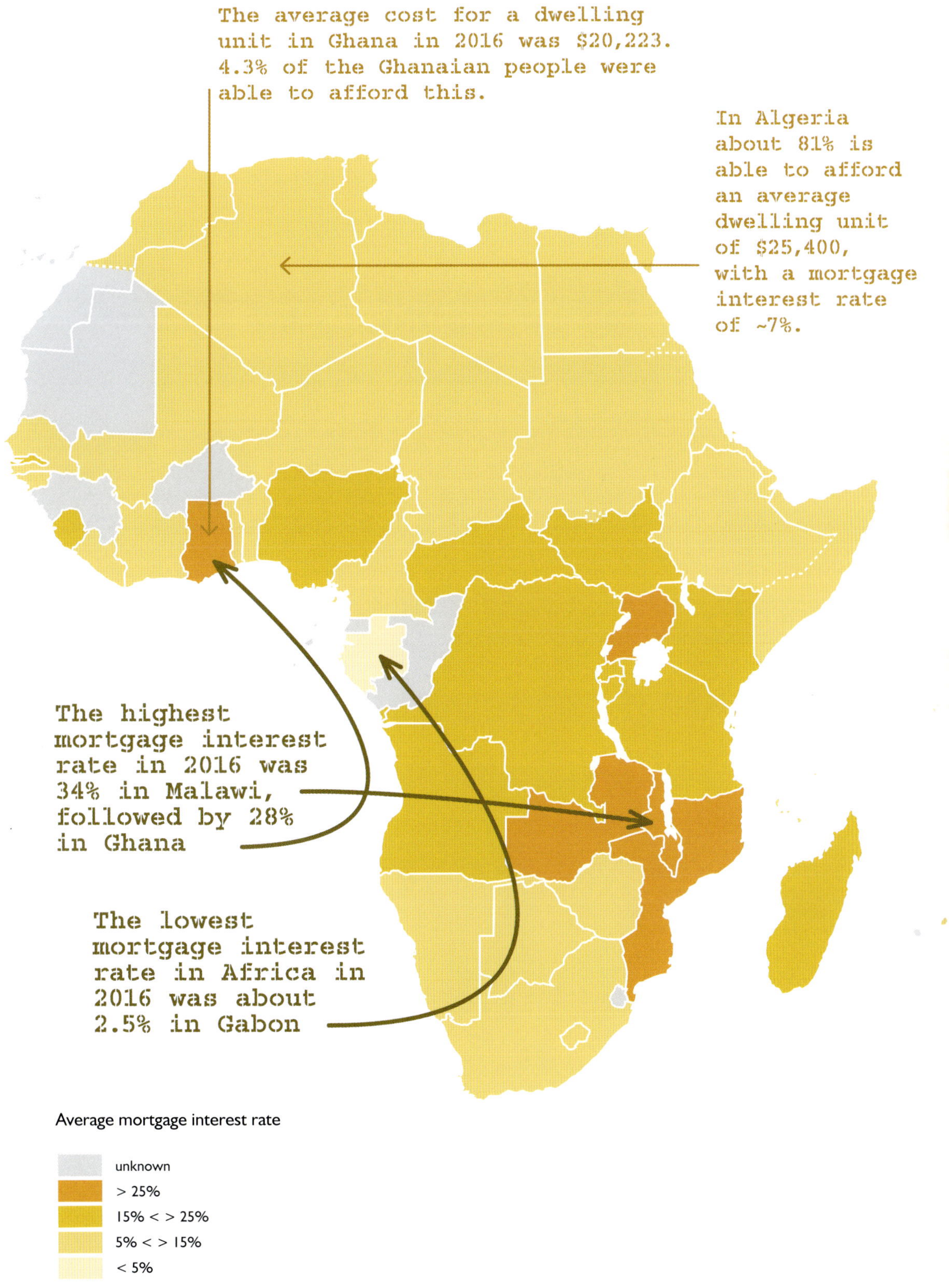

CAHF Research (2016)

Tema (1960), Ghana. (Photo: M. Provoost, 2007)

6th of October (1979), Egypt (Photo: R. Keeton, 2016)

Ville Verte Mohammed VI (2010), Morocco. (Photo: R. Keeton, 2017)

City Passports

Introduction

The City Passports expand on quantifiable data related to 31 New Towns, selected from the inventory of 148 New Towns based on their geographic diversity, data availability, and distribution over time. This includes size, density, projected population, real population, location and dates of development, urban morphology, and also (if known) information on the housing types, infrastructures, and urban amenities. We have also included a short description of each New Town, its development, and its challenges.

Additionally, we examined the urban morphology of these New Towns. To be able to identify trends in the urban design and character of the cities we categorised their urban models and fabric, using typological characterisations of street patterns (such as 'warped grid', 'orthogonal grid', 'composite' and 'loops and lollipops'), and urban forms (such as 'grid', 'polycentric', 'radial', 'linear', 'township', and 'skyline'). Since about 2000, we see a growing number of the 'skyline' New Towns modelled on the glittering images of Dubai or Singapore. Most of these cities can be considered commercial cities, and they may express this through business or ICT parks at the heart of the project.

For the City Passports, it was not always possible to find or verify all relevant data.

Legend

By whom:

This graph indicates who initiated, built and financed the New Town. According to the position in the graph, the symbols show if the New Town is public or private and if it is national or international. However, data on the finances behind the majority of New Towns is not always transparent.

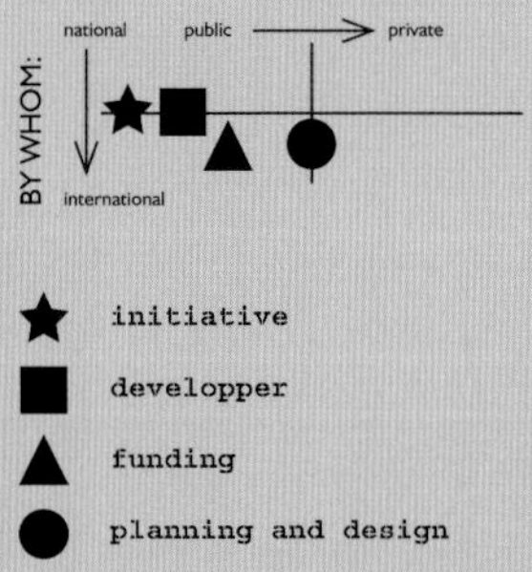

For whom:

This graph depicts for whom the New Town was built. The size of the dots indicates the relative amount of housing for the relevant income group. For reasons of clarity the dots are restricted to three sizes: small, medium and large. No dot indicates a lack of housing for this income group.

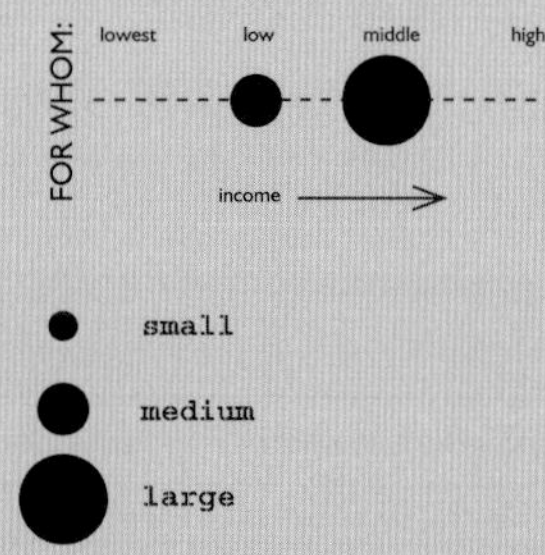

The data for this graph is mainly based on information from the original masterplans and literature. We interpreted the available information based on our historical knowledge and experience. Nonetheless, in each period and in each country the definition of income classes varies widely and this interpretation should be regarded as an impression.

Quantities:

The square indicates the size of the urban area of the New Town in km^2.
The light circle indicates the target population.
The dark circle indicates the number of inhabitants.
The exact numbers are shown in the list.

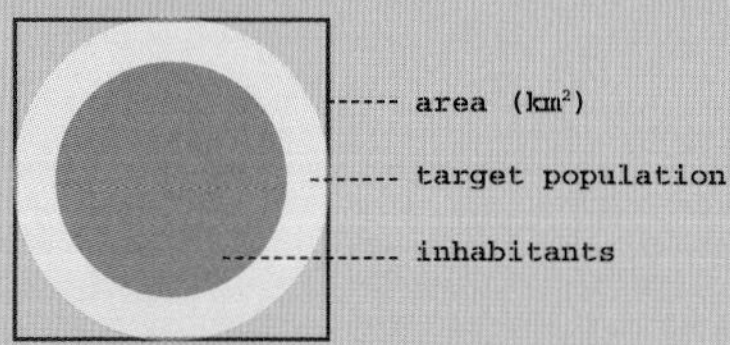

In the principles of UN-Habitat, 15,000 inhabitants per km^2 is considered an ideal urban density. In that case the circle fits perfectly in the square. For example a big square with a small circle would indicate a less dense city, while a small square with a larger circle would indicate a city with a higher density than recommended by UN-Habitat.

COUNTRY	Mauritania
DEVELOPMENT	**Nouakchott New Town**
YEAR	1957 (1958-1970 / 1970-1983 / 1983-2003 / 2003-2020)

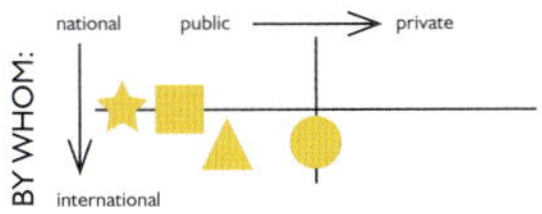

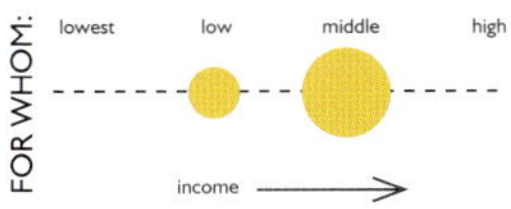

INITIATIVE / CLIENT	French government, Mauritian government
DEVELOPERS	Mauritania government, French Development Agency
PLANNING AND DESIGN	Governor Mouragues (France), M. Hirsch (France), Cerutti Marri (France), Lainville (France), Leconte and Lafon (France), 1970: SMUH (Secretariat des Missions d'Urbanisme et d'Habitat, France), 1983: BCEOM (France), 2003: Urbaplan, (Switzerland)

CITY TYPE	Capital
URBAN FABRIC / TYPOLOGY	Warped grid, low to mid rise

TARGET POPULATION	15,000
INHABITANTS	968,000 (2015)
SIZE	1,000 km^2

SHORT DESCRIPTION

Until 1960, Mauritania was ruled remotely by the French from Saint-Louis, Senegal, some 300 kilometers to the south. After winning independence, Mauritanian President Moktar Ould Daddah chose Nouakchott as the site for a new capital that would reflect the nascent country's modernity and unity. Plans for the New Town were modest, with an original target population of just 15,000. That number has proven to be grossly underestimated, as climate variability and desertification have driven nearly one third of all Mauritanians (roughly one million), to the seaside capital. As a result, Nouakchott is known for its kébbés or informal settlements, with an estimated 80% of residents living in slums (UN-Habitat 2014). Nouakchott is also threatened by rising sea levels, and government officials have estimated that the capital could be completely submerged by 2030. Additionally, the non-renewable fresh water reservoir below the city is expected to run dry by 2050, compounding the city's already serious challenges.

COUNTRY	Ghana
DEVELOPMENT	**Tema**
YEAR	1960 (1960-2015)

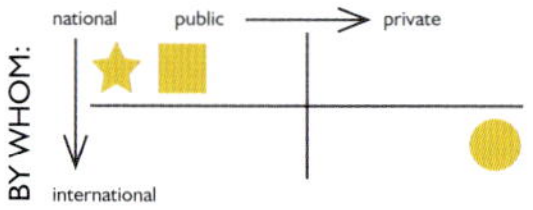

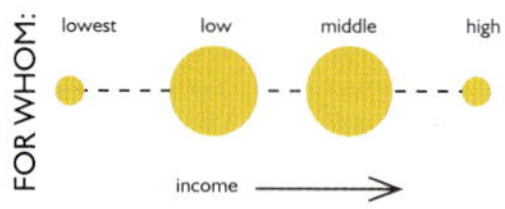

INITIATIVE / CLIENT	Government of Ghana, under the presidency of Kwame Nkrumah
DEVELOPERS	Government of Ghana
PLANNING AND DESIGN	Doxiadis Associates (Greece)
CITY TYPE	Industrial
URBAN FABRIC / TYPOLOGY	Warped grid, low to mid rise
TARGET POPULATION	250,000
INHABITANTS	139,784 (2010)
SIZE	166 km^2
% OR AREAS FOR ZONING	42.2% residential / 10.9% circulation and movement / 6.1% schools / 6.1% Central area / 34.5% open spaces

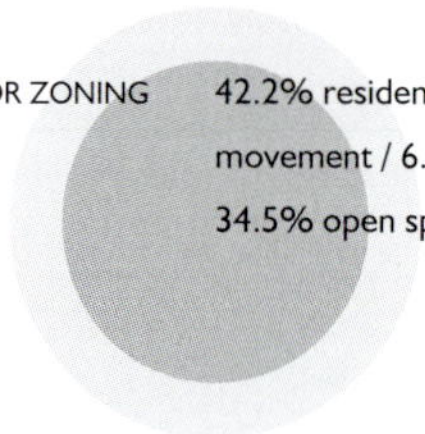

SHORT DESCRIPTION

The port city of Tema was the brainchild of Ghana's first President Kwame Nkrumah and Greek planner Constantinos Doxiadis. Tema was originally conceived as an industrial city about 30 kilometers from Accra. The New Town was designed to provide housing for workers and middle class families, embodying the ambitions of the independent nation state with beautiful architecture, ample public services, and a modern lifestyle. Today, the New Town's image of a low-rise tropical city amongst the trees is changing into a high-rise business metropolis. The harbour activities have tripled in the last decade and the quays and basins are being expanded to turn Tema into the biggest port in West Africa. The planned and organised housing neighbourhoods are popular and the price of real estate shows a steep line upwards. Designed as a city for all income levels, the diversity of its population is now under pressure. Tema is in the middle of replacing the older worker neighbourhoods with apartment blocks, gradually becoming a middle-class city surrounded by unregulated urban growth that has all but filled up the area between Accra and Tema. Instead of being a well-connected but autonomous spatial entity, Tema is now intricately interwoven with the unstoppable urbanisation of Africa's West Coast.

COUNTRY	Botswana
DEVELOPMENT	**Gaborone**
YEAR	1963 (1963-1971)

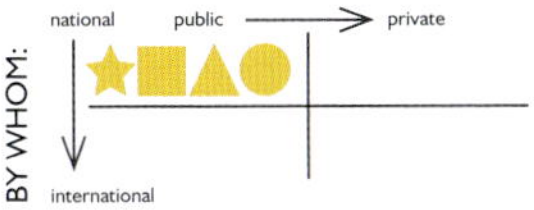

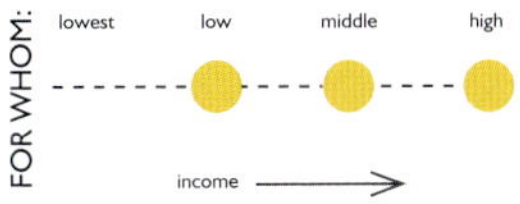

INITIATIVE / CLIENT	Legislative Council of Botswana Protectorate
DEVELOPERS	Colonial Administration
PLANNING AND DESIGN	Public Works Department in Mefikeng

CITY TYPE	Capital
URBAN FABRIC / TYPOLOGY	Half radial with loops and lollipops

TARGET POPULATION	20,000
INHABITANTS	269,400 (2018)
SIZE	169 km^2

SHORT DESCRIPTION

Initiated as a capital city for newly-independent Botswana, Gaborone was planned based on Garden City principles. The location for the new capital was chosen because it was well-situated along the Notwane River and free of complicating tribal affiliations. Intended to be a walkable, green city with verdant public spaces, Gaborone was originally planned for 20,000 residents. Most of the capital was constructed in just three years, which required a huge labour force from rural areas. Most labourers remained in the capital after construction was complete, creating informal settlements in peri-urban areas. The New Town has since grown into Botswana's largest urban centre, and houses roughly 10% of Botswana's total population, with more than 269,400 residents (2018).

COUNTRY	Cote d'Ivoire
DEVELOPMENT	**Yamoussoukro**
YEAR	1965 (1970-1983 / In 1983 Yamoussouko became the new capital)

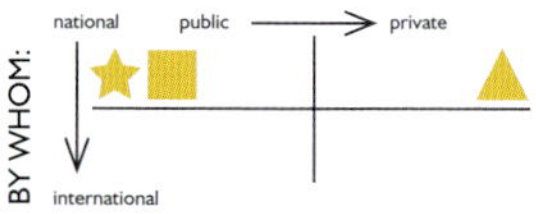

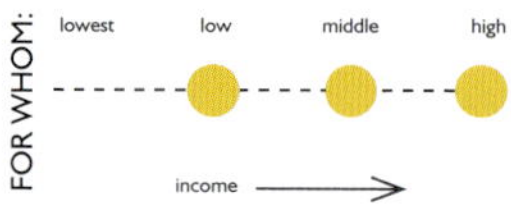

INITIATIVE / CLIENT	Ivorian Government under the presidency of Félix Houphouët-Boigny
DEVELOPERS	Government of Cote d'Ivoire
CITY TYPE	Capital
URBAN FABRIC / TYPOLOGY	Warped grid, low to mid rise
TARGET POPULATION	200,000
INHABITANTS	355,573 (2014)
SIZE	453 km^2

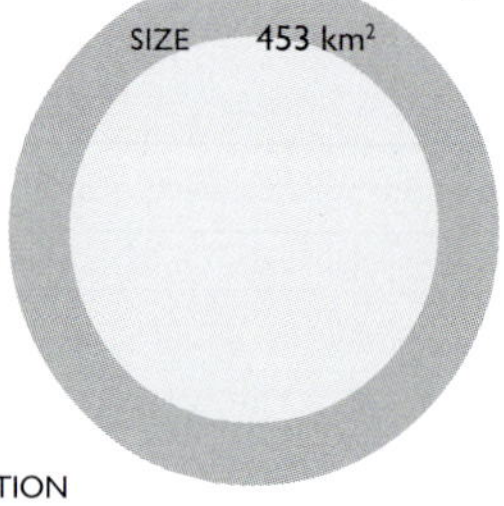

SHORT DESCRIPTION

The birthplace of former President Houphouët-Boigny, Yamoussoukro replaced Abidjan as the capital of Côte d'Ivoire in 1983. The New Town is 275 kilometers northwest of Abidjan, which lies on the Atlantic coast. Unlike other post-independence African captials, Yamoussoukro was not chosen for its neutral tribal affiliations or geographic centrality. Rather, Houphouët-Boigny oversaw investment and infrastructure in his birthplace for two decades before convincing the government to relocate the capital. It has been called the 'African Versailles': a personal prestige project for a despot ruler. Today, Yamoussoukro functions as the nation's administrative capital but the local economy is primarily based on fishing and forestry, and the transfer of government offices has been slow. Abidjan remains the economic and business heart of the country. According to the 2014 census, Yamoussoukro had a population of about 355,000 residents, while Abidjan stood at 4.7 million.

COUNTRY Malawi

DEVELOPMENT **Lilongwe**

YEAR 1965-1969 (Start in 1969 / In 1975 Lilongwe became the new capital)

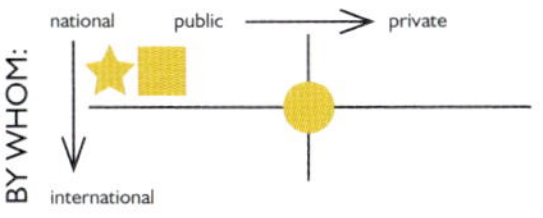

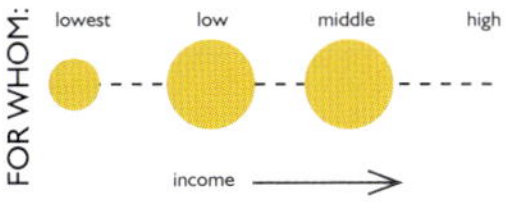

INITIATIVE / CLIENT Government of Malawi

DEVELOPERS Capital City Development Corporation

PLANNING AND DESIGN Brian Colquhoun and Partners (UK), Imex (Pty) of Jo'burg (South Africa), Town Planning Department of the Ministry of Works and Supplies

CITY TYPE Capital

URBAN FABRIC / TYPOLOGY Curvilinear loops and lollipops, mixed rise

TARGET POPULATION 500,000

INHABITANTS 1,161,400 (2017)

SIZE 456 km^2

% OR AREAS FOR ZONING Low Density Residential (LDR)-2,670ha / Middle Density Residential (MDR) 1,987ha / High Density Residential (HDR) 6,795 ha / Quasi- Residential 6,171ha / High-rise flat area 1,155ha / Commercial 1,611ha / High-rise commercial 219ha / Heavy / Large scale industry 1,280ha / Light industry 616ha Government 1,836ha / Airport 358ha / Nature Sanctuary 137ha / Park and recreation 1,149 ha Greenery/natural open space 6,840ha / Agriculture 4,309ha / Forestry 9,564ha / Cemetery 701 ha

SHORT DESCRIPTION

In 1968, President Hastings Banda chose Lilongwe as the site of the Malawi's new capital. Lilongwe replaced Zomba as all government offices were relocated 284 kilometers north to the new site in the geographical centre of the country. Formerly a small fishing and trading centre along the banks of the Lilongwe River, the new capital became the symbol of a new national identity. For its first two decades, Lilongwe struggled to compete with Blantyre, a major metropolis some 300 kilometers to the south. Finance challenges, planning delays, housing provision, employment and delivery of public services remained serious problems until the 1990s. Over time, industry and capital slowly found the city, which is now a bustling urban centre.

COUNTRY	South Africa
DEVELOPMENT	**Mitchell's Plain**
YEAR	1970 (1974-1984)

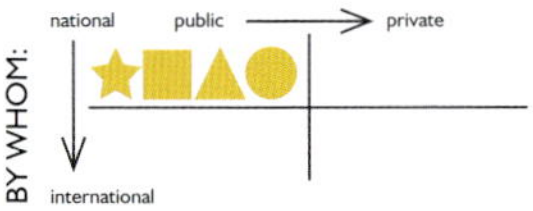

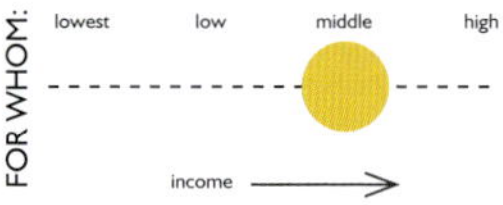

INITIATIVE / CLIENT	City of Cape Town
PLANNING AND DESIGN	City of Cape Town, Department of Engineering, Planning unit
CITY TYPE	Apartheid
URBAN FABRIC / TYPOLOGY	Warped grid, low rise
TARGET POPULATION	250,000
INHABITANTS	310,485 (2011)
SIZE	31 km^2

SHORT DESCRIPTION

Mitchell's Plain is a New Town situated 27km southeast of the central business district of Cape Town in the Cape Flats. Constructed in the 1970s by the City of Cape Town and the South African government with the aim of providing a complete, uplifting residential environment, it was restricted to 'coloureds' only during the apartheid era. Today, Mitchell's Plain is entirely dependent upon economic activities in other parts of the metropolitan area, particularly the central business district of Cape Town, and is segregated along economic lines and characterised by few job opportunities, a decayed built environment, poverty, and crime.

COUNTRY	Tanzania
DEVELOPMENT	**Dodoma**
YEAR	1973 (1976-2000)

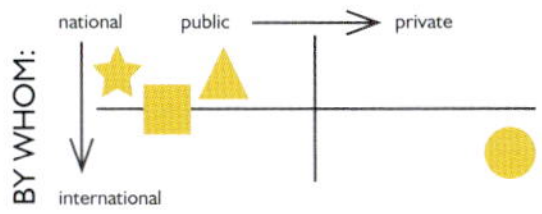

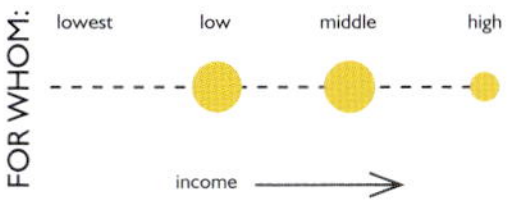

INITIATIVE / CLIENT	Government of Tanzania, under the presidency of Julius Nyerere
DEVELOPERS	Government of Tanzania, United Nations
PLANNING AND DESIGN	Project Planning Associates (Canada), James S. Rossant (USA)
CITY TYPE	Capital
URBAN FABRIC / TYPOLOGY	Composite curvilinear polycentric, low to mid rise
TARGET POPULATION	350,000
INHABITANTS	213,636 (2012)
SIZE	2,576 km^2 (625 km^2 urbanized)

SHORT DESCRIPTION

Dodoma was initiated by President Julius Nyerere as new capital in the geographic heart of the nation, 450 kilometers west of Dar es Salaam. At the time, Dar es Salaam was experiencing uncontrolled population growth following independence and Dodoma was seen as a way of decentralising national development and showcasing the Tanzanian concept of *ujamaa*, or African socialism. It was designed as a collection of urban villages of about 7000 residents each, in a clustered organisation, with spatial concepts regarding collective production, farming, and self-reliance. The new capital did not grow as planned, and government representatives continue to resist the remote New Town by flying in for ministerial debates and then returning to bustling Dar es Salaam. As a result, Dodoma has expanded in fits and starts, despite renewed government relocation programmes as recently as 2016 and 2018. Tanzania's 2012 census recorded only 213,636 residents in Dodoma, while Dar es Salaam remains a major metropolis with more than four million residents.

COUNTRY Egypt

DEVELOPMENT **10th of Ramadan**

YEAR 1976 (1976-2000)

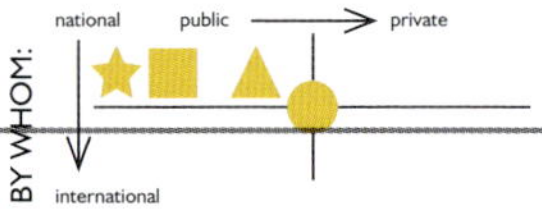

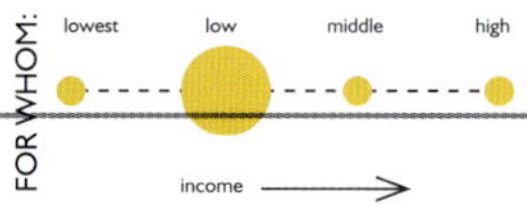

INITIATIVE / CLIENT Government of Egypt, NUCA

DEVELOPERS New Urban Communities Authority (NUCA) within the Ministry of Housing (MHUDD)

PLANNING AND DESIGN NUCA, Sweco (Sweden), Shawky-Zeitoun (Egypt)

CITY TYPE Industrial

URBAN FABRIC / TYPOLOGY Polycentric loops and lollipops with low to mid rise

TARGET POPULATION 500,000

INHABITANTS 219,442 (2017 census)

SIZE 383 km²

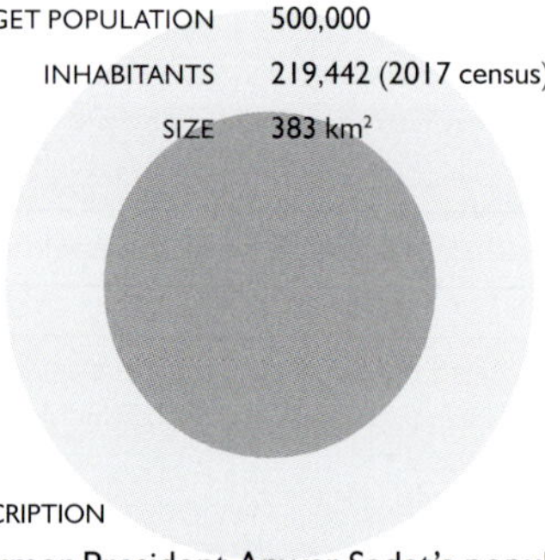

SHORT DESCRIPTION

Part of former President Anwar Sadat's populist bid to build support for his leadership in the 1970s, 10th of Ramadan was intended as an industrial city to provide jobs and bring development opportunities to this desert area. 10th of Ramadan is still Egypt's main manufacturing hub, and competitive corporate tax rates and customs incentives continue to attract both foreign and national investment. The social and 'youth' housing has also attracted residents, and the city functions autonomously of Cairo with a vibrant daily life. However, much of the housing stock has proven too expensive for low-level factory workers. As a solution, nearly every factory runs private bus shuttles to desert villages in surrounding areas, and large extended families may work at a single factory. While intended to be symbiotic, the industrial zones and the rest of the city have become relatively independent as a result of this mismatch between jobs and housing provision.

2018 GoogleEarth

COUNTRY	Nigeria
DEVELOPMENT	**Abuja**
YEAR	1976 (1984-1991, Abuja was formally inaugurated as capital city in 1991)

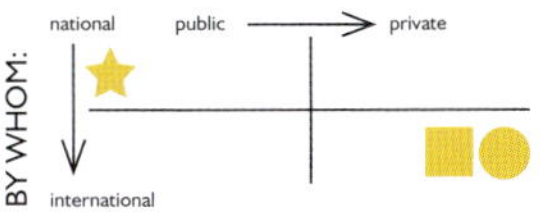

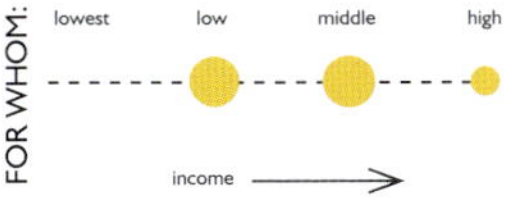

INITIATIVE / CLIENT	Government of Nigeria
DEVELOPERS	American, Japanese, British, Greek
PLANNING AND DESIGN	Masterplan: International Planning Associates (USA), a cooperation between Planning Research Corporation, Wallace, McHarg, Roberts and Todd and Archisystems. City centre: Kenzo Tange (Japan). Regional scale plan: Doxiadis Associates (Greece). Suburbs: Milton Keynes Development Corporation (UK)
CITY TYPE	Capital
URBAN FABRIC / TYPOLOGY	Curvilinear, mixed rise
TARGET POPULATION	3,000,000
INHABITANTS	2,440,000 (2015)
SIZE	713 km^2

SHORT DESCRIPTION

Abuja officially replaced Lagos as the capital of Nigeria in 1991. The plan was initiated by General Murtala Mohammed and Abuja's location in the geographic centre of the country was chosen to express unity among the country's tribes. However, the land necessary for development was inhabited by roughly 500,000 villagers in small communities. The costs associated with this scale of resettlement were unacceptable, and the impacts of sloppy resettlement policies have continued to plague the city. Abuja is one of the fastest growing cities in the world. The capital currently houses almost 2.5 million, although the entire metropolitan area has more than 6 million residents. Until 2003, Abuja did not grow according to the masterplan, with civic leaders often turning a blind eye to illegal neighbourhoods and expansions. In 2003 political leaders decided to adhere closely to the masterplan, effectively rendering masses of the population illegal squatters. The struggle between a formalised urban environment and the rights of the urban poor remains one the city's biggest challenges.

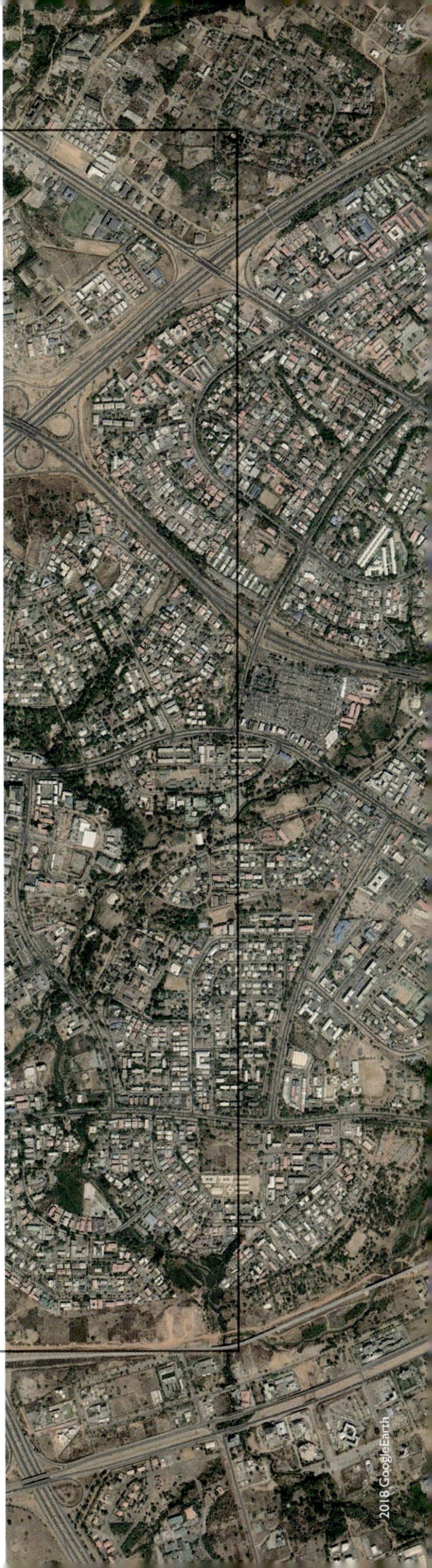

COUNTRY	Libya
DEVELOPMENT	**New Brega**
YEAR	1984 (1986-1993)

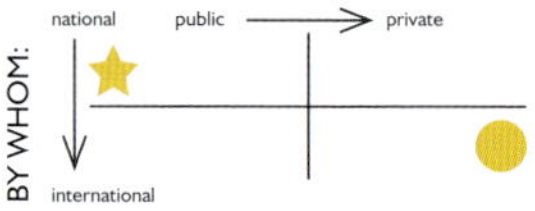

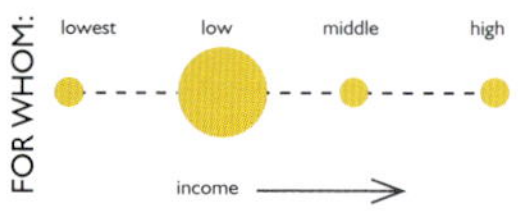

INITIATIVE / CLIENT	Ministry of Petroleum, secretariat of Heavy Industries
PLANNING AND DESIGN	ENKA Teknik (Turkey)
CITY TYPE	Industrial
URBAN FABRIC / TYPOLOGY	Curvilinear polycentric low rise
TARGET POPULATION	45,000
INHABITANTS	7,000 (2006)
SIZE	10.48 km^2
% OR AREAS FOR ZONING	25.62ha green areas and parking / 13.4 ha cultural amenities / 13.9ha public amenities like hospital, administrative areas / 90.7ha for light industries

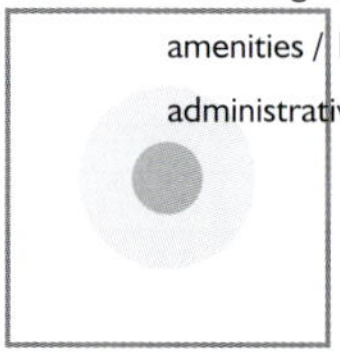

SHORT DESCRIPTION

Marsa el Brega, planned in the 1960s, became home to Libya's second largest hydro-carbon complex. To the east of the city, Brega New Town was built as part of the Petroleum Ministry of Libya's Mega Housing Project of the 1980s. Conceived as a ready-made town to support the important oil refinery and major oil export hub for Libya, the New Town was completed to turnkey detail, with single-family houses, schools, supermarkets, healthcare services, cultural centres, leisure facilities and complete infrastructure. An efficient prefab system developed by ENKA, a Turkish engineering firm, allowed for completion of the project within 5 years. Because of its strategic position in Libya's oil export network, Marsa el Brega fell to the Libyan Opposition forces in 2011, and the New Town was all but abandoned during the Libyan civil war.

COUNTRY Algeria

DEVELOPMENT **Ali Mendjeli**

YEAR 1988 (1993-1999 / 2000-2005)

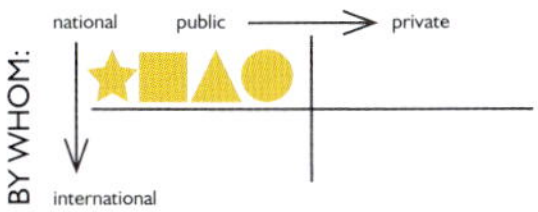

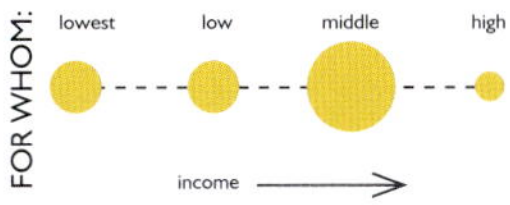

INITIATIVE / CLIENT

DEVELOPERS Wilaya (province) de Constantine

Private and public parties (AADL, CNEP, OPGI,

PLANNING AND DESIGN EPLF)

URBACO (Centre d'études et de réalisations en urbanisme de Constantine)

CITY TYPE

URBAN FABRIC / TYPOLOGY Decentralisation

Composite curvilinear grid

TARGET POPULATION

INHABITANTS 335,000

SIZE 64,120 (2008)

% OR AREAS FOR ZONING 15 km²

77% residential / 8% buisness / 8% multiple activities zone / 5% recreational park / 1.5 % public urban park / In 2010, 10,500 (65%) of 16,178 housing units were intended for middle- and high-income households

SHORT DESCRIPTION

Initiated with the intent to reduce congestion and housing pressure in Constantine, Ali Mendjeli was designed to ensure a more balanced spatial distribution of urban inhabitants, including the lowest income groups. The New Town faced numerous delays and financial struggles during development, and its ability to attract new residents has continued to decrease over time. Ali Mendjeli now primarily functions as a bedroom community, with most working residents commuting to Constantine during the day. Some observers have attributed the New Town's growing pains to the ad hoc relocation of Constantine's urban poor. Gang violence appears to be on the rise among unemployed youth and as a result the satellite city has developed a poor reputation over the course of its short existence. Inadequate maintenance, homogenous architecture, and a sterile urban environment have contributed to the New Town's stigma.

COUNTRY	Egypt
DEVELOPMENT	**Sheikh Zayed**
YEAR	1995 (1976-2000)

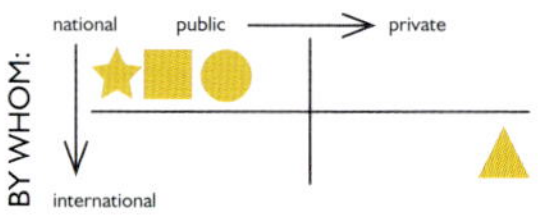

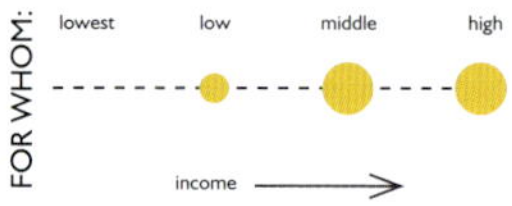

INITIATIVE / CLIENT	Government of Egypt funded by Al Sheikh Zayed Ibn Sultan Al Nahyan, late president of the United Arab Emirates
DEVELOPERS	New Urban Communities Authority (NUCA) within the Ministry of Housing (MHUDD)
PLANNING AND DESIGN	ACE consulting engineers (Egypt)
CITY TYPE	Decentralisation
URBAN FABRIC / TYPOLOGY	Half radial with loops and lollipops, mixed rise
TARGET POPULATION	675,000
INHABITANTS	90,997 (2017 census)
SIZE	49 km^2
% OR AREAS FOR ZONING	20 residential districts, with four neighbourhoods in each district.

SHORT DESCRIPTION

Although it began with clear intentions to provide low-cost housing to Cairenes living in cramped and overcrowded conditions, Sheikh Zayed New City evolved during development to have many more expensive gated communities than planned. This was an effect of NUCA's new policy to sell large tracts of land to private developers, who in turn developed housing while NUCA continues to provide main infrastructures. The gated communities in Sheikh Zayed now offer a range of luxe dwellings and private leisure facilities. Outside the gates, the city offers very few amenities to lower-income groups. Most of the commercial and recreational spaces target higher-income groups and are situated in private 'plazas' or outdoor malls. The city is so vast and of such low density that a car is required to travel around town. Residents of social housing areas rely on limited public transport in the form of microbuses and shared taxis. The New Town remains closely tied to Cairo, with most working residents commuting daily to downtown Cairo.

COUNTRY	Equatorial Guinea
DEVELOPMENT	**Djibloho / Oyala New Capital**
YEAR	2000 (2000-2020)

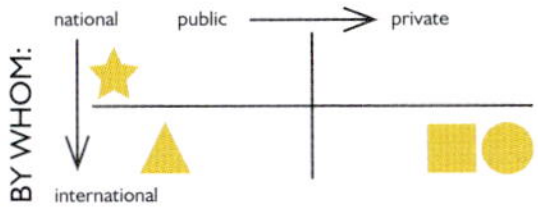

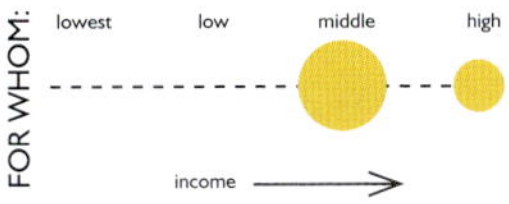

INITIATIVE / CLIENT	Government of Equatorial Guinea
DEVELOPERS	Government of Equatorial Guinea, Somagec, Arab Contractors, Besix, Sinohydro, CMEC, Seguibat
PLANNING AND DESIGN	IDF-Ideias do Futuro, IDF Lisboa architects, Egis Route, ARG infrastructures, Bouygues, Besix group, Piccini
CITY TYPE	Capital
URBAN FABRIC / TYPOLOGY	Warped grid, low to mid rise
TARGET POPULATION	200,000
INHABITANTS	0
SIZE	81.5 km^2

SHORT DESCRIPTION

Djibloho was designed to replace Malabo as Equatorial Guinea's new capital city. Located in the dense equatorial forrest along the Wele River, and surrounded by national parks, the site of the city is about 100 kilometers inland from the east coast. Although far removed from the old capital and coastal cities, the location is just 20 kilometers from a new airport and connected to the national road network. President Obiang, who has faced both coup and assignation attempts, has also cited security as a reason for the move. Djibloho was designed by the Portuguese firm Future Architecture Thinking to embrace the site's natural beauty and accommodate the needs of a new capital city. At the President's request, the plan brings together traditional cultural values and state-of-the-art amenities. Still under construction as of 2018, the new capital has grand ambitions.

COUNTRY	South Africa
DEVELOPMENT	**Waterfall City**
YEAR	2001 (2006-ongoing)

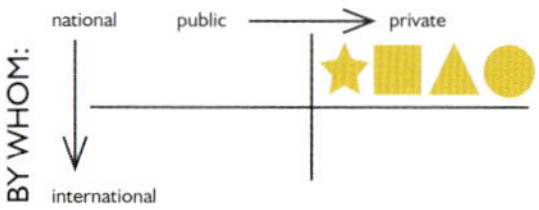

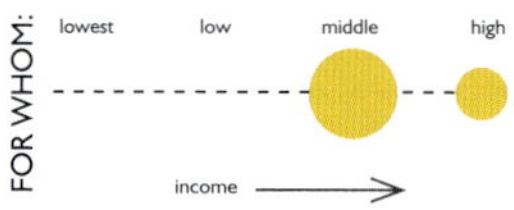

INITIATIVE / CLIENT	Waterfall Investment Company, Waterfall Islamic Institute Trust
DEVELOPERS	Waterfall Investment Company, Waterfall Islamic Institute Trust, Century Property Developments, Sanlam Properties, Investec Property Group, Growthpoint Properties, Zenprop, Group Five, Netcare, Atterbury Property Group (South Africa)
PLANNING AND DESIGN	Bentel Associates International (South Africa), Boogertman and Partners (South Africa), MDS Architecture (South Africa)
CITY TYPE	Commercial
URBAN FABRIC / TYPOLOGY	Composite curvilinear grid, skyline city, mixed rise
TARGET POPULATION	150,000
INHABITANTS	678 (2011)
SIZE	22 km^2

SHORT DESCRIPTION

Waterfall City is strategically located about 30 kilometers north of Johannesburg and 36 kilometers south of Pretoria. This distance allows the New Town to function autonomously, while reaping the benefits of a position between two well-established urban nodes. The New Town is a modern mix of industry, office parks, business, retail and residential areas. A completely private development, Waterfall City was initiated by The Waterfall Islamic Institute Trust, a private family company. The New Town has private governance structures that effectively replace municipal management. Management of the New Town is informed by traditional Islamic values and The Waterfall Islamic Institute Trust retains ownership of all the property in the development. Attacq Waterfall Investment Company (WIC) holds development rights to the entire city, creating a monopoly on real estate. Almost like a scaled-up gated community, Waterfall City is a private enclave under private governance. The model is new, but may become familiar as more private corporations take on public oversight.

COUNTRY	Uganda
DEVELOPMENT	**Akright City**
YEAR	2002 (2002-2020)

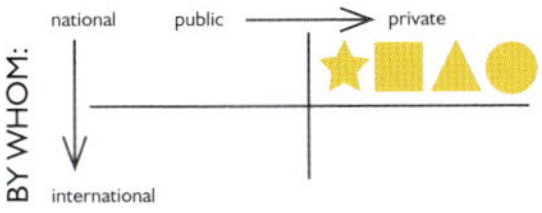

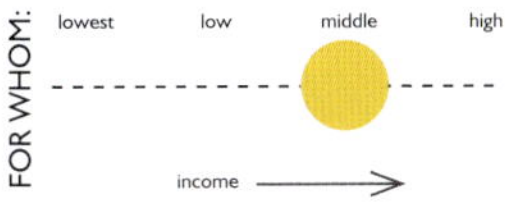

INITIATIVE / CLIENT	Akright Projects Limited
DEVELOPERS	Akright Projects Limited
PLANNING AND DESIGN	Akright Projects Limited
CITY TYPE	Commercial
URBAN FABRIC / TYPOLOGY	Orthogonal grid, low rise
TARGET POPULATION	144,000
INHABITANTS	0
SIZE	5.2 km^2
% OR AREAS FOR ZONING	12 neighbourhoods

SHORT DESCRIPTION

Privately developed by one of Uganda's largest developers, Akright Projects Ltd., Akright City is a mixed-use development offering residents integrated infrastructure and services. Located 18 kilometers southwest of Kampala, Akright City is the brainchild of Anatoli Kamugisha, who sees the development as way of providing an organised urban environment to Kampala's frustrated middle class. Originally conceived as a semi-autonomous live-work-play New Town, Akright City has faced financial problems that have led to a slowdown in construction. For now, the New Town functions as a dormitory town for Kampala, with working residents commuting to the capital, while awaiting development at home.

COUNTRY	Nigeria
DEVELOPMENT	**Eko-Atlantic**
YEAR	2003 (2010-ongoing)

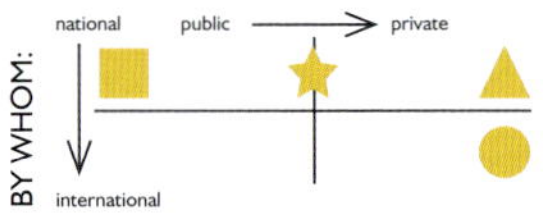

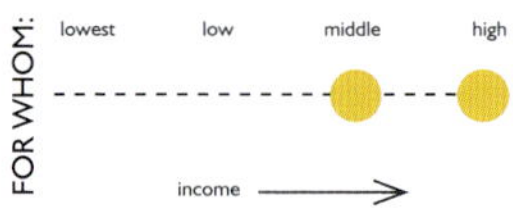

INITIATIVE / CLIENT	Lagos State Government in partnership with Chagoury group, South Energyx
DEVELOPERS	Lagos State Government, Federal Government, South Energyx (Nigeria)
PLANNING AND DESIGN	Royal HaskoningDHV (Netherlands), Dar Al-Handasah (Shair and Partners, Lebanon), AR+H Architects, MZ Architects (Qatar), China Communications Construction Group (China)
CITY TYPE	Commercial
URBAN FABRIC / TYPOLOGY	Skyline warped grid, mixed rise
TARGET POPULATION	250,000 (+ 150,000 commuters)
INHABITANTS	0
SIZE	10 km²
% OR AREAS FOR ZONING	7 districts

SHORT DESCRIPTION

Eko-Atlantic represents an ambitious public-private-partnership financed by South Energyx Nigeria Limited and supported by the Lagos State Government and Federal Government of Nigeria. Eko-Atlantic is a new peninsular extension to Victoria Island, just 18 kilometers from downtown Lagos. Eko-Atlantic is conceived as a new financial and business hub with luxe residential addresses and state-of-the-art service infrastructure. The New Town will be connected to the mainland by public transport, ferry, and a high-speed roadway, with the likely result that Eko-Atlantic will function as a massive new business district rather than an autonomous New Town. Built on 9 km^2 of new land reclaimed from the Atlantic Ocean, the development will be surrounded by seawalls to protect it from ocean surges. Critics have questioned the impact of the seawall, or 'Great Wall of Lagos', on nearby islands and low-lying informal settlements, bringing the city's rising inequality into sharp focus.

2018 GoogleEarth

COUNTRY	Algeria
DEVELOPMENT	**Boughezoul**
YEAR	2004 (2004 - 2030)

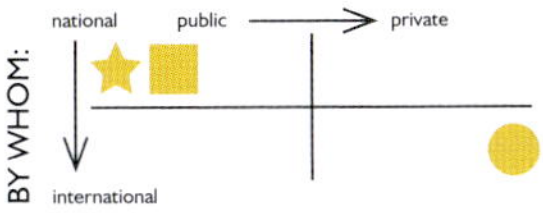

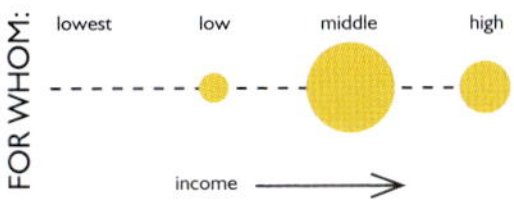

INITIATIVE / CLIENT	Algerian Ministry of Spatial Planning, Environment and Tourism
DEVELOPERS	Algerian Government, Global Environment Facility, UNEP, EPIC
PLANNING AND DESIGN	Korean enterprises: Daewoo Engineering & Construction (50%), Samwhan Corporation (30%) and Woolim Construction Co., Ltd (20%).
CITY TYPE	Capital
URBAN FABRIC / TYPOLOGY	Orthogonal grid, mixed rise
TARGET POPULATION	350,000
INHABITANTS	0
SIZE	17.5 km^2
% OR AREAS FOR ZONING	533 ha for tertiary sector and services / 3653 ha for urban area, 22% for housing projects / 500 ha for airport / 1886 ha for lake / 1839 ha for agriculture 2578 ha as protection area / 300 to 700 ha as green areas

SHORT DESCRIPTION

As Algiers faced massive population growth with inadequate resources, seismic threats, and the restlessness of overcrowded residents, the Algerian government announced a simple solution: 160 kilometers south, a new capital city would be built. The distance was intended to force the resulting capital into autonomy by preventing daily commutes. Situated adjacent to a Ramsar-protected wetland, government bodies responsible for Boughezoul committed to a zero-emissions development strategy, aiming to provide an example for future new cities. Since the site was selected, progress has been slow. Algeria's dependence on the oil and gas sector seems to indicate that the fate of the new capital is tied to global petroleum prices. It is also unclear what will happen to the 14,000 residents of the existing village of Boughezoul as their community makes way for the new development.

COUNTRY Algeria

DEVELOPMENT **Sidi Abdallah**

YEAR 2004 (2004-2030)

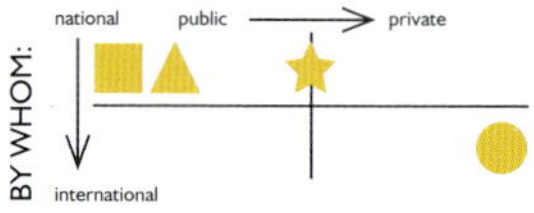

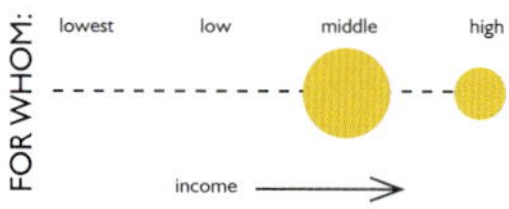

INITIATIVE / CLIENT Établissement Publique pour l'Aménagement de l'Agglomération Nouvelle de Sidi Abdellah (EPA-ANSA), Algeria and the Canadian International Development Agency (CIDA)

DEVELOPERS Algerian Ministry of Housing and Urbanism

PLANNING AND DESIGN Illo space design group (South Korea), Architect Jean-Jacques Deluz (Switzerland), Dessau (Canada), Fairbanks Architectos (Spain)

CITY TYPE Smart

URBAN FABRIC / TYPOLOGY Radial grid, mixed rise

TARGET POPULATION 500,000

INHABITANTS 100,000

SIZE 18.7 km^2

% OR AREAS FOR ZONING El Boustène (86ha) / Sidi Bennour (51ha) / Western Mahelma (54 ha) / Cyber Park (94ha) / Zones of habitat (100 ha)

SHORT DESCRIPTION

Sidi Abdellah was presented by authorities as a way to curb Algeria's population growth and alleviate housing problems. The plan envisaged a sophisticated 'smart city' that would become a centre of technological excellence with a university and multiple scientific research centres. In reality, however, Sidi Abdellah has become more of a quiet dormitory town, with middle class residents living in repetitive concrete apartment blocks. Home ownership rates are high, made possible by generous state subsidies. Part of the challenge for this New Town has been securing autonomy from Algiers. Located just 25 kilometers west of the capital, commuting for work (or leisure) remains relatively easy. As a result, commercial facilities and other amenities are still lacking in Sidi Abdellah. Access to public services, such as water, has been unreliable, causing some residents to stop paying fees and feeding distrust of municipal institutions. The city appears to be in limbo, with the earliest constructions already needing maintenance and other areas still sandy construction sites.

COUNTRY Morocco
DEVELOPMENT **Tamansourt**
YEAR 2005 (2005-ongoing)

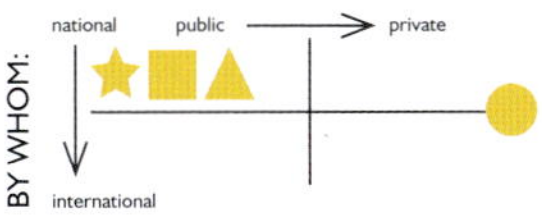

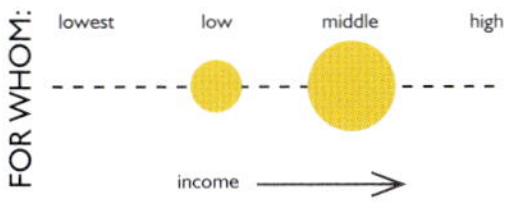

INITIATIVE / CLIENT Government of Morocco, Ministry of Housing and Urban Planning
DEVELOPERS Al Omrane Tamansourt Development Company
PLANNING AND DESIGN Mikou Studio (France), six Morrocan architecture firms

CITY TYPE Decentralization
URBAN FABRIC / TYPOLOGY Composite curvilinear grid

TARGET POPULATION 250,000
INHABITANTS 60,000 (2016)
SIZE 19 km^2

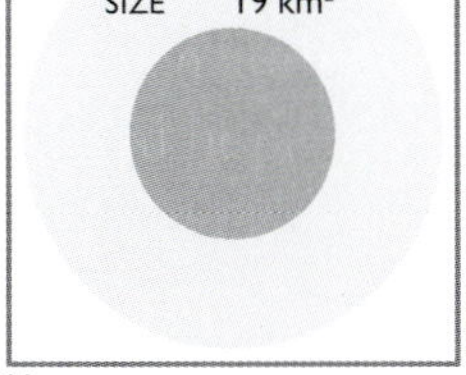

SHORT DESCRIPTION

Initiated under the patronage of King Mohammed VI, Tamansourt was intended to help decongest Marrakesh. Tamansourt is part of a larger national New Town building programme launched in 2004. Fifteen New Towns were planned, of which four have been (partially) constructed. The developer responsible for the New Town, Al-Omrane, cited two main goals: the creation of a low-density, green city, and the realization of a successful social mix among residents. The New Town is about 20 kilometers northwest of Marrakesh, with religious, leisure, commercial and recreational facilities. The new Casablanca-Agadir highway directly connects Tamansourt to Marrakesh, shortening commute times to about 15 minutes. That proximity is largely responsible for Tamansourt's self-imposed nickname: *cité-dortoir* (dormitory city). Social and affordable housing make up the majority of Tamansourt, but inadequate job opportunities and urban amenities as well as limited public transport links (one bus line to Marrakesh) are already causing the New Town some growing pains.

COUNTRY Nigeria

DEVELOPMENT **Lekki**

YEAR 2006 (2008-2015)

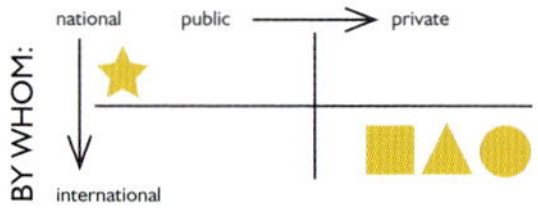

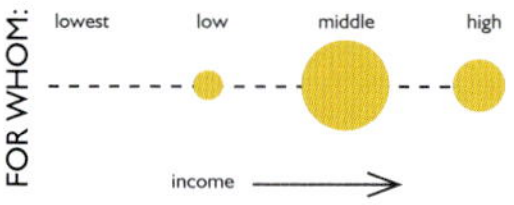

INITIATIVE / CLIENT Lagos State Ministry of Urban Planning and Physical Development

DEVELOPERS China-Africa Lekki Investment (CALI, China)

PLANNING AND DESIGN Dar al Handasah, Shair and Partners (Qatar)

CITY TYPE Commercial

URBAN FABRIC / TYPOLOGY Skyline composite, radial composite, mixed rise

TARGET POPULATION 3,400,000

INHABITANTS 401,272 (2011)

SIZE 755 km^2 (total peninsula development)

% OR AREAS FOR ZONING 4 sectors of development: 1 commercial and service area, 2 industrial park, 3 General Development Area, 4 logistic and warehousing area

SHORT DESCRIPTION

The Lekki peninsula stretches about 80 kilometers across the southern coast of Nigeria. The western tip of Lekki is home to luxury residential developments in posh Victoria Island. At the eastern edge, the peninsula connects to the mainland near the coastal village of Aiyetoro. Much of the area in between is currently farmland, wetlands, and sandy plots marked out for development. All of this is set to change very quickly. Huge new developments like the 155 km^2 Free Trade Zone at the peninsula's eastern edge will connect this area to the world through the future Lagos international airport, and a new deep-sea port. The first phase of the Free Trade Zone will be the site of a city for 120,000 residents, most of whom will work in new industrial areas.

Other New Towns are also coming. In the northwest part of the peninisula, Alaro City is Rendeavour's latest project. This 20 km^2 mixed-use, mixed-income project has been fast-tracked by the national government. The Elegushi Royal Family and private developer Channeldrill Resources Limited have also initiated the Imperial International Business City, touted as an 'eco-friendly, smart business city' along the Lekki-Epe axis. Coastal City Lekki and Iberekodo Industrial Town are additional Lekki New Towns targeting about 60,000 residents each. Smaller developments are also underway. The national government has undertaken massive new road, electric, drainage, and water networks to encourage these private developments.

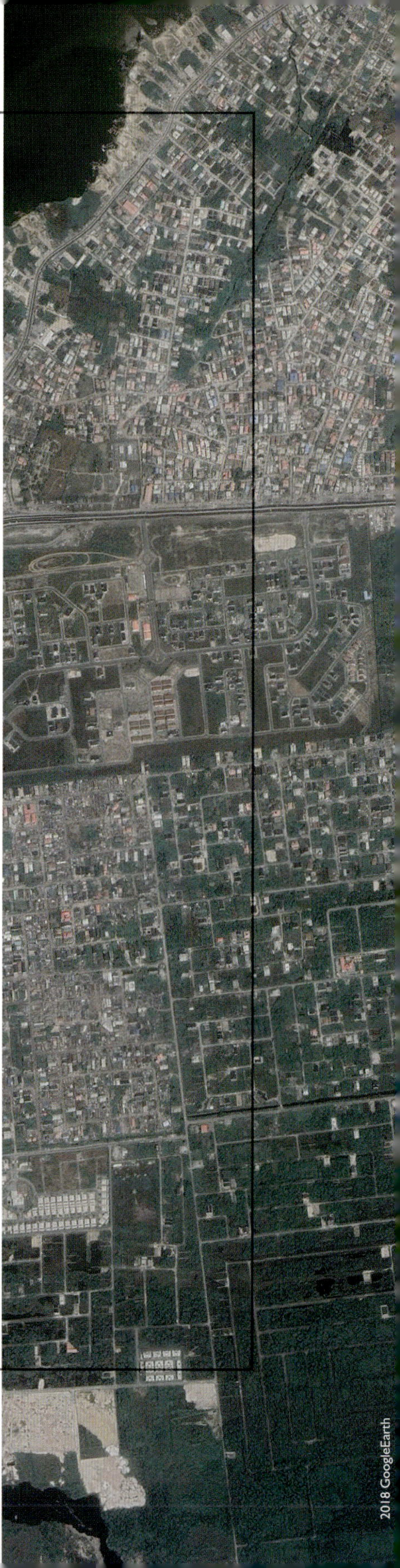

COUNTRY Angola

DEVELOPMENT **Zango**

YEAR 2007 (2008- ongoing)

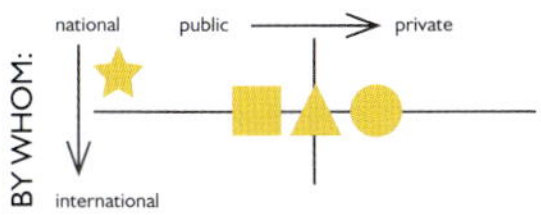

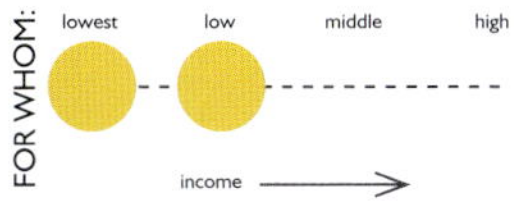

INITIATIVE / CLIENT SONIP (Sonangol Imobiliária e Propriedades, Lda)

DEVELOPERS SONIP (Sonangol Imobiliária e Propriedades, Lda), TPF Group

PLANNING AND DESIGN China Guangxi International Construction Engineering Corporation, SECAN – Sociedade de Engenharia e Consultoria, TPF consultores, OOIIO Architecture- Zango boulevard

CITY TYPE Decentralisation

URBAN FABRIC / TYPOLOGY Warped grid, low rise

TARGET POPULATION 254,000

INHABITANTS 200,000 (2017)

SIZE 4.16 km^2

% OR AREAS FOR ZONING Social housing project

SHORT DESCRIPTION

Since the end of the civil war in 2002, the Angolan government has engaged in many large-scale rehousing projects. Zango was initially intended to house resettled residents from 'high risk' informal settlements (*musseques*) in Luanda. Zango was designed based on the South African township model, with single family homes on individual plots. The social housing units have been modified and personalised, but the basic unit offers three bedrooms, a living room, kitchen, and bathroom. To overcome a lack of amenities, some homes along the main roads have been transformed into shops, beauty salons, or mechanics' garages – despite fines for flouting regulations. Critics have been vocal about the New Town's remote location, 38 kilometers from Luanda's *baixa* (down town). Zango also lacks efficient operation of basic infrastructures, particularly electricity and water supply. Despite these shortcomings there is a strong market for housing.

COUNTRY	Angola
DEVELOPMENT	**Kilamba**
YEAR	2008 (Phase I finished, next phases ongoing)

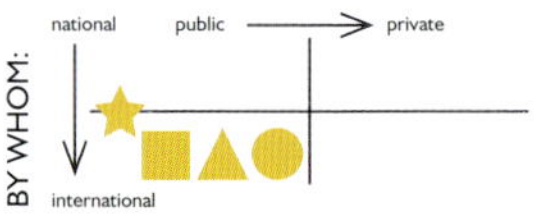

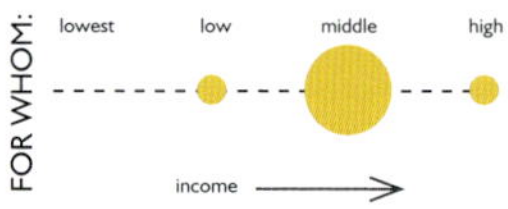

INITIATIVE / CLIENT	Ministério do Urbanismo e Habitação de Angola, SONIP (Sonagol Imobiliaria e Propriedades Lda)
DEVELOPERS	Government of Angola in partnership with SONIP (Sonangol Imobiliária e Propriedades, Lda), Haishan International Trade Co Ltd, TPF Group
PLANNING AND DESIGN	CITIC (China International Trust and Investment Corporation), Chinese Academy for Urban Planning and Design (CAUPD), Development Workshop, Overseas Design Insititute (Beijing Urban Construction Design and Development Group)
CITY TYPE	Decentralisation
URBAN FABRIC / TYPOLOGY	Orthogonal grid, mid rise
TARGET POPULATION	100,000 (1st phase)
INHABITANTS	80,000 (2015)
SIZE	8.8 km^2 (1st phase)
% OR AREAS FOR ZONING	44 neighbourhoods / central area: buisness, trade and service area, including green areas.

SHORT DESCRIPTION

Kilamba was proposed by the Chinese government at a time when Angola desperately needed alternative housing for Luanda's teeming population. Chinese planners collected data and offered designs that reflected a functional approach to city-building: three types of apartments in 720 mid-rise tower blocks. The resulting city was built quickly and efficiently, but stood empty for two years as the Angolan government scrambled to invent an appropriate housing finance system that would give more Angolans access to this new development. In 2013, former President Jose Dos Santos announced that the apartments in Kilamba would be subsidised by nearly 50%, triggering a wave of housing applications that quickly filled the New Town to capacity. While Kilamba is no longer a ghost town, operational challenges remain. The city government struggles to maintain infrastructure and public services, while overlapping responsibilities among four different governing bodies cause delay and ambiguity.

COUNTRY Congo DRC

DEVELOPMENT **La Cité du Fleuve**

YEAR 2008 (2009 - ongoing)

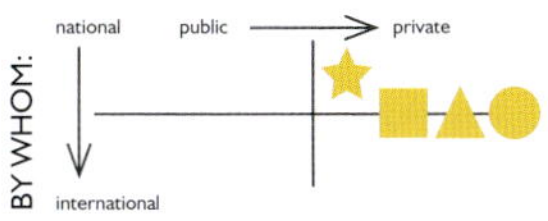

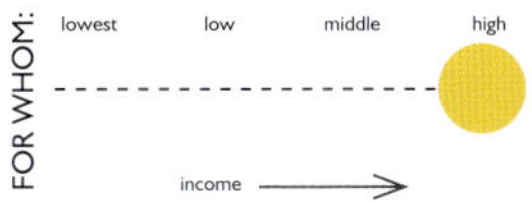

INITIATIVE / CLIENT Hawkwood Properties

DEVELOPERS Hawkwood Properties, Mukwa Investments (Zambia)

PLANNING AND DESIGN Rent-A-Port (Belgium), Egis (France), ATCO (DRCongo), Asmec Africa (Zimbabwe), Dispromalt (DRCongo)

CITY TYPE Commercial

URBAN FABRIC / TYPOLOGY Composite radial grid, mixed rise

TARGET POPULATION 250,000

INHABITANTS 2,500 (2017)

SIZE 3.75 km^2

% OR AREAS FOR ZONING 200 villas / 10,000 apartments / 10,000 offices / 2,000 shops / 15 diplomaic missions / 3 hotels / 2 churches / 1 university / 3 healthcare centres / 1 shopping centre

SHORT DESCRIPTION

La Cité du Fleuve is located on two artificial islands in the Congo River at the eastern edge of Kinshasa. Due to its location, the development is likely to function as a bedroom community, with working residents commuting to downtown Kinshasa during the day. La Cité du Fleuve is a private development initiated by Zambia-based Hawkwood Properties and embraced by both local Congoloese elite and members of the diaspora. The development aims to provide luxury housing supported by first-class amenities and infrastructure. That combination is seen as greatly desired in a city of twelve million people where overcrowding and inadequate infrastructure is the norm. Because the Democratic Republic of the Congo has a nascent home financing market, Hawkwood Properties is working to establish a bank that would provide home loans, and thus greater access to home ownership in La Cité du Fleuve.

COUNTRY	Tanzania
DEVELOPMENT	**Kigamboni**
YEAR	2008 (2011-2030)

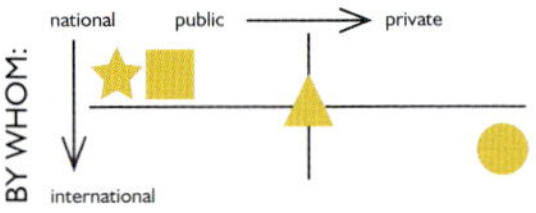

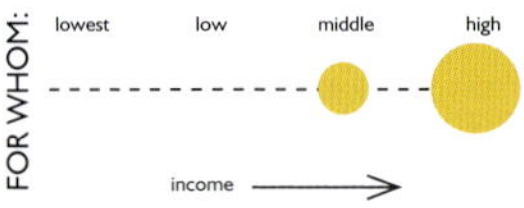

INITIATIVE / CLIENT	Tanzania Ministry of Lands, Housing and Human Settlements Development
DEVELOPERS	Kigamboni Development Authority (until 2017), Kigamboni Municipal Council
PLANNING AND DESIGN	Land and Housing Consortium (Korea)
CITY TYPE	Decentralisation
URBAN FABRIC / TYPOLOGY	Linear skyline city, mixed rise
TARGET POPULATION	500,000
INHABITANTS	97,000 (2014)
SIZE	65 km^2
% OR AREAS FOR ZONING	5 zones residential 36.2% / industrial 7.7% / tourism 8.3% / international buisness 5.6% / public facilities and open areas 40.2%

SHORT DESCRIPTION

Kigamboni was envisioned as a development that would increase the quality of life for residents of Dar es Salaam. The New Town was situated in Temeke district of the Dar es Salaam region, on the southern bank of the Kurasini Creek. The area is currently a popular location, with mixed usage and access to downtown Dar es Salaam facilitated by ferry. Plans for redevelopment of Kigamboni show the government's renewed interest in steering urban development. However, the top-down, technocratic approach taken in Kigamboni caused tension with residents and local activists. Redevelopment required resettlement and compensation of 97,000 Kigamboni residents. At the time of writing, resettlement issues, financial complications and other delays have brought the project to a standstill, and the future of Kigamboni remains unclear.

COUNTRY	Kenya
DEVELOPMENT	**Konza Tech City**
YEAR	2008 (2013-2030)

INITIATIVE / CLIENT	Government of Kenya
DEVELOPERS	Tetra Tech (US), Ministry of Information and Communications, TheCityUK, CMA, Kenya National Government
PLANNING AND DESIGN	SHoP Architects (USA), HR&A Advisors (USA), Center for Urban and Regional Planning (Kenya), OZ Architecture (USA), Tetra Tech (USA)
CITY TYPE	Smart
URBAN FABRIC / TYPOLOGY	Linear skyline city, mixed rise
TARGET POPULATION	250,000
INHABITANTS	0
SIZE	20 km^2
% OR AREAS FOR ZONING	3.2 million m^2 of residential developments / 130,000 m^2 in the business corridor / 230,000 m^2 in our technology park / 200,000 m^2 of parks, playgrounds and open spaces / 75,000 m^2 of hospitals and health facilities / 650,000 m^2 of light industrial and warehousing facilities / 445,000 m^2 of school sites

SHORT DESCRIPTION

Konza Tech City was initiated in 2008 as a flagship Kenya Vision 2030 project. The aim of Vision 2030 was to support development within Kenya, increase quality of life, and cultivate a globally competitive nation. Located 60 kilometers south of Nairobi, Konza was envisioned as a 'smart city' that would revolutionise Kenya's ICT sector. The location on the former Malili Ranch was chosen for its proximity to existing road networks. Konza was originally proposed as a technology park with world-class infrastructure that would support growth. In 2012 a comprehensive plan was developed that expanded the project into 'Africa's Silicon Savannah'. After delays due to political changes, Konza was fast-tracked by the Kenyan government in January 2016. Construction began in late 2016.

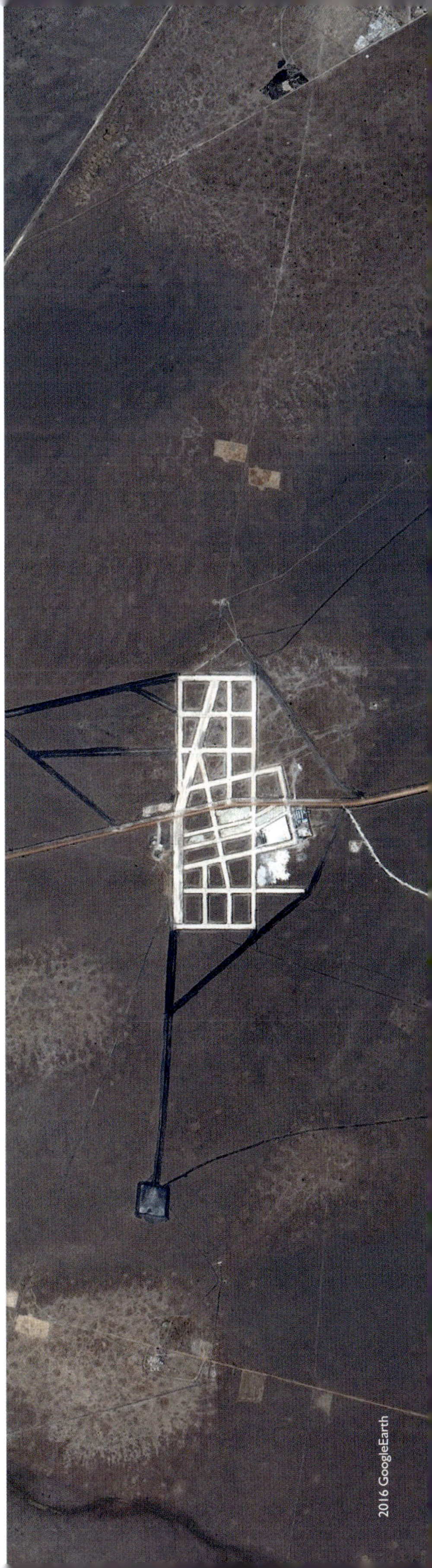

COUNTRY Ethiopia
DEVELOPMENT **BuraNEST**
YEAR 2010 (2017-ongoing)

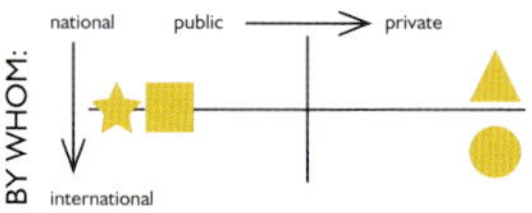

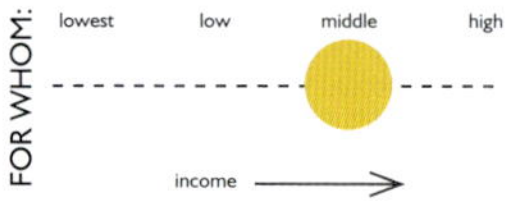

INITIATIVE / CLIENT Government of Ethiopia
DEVELOPERS Authorities of the region of Amhara, NESTown group (ETH Zurich)
PLANNING AND DESIGN NESTown Group

CITY TYPE Eco
URBAN FABRIC / TYPOLOGY Warped grid, low rise

TARGET POPULATION 40,000 (6,835 phase I)
INHABITANTS 16
SIZE 1.25 km^2
% OR AREAS FOR ZONING town core and 4 quarters: education nucleus to implement education and sports, energy nucleus operation centre, market nucleus start up initiative for new buisnesses, environmental nucleus to implement ecology and securety

SHORT DESCRIPTION

Initiated as a collaboration between Ethiopian and Swiss planners and architects, BuraNEST was conceived as a socially, environmentally and financially sustainable New Town. The entire process of city-making was thoroughly examined and presented to the regional government of Amhara State as an opportunity to bring the benefits of development to a rural area. The site in Bura kebele, Libokemkem woreda, was chosen by the government, rather than the architects and presented various new challenges. Since the project was initiated in 2010, the project leaders have spent years conducting workshops, interviews, and charrettes with members of the local farming community. From the beginning, they faced resistance from subsistence farmers with traditional values. But over time, the project's benefits have become clear, and as the first public buildings, educational gardens, and multi-family housing structures have taken shape, local families have signed on with increasing rapidity. With the support of the local community and the regional government securely in place, project leaders expect the next project phases to go more quickly.

COUNTRY	Kenya
DEVELOPMENT	**Tatu City**
YEAR	2010 (2008-2020)

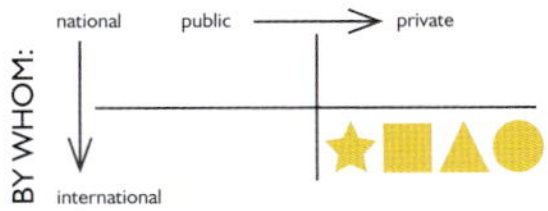

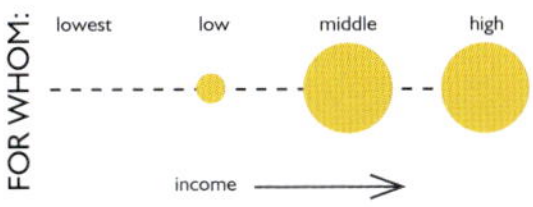

INITIATIVE / CLIENT	Rendeavour
DEVELOPERS	Rendeavour
PLANNING AND DESIGN	DLC Group (South Africa), SOM (USA), Lariak Landscapes (Kenya)
CITY TYPE	Commercial
URBAN FABRIC / TYPOLOGY	Curvilinear warped grid
TARGET POPULATION	150,000 inhabitants (40,000 commuters)
INHABITANTS	0
SIZE	10.12 km^2
% OR AREAS FOR ZONING	64% residential area / 9% education facilities / 13% light industies / 5% technological park / 3% buisness district / 4% parks playgrounds and open spaces / 2% healthcare facilities

SHORT DESCRIPTION

Tatu City was initiated by international developer Rendeavour according to a planning model that the company applies to each of their (currently) seven urban developments in five African countries. Included in Nairobi's Vision 2030, the city is capitalising on its sharp contrast to Nairobi's dilapidated infrastructure, pollution, overcrowding, and crime. Located in the quickly urbanising northern part of Nairobi, Tatu City is close to the highway connecting the New Town to Nairobi centre.

For a long time, the city's construction was hampered by legal disputes, but since construction started in 2015, things have gone more smoothly. The city has acquired the status of Special Economic Zone, providing benefits such as reduced taxes, and the vast industrial terrain in Tatu City is attracting international companies and filling up. Services such as schools and a Training Academy for local construction workers have opened. Residential areas are being built, providing gated communities with serviced plots as well as more affordable housing in apartment blocks.

COUNTRY Morocco

DEVELOPMENT **Ville Verte Mohammed VI**

YEAR 2010 (2010-2040)

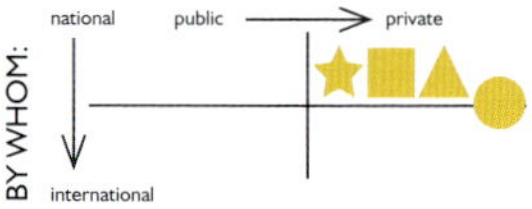

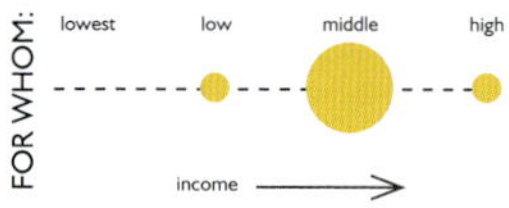

INITIATIVE / CLIENT OCP Group (Office Cherifien des Phosphates)

DEVELOPERS OCP Group (Office Cherifien des Phosphates)

PLANNING AND DESIGN OCP Group (Office Cherifien des Phosphates), University Campus: RBTA (Ricardo Bofill Taller de Arquitectura, Spain)

CITY TYPE Eco

URBAN FABRIC / TYPOLOGY Warped grid, mixed rise

TARGET POPULATION 130,000

INHABITANTS 10,000-25,000

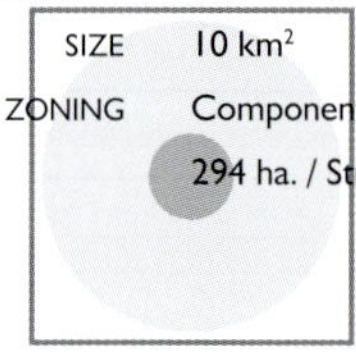

SIZE 10 km^2

% OR AREAS FOR ZONING Components: 819 ha. / Forest and green spaces: 294 ha. / Strategic Reserve: 186 ha.

SHORT DESCRIPTION

Ville Verte Mohammed VI (VVM6) is initiated, financed, designed and constructed by Office Chérifien des Phosphates (OCP), a private Moroccan company and the world's largest exporter of phosphate fertilisers. The New Town is intended to showcase OCP's commitment to environmental responsibility, and is the first city in the African continent to participate in the Leadership in Energy and Environmental Design (LEED) Neighborhood Development certification process. In 2015 the development received a LEED rating of Silver. Inspired by Cambridge, Massachusetts, VVM6 is designed around the new University Mohammed VI Polytechnic (UM6P), which was built first and housed students and staff before construction began on the rest of the New Town. By combining an engineering university with a platform for city-scale experiments in renewable energy techniques, VVM6 hopes to continue pushing for eco-innovation and set a precedent for green building in Morocco.

COUNTRY	Ghana
DEVELOPMENT	**Appolonia**
YEAR	2012 (2017-ongoing)

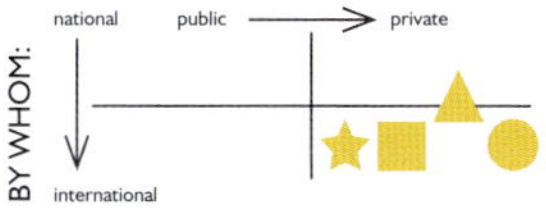

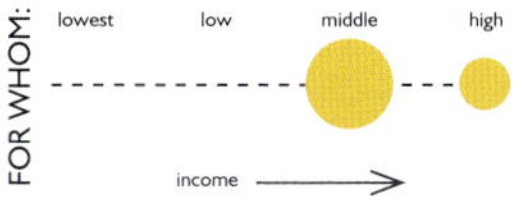

INITIATIVE / CLIENT	Rendeavour
DEVELOPERS	Rendeavour
PLANNING AND DESIGN	Rendeavour, DLC Group (South Africa)
CITY TYPE	Commercial
URBAN FABRIC / TYPOLOGY	curvilinear loops and lollipops, low rise
TARGET POPULATION	88,000
INHABITANTS	0
SIZE	9.5 km^2
% OR AREAS FOR ZONING	70% residential development / 10% school and hospital services / 6% light industries and warehousing facilities / 7% central buisness district / 8% buisness corridor

SHORT DESCRIPTION

Appolonia was initiated by Rendeavour as a model to offer middle- and high-income groups in Ghana an alternative to the flooding, congestion, and poor housing construction quality in Accra. The result is a partnership between Rendeavour and Ghana Home Loans that combines built housing with new housing finance models to allow greater access to the project. About 28 kilometers northeast of Accra, Appolonia is currently under construction and will likely function as a bedroom community for Accra as the first phase is completed. The mixed-use plan incorporates schools, light industry, commercial facilities, and healthcare, in addition to mixed residential communities. There is also the possibility to purchase a plot and construct housing privately, albeit within certain design parameters. That freedom is unusual for this generation of New Towns. As the largest urban developer in Africa, Rendeavour has the advantage of experience in other African countries, and a willingness to experiment.

COUNTRY	Egypt
DEVELOPMENT	**Wedian City**
	New capital city
YEAR	2015 (2016-2040)

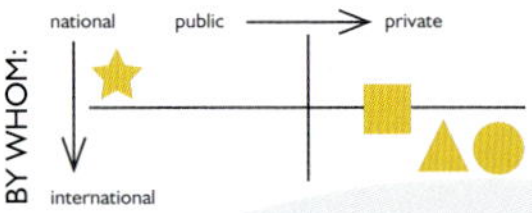

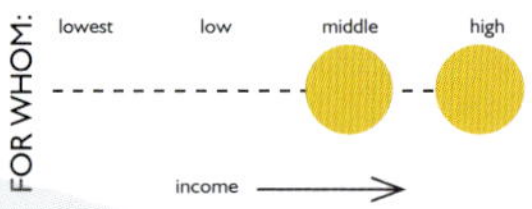

INITIATIVE / CLIENT	Government of Egypt, Ministry of Housing, Ministry
DEVELOPERS	Government of Egypt in partnership with Capital City Partners (Dubai), China State Construction Engineering Corporation (China)
PLANNING AND DESIGN	SOM Architects (USA), Urban Design Consortium +5 (Egypt)
CITY TYPE	Capital
URBAN FABRIC / TYPOLOGY	Curvilinear polycentric, mixed rise
TARGET POPULATION	5,000,000
INHABITANTS	0
SIZE	700 km^2
% OR AREAS FOR ZONING	21 residential districts and 25 'dedicated districts' / 490 km^2 available for development / 91 km^2 renewable energy farms / 140 km^2 new streets / 16 km^2 airport area / 5.6 km^2 buisness district / 4.2 km^2 shopping mall / 4 km^2 leisure park

SHORT DESCRIPTION

When the Egyptian government announced plans for a new administrative capital in 2015, media outlets and academics were vocal in their opposition. Egypt's history of New Town building is long and varied, but since the 1970s the New Urban Communities Authority (NUCA) has struggled to fill dozens of New Towns along the Nile corridor. The plan for a new capital was greeted as a waste of money, and another excuse to prop up the military construction arm. Since then, the new capital has become a reality, with infrastructure already on the ground at the desert site 70 kilometers east of Cairo. The new capital is intended to function as the administrative heart of government, but also as an autonomous and vibrant city. Many of Cairo's 19.5 million residents live in overcrowded conditions and Wedian City is seen as a way of decentralising Egypt's population, creating jobs, and emphasizing Egypt's status on the world stage.

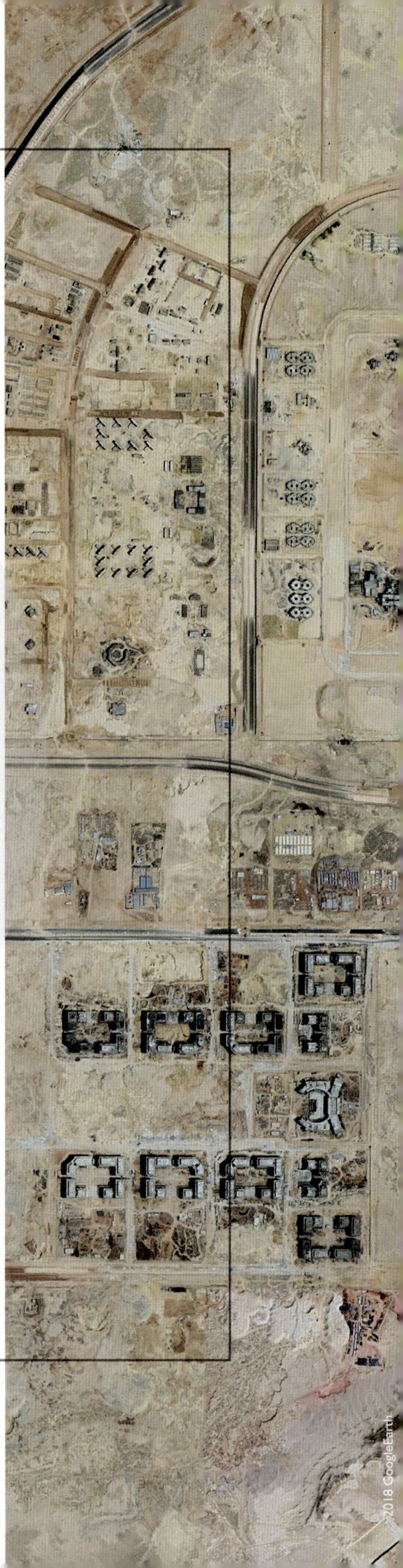

COUNTRY	Ghana
DEVELOPMENT	**Ningo-Prampram**
YEAR	2015 (Approved in 2016)

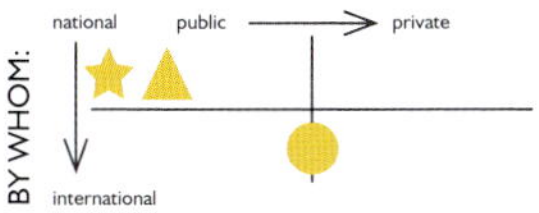

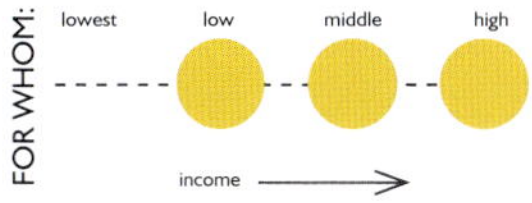

INITIATIVE / CLIENT	Ningo-Prampram District Authorities
PLANNING AND DESIGN	UN-Habitat Urban Planning and Design Labs FABRICations, MLA+, Mixst Urbanisme, More Architecture, OKRA Landscape Architects
CITY TYPE	Decentralisation
URBAN FABRIC / TYPOLOGY	Orthogonal grid, poly centric, mixed rise
TARGET POPULATION	1,500,000
INHABITANTS	83,603 (2018)
SIZE	150 km^2

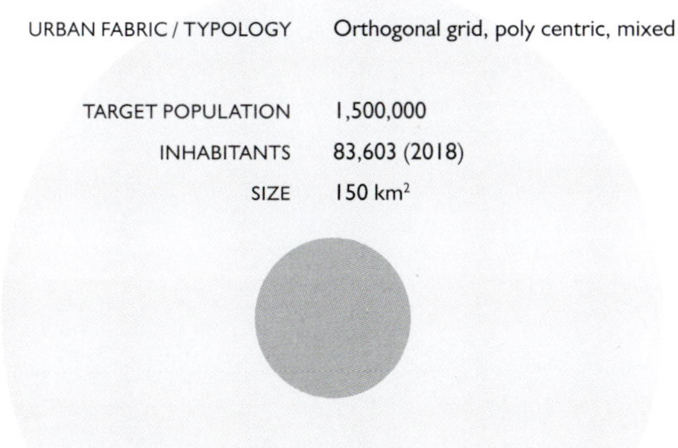

SHORT DESCRIPTION

Ningo-Prampram began in 2015 with an Urban Lab co-organised by UN-Habitat and the Dutch Creative Industries Fund. Dutch planning firms MLA+, More Architecture, FABRICations, MIXST Urbanisme, and OKRA jointly designed a plan that addresses the ad hoc urban sprawl of the Accra region in an evolutionary and flexible way. The design is informed by a grid that breaks apart at natural features such as a rivers, allowing for food production and water retention. Ningo-Prampram is one of the first New Towns to incorporate urban farming in the design, and its proximity to Accra would allow for exchange between the two areas. The plan for Ningo-Prampram was officially approved by the Statutory Planning Authority of the Ningo-Prampram District Assembly (NiPDA) and ground was broken during a ceremony in September 2017.

2017 GoogleEarth

FOR WHOM WAS THE NEW TOWN BUILT:

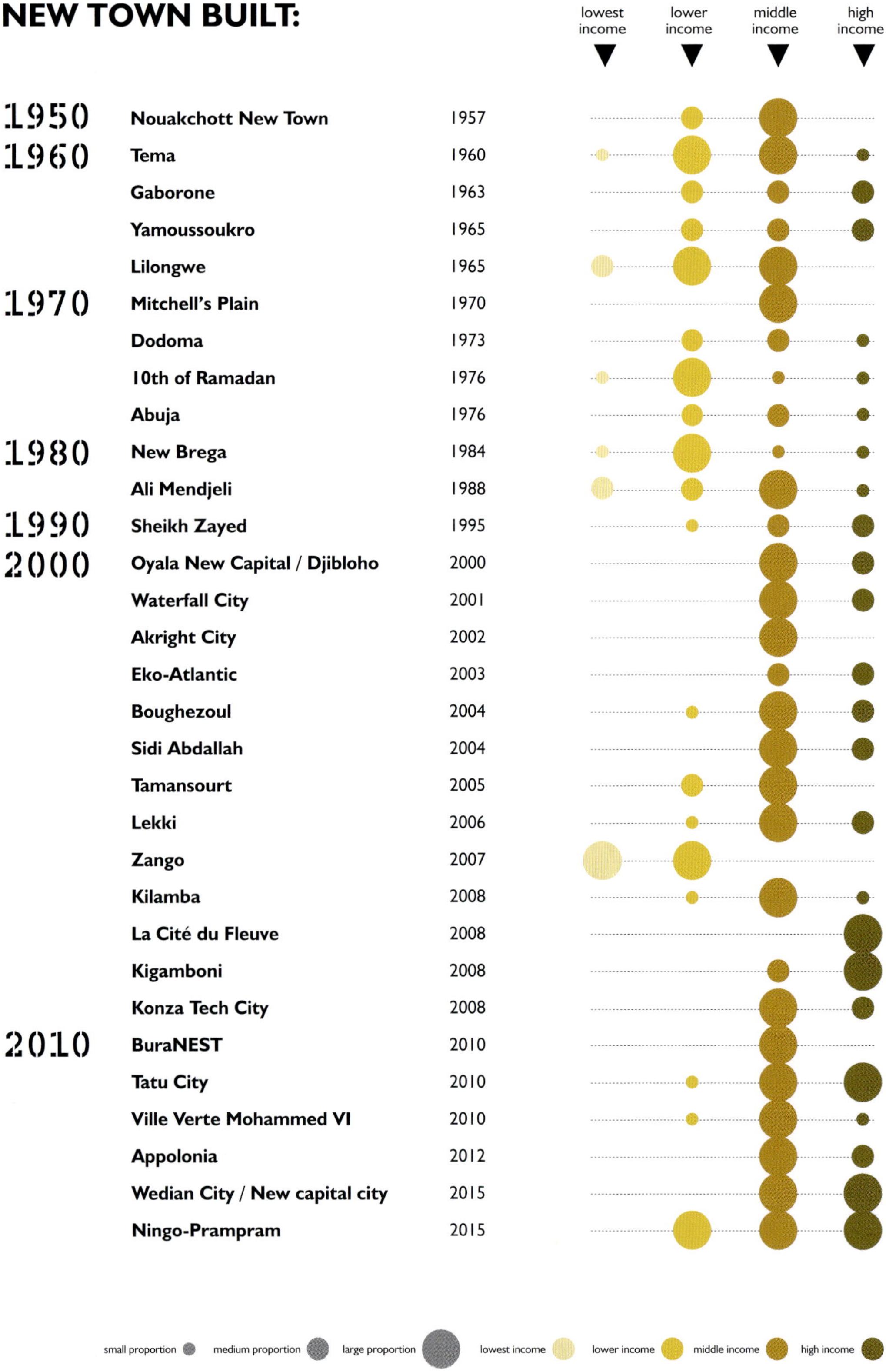

WHO INITIATED, BUILT AND FINANCED THE NEW TOWN:

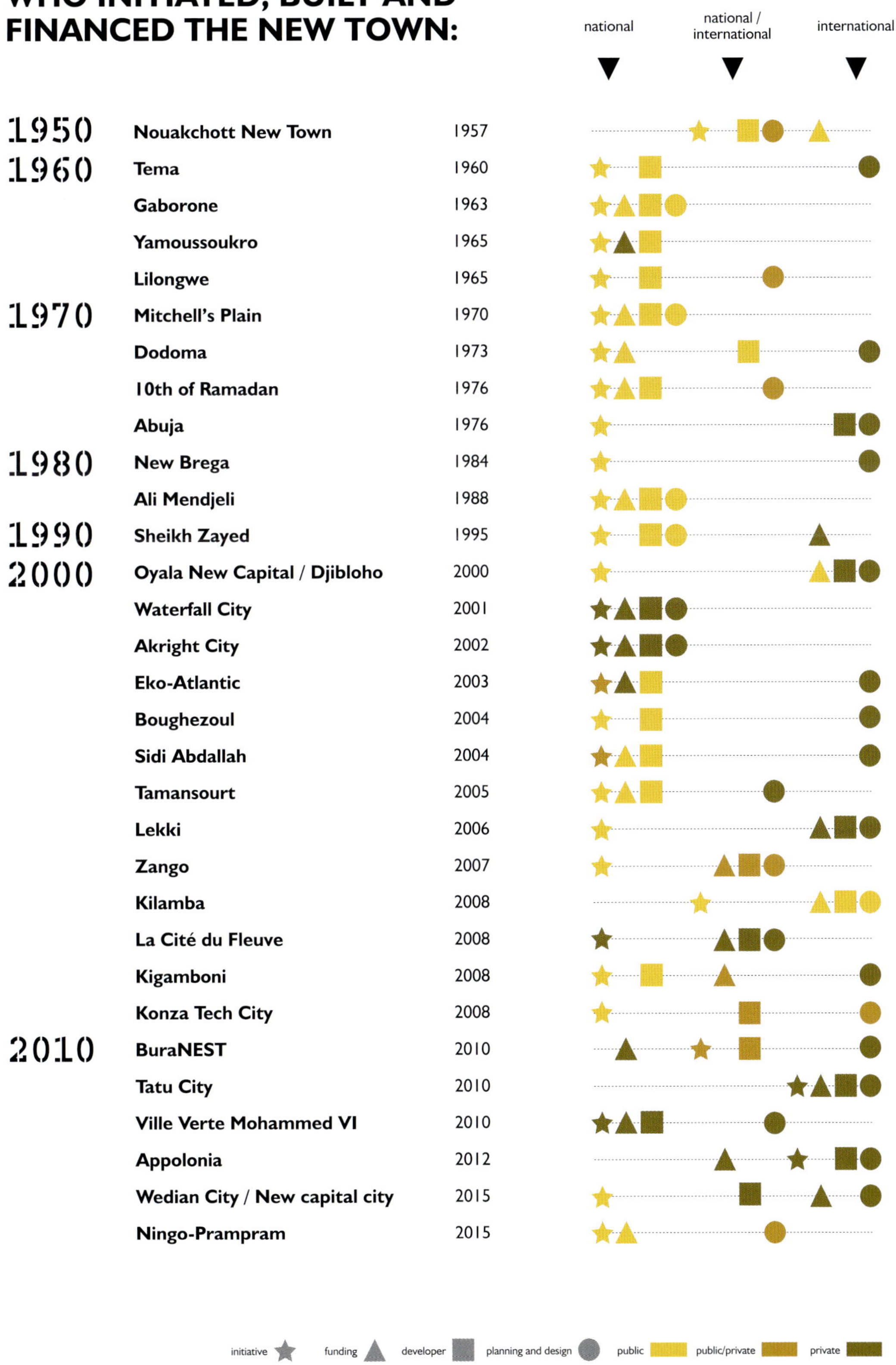

FOREIGN INFLUENCES
DESIGN, FINANCE AND ENGINEERING FROM ABROAD IN 31 NEW TOWNS

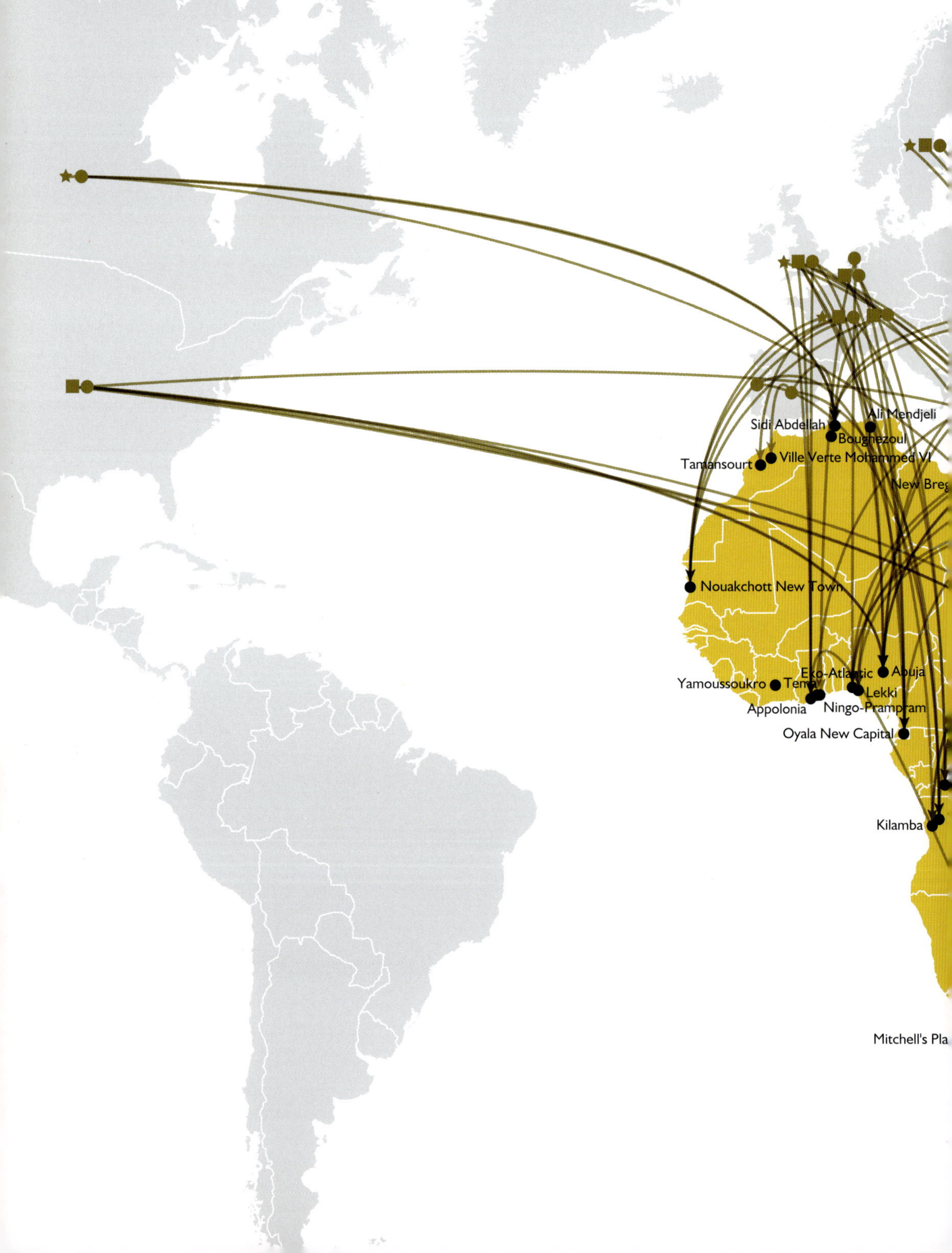

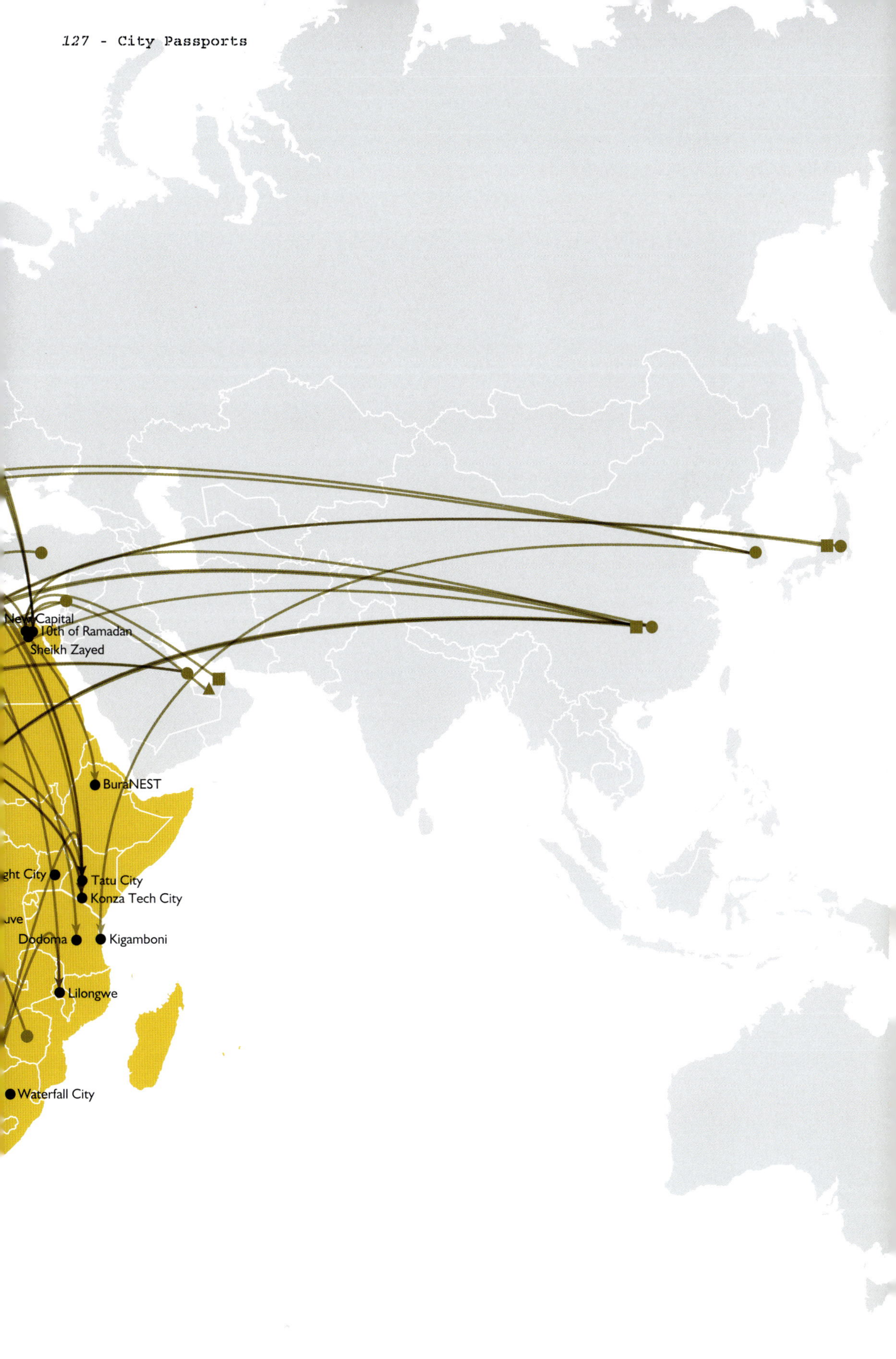
New Capital
10th of Ramadan
Sheikh Zayed
BuraNEST
ght City
Tatu City
Konza Tech City
Dodoma
Kigamboni
Lilongwe
Waterfall City

QUANTITATIVE COMPARISON
TARGET POPULATION, INHABITANTS AND SIZE OF 31 NEW TOWNS

In the principles of UN-Habitat, 15,000 inhabitants per km^2 is considered an ideal urban density. In that case the circle fits perfectly in the square.

Nouakchott New Town, 1957

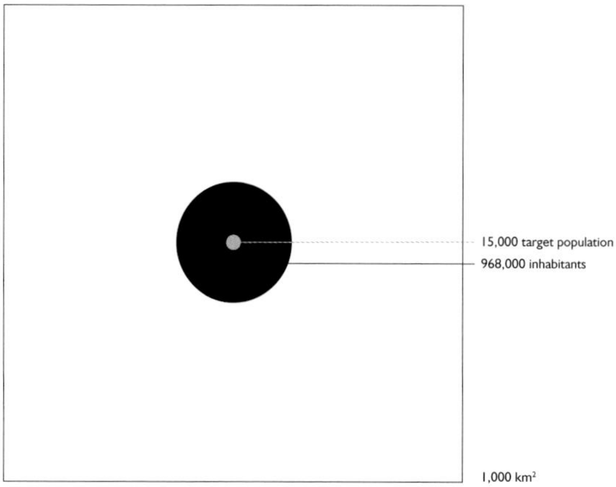

Tema, 1960

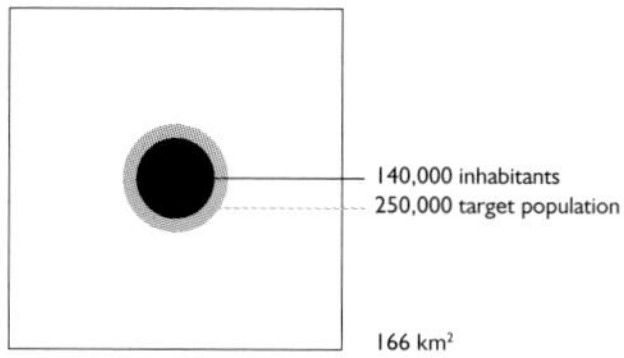

Gaborone, 1963

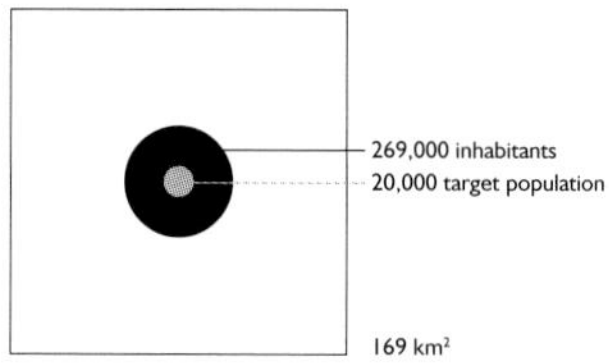

Yamoussoukro,1965

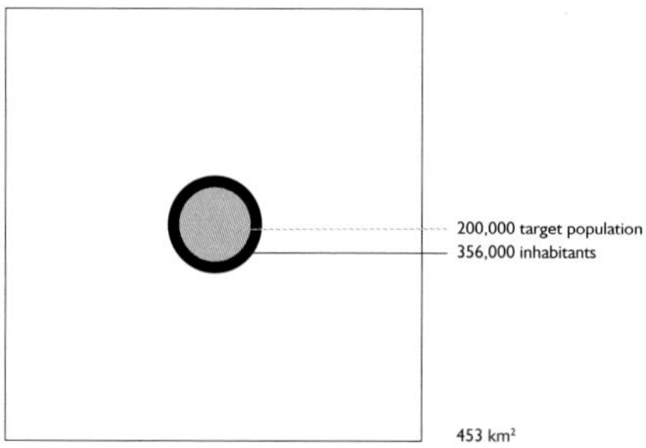

Lilongwe, 1965

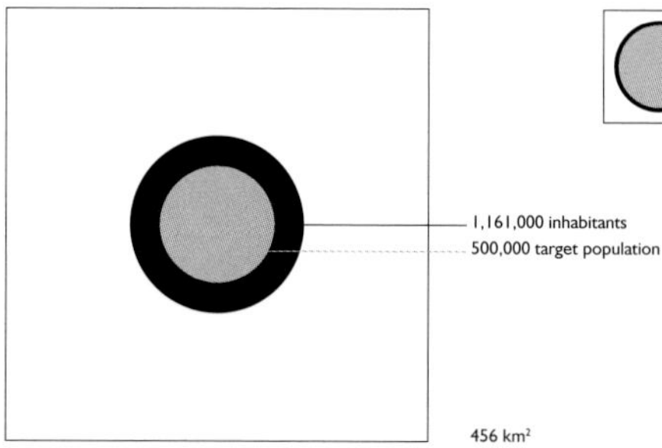

Mitchell's Plain, 1970

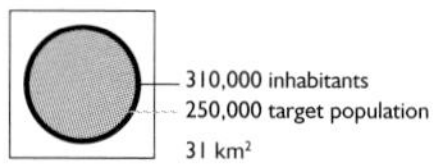

Dodoma, 1973

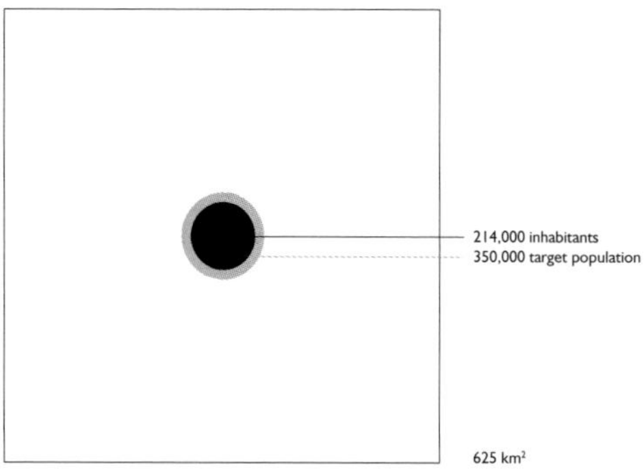

10th of Ramadan, 1976

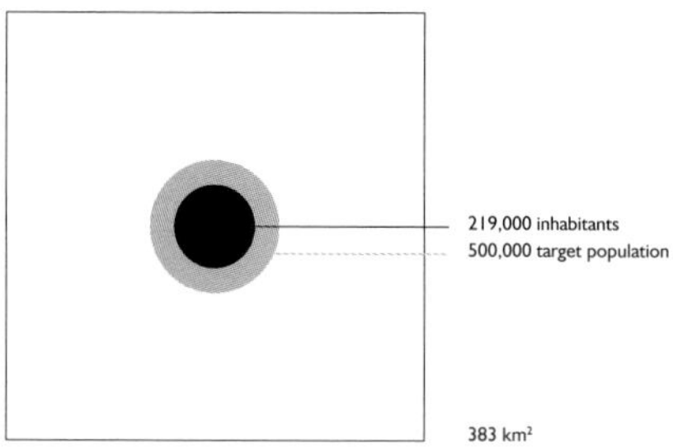

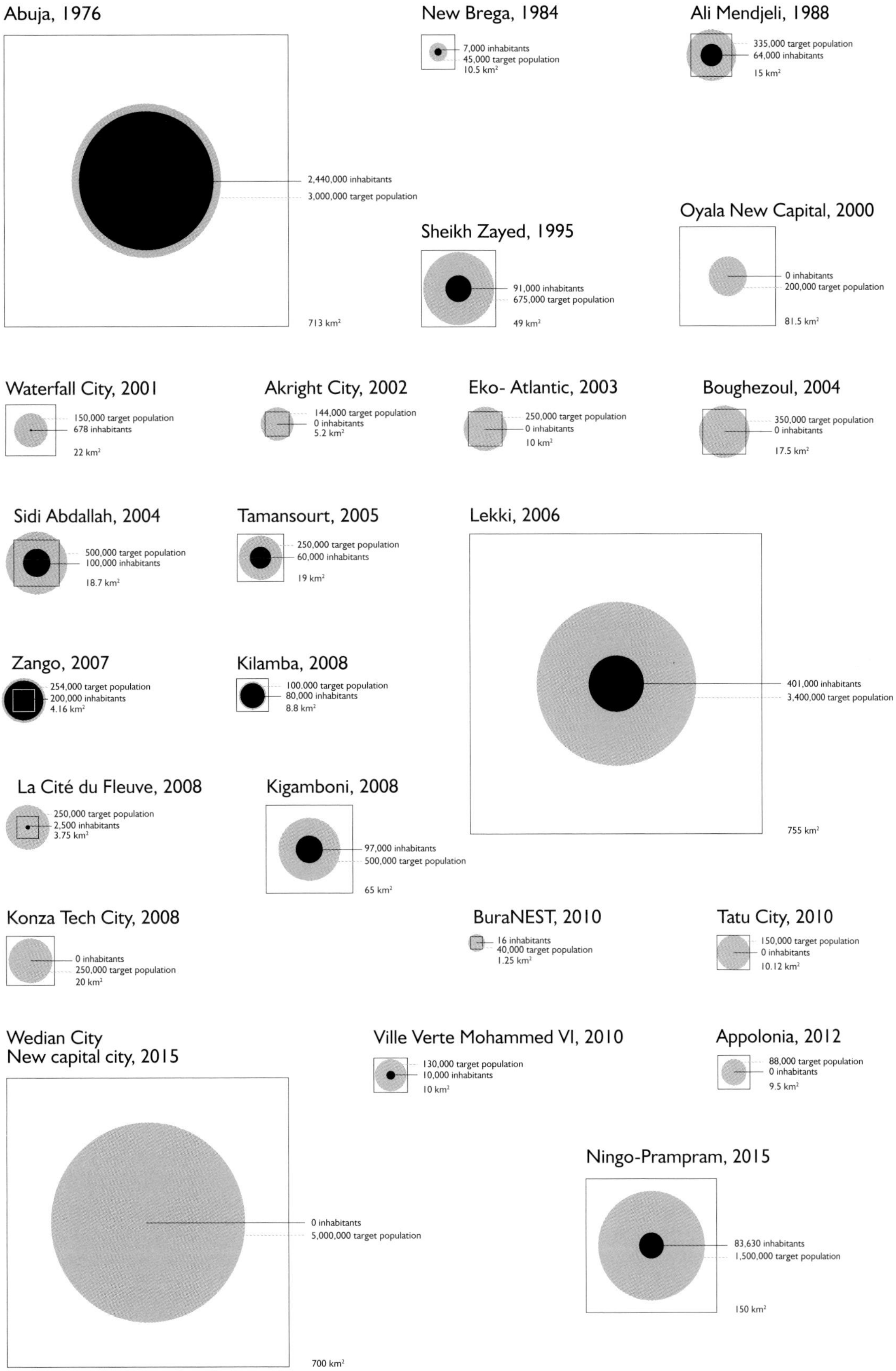
Abuja, 1976
2,440,000 inhabitants
3,000,000 target population
713 km²
New Brega, 1984
7,000 inhabitants
45,000 target population
10.5 km²
Ali Mendjeli, 1988
335,000 target population
64,000 inhabitants
15 km²
Sheikh Zayed, 1995
91,000 inhabitants
675,000 target population
49 km²
Oyala New Capital, 2000
0 inhabitants
200,000 target population
81.5 km²
Waterfall City, 2001
150,000 target population
678 inhabitants
22 km²
Akright City, 2002
144,000 target population
0 inhabitants
5.2 km²
Eko- Atlantic, 2003
250,000 target population
0 inhabitants
10 km²
Boughezoul, 2004
350,000 target population
0 inhabitants
17.5 km²
Sidi Abdallah, 2004
500,000 target population
100,000 inhabitants
18.7 km²
Tamansourt, 2005
250,000 target population
60,000 inhabitants
19 km²
Lekki, 2006
401,000 inhabitants
3,400,000 target population
755 km²
Zango, 2007
254,000 target population
200,000 inhabitants
4.16 km²
Kilamba, 2008
100.000 target population
80,000 inhabitants
8.8 km²
La Cité du Fleuve, 2008
250,000 target population
2,500 inhabitants
3.75 km²
Kigamboni, 2008
97,000 inhabitants
500,000 target population
65 km²
Konza Tech City, 2008
0 inhabitants
250,000 target population
20 km²
BuraNEST, 2010
16 inhabitants
40,000 target population
1.25 km²
Tatu City, 2010
150,000 target population
0 inhabitants
10.12 km²
Wedian City
New capital city, 2015
0 inhabitants
5,000,000 target population
700 km²
Ville Verte Mohammed VI, 2010
130,000 target population
10,000 inhabitants
10 km²
Appolonia, 2012
88,000 target population
0 inhabitants
9.5 km²
Ningo-Prampram, 2015
83,630 inhabitants
1,500,000 target population
150 km²

BuraNEST (2010), Ethiopia. (Photo: R. Keeton, 2017)

6th of October (1979), Egypt. (Photo: R. Keeton, 2016)

Kilamba (2008), Angola. (Photo: R. Keeton, 2016)

Atlantis (1972), South Africa. (Photo: M. Provoost, 2014)

Tema (1960), Ghana. (Photo: M. Provoost, 2015)

SUZUKI

10th of Ramadan (1976), Egypt. (Photo: R. [illegible]eton, 2016)

PART 2. A MANUAL

The principles presented in this Manual are distilled from various research strands: first, they are based on historic research through close consideration of 20th century African New Towns. Second, they draw on our experiences with New Towns worldwide. Third - and most importantly - we have used our analysis of current and contemporary plans in Africa to identify the most common critical aspects in the planning of New Towns in Africa and have geared the principles towards these issues.

The principles have been developed as an addition to the *New Urban Agenda* by the United Nations (2017). Underlining the general recommendations for planning and urban design in this document, there are a number of issues that specifically apply to the physical planning and design of New Towns, which have not been addressed in the *New Urban Agenda*. This Manual hopes to rectify this omission and offer advice on essential steps in the planning and design of New Towns.

An early draft of these principles was first presented at the first International New Town Day in Almere, the Netherlands, 2016. Later in 2016 they were presented in Quito, Ecuador at Habitat III. Following that, they were further tested through workshops with New Town stakeholders, reviewed by multi-disciplinary experts, and refined through extensive discussion with planners, developers, politicians, and residents of African New Towns.

1. Planning is an ongoing process

No city is permanent or static, and everything that was once modern eventually becomes outdated. The cities that are most effective are those that reflect and adapt to changes over time. New Towns should be conceptualised as a very long-term process, rather than a short-term product. They need time to develop into complete and vital urban environments. All cities continuously evolve over time, and this evolution should be clearly addressed in terms of phasing, sequencing, maintenance, and financing.

To do so, the (master) planning documents must be re-evaluated at key stages, and especially when growth-related, large infrastructural or programmatic choices are being considered. Monitoring and evaluation should be ongoing throughout the New Town's life cycle, so that current conditions are understood, changes are documented and their consequences can be processed in consecutive planning phases. It usually takes New Towns at least 50 years after initiation and sometimes longer to reach maturity. Private developers should therefore work with local governments to achieve long-term results. No city is ever finished.

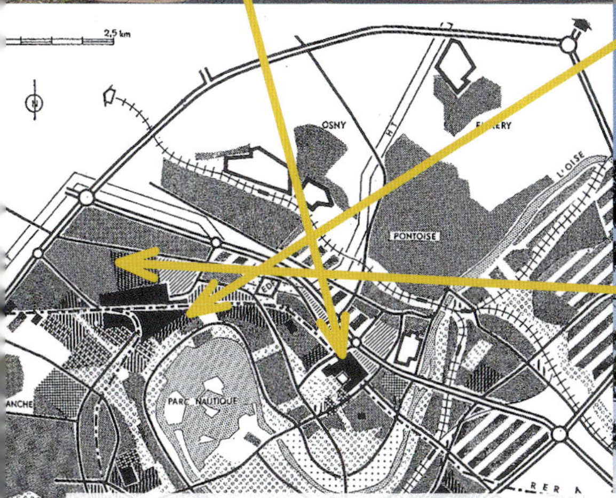

Cergy Pontoise, France, one of the Villes Nouvelles around Paris, is based on a Masterplan designed in 1970, allowing for continuous growth of the city (presently 200,000 inhabitants) within the infrastructural framework of the plan. The programme, density, design and architecture of the individual districts is adjusted according to the demand, economy and financial possibilities of the moment. Therefore, the identity of each district differs greatly, reflecting the needs and zeitgeist of each decade. Fifty years after the initial masterplan, the framework is still being used to expand the city, while the urban design of the new districts is completely contemporary.

(Photos: M. Provoost, 2014)

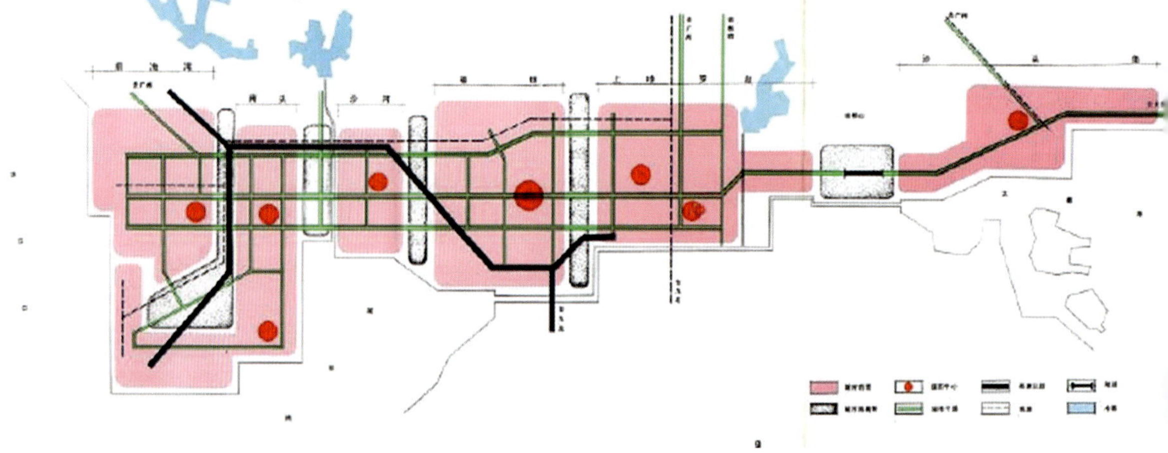

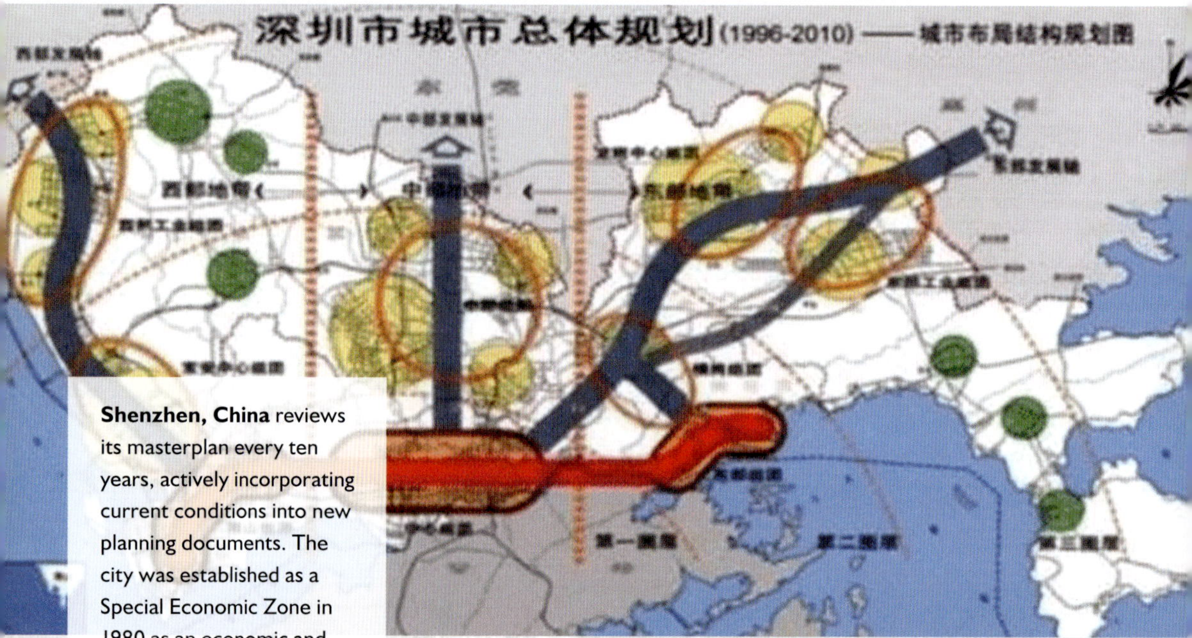

Shenzhen, China reviews its masterplan every ten years, actively incorporating current conditions into new planning documents. The city was established as a Special Economic Zone in 1980 as an economic and political experiment. The first masterplan was quite rudimentary and mapped the outline of the new city as a linear city developing along a few main highways. Subsequent masterplans have been issued every decade to cope with the fast pace of development of the city: To steer the development, but also to invite it; to not frustrate development; and to make negotiations and detailed plans possible on more detailed levels.

(Source: Urban Planning, Land & Resource Commission of Shenzhen Municipality)

Abuja, Nigeria was originally developed according to a comprehensive masterplan. However, as the city grew, certain officials looked the other way as illegal neighbourhoods and squatter settlements mushroomed within areas slated for other development. That relaxed attitude has shifted significantly in the last two decades. Beginning in 1999, the masterplan was revised regularly, in 2006 and 2016. Each review has been followed by new commitments to safeguard green space and subsequent shanty demolitions and resettlement projects. In 2018, the city's administration commenced another resettlement programme to move indigenous communities living in the Federal Capital City to peri-urban areas. The programme has been met with active resistance and questions regarding fair compensation.

(Photo: AP Photo/Sunday Alamba)

2. Plan for adaptivity

When a city is conceived according to a masterplan aimed at a single, final result, it limits the New Town's capacity for change. For this reason, New Towns have historically struggled with the need to adapt to dynamic economic or social conditions. Their masterplan was conceived at a single moment in time, and because planning inevitably reflects the conditions at that one moment, a masterplan is frequently obsolete before it is even realised.

Demographic projections indicate continued urban growth over the next century throughout the African continent. The masterplan for Abuja, Nigeria (1979), for example, was planned for a projected population of three million after 25 years, but its metropolitan area currently has six million residents. Others, like Dodoma, Tanzania, have never reached the population size they expected to achieve. To adapt successfully, New Towns must be able to absorb influxes (of varying sizes) through increased density and/or extension, becoming increasingly compact over time without degrading public and green spaces.

Demography is just one of many factors that may not crystalise as expected. New Towns will also have to address future issues that we simply cannot anticipate. The organising urban form should therefore create spatial conditions that enable adaptation to a number of variables, including: demographic, economic, and environmental. Urban planning should leave space for reinterpretation over the course of time. A masterplan should not create a final image, or a blueprint that needs to be realised, but rather a spatial vision for the future and a solid framework to reach this goal while leaving space for new insights and infill. Planning for adaptivity requires the capacity to accept uncertainty.

Source: UN-Habitat

Ningo-Prampram, Ghana is a plan for a new city of 1,500,000 inhabitants in the fast urbanising coastal area east of Accra, co-designed by UN-Habitat. Rather than a masterplan, this is a strong framework for the development of a naturally growing city. Based on an infrastructural grid system coupled with ribbons of green and water, this design addresses the need for inclusive housing areas, the need to accommodate excess flooding during peak rain season and the explosive urban sprawl in the Accra region.

Aranya, Indore, India, is a township planned for 60,000 people of low and middle income by means of a sites and services strategy. To make housing available for modest incomes, the government of Indore provided plots, foundations and infrastructure and offered a toolkit for people to build their own house. Depending on their savings the size, materials and construction varied and the township grew incrementally. A demonstration project of 80 houses showcased the options. Just like the masterplan and the financial processes and all other aspects, these houses were designed in 1983 by the Vastu Shilpa Foundation and Balkrishna V. Doshi. To this day, the Aranya housing area continues to grow and evolve.

(Source: Vastushilpa Consultants)

Fig. 27
Accra-Tema metropolitan area: a Dynametropolis with three nuclei growing parallelly

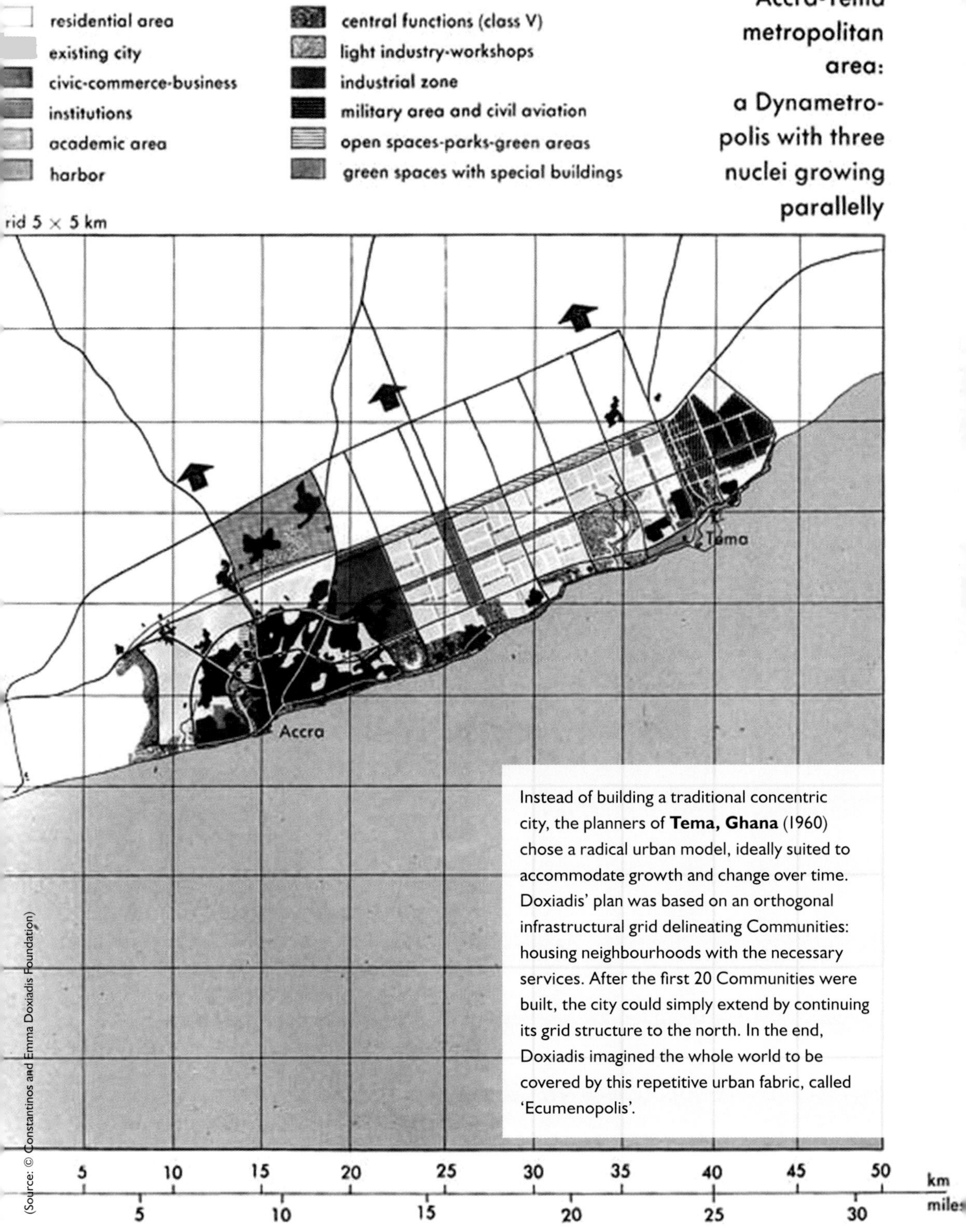

Instead of building a traditional concentric city, the planners of **Tema, Ghana** (1960) chose a radical urban model, ideally suited to accommodate growth and change over time. Doxiadis' plan was based on an orthogonal infrastructural grid delineating Communities: housing neighbourhoods with the necessary services. After the first 20 Communities were built, the city could simply extend by continuing its grid structure to the north. In the end, Doxiadis imagined the whole world to be covered by this repetitive urban fabric, called 'Ecumenopolis'.

(Source: © Constantinos and Emma Doxiadis Foundation)

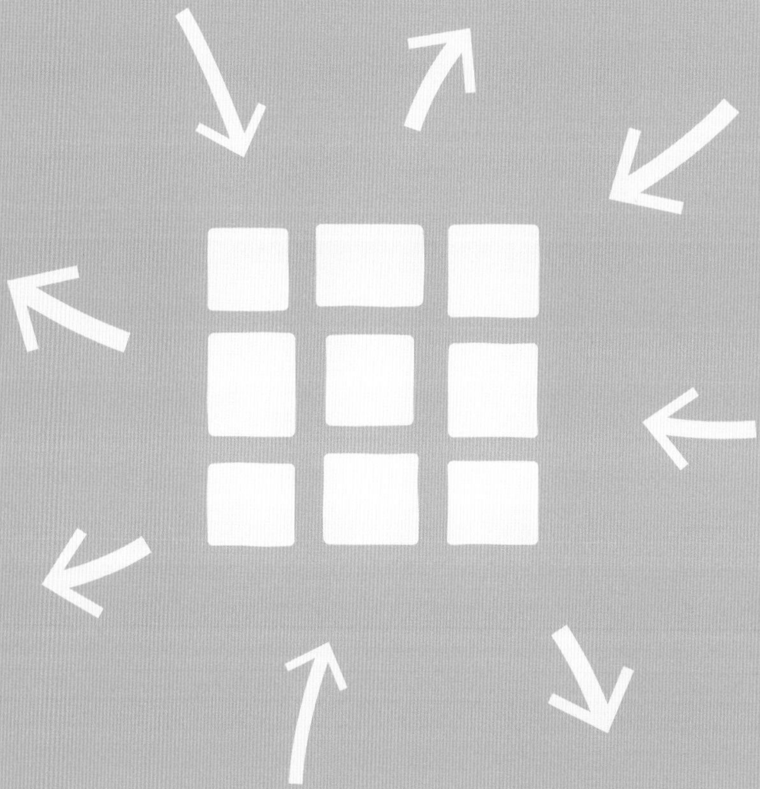

3. No New Town is an island

Many New Towns in Africa are developed on sites that are chosen for their low price, the transparency of ownership, or relationship to a person with political influence. This can cause problems related to access as New Town residents find themselves with long commutes to and from a 'mother city'. A location that is not connected by existing infrastructure can also seriously limit the New Town's growth: residents or businesses are less likely to move to a New Town that is difficult to access.

The site selection phase is therefore critical to the future success of the New Town. Potential locations must be considered within their regional and national contexts. The sites should be selected based on accessibility (efficient infrastructural connections to surrounding urban areas), local needs, geographic conditions, potential for growth, and position in existing social, financial and production networks.

Planning New Towns requires a thorough evaluation of the position of the city with respect to regional, national, and global flows. To ensure their success, future New Towns should be based on a comprehensive national spatial policy and not planned as isolated projects.

Milton Keynes, United Kingdom has become one of the most popular British New Towns, largely in part because of its strategic location halfway between London and Birmingham. This proximity facilitates labour and economic flows between the New Town and two large 'mother cities', while at the same time preventing the New Town from becoming a bedroom community.

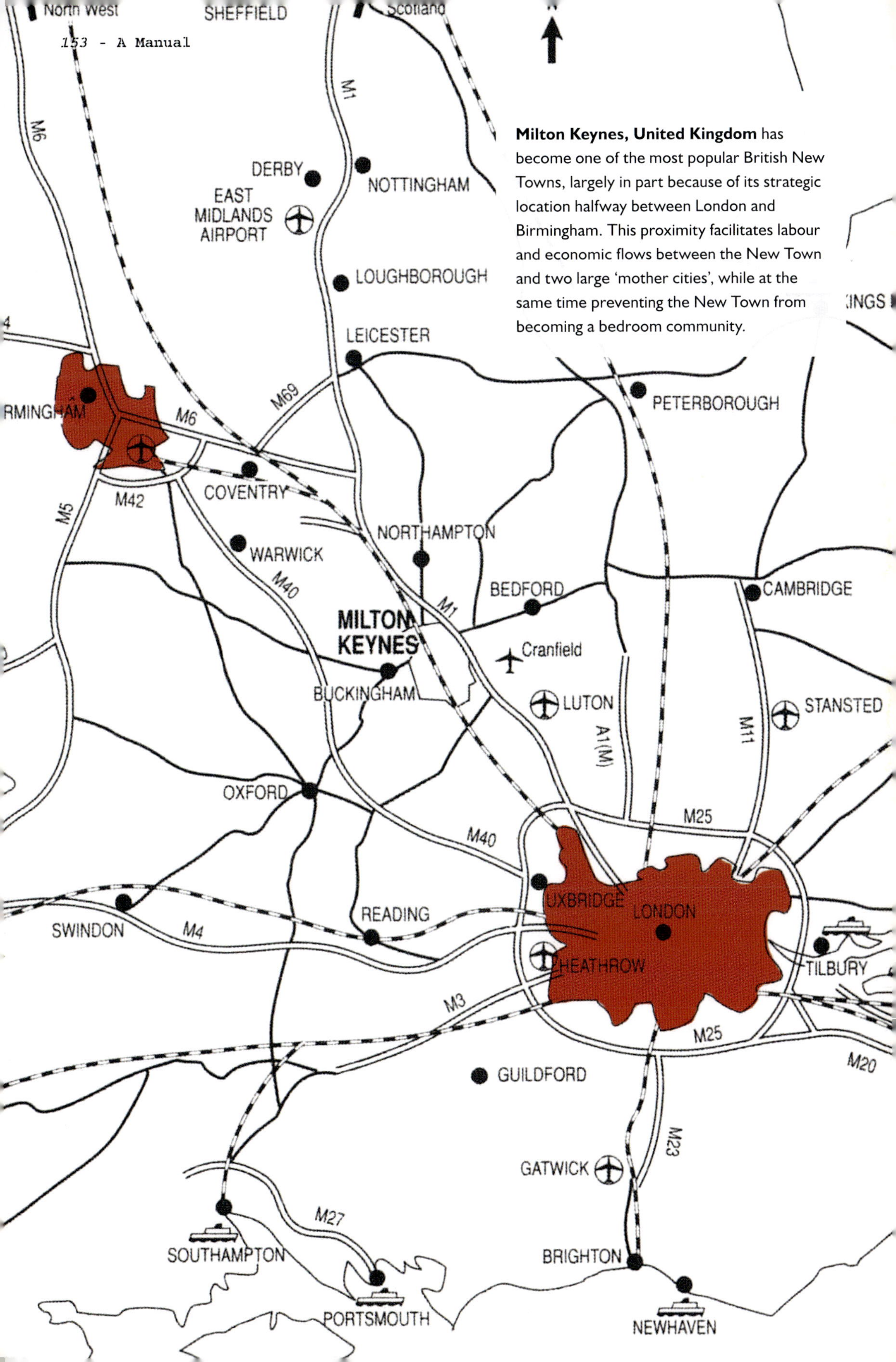

planoluanda
viva a nossa cidade

ESTRUTURA DE DESENVOLVIMENTO E CONCEITOS

DEVELOPMENT FRAMEWORK & CONCEPTS

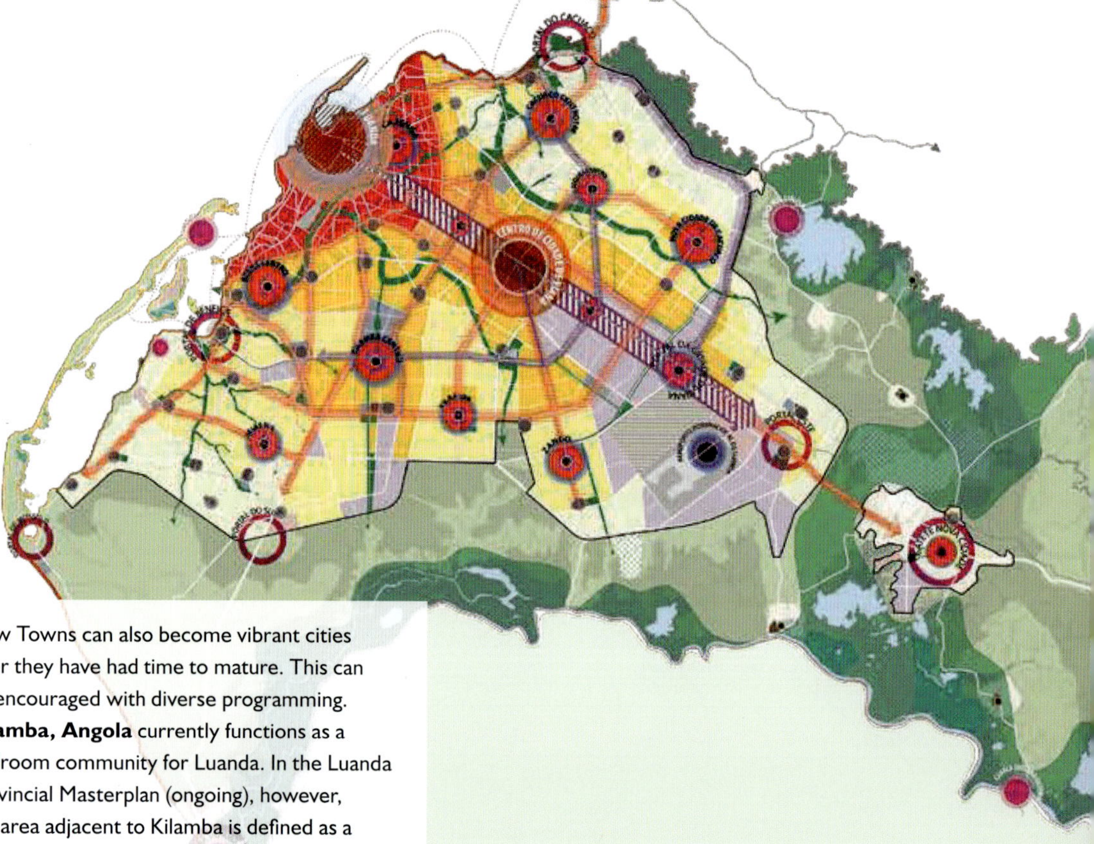

New Towns can also become vibrant cities after they have had time to mature. This can be encouraged with diverse programming. **Kilamba, Angola** currently functions as a bedroom community for Luanda. In the Luanda Provincial Masterplan (ongoing), however, the area adjacent to Kilamba is defined as a new central business district and will be more efficiently connected to the existing downtown by a highway and new train connections.

(Source: Broadway Malyan, 2016)

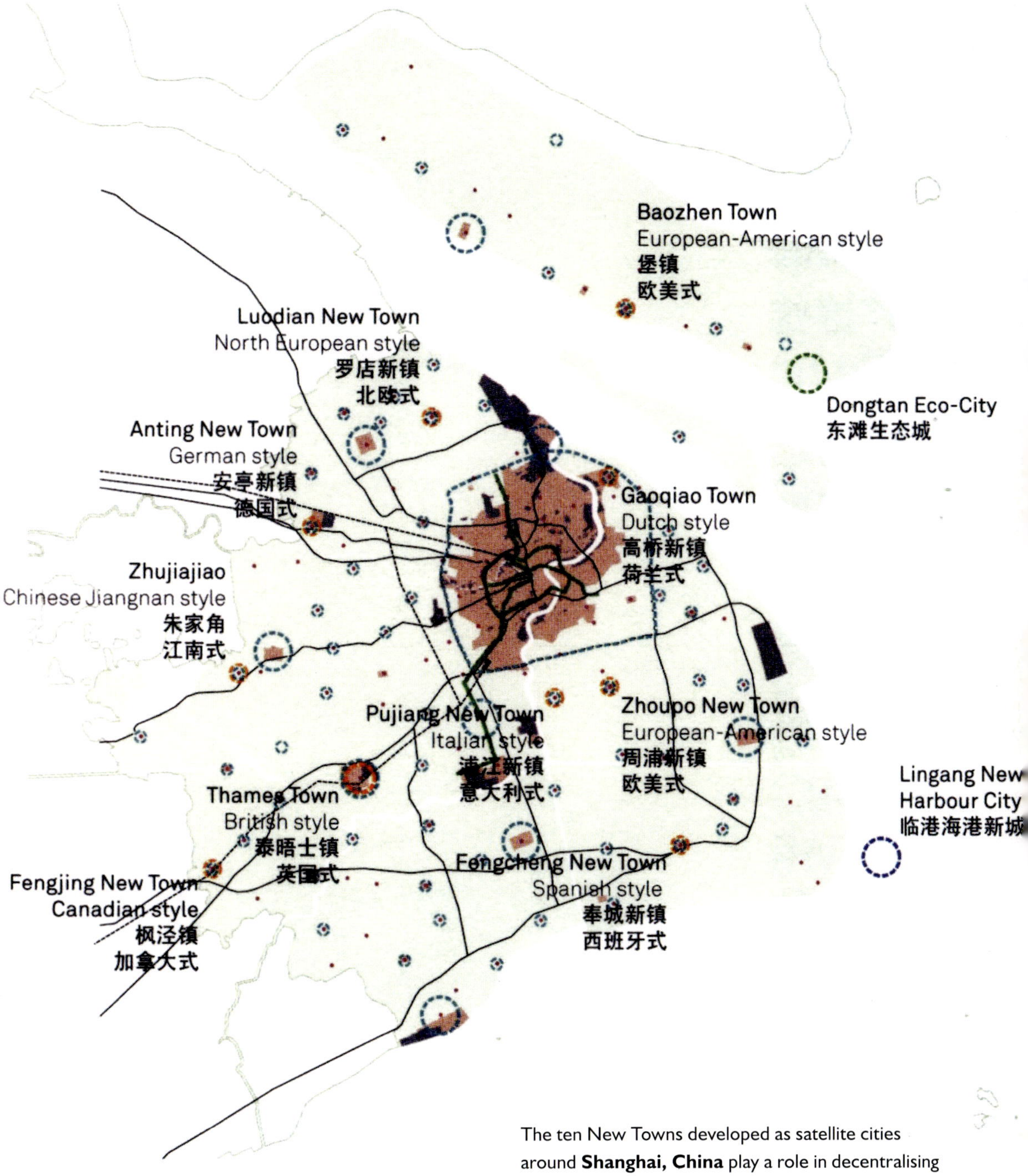

The ten New Towns developed as satellite cities around **Shanghai, China** play a role in decentralising the development and mitigating population growth of Shanghai. They are close enough that residents can commute easily, and well-connected via public transport. They are also far enough from Shanghai that the New Towns must provide adequate urban amenities and commercial facilities in order to survive.

(Source: H. den Hartog, 2010)

Access is defined by distance as well as availability and price of transport. Increasing access can be as simple as supplying adequate public transportation options. Cape Town recently extended their Integrated Rapid Transit (IRT) network to include a new bus line to Atlantis, South Africa, a New Town (presently 70,000 inhabitants) that was planned in the Apartheid era and subsequently valued isolation of the 'black and coloured' population more than the connection to Cape Town, 40 km to the south. The new bus service provides residents with safe and frequent service to other parts of the city.

(Source: www.capetowngreenmap.co.za/blog/myciti-bus-service-operating-atlantis)

4. Use no cut-and-paste universal model

There is no one-size-fits-all model for New Towns: models from one part of the world don't guarantee success when exported to another part. The economic acceleration of a city like Dubai doesn't mean that a similar model can be equally successful or appropriate in African countries with completely different economic and demographic compositions. However, we are witnessing a growing number of planned cities in Africa that take models from the Middle East and Asia as archetypes to emulate.

**The reason for this is that international companies have pinpointed urbanisation in Africa as the next global opportunity for profit. Not only private companies, but also state-owned companies in China, South Korea, and Singapore aim to prolong their success in other parts of the world by exporting standard urbanisation models from their own countries.
As a result, the influx of foreign parties also results in the import of foreign urban concepts, often uncritically adopted by local governments. This shows how global capitalism has become perhaps the most powerful force for homogenization of contemporary urban environments. It also helps explain the uniformity of the African New Towns presented in this book, and their strong similarities with New Towns in parts of the world such as Asia, Latin America or the Middle East.**

Instead of accommodating this imported uniformity, every country should be capable of developing its own urban models based on local culture, climate, politics, social needs and financial possibilities. To support this contextualization, local capacity-building within the planning discipline, planning and design education, and training are necessary and should be stimulated at national, regional, and local levels. Next to that, there is a need for a mentality change to inform future urban design, including an awareness of the incredibly diverse African urban traditions and the unique characters of present day urbanisation processes in Africa.

Trade Cente

5. Embrace new ideas

The culture of New Towns is forward-looking, with an emphasis on innovation and experimentation. This ambition is optimistic and should be fostered. Every New Town in history has attempted to surpass cities of the past and showcase state-of-the-art urban design, technology, finance, or architectural techniques. Recent innovations have included experiments in the fields of sustainability, climate change response, and energy, as well as social changes such as participatory design, resident engagement, and revisions of the relationships between government and residents.

For future New Towns this means the development of new solutions (not only in technology but also social, cultural, political and financial innovation), should be supported in order to improve the fairness and competitiveness of the city. New Towns can be excellent laboratories for experimentation, as well as implementation of the sustainable urbanism goals outlined in the New Urban Agenda.

(Source: Wikimedia, photo: Romita05)

Magarpatta, India– A farming community outside of Pune watched as urbanisation spread towards them. Other farmers were selling off land to developers for small sums, but then struggling without long-term sources of income. Aware of this, the Magar clan pooled their land and became developers themselves, thus retaining ownership of what eventually became the New Town of Magarpatta. By maintaining ownership through collective action, the farmers have ensured a profitable future for themselves, and become active participants in decision-making processes related to Magarpatta's growth.

The future city of **Vinge** is currently **Denmark**'s largest urban development project, combining nature and technology. The intention is that Smart Grids and Smart Technology come into play when monitoring energy consumption, rainfall, humidity and so forth, enabling the community to strive for a sustainable lifestyle. In addition, technology should serve as a tool to use decentralised renewable energy, to develop low carbon mobility, to optimise the operation of infrastructure and services, to create distributed places of work and learning and to organise participatory governance and planning. Citizens should be able to communicate with each other and share ideas and visions with the planners through various digital platforms, thus becoming active participants in the creation of their future city.

(Visualization: Henning Larsen Architects and Third Nature)

(Source: www.curitiba.pr.gov.br/)

Curitiba, Brazil, has become well-known as an innovative and sustainable city. Without a budget for standard waste recycling plants, the city started the 'Lixo que nao è Lixo'; (garbage that is not garbage) and 'Cambio Verde' (green exchange) programmes, both dealing with waste management. With 'Lixo que nao e Lixo' the city established complementary currencies to reward people for separating their organic and non-organic recyclable wastes and bringing them to waste stations, where they can be exchanged for public transport tickets, food, and school-books. 'Cambio Verde' is a programme where citizens receive locally grown, organic, healthy foods in exchange for their recyclable waste or can buy them at 30 percent cheaper prices than in regular stores. This way, the city combines waste management and promotes healthy food consumption at the same time.

One of the first 'eco-cities' to be constructed, **Masdar City, United Arab Emirates** was envisioned as an environmentally sustainable New Town, using state-of-the-art technologies to aim for carbon neutrality in a country powered by petroleum profits. Masdar planners Foster and Partners designed both passive and active energy solutions for the New Town, including building-mounted solar panels, shaded pedestrian walkways, narrow spaces to capture prevailing winds, an electric 'pod' transport system, and water conservation techniques. These innovations were ambitious and ground-breaking, and while Masdar has not grown to be the carbon-neutral city that was promised, it remains an inspirational example of how a New Town can function as a laboratory for experiments aiming for new standards, rather than repeating what has been done before.

(Photo: R. Keeton, 2015)

6. Infrastructure and mobility for all, from the start

New Towns are usually located at a short distance from their 'mother city' but still programmatically connected when it comes to work and services. Strong and diverse transportation connections are therefore essential. Many New Towns begin phased development with housing construction, leaving public transport for a later moment, and usually this has proven to be a mistake. The provision of public transport within the city and to surrounding cities from the immediate start of development is a main factor in the success or failure of New Towns. Without good and efficient mobility options the image and attraction of the New Town will suffer in a way that is hard to overcome at a later stage. To combat this, services, amenities, road infrastructure, and public transport must be provided and should be initiated before housing becomes available. Various constructions have been developed to support this approach, such as temporarily reduced rents for early service providers.

Transport and mobility plans should be an integral part of the urban design and overall territorial plans, connecting the density and programme to the availability of transit options (commonly called transit-oriented development, or TOD). The urban plan should promote a wide range of mobility options and not prioritise cars over other transit types. It should include mass transit options such as trains, trams, or buses, and encourage slow traffic by providing distinct routing for carts, bicycles and pedestrians. Increasing the diversity of transport options makes mobility safe, efficient and accessible for a wider range of users.

Both the masterplans of **Almere, NL** (1976) and **Runcorn, UK** (1967) were designed on the basis of a separate bus lane. With this experimental basis, public transport became the fundament and the structuring element of the masterplan. It connects all local centres and the stops are at a short distance, so no inhabitant ever has to walk more than 5 minutes (400 metres). The bus lanes are separated from car and bicycle traffic and have priority at intersections, which makes their itinerary more reliable and efficient. That way, the bus becomes competitive to a journey by car.

ource left: Busfoto.net, photo: Michiel van Dijk)

The capital of **Austria**, Vienna, is preparing itself for a large increase of inhabitants and has started to develop **Aspern Seestadt**, (Aspern Lake City) on the north bank of the Danube. To make this mixed use development attractive for its 20,000 future residents and many businesses, Vienna invested heavily in a metro line and station, which were ready when the first inhabitants arrived. Now the metro offers a comfortable transport to all layers of society and a 25 minute ride to downtown Vienna as well as to the Slovakian capital Bratislava.

(Photo: ©Ralf Roletschek / roletschek.at)

The functioning of **Curitiba, Brazil** depends heavily on its Bus Rapid Transit (BRT) system which has become a textbook example of the introduction of public transport in a developing country. It was introduced in 1974 as part of a comprehensive masterplan for the city and consists of 81 km of dedicated bus lanes on major streets, serving more than 2 million daily commuters. Not only is it efficient, frequent (up to every 90 seconds) and reliable, but the attractive design of the tubular stations also adds to its good reputation. With growing congestion in Curitiba, the city is now looking to develop a bicycle path network as an addition to car and bus traffic.

(Source: Wikimedia Commons, photo: WeWahWai)

In the 1960s, the fast and unruly economic development of **Hong Kong, China**, caused congestion. The Mass Transit Railway (MTR) and nine New Towns (presently: 3 million inhabitants) were initiated to decentralise the dense population. The MTR opened in 1979 and at this moment has more than 200 kilometres of rail. It is not only the most popular means of transport in Hong Kong, it also makes a profit. The stations of the MTR epitomise the mixed-use approach that has become the slogan of Hong Kong's urban model. A vertical succession of decks contains functions of every kind, from transport junctions on the lower levels to shopping malls, offices, hotels and homes on the higher levels. While the stations involve an extremely high density, in between them there is a lower urban density.

The city of **Milton Keynes, UK**, is mostly known for its invention of the car-based grid structure. But it was also designed with an experimental bicycle-network: in the vast green areas, safely separated from the car traffic by underpasses and viaducts, a 273 kilometers long network stretches to all corners of the city. Though well suited for leisure it can be argued however that the Redways (named after the colour of their tarmac) are not ideally laid out for functional commuter needs.

(Source: MK Cycling Map)

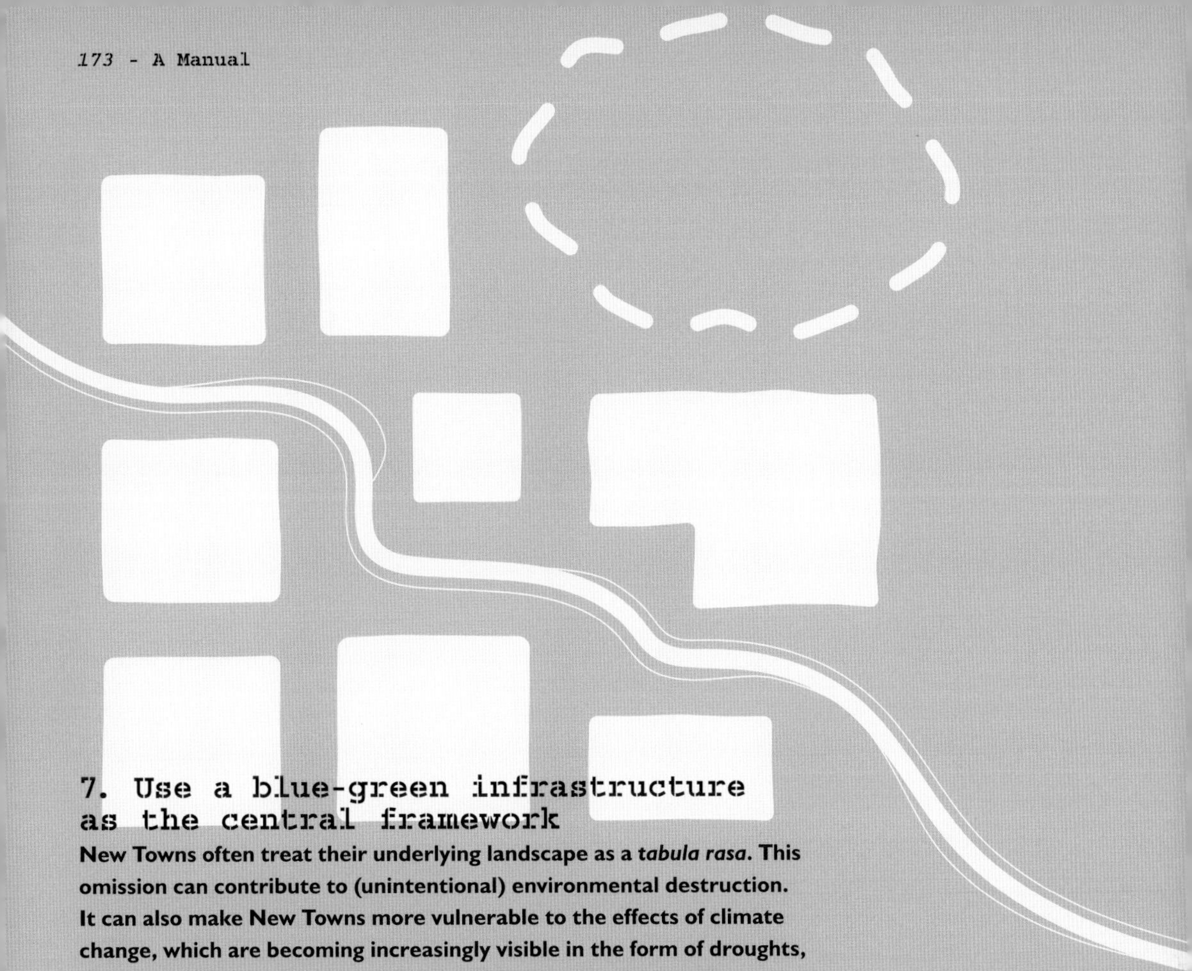

7. Use a blue-green infrastructure as the central framework

New Towns often treat their underlying landscape as a *tabula rasa*. This omission can contribute to (unintentional) environmental destruction. It can also make New Towns more vulnerable to the effects of climate change, which are becoming increasingly visible in the form of droughts, floods, and natural disasters. It is critical to consider the specific opportunities and limitations offered by individual sites, especially in areas facing rapid urbanisation or located near water systems. A solid backbone of (green) open spaces and a (blue) water network can provide a robust and distinctive organisational framework for a New Town.

According to UN-Habitat's urban design principles, green spaces should account for 30 percent of total area and offer safe, quality public spaces that are open and accessible to all. Green spaces should be multifunctional areas for social interaction and cultural exchange. This network should underpin every New Town design by combining ecology, flood prevention, and water retention with public space and leisure.

Spatial planning (where to build) and urban design (how to build) are powerful instruments to increase a New Town's resilience. Any urbanisation puts a burden on local resources and environmental conditions, and increases the demand for water. This can result in competition (with industry and agriculture) for limited natural resources, and it may also increase waste, pollution, the risk of flooding, and depletion of non-renewable groundwater. The scarcity of drinking water, wastewater treatment, and the ecological quality of aquatic ecosystems in any New Town and its immediate surroundings are therefore important considerations for the design of an urban plan.

The backbone of **Vinge, Denmark**, a new development of 370 ha that is expected to have 20,000 inhabitants and 4000 jobs when fully built, consists of green and blue landscape. This elongated ecological zone connects all the different housing neighbourhoods. While providing structure and handling rainwater, it also offers spaces for leisure and roads for slow traffic, combined with collective services, shops, and schools. Even the train station is connected to this central green zone.

(Visualization: Henning Larsen Architects and POWER)

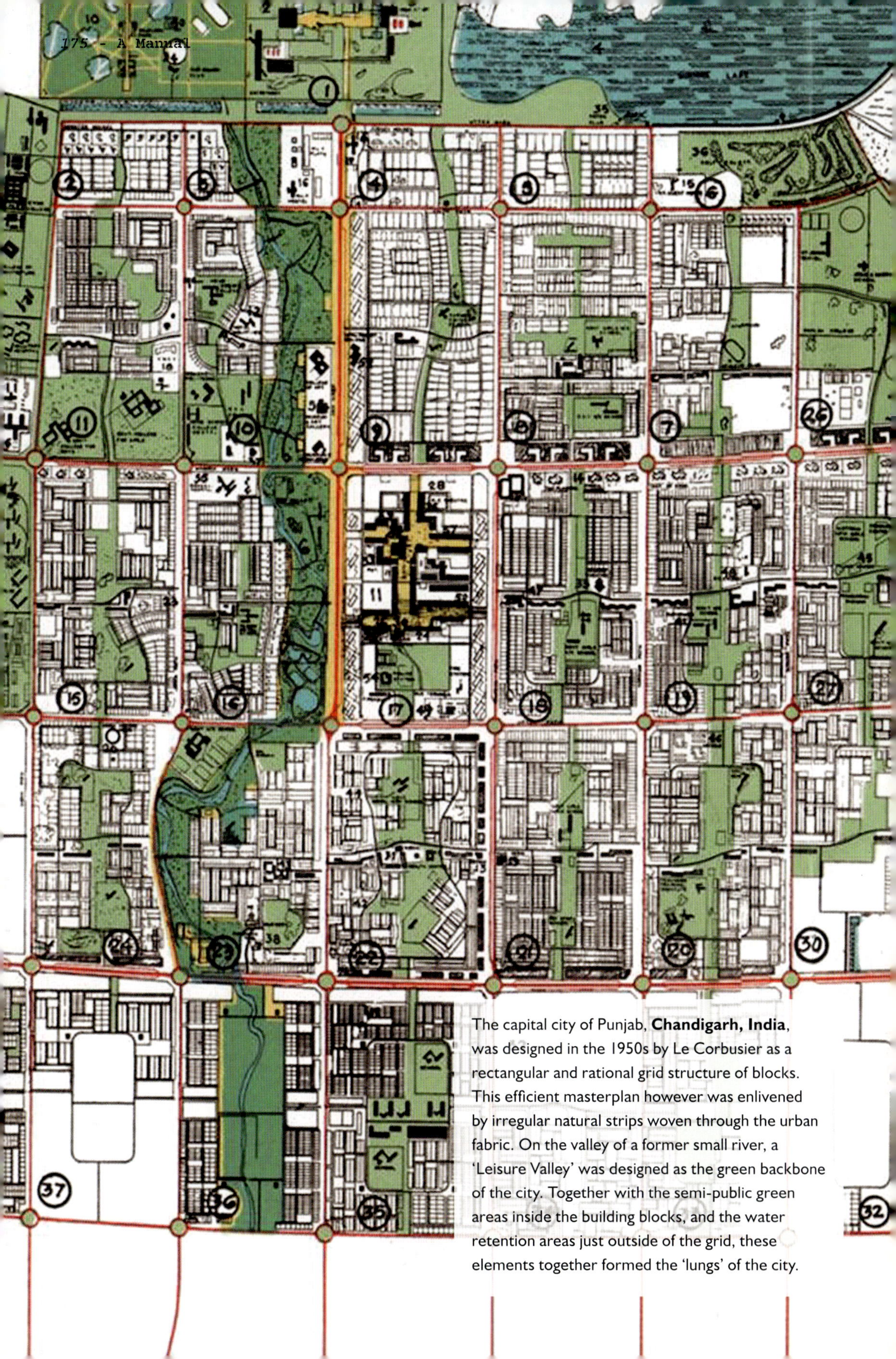

The capital city of Punjab, **Chandigarh, India**, was designed in the 1950s by Le Corbusier as a rectangular and rational grid structure of blocks. This efficient masterplan however was enlivened by irregular natural strips woven through the urban fabric. On the valley of a former small river, a 'Leisure Valley' was designed as the green backbone of the city. Together with the semi-public green areas inside the building blocks, and the water retention areas just outside of the grid, these elements together formed the 'lungs' of the city.

Surrounding foodsheds should be protected and growth should be structured so that it does not threaten productive agricultural land. **Nakuru, Kenya** is an example of a city successfully combining urban and rural fabrics. Nakuru is organised like an African version of Frank Lloyd Wright's Broadacre City, a grid structure with houses on large plots of land. The town provides urban amenities but also protects and preserves adjacent agricultural fields, ensuring the town's continued food security as it grows.

(Photo: S. Rots, 2015)

(Photo: R. Keeton, 2017)

Climate change and variability will create extreme situations in the African context and urban planning must address and mitigate these threats. Long-term impacts of climate change (flooding, desertification, etc.) should be reflected in design decisions.

Water retention and release are critical issues for any urban area. Excessive rainfall can cause flooding when surfaces are unable to absorb water. Residents at **BuraNEST, Ethiopia** planted a eucalyptus forest adjacent to the New Town. This acts as a natural sponge, absorbing water as well as holding soil in place to prevent landslides and erosion.

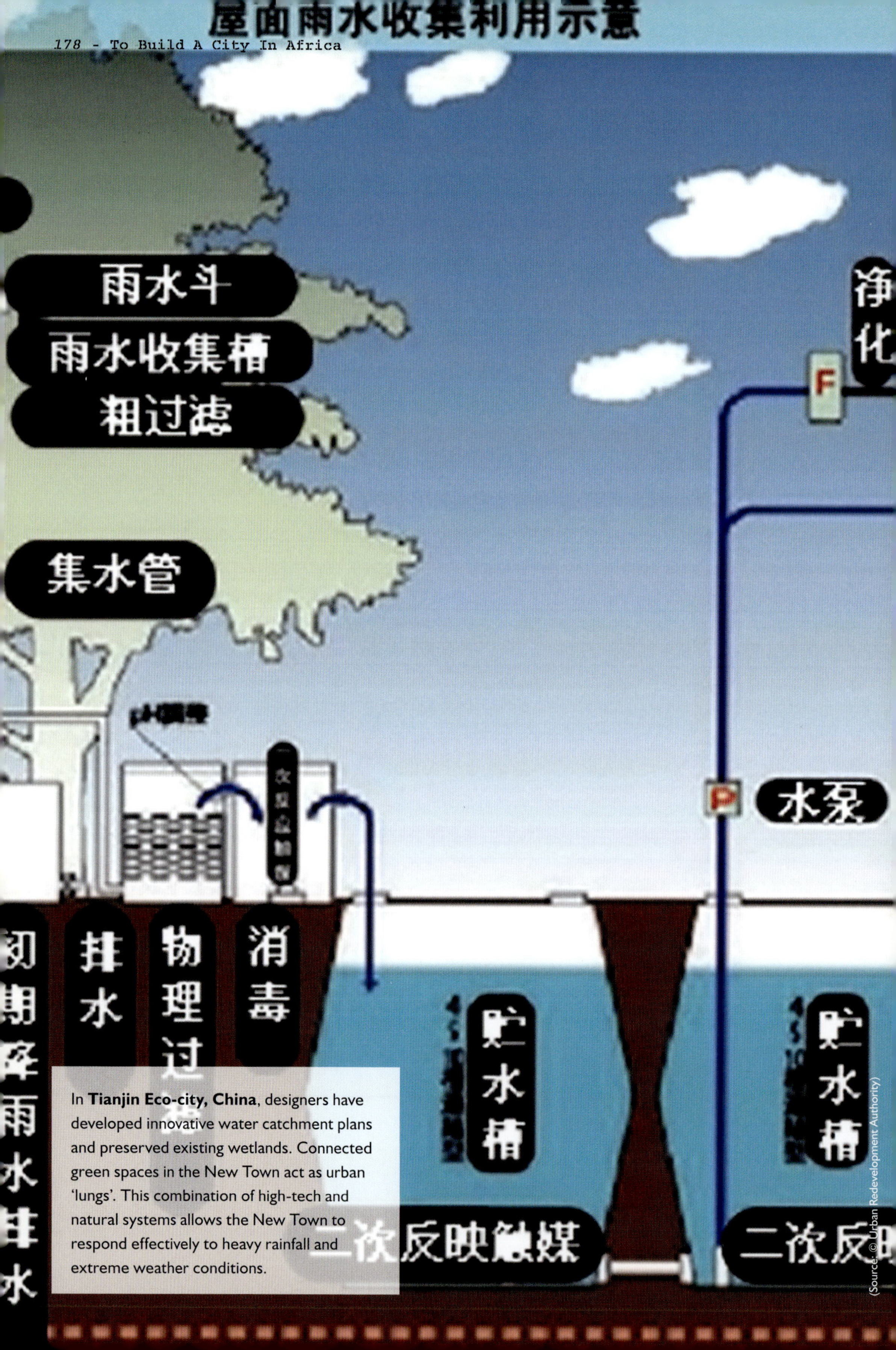

In **Tianjin Eco-city, China**, designers have developed innovative water catchment plans and preserved existing wetlands. Connected green spaces in the New Town act as urban 'lungs'. This combination of high-tech and natural systems allows the New Town to respond effectively to heavy rainfall and extreme weather conditions.

(Source: © Urban Redevelopment Authority)

8. Incorporate local cultural heritage(s)

Many contemporary New Towns are developed by international companies with limited knowledge of the local context. This can result in New Towns that use generic urban models and architecture and miss opportunities to provide more vibrant and authentic urban environments. Alternatively, embracing local heritage has the power to stimulate the inclusion of more groups of people, and increase the connection between people and place. Heritage can be architectural monuments or natural landmarks; it can also be local habits and histories or local building techniques and traditions.

Cultural heritage, whether tangible or intangible, is an enrichment in the development of any New Town. Incorporating heritage can help create unique and authentic environments that people can identify with, and that are instantly recognizable. Cultural assets of local populations should also be integrated in plans and researched throughout the planning process. This supports the development of both identity and community. Spiritual connections to sacred spaces (waterways, trees, etc.) should be well-understood, respected, and celebrated. No-go sacred spaces should be zoned appropriately. Customary laws, social norms, and taboos should be researched and accommodated through design.

Incorporating appropriate cultural symbols into public space can add meaning for existing and new residents. The developers of the masterplan for **Tatu City, Kenya** commissioned research on the historical and cultural meaning of an existing Mugumo tree for local communities. The tree was the place where the first president of the country, Yomo Kenyatta, rested on his travels to Nairobi. For ages it has been the gathering place of men and elders in the area. In the masterplan for Tatu City, the impressive tree was incorporated into the plan, where it will be the centerpiece of a new public square.

(Photo: S. Rots, 2016)

Understanding how New Town residents use existing spaces can help designers adjust infrastructural frameworks at smaller scales. The Greek planner Constantinos Doxiadis incorporated 'gossip squares' into his 1955 masterplan for **Baghdad, Iraq**. Building on existing cultural customs in Iraqi villages he included these small intimate squares for everyday life, for people to meet and interact and thereby also easing the transition from being a villager to becoming a member of the urban community.

(Source: Constantinos A. Doxiadis Archives. Archive Files 23970 © Constantinos and Emma Doxiadis Foundation.)

The small **New Gourna Village, Egypt** (174 households) was designed by the Egyptian planner Hassan Fathy in 1946. He used traditional materials (mostly bricks from local mud) and ancient vault building techniques and combined them with modern architectural principles. Next to this sensitivity to local and ethnic traditions, he was also a pioneer in participation, involving every single family in the process of resettlement.

(Source: Wikimedia, photo: Marc Ryckaert)

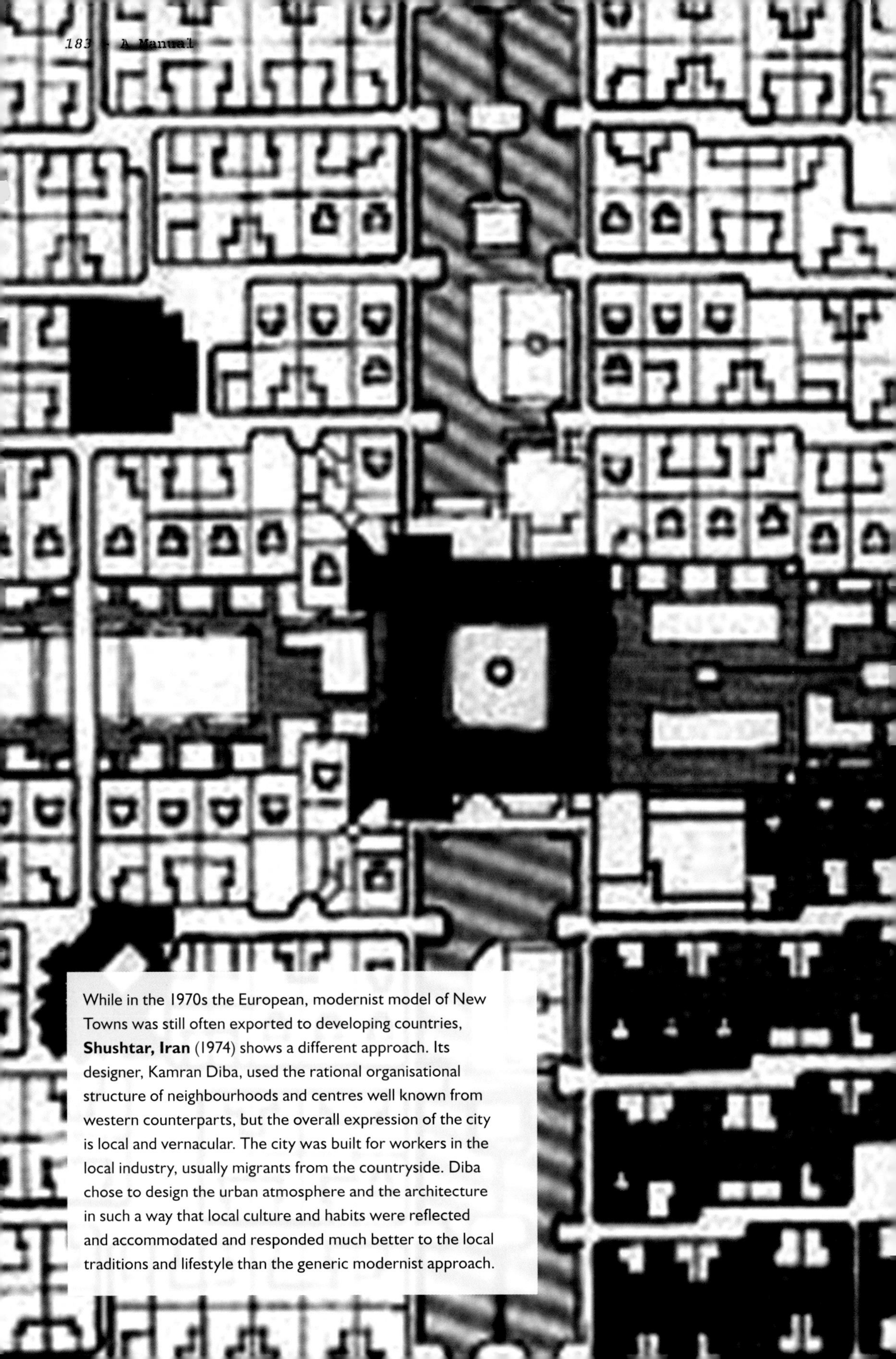

While in the 1970s the European, modernist model of New Towns was still often exported to developing countries, **Shushtar, Iran** (1974) shows a different approach. Its designer, Kamran Diba, used the rational organisational structure of neighbourhoods and centres well known from western counterparts, but the overall expression of the city is local and vernacular. The city was built for workers in the local industry, usually migrants from the countryside. Diba chose to design the urban atmosphere and the architecture in such a way that local culture and habits were reflected and accommodated and responded much better to the local traditions and lifestyle than the generic modernist approach.

Research into local conditions can provide valuable insights during the decision-making process related to site location. For example, one of the original design proposals for **Konza Tech City**, Kenya incorporated wildlife migration patterns, informality and integrated public transport options into the masterplan for Nairobi and its surrounding metropolitan region (Vision 2030). Designed by local planning office The Centre for Urban and Regional Planning, this proposal illustrated local knowledge of the area that was either unknown to, or ignored by competing international proposals, including the winning design by Consult Engineering Services, an Indian design firm.

(Photo: Muoki Kioko)

9. Combine top-down and bottom-up

New Towns by definition share a largely top-down approach, with a fixed hierarchical relationship between the government or private party developing the city and the residents who live there. These cities are based on masterplans that often regard the site as a clean slate, depicting surrounding areas as a white void. In reality, a *tabula rasa* simply does not exist: there is always an underlying landscape, and farmers, nomads, or other residents can usually be found on or near the site. To become more resilient and fair, and to unleash the vital dynamics that can season a new urban area, New Towns should provide for a more inclusive and participatory approach. To that end, existing villages or (temporary) communities using the development site should be respected as pre-existing elements of the plan. The plan should actively prevent illegal and unfair displacement of people.

The first phases of a New Town are often managed by large organisations. This is generally a heavily top-down period. To encourage more democratic opportunities for public participation, New Towns should move towards municipal governance as soon as possible. This allows for more representative governance, and a greater diversity of feedback loops for urban managers and planners. Early on, there should be room for many voices: residents' committees should be representative and engagement should be encouraged.

European and American New Towns have shown that after a few decades they can become too vulnerable when dependent on just one institutional owner or developer. During the course of the city's development it will benefit from residents' involvement and private building, economic, and cultural initiatives. The planning process should take this into account and provide the opportunity for more stakeholders to become part of the process of making a new city.

Almere, NL, is experimenting with a complete reversal of roles in which the city is expanded not by top down plans but by the actions of its citizens. The development of a greenfield neighbourhood in the polder, called Oosterwold is part of a city-wide programme to become greener and more participatory. Contrary to almost all other New Towns, there is no masterplan underlying this development, only a set of rules, developed by the Dutch architecture firm MVRDV. Safeguarding the green and ecological character of the area, the rules provide for an organic development of the area in which residents not only build their own housing, but also cooperatively construct roads and other shared infrastructures.

(Source: MVRDV)

The settlement of **Dandora, Kenya**, started with 6000 plots built in 1977 with the aid of the Worldbank. Thirty years later, the streets, parking spaces, gutters and squares of Dandora had disappeared under a vast layer of sand, mud and ashes from the burning of waste at the nearby dump site. Crime rates and unemployment soared, the streets were filthy and dangerous. In 2014, started by local youths calling themselves Mustard Seeds and later developed in the Dandora Transformation League, the young generation initiated a clean-up operation, uncluttering drainage and unearthing courtyards, making public space attractive and safe again (crime is down by 70 percent) and creating community and jobs while doing so. Using workshops with residents and professionals, their success has attracted NGO's and foreign support, making it possible to strengthen and expand the programme.

(Source: placemakers.nl)

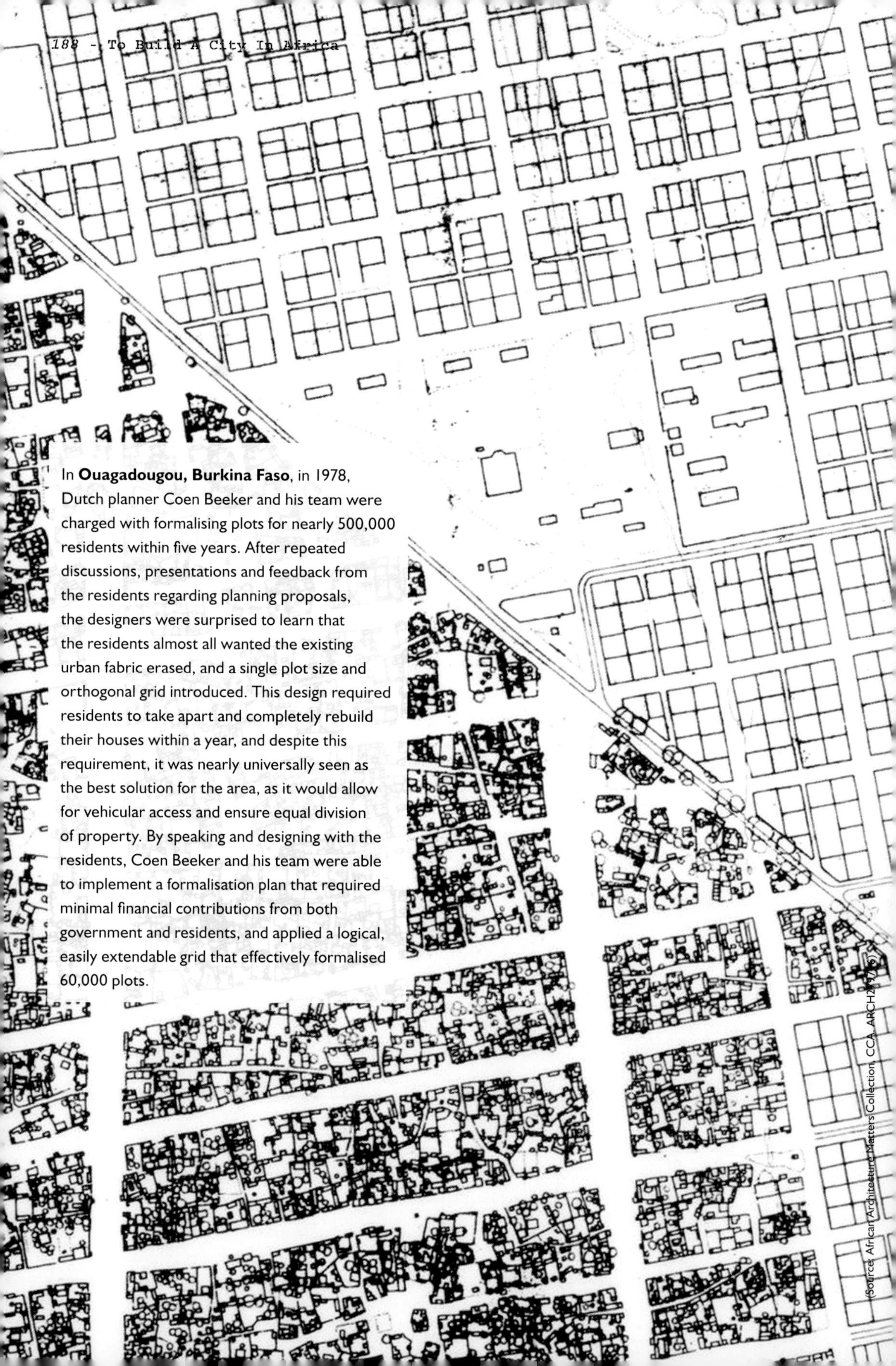

In **Ouagadougou, Burkina Faso**, in 1978, Dutch planner Coen Beeker and his team were charged with formalising plots for nearly 500,000 residents within five years. After repeated discussions, presentations and feedback from the residents regarding planning proposals, the designers were surprised to learn that the residents almost all wanted the existing urban fabric erased, and a single plot size and orthogonal grid introduced. This design required residents to take apart and completely rebuild their houses within a year, and despite this requirement, it was nearly universally seen as the best solution for the area, as it would allow for vehicular access and ensure equal division of property. By speaking and designing with the residents, Coen Beeker and his team were able to implement a formalisation plan that required minimal financial contributions from both government and residents, and applied a logical, easily extendable grid that effectively formalised 60,000 plots.

(Source: African Architecture Matters Collection, CCA, ARCH2[illegible])

(Photo: M. Provoost, 2016)

Alamar, Cuba, is a satellite city of Havana built during the 1970s. This prefab city started out as the embodiment of the communist spirit but fell into decay after the collapse of the Soviet Union in 1989. However, with original masterplans for the central zone left unexecuted, Alamar has unintentionally grown into a unique case of urban planning, intertwined with urban agriculture. Out of necessity, citizens have developed the open plots in the centre into large scale urban gardens (*organoponicos*) which now provide for 95 percent of all vegetables consumed in Alamar, while bringing social cohesion to the communities. Closely connected to the local universities and knowledge organisations, this organic agricultural practice is considered exemplary by international experts.

10. New Towns need diversity

When cities are diverse in their programme, economy and population, they are more resilient, more just, and less vulnerable. Cities that have been built for only one economic group become vulnerable to small fluctuations. Cities that have been built with extremely limited housing types for only a few target groups do not offer enough choice for healthy long-term development. Cities grow and mature because residents stay (and change), and new residents migrate to the city. There must be room for these residents to live, work, and establish their place in the culture of a city.

Cities should be built for a representative cross-section of society, including low-income and no-income groups. There is a need for new financial models to achieve inclusiveness and for policies to guarantee this. Especially in Africa, urban planning must incorporate and facilitate incremental settlements, since they will make up the largest part of urbanisation, and because spatial segregation is a threat to societal cohesion. Developing different sites to varying degrees of completeness can offer financially attractive options to multiple income groups. The spatial components of the local 'informal' economy (i.e. kiosks, transport options, markets, etc.) should also be accommodated in spatial plans and engaged as a productive part of urban life.

Kilamba, Angola, has responded to economic realities by drastically lowering the price of housing in response to public outcry. In 2013 then-President dos Santos nearly halved prices, cutting the cost of the smallest apartment from USD 125,000 to USD 70,000. That intervention allowed more middle-class Angolans access to the New Town, and improved the mix of residents. Despite this, Kilamba remains out of reach for the vast majority of Angolans, and an informal settlement has grown concurrently with the New Town along its borders. The economic interdependencies between the two communities are complex and manifold, but the separation of physical spaces remains clear.

(Photo: R. Keeton, 2016)

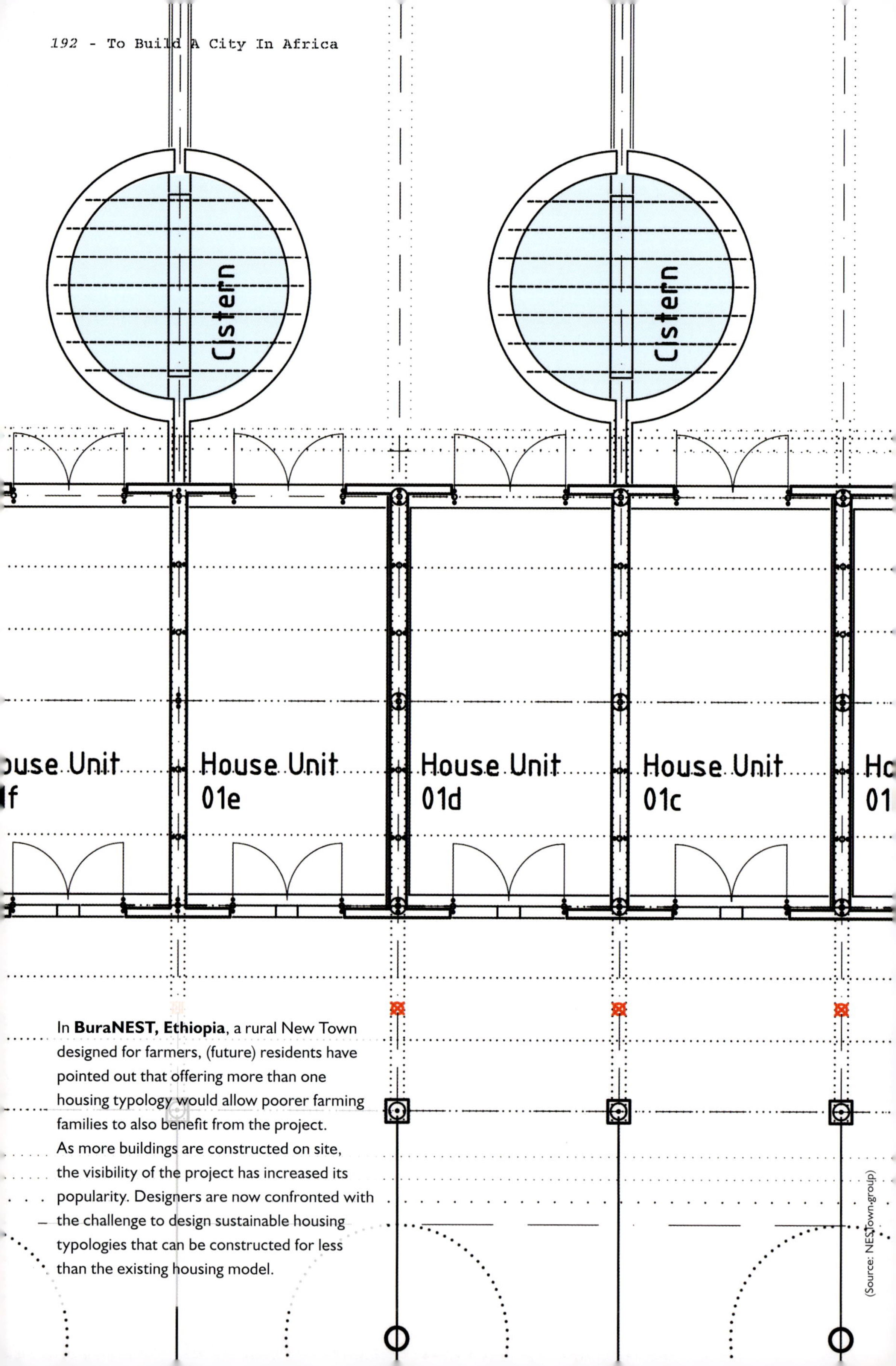

In **BuraNEST, Ethiopia**, a rural New Town designed for farmers, (future) residents have pointed out that offering more than one housing typology would allow poorer farming families to also benefit from the project. As more buildings are constructed on site, the visibility of the project has increased its popularity. Designers are now confronted with the challenge to design sustainable housing typologies that can be constructed for less than the existing housing model.

(Source: NESTown-group)

1964

1967

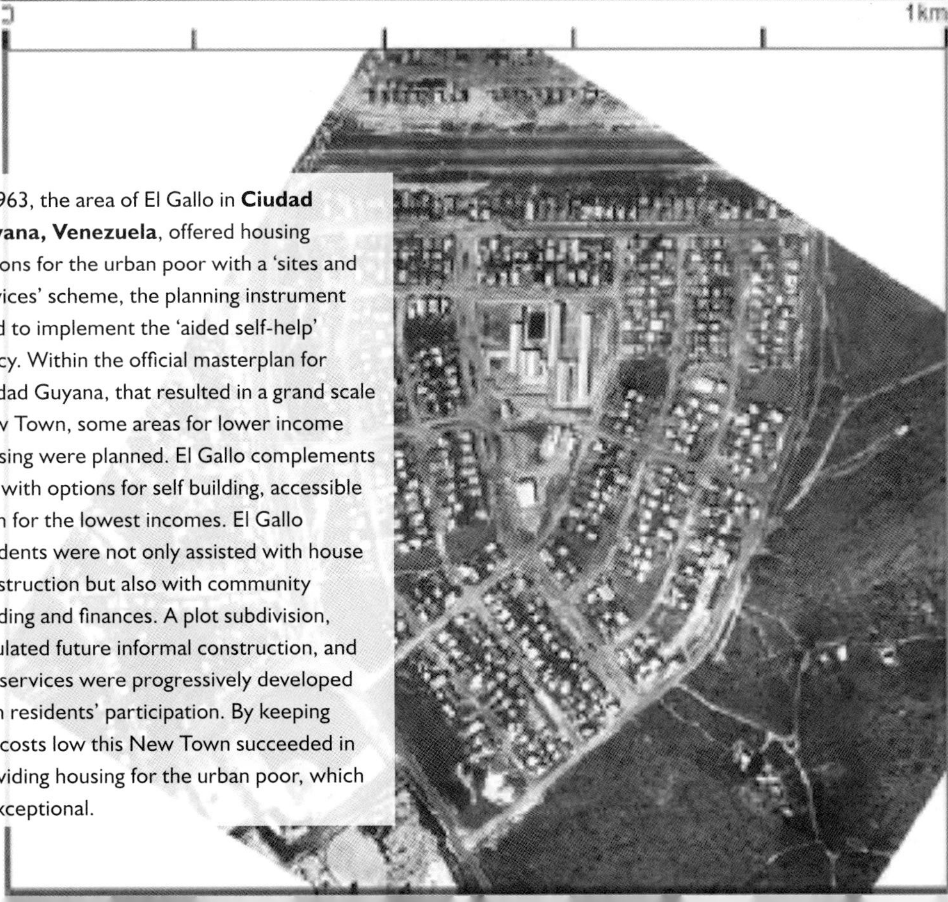

In 1963, the area of El Gallo in **Ciudad Guyana, Venezuela**, offered housing options for the urban poor with a 'sites and services' scheme, the planning instrument used to implement the 'aided self-help' policy. Within the official masterplan for Ciudad Guyana, that resulted in a grand scale New Town, some areas for lower income housing were planned. El Gallo complements this with options for self building, accessible even for the lowest incomes. El Gallo residents were not only assisted with house construction but also with community building and finances. A plot subdivision, regulated future informal construction, and the services were progressively developed with residents' participation. By keeping the costs low this New Town succeeded in providing housing for the urban poor, which is exceptional.

(Source: Caminos H., Turner J.F.C, Steffian J., Urban Dwelling Environments, an elementary survey of settlements for the study of design determinants, M.I.T. report no. 16, MIT Press, 1969)

In **Spijkenisse, The Netherlands**, a large-scale investment in the reinforcement of social and cultural structures has transformed the city centre into the 'living room' of the New Town.

The town centre, built in the 1980s, lacked attractiveness and atmosphere; in the 2000s the city decided to rebuild it. Crucial elements in the social and cultural programme of the centre are the new theatre and the new library. These both have a distinctive architecture, and were designed by top-class architects. They are not only cultural centres, but also serve as places for different groups of inhabitants to meet and have become iconic landmarks for Spijkenisse.

(Photo: Daria Scagliola and Stijn Brakkee)

In **Shenzhen, China**, the urban villages are the place where new migrants from the countryside, workers but also young professionals, find a cheap place to live surrounded by an abundance of urban amenities such as shops, restaurants and services. Located in the middle of new high-rise developments, these services also attract office workers and function as lively urban centres. While before, Shenzhen regarded these urban villages merely as overcrowded and unwanted, the positive urban value of these areas is becoming increasingly recognised.

(Photo: M. Provoost, 2018)

Milton Keynes, UK was built in 1967 for a largely homogeneous population, but has since grown into a culturally and ethnically diverse city. Since its beginnings, grassroots volunteer cultural organisations have been active in building Milton Keynes's vibrant art scene, and it is these groups that the City Council is now turning to as a way of strengthening cultural exchange and social cohesion. Their initiatives include the MK Museum, the annual Art in the Park events, and the African Diaspora Day. These residents' initiatives, supported by the city, bring people together and shape MK's cultural identity.

(Source: CMK Town Council)

PART 3. A HISTORY

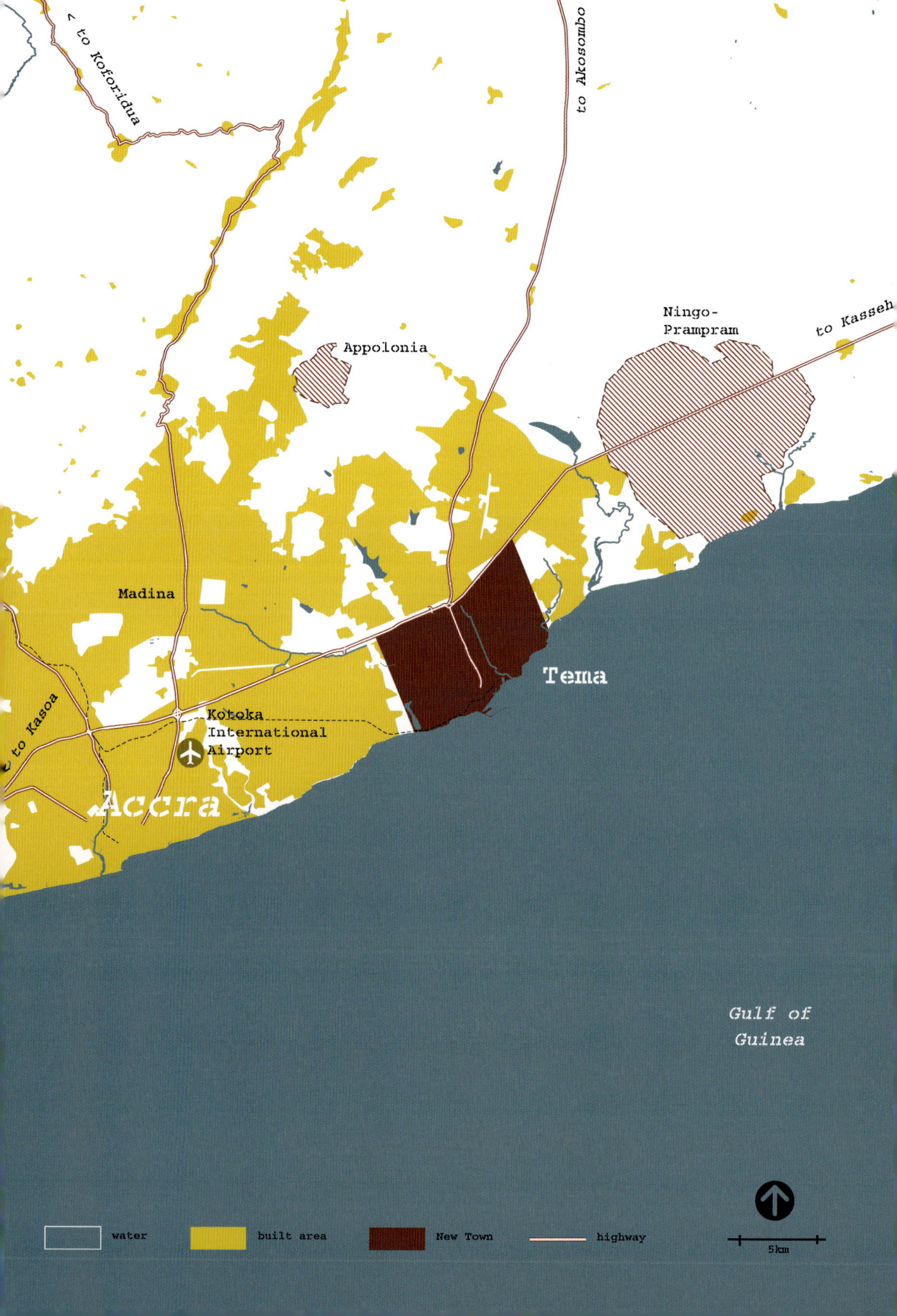
< to Koforidua
to Akosombo >
Appolonia
Ningo-
Prampram
to Kasseh
Madina
to Kasoa
Kotoka
International
Airport
Accra
Tema
Gulf of
Guinea
water
built area
New Town
highway
5km

CASE STUDY

Tema, Ghana

'After you've built it, can you maintain it?'

Tema, built immediately after Ghana's independence in 1957, is the first city of post-colonial Africa. At that moment, the predicted demographic growth and accompanying urbanisation were unprecedented; the end of the colonial era, the creation of new nation states, industrialisation and economic development caused a major demographic concentration in existing urban centres. Not only in Africa but also in the Western world the growth figures were enormous during the 1960s. This led urban planners worldwide to focus on the question: how do you design for the big numbers? How do you create urban environments and cities for large amounts of people?

It is interesting to look back at the cities dating from the 1960s and what experiences have been gained in the 50 years of their existence. Currently, with the increasing speed of urbanisation, we face many of the same questions that Ghana was confronting in 1960. Large scale migrations, problems with landownership and land rights, lack of funds, rapid growth of informal settlements, a lack of inclusivity, the difficulty of creating efficient institutions, these were all present when Nkrumah and his team started the project of Tema. What lessons can we draw from Tema for the future of urban Africa? What is the relevance of 1960s urbanism for twenty-first Century urbanism?

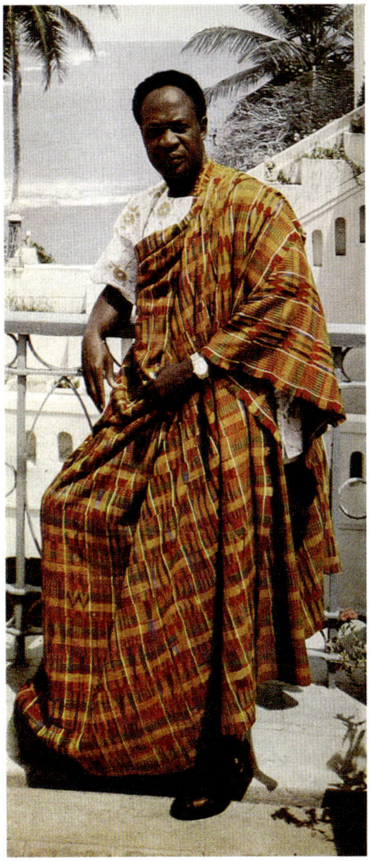

Portrait of President Kwame Nkrumah, 1959. (Source: 'Ghana. Ten Great Years 1951-1960', Ghana Information Services, Accra 1960. Photo: Arnold Newman)

Industrialisation of the new nation state

The city of Tema can only be understood as an instrument of Kwame Nkrumah's policies to develop the new nation state Ghana. Not only was the decision to build the city and the port an integral part of his modernisation and industrialisation plans, the image of modernity with which the city presented itself was also strongly influenced by Nkrumah's personal ambitions.

Kwame Nkrumah's time in power began in 1952, when he became the first elected leader of the Gold Coast Parliament, and lasted until his deposition as president of Ghana during a military coup in 1966. Over the years, his reputation changed diametrically several times. He was honoured as a great statesman in Ghana itself, as one of the country's founding fathers, the champion of independence and of the pan-African ideal. From the 1952 election onward, when an overwhelming majority elected the imprisoned political activist and the British rulers released him from the prison where he was held as a political prisoner, he grew into a popular hero. Nkrumah, a Marxist socialist who had studied economics, sociology and psychology in the USA, reached star status in Ghana in no time.

The Volta Dam.
(Source: Information Centre Volta Dam, Ghana)

Although Nkrumah's economic policies would later elicit much criticism, some of his investments and modernisation plans keep the country afloat to this day, for example, the Volta River Dam that produces the lion's share of Ghana's electricity. Nkrumah believed that an independent Ghana would achieve progress and modernisation by turning itself into a state-run industrial power. Cacao export, previously the mainstay of the Ghanaian economy, of course remained important.

However, the country's industrialisation was the showpiece of his modernisation efforts. His five-year plans included an impressive number of state enterprises, the most famous of them the Kwame Nkrumah Steelworks, followed by the State Fishing Corporation, the Ghana National Construction Corporation, the State Gold Mining Corporation, the State Fibre Bag Corporation and the Vegetable Oils Corporation. Then there were the factories for the production and processing of cacao, oil, rice, fruit, meat, sugar, pharmaceuticals, shoes and textiles.[1] Nkrumah wanted to kick-start Ghana's development and achieve striking results quickly.

One of the main requirements towards industrialisation was sufficient electricity and an adequate port. Therefore, Nkrumah prioritised a plan for a hydroelectric dam that the British had been preparing since the 1940s. This was to result in the most extensive building project in the history of Ghana: at the time, the Volta River Dam was the largest dam in the world, financed by mega-loans from the UK, the USA and the Worldbank.[2] Nkrumah saw constructing the dam as a way for Ghana to leapfrog into a developed country.

A port was necessary for the import and export of aluminium, cocoa beans, printed fabrics and all other raw materials and products. A location was chosen just east of Accra, occupied at that time by a small village called Tema, inhabited by the Ga tribe. Given the level of ambition, the scope of the modernisation and the importance to the national economy, it is not surprising that authorities took a radical decision: the village of Tema had to go. Like so many other New Towns, Tema can be interpreted as an inseparable part of an infrastructural and industrial complex — in this case of the Volta River Dam and the connected regional planning.

Industrialisation and the new harbour of Tema, part of Nkrumah's modernisation plans for Ghana. (Source: 'Ghana. Ten Great Years 1951-1960', Ghana Information Services, Accra 1960)

From Garden City to Ecumenopolis

The decision to construct the prestigious port had already been made by the British colonial powers in 1951, and they had made the whole repertory of British planning tools available to the Gold Coast. Not only spatial planning and the connected, underlying social and political values, but the institutional organisation as well: they made a package that was transplanted straight from the motherland to Ghana. It was taken for granted that spatial planning, urban development and infrastructure construction were approved and managed by the British rulers: British architects and engineers designed the towns, streets and bridges.

The Ministry of Housing and Town and Country Planning was responsible for the planning of the new resettlement village for the inhabitants of Tema village (called Tema Manhean).[3] A special Port Authority was commissioned to plan the port, the railways and the highway. These

1 Ghana had more than 50 state companies by 1960. See: Meredith, M. (2005) *The State of Africa, A History of Fifty Years of Independence*, London. P. 185.

2 Gill, M.S., (2005) *Immortal Heroes of the World*, New Delhi. P. 186; Nkrumah, K. (1963) 'Presenting the Volta River project, Accra', 25 March, www.nkrumahinfobank.org/article.php?id=431&c=51.

3 An insightful publication was written on the resettlement of the Tema-villagers: Amarteifio, G.W., D.A.P. Butcher, Whitham, D. (1966) *Tema Manhean, a Study of Resettlement*, Ghana Universities Press, Accra.

4 Initial Proposals for the Development of the New Town of Tema by the Town Planning Adviser, Tema 1952. To design the plan, Alcock collaborated with Helga Richards and Denis C. Robinson.

organisations were established in 1952, the year that Nkrumah was elected president. To prevent land speculation, the government issued an ordinance to expropriate a 163 km^2 area for the construction of Tema's city, port and industrial zone. Another ordinance decreed the creation of a special body for the building of the city: the Tema Development Corporation. This organisation was copied from the British New Town administrative bodies.

The British planner Alfred E. S. Alcock presented a design for the port city that very year.[4] He designed a city modelled on the British New Towns comprising five neighbourhoods with a total population of 50,000 residents. British architects Maxwell Fry and Jane Drew received the commission to design the housing for the resettlement of Tema village. Both projects, the new village and the new city were developed simultaneously in the period from 1952 to 1960.

The building of the first three Communities (large neighbourhoods or boroughs) in the new port city began in 1954. A team of British architects led by Ghanaian architect and planner T.S. Clerk designed a series of standardised dwellings, with 80% of them meant for the lowest incomes:

The original village of Tema just before demolition. (Source: Keith Jopp, 'Ghana's new town and harbour Tema', Ghana Information Services, 1961

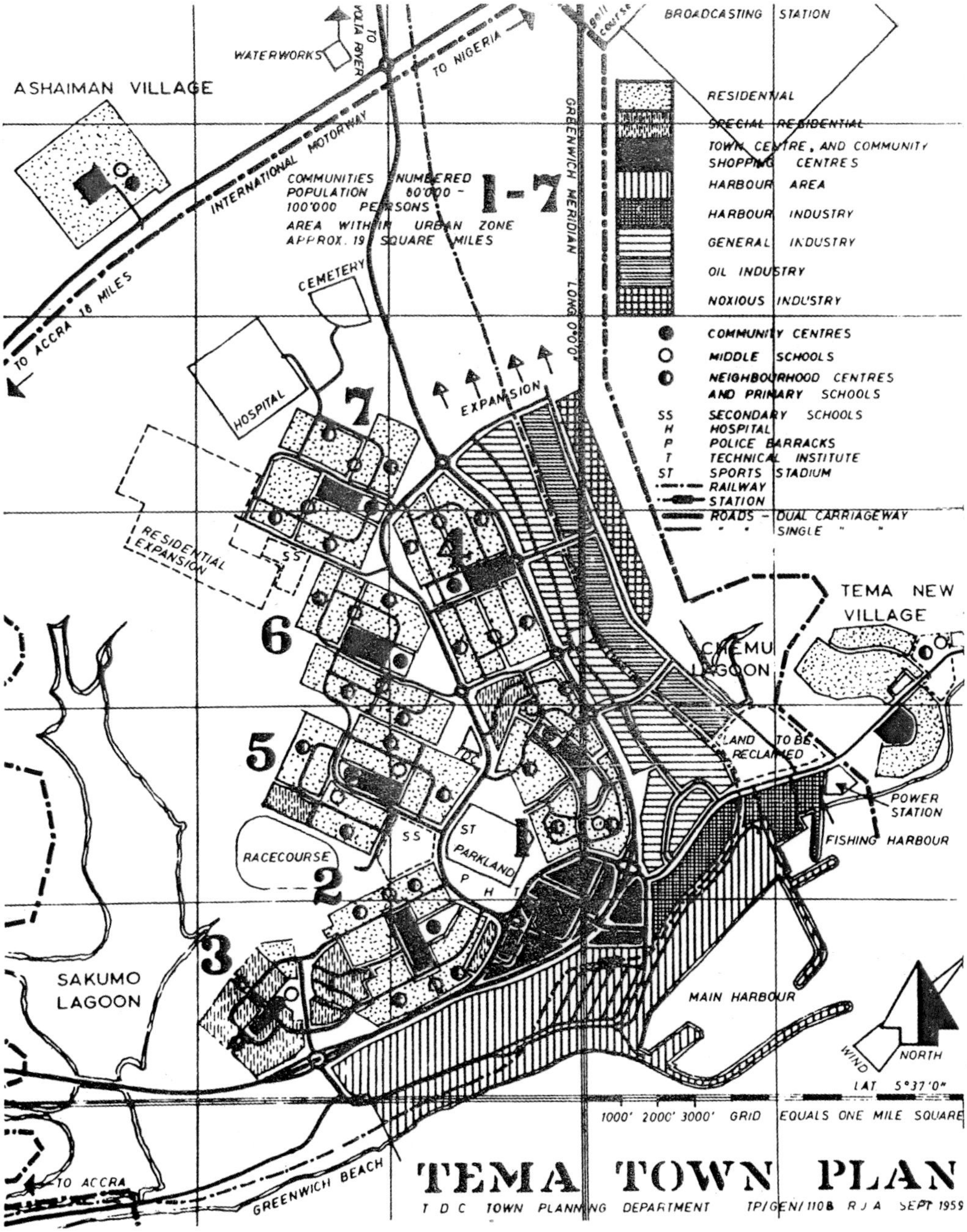

First masterplan for Tema, 1954.
(Source: 'Overseas Building Notes', May 1963, no.87)

small low-rise dwellings that had to meet the acute housing demand from dockworkers and others. However, the care and detail with which they worked would soon be obsolete due to the wave of urbanisation the project itself brought on. The 'ordinary' tools of urban planning and architecture known from the (much smaller and less complex) first generation of British New Towns were inadequate to develop Tema.

In the mid-1950s, when construction of the port and the city was clearly growing into a major economic project, people from all over Ghana flocked to Tema. These were mostly impoverished rural migrants who came to find work as labourers. The temporary barracks that the British planners had built in Community 1 soon became inadequate.[5] Many migrants built huts on the fringes of the planned area, near the village of Ashaiman, where an extensive slum without infrastructure, running water or sewage soon emerged. The draw of the port and the new city were obviously beyond the absorptive power of both the existing urban plan and the Tema Development Corporation's building capacity. Prognoses on the estimated number of residents were radically revised upwards: to 120,000 inhabitants (rather than 84,000). And the number would continue to rise: in 1960, estimates mentioned 200,000 and later during that same year, even 250,000.[6] These figures gave rise to a call for a different planning approach. The Greek planner Constantinos Doxiadis was asked to step in by Nkrumah himself.

Portrait of Constantinos Doxiadis. (Source: Constantinos A. Doxiadis, 'Ekistics. An introduction to the science of human settlements', Oxford University Press, New York 1968 (jacket). © Constantinos and Emma Doxiadis Foundation)

Doxiadis was a major exponent of the trend towards internationalisation of the urban development and architecture in developing countries. When he began to work outside of Europe, Doxiadis was confronted with issues that largely had to do with the enormous demographic and economic growth of that era. To deal with the new scale, Doxiadis developed an extremely hermetic, theoretical design and engineering system he called 'Ekistics, the Science of Human Settlements'. It was a rational and scientific alternative to the existing historical cities with their congested cars and people.[7] Instead, Doxiadis proposed a gridiron city model that would provide a human-scaled environment and at the same time facilitate unlimited growth. This model still had its roots in the accepted hierarchic ordering of the New Town model, but raised it to another scale. The neighbourhood units were standardised and enlarged; they were submerged in an ever-expanding grid, which was not supposed to contain or limit growth, as were the original British New Towns, but on the contrary: to facilitate ordered growth. At the same time, he recognised the need to offer the new urbanites of the city

5 The barracks were intended as temporary housing, but are still standing in the year 2015.

6 Kirchherr, E.C. (1968) 'Tema 1951-1962: The Evolution of a Planned City in West Africa', Urban Studies Vol 5, No 2: 207-217.

7 Doxiadis, C.A. (1968) Ekistics. An Introduction to the Science of Human Settlements, New York.

a stable and dependable framework, both spatially and socially. Aware of the existing local social structures as well as of future global urbanisation, he proposed the rather generic approach of Ecumenopolis, the world-encompassing city, as the solution. Doxiadis was possibly the leading advocate of the explicit application of comprehensive modernist planning models as vehicles for freedom, peace and progress.

8 Letter by Ftenakis to the Hon. Minister of Work & Housing, Accra, 12 October 1959, Ghana Correspond C-GhC 1-232 September 1959-December 60, Vol 7, Constantinos A. Doxiadis Archives.

The Doxiadis Masterplan

Doxiadis Associates explained their role as acting 'not merely as a Consulting Firm, but mainly as Pioneers. We are pioneers of a new science —developed mainly by Dr C.A. Doxiadis, our president— the science of Ekistics. . .'[8] Ekistics was the preferred method to deal with the tremendous problems that developing countries faced, including industrialisation, modernisation and urbanisation. Of the many foreign consultants that worked in Ghana, Doxiadis was the one who succeeded in convincing Nkrumah, no doubt by his large-scale approach that, focusing on radical progress, was visionary on the scale of the whole of Africa. This vision was the infrastructural equivalent of Nkrumah's pan-African political ambitions.

Masterplan with lay-out of the first 19 Communities within the Tema Acquisition area, Doxiadis Associates 1960. (Source: © Constantinos and Emma Doxiadis Foundation)

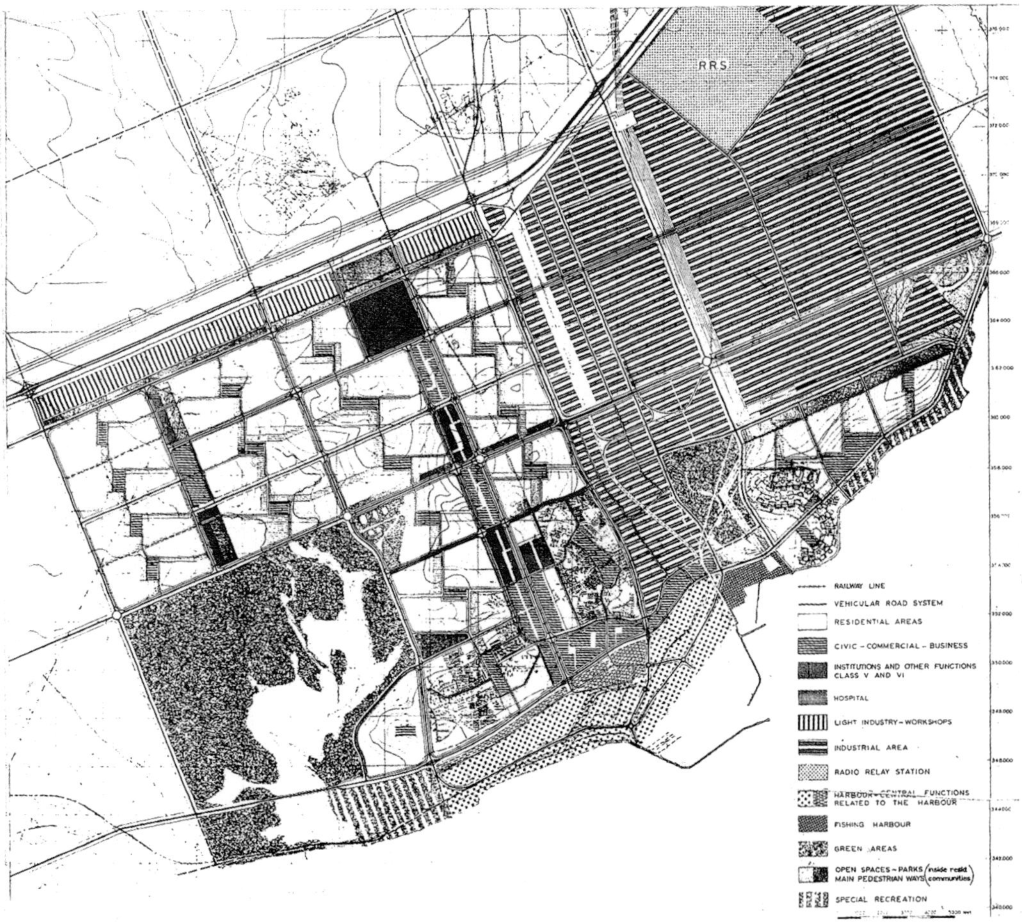

2019 GoogleEarth

light industry
heavy industry
harbour
fishing harbour
public green
ecological green
water
infrastructural
administrative
railroad
mixed use
commercial
residential low income
residential middle income
residential high income
educational
medical
1km

Doxiadis' visit to Ghana in early 1960 marked the official start of the surveys that collected the data necessary to plan for the region as well as for Tema. This was part of the thorough Ekistic method, which had universal principles, but the solutions had to be adapted to the particular situation. Therefore each project started with an 'on the spot investigation and survey of a host of factors covering history, tradition and custom, climate and geography, population characteristics and movements, sociology, economy...'[9] A small interdisciplinary team made up of an economist, a planner and a hydraulic engineer began collecting data, photos, maps and information and subsequently fed these back to Doxiadis' team in Athens.

At that time, the first Communities built in Tema already housed 26,860 people.[10] The construction of facilities at the neighbourhood and city level, however, was trailing behind.[11] In 1960, as a result, Doxiadis Associates received the commission to redesign the city centre and the road network, which according to Doxiadis were a complete mess.[12] He was also very critical of the housing and the dockworkers' dwellings in Community 2 met with his disapproval: he judged they were monotonous and unpleasant. Doxiadis proposed to take a radically different course, which he presented in his masterplan for Tema, in August 1962.[13]

While Maxwell Fry and Jane Drew, who designed and planned the resettlement village for the Tema residents, took a cautious approach, talking to chiefs and inhabitants and analysing the local culture, Doxiadis' attitude was different. His assignment was also different in the sense that he was planning for a largely unknown population. Nonetheless, it was indicative of his work that he did not start by zooming in, but by zooming out, namely by designing a plan for the whole Accra-Tema region. He surveyed the economic, demographic, geological, hydrological and traffic developments in the region and applied his theories of Dynapolis. He envisioned the future of the region as being dynamic and growing. While filling in the area between Accra and Tema with a repetition of similarly sized neighbourhoods, the arrows on his map showed how the metropolis could grow and extend to the north in the future. On an even larger scale, he pictured the new motorway from Accra to Tema as the first part of the pan-African highway, connecting the newly independent countries by land and not by sea, which was perceived as the colonial way.[14]

The design for Tema was based on a mathematical system that was rigidly hierarchical, with roads in eight different, numbered classes ranging from footpaths between houses (Road I) to highways (Road VIII). The residential areas ranged from a small cluster of houses (Community Class I) to the city as a whole (Community Class V) and even to the metropolitan region (Community Class VI). Tema is easily recognisable as part of the same family as Doxiadis's other urban plans in Khartoum, Islamabad or Baghdad; to a high degree it was a generic system, with its neutrality as the container for a complex of social goals like community creation, emancipation, modernisation and economic progress. Only a limited influence of local factors was allowed, most of which did not

9 Letter from Ftenakis to the Hon. Minister of Work & Housing, Accra, 12 October 1959, Ghana Correspond C-GhC 1-232 September 1959-December 60, vol. 7, Constantinos A. Doxiadis Archives.
10 DOX-GHA 3 8.7.1960, p. 2, Constantinos A. Doxiadis Archives.
11 'There is an urgent need to construct the first parts of the centre as shown by the fact that houses have already been completed without the corresponding central facilities', DOX-GHA 3 8.7.1960, p. 77, Constantinos A. Doxiadis Archives.
12 The road network was not designed to cope with the anticipated turbulent regional development, it hindered the further growth of the centre and was inadequately structured for the different traffic types. 'The Main Roads of Tema', DOX-GHA 6 10.2.1961, p. 1, Constantinos A. Doxiadis Archives.
13 Work on the masterplan began in 1960, and from May 1961 Doxiadis had full responsability for the development of Tema. Tema. The Final Master Plan, 15-8-1962, DOX-GHA 65, Doxiadis Archives.
14 'Toward an African Transport Plan', DA Monthly Bulletin February 1964, No 63.

'A typical Community Class IV', cover of Doxiadis Associates' magazine 'Ekistics', March 1962. (Source: © Constantinos and Emma Doxiadis Foundation)

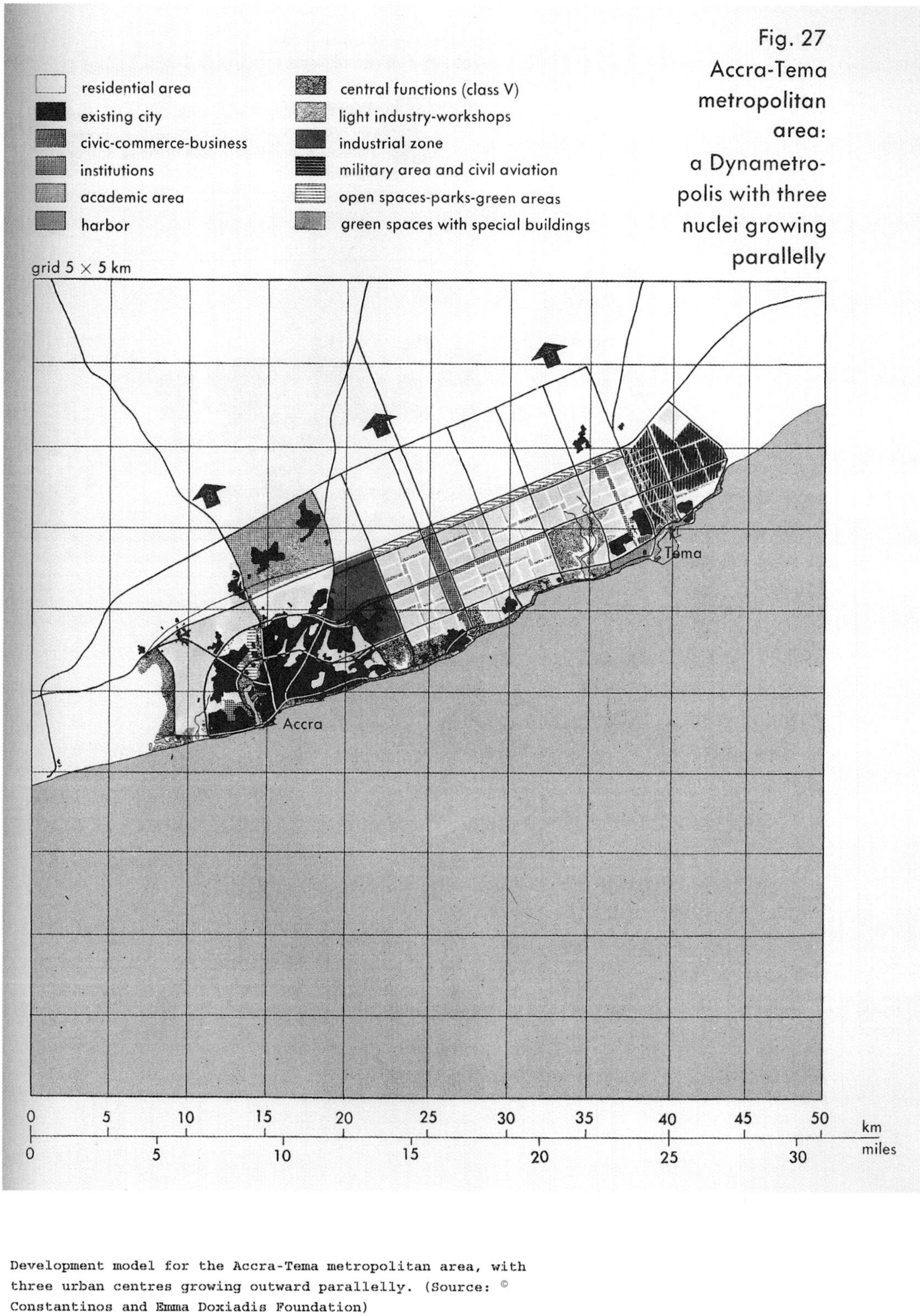

Development model for the Accra-Tema metropolitan area, with three urban centres growing outward parallelly. (Source: © Constantinos and Emma Doxiadis Foundation)

involve cultural factors, but rather local building traditions or the climate. In the case of Tema this involved the striking diagonal orientation inside the communities, which had to do with taking the most advantage of prevailing winds.

The picturesque winding roads of Alcock's Garden City were rationalised wherever possible. Doxiadis systematised and took all whimsicalities and irregularities out of the plan. The already existing first Communities were incorporated in an orthogonal grid of main roads, which delineated a series of identical Communities IV, each with their own centre, including shops, high schools and government buildings. Every Community was divided into four smaller neighbourhoods, again each with its own centre containing daily shops and primary schools.

One of Doxiadis's most important goals was to facilitate social cohesion within the Communities; a necessary goal in a country with ongoing differences and feuds between tribes and essential for a city in which every inhabitant was a newcomer without existing social structures to fall back on. The design of public buildings and public space was therefore a priority. These were carefully standardised: schools, marketplaces, shopping streets, cinemas, (municipal) offices and public services, as well as roads, paths and squares, along with landscaping and trees.

Schools

Besides industrialisation, another priority of Nkrumah's policy was the improvement of the education system. The country boasted a high education budget: 'Ghana is one of the few countries in the world today that spends more on education and social services than on armed forces and armaments.'[15]77 Nkrumah wanted this policy to produce results fast, and designated Tema as a pilot project dedicated to Ghana's educational reform. The entire organisation of the Communities was based on the positioning of the schools: one primary school per Community Class III (2,000-3,500 people), placed so that every child could reach the school without having to cross any motorways; the maximum distance was half a kilometre.

The education system was improved and the age to which school attendance was compulsory rose. Primary and secondary schools were compulsory and free of charge. The number of pupils attending primary school increased dramatically, from 154,000 in 1951 to 1,480,000 in 1966.[16] Courses in Tema were to be tailored to the needs of the large group of young migrants, including 'evening schools, technical training, basic reading and writing courses, help in adjustment to the new urban environment'.[17] Nkrumah also increased the range of secondary schools to create the university-educated population he needed to build and develop the new Ghana.

Doxiadis designed standardised schools with extensive sports facilities and classrooms for 35 to 40 pupils, which was below the number of 46

15 *Ghana Reports* July-December 1960, Report 47 (18 June 1962), 7, Constantinos A. Doxiadis Archives.
16 Vallin, H. (1966) 'Nkrumah's Downfall', *International Socialist Review*, Vol 27, No 3: 115-120.
17 *Ghana Reports* July-December 1960, Report 47, 18-6-1962, P. 10, Constantinos A. Doxiadis Archives.

Standard elementary school.
(Photo: J. den Hollander, 2007)

that was common in Ghana. They were 'modern and modest' buildings, designed especially with an eye to the functionality of light, climate (cross ventilation) and circulation. The orientation of the classrooms, with their glassless windows, took advantage of the prevailing winds and filtered sunlight. With their characteristic scale roofs, the school buildings feature as primary schools in every neighbourhood and as middle schools in every borough and are thus recognisable elements throughout the New Town.

Flora

Doxiadis attached great importance to the design and planting of the public space. In his mind's eye, he saw Tema as a low-rise city surrounded by green, following and accentuating the lines of the landscape. This not only applied to the Communities, but also to the vast industrial area: Doxiadis imagined an industrial park with low-rise factories amid the green, 'modern and modest, you won't be able to tell if they're schools or industries or anything else'. Regulation of plant construction on the basis of a study of the existing landscape would ensure that the residents would not end up overlooking an ugly industrial estate.

The team made extensive and detailed plans for the planting and design of the public space using different types of trees, streets and paths with shrubs and other plants, and fences consisting of hedges. Today, unfortunately, it is no longer easy to see how Doxiadis intended his design of the public space to work out. On the one hand this is because much of it soon fell victim to budget cuts. On the other hand, Tema's public space was under permanent pressure because the city was overcrowded.

Schools and churches were planned as central elements in the Communities. (Photo: M. Provoost, 2007)

Public space was the first thing that was sacrificed in the search for extra residential space.

City centre

Doxiadis's design for the city centre is somewhat curious, given that he appreciated modesty. In the 1950s, British planners had already decided on a Western city centre model on the location of the former Tema-village adjacent to the port. It comprised a fully elevated pedestrian plateau underneath which cars could pass freely, its size unprecedented in Ghana. Doxiadis, however, took things a step further. Unsurprisingly, however, the megalomanic complex of 'shops, department stores, office blocks, cinemas and theatres, a Magistrate's Court and headquarters buildings for police and other local authorities, a Town Hall, museum, art gallery, three hotels, a public library and a pavilion for special exhibitions' he designed failed to actually materialise.[18] And this was only meant to be the beginning! According to Doxiadis, the centre on the site of the old village was only the first of a series of sub-centres that would grow along the central axis and eventually unite key commercial, cultural and educational institutions into one elongated centre that would extend to the motorway to Accra.

Although the Meridien hotel, the Ghana National Bank and some other buildings were built, scattered across the centre, that is where implementation and the masterplan diverged.

18 'Ghana. Accra-Tema-Akosombo Regional Development', DA review, November 1968. P. 8, Constantinos A. Doxiadis Archives.

CREATOR
SCHOOL

Behind the lush trees and the many added kiosks the original terraced housing is barely visible. (Photo: M. Provoost, 2007)

19 'Thoughts on the formation of Tema', Ghana Reports July-December 1960 Vol 9, Report 27: 1, Constantinos A. Doxiadis Archives.

20 Ghana Reports July-December 1960 Vol 9, Report 22, Constantinos A. Doxiadis Archives.

Housing for the lowest incomes

One of the main reasons Doxiadis got involved in the construction of Tema was because the shortage of housing for labourers held back the growth of the port and industry. Companies wanted to locate in places where housing was available, and complained bitterly when it was not. Even in 1958, there were concerns about the increase in squatter settlements and illegal workshops near Tema. Thousands of requests for rental housing could not be granted and, moreover, the Communities that were under construction had no community facilities yet: no schools, community centres or markets, no playgrounds, local squares or public toilets. The threatening overpopulation, caused by the fact that many people sub-let their rooms, with several families jointly inhabiting a single house, was a thorn in the authorities' side.[19] In addition, all kind of illegal land use occurred, especially by furniture makers and sellers and car hire and garage services. They were all drawn to the new city, even though they were unable to rent an official place of business.

Different housing types from the experimental scheme. (Source: © Constantinos and Emma Doxiadis Foundation)

HOUSE TYPE A 01 S 1-ROOM

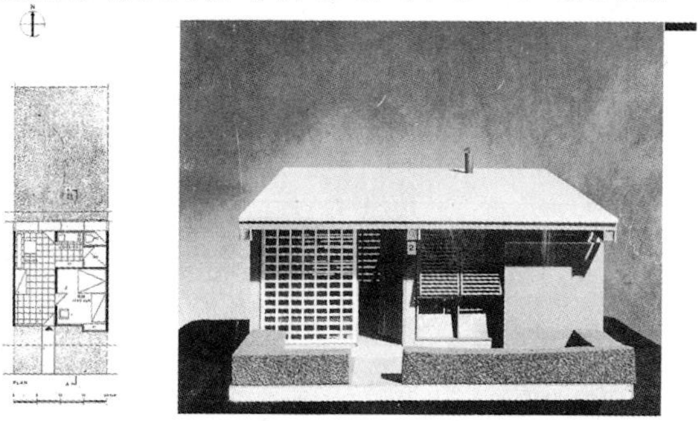

HOUSE TYPE A 03 S 2-ROOM

HOUSE TYPE B 05 S 2-ROOM

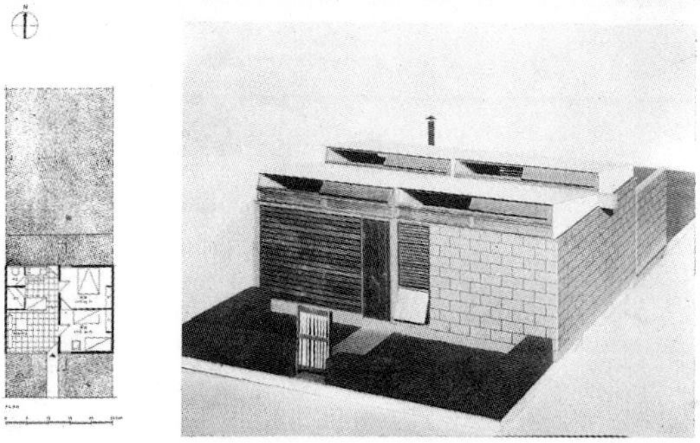

The acute shortage of cheap housing had to be resolved to prevent the advent of urban chaos through self-built slums. Doxiadis identified 'hurrying up' as his main objective and introduced a new approach for Community IV which was the first realised in accordance with the new masterplan. To this day, it is also the Community that best reflects Doxiadis' ambitions.

In a 1:1 low-cost housing pilot varieties of all aspects involved in house building were tested: construction method, plan, materials, prefabrication, use of the work force, construction time, organisation of the construction site and urban layout.[20]

The pilot area, completed in June 1963, consists of low-rise terraced housing with playgrounds and squares, a congenial environment with houses on pleasant, intimate pedestrian streets. The design of collective life clearly had priority here. The small squares with playgrounds, sandboxes, trees and seating between the low-rise dwellings can only be described as 'cosy' and are still very much in use.

The dwellings were small and simple. Their design was modern, but their typology was entirely different from that of Western houses. Though walls enclosed bedrooms,

Housing in the Experimental Housing Scheme in Community IV. (Photos: M. Provoost, 2015)

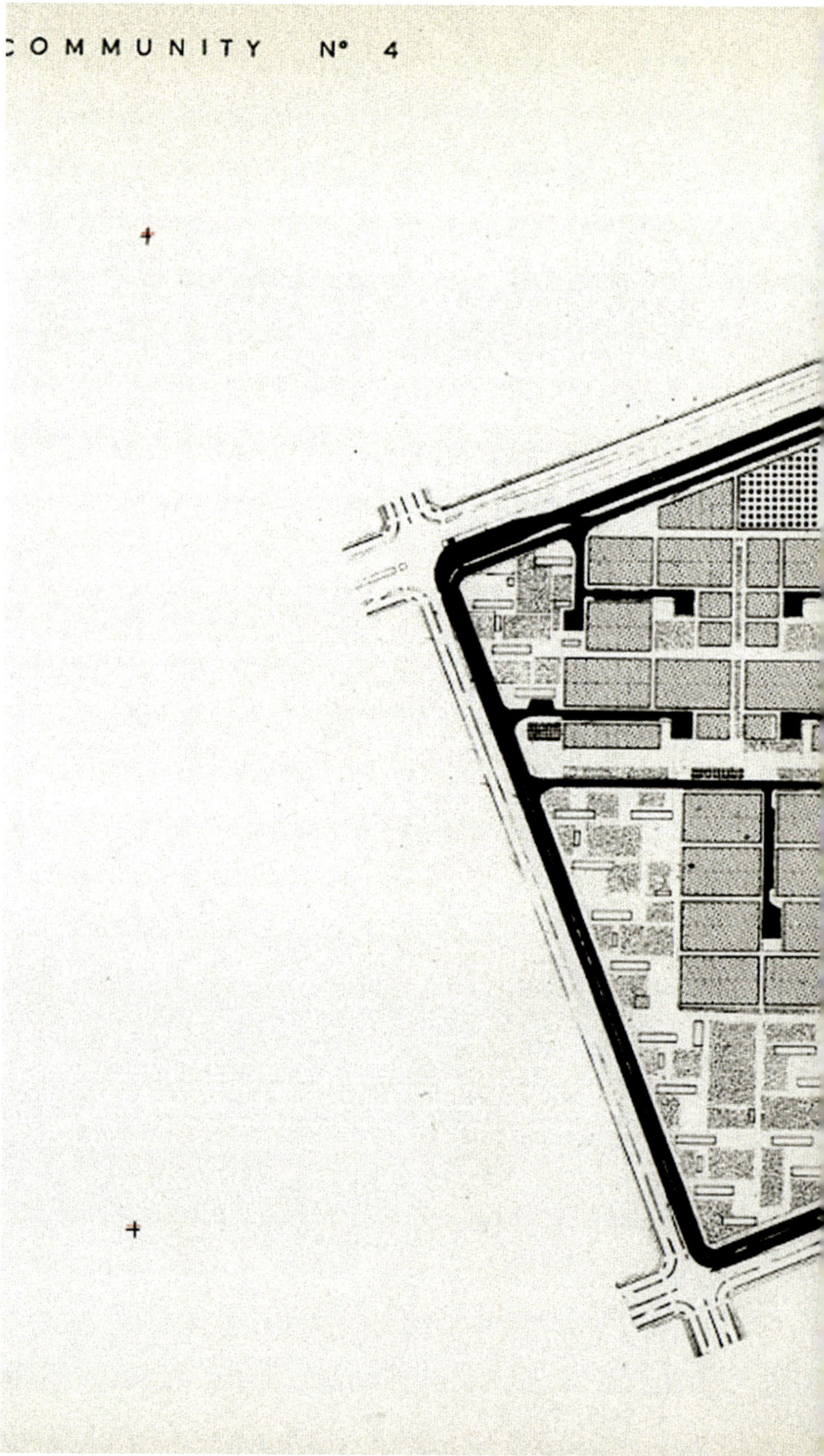

'Layout of the initial nucleus of experimentation' in Community 4. (Source: Constantinos A. Doxiadis Archives, Reports Tema DOX-GHA 22, p.9 © Constantinos and Emma Doxiadis Foundation)

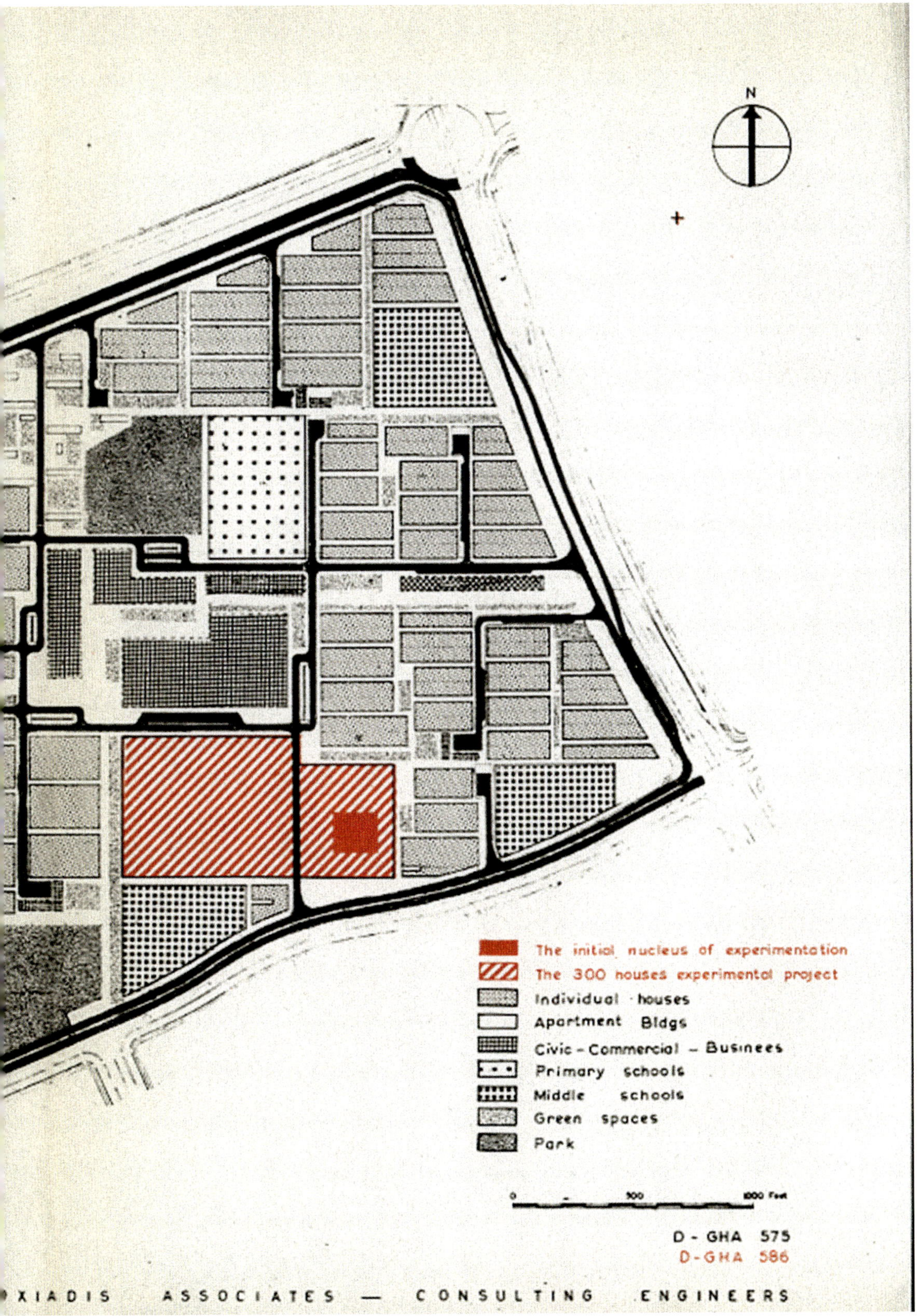
N
The initial nucleus of experimentation
The 300 houses experimental project
Individual houses
Apartment Bldgs
Civic - Commercial - Businees
Primary schools
Middle schools
Green spaces
Park
0
500
1000 Feet
D - GHA 575
D - GHA 586
XIADIS ASSOCIATES — CONSULTING ENGINEERS

The urban design of the footpaths and public-private spaces in the lower income areas in Community 7. (Source: © Constantinos and Emma Doxiadis Foundation)

The urban design is still effective in creating a pleasant living environment. (Photo: M. Provoost, 2007)

toilet and shower, the other spaces under the roof were open to the sky in one way or another, mostly only separated from the outside world by slats. In addition, there was a lot of outdoor space: a terrace at the front and a garden or small yard at the back. Most roofs were pitched, with a slot kept open at the peak for ventilation. The team built a total of 300 experimental houses and after evaluation, the successful ones were copied in the other Communities.

In Community VIII, for example, some 1,000 of the smallest and cheapest dwellings were built for residents in the 'very low income' category. The aim was to build as many dwellings for as little money as possible. The affordability of the dwellings remained problematic nevertheless. Though some terraced houses were designed as duplexes, for one family on each floor, it was impossible to lower the rent to such an extent that workers

Kaiser- and Segecoflats on Hospital Road, Community 4. (Source: © Constantinos and Emma Doxiadis Foundation)

Kaiserflats in 2007. (Photo: M. Provoost)

Single family housing in Community IV. (Source: © Constantinos and Emma Doxiadis Foundation)

Single family housing in Community IV, 2007. (Photo: M. Provoost)

that made only 78 cents per day could afford to pay it: 'Although lower income houses are subsidised by the Corporation, the majority of people cannot afford to pay rents which range from G£ 3 to G£ 5 monthly per residence.'[21]

As a final resort, barracks offered some relief, though built in nearby Ashaiman rather than in Tema. This small, seventeenth-century village had mushroomed since the building of Tema began, with an expanding self-organised settlement forming on a rudimentary road network. In 1966, the TDC decided to build a large number of barracks there for workers who would never be able to afford a house in Tema. The barracks were simple, consisting of rooms without kitchens, with verandahs, shared toilets and shower blocks.[22]

The development of the housing types in Community IV shows how Doxiadis rejected the traditional compound house for extended families; in the many series of experimental houses he developed, there were bungalows, row houses and apartment buildings. Every possible variation was tested, but they were all geared to the Western, nuclear family. Doxiadis and also Nkrumah decided the local housing habits were unfit for a modern industrialised society. Tema was not just a large-scale urban project, but also a large-scale example of social engineering, in which people of different tribes and different social and cultural backgrounds would be united in a new urban community, serving the modernisation ambitions of Nkrumah.

Doxiadis was well aware of the risks of cities that were too homogeneous: 'Specialised settlements always prove a failure both socially and economically.'[23] Therefore, building in Tema focused on housing for mixed incomes: not only for the workers in the port and industry, but also for merchants, doctors, teachers and engineers.[24] Expats were a category by themselves: a reasonably large number of foreigners worked in Tema, who were mostly housed in high-rise buildings that were more expensive to build, like the walk-up Kaiserflats in Community IV, adjacent to the central axis of Tema.

Sites and services

In Tema there was also an attempt to provide for the lowest income group by including areas in which migrants could build their own houses; this programme was called Firm Foundations and was an example of 'sites and services'. This approach was made popular in the 1970s by John Turner, a British architect who advocated self-organised building.[25] Doxiadis had already worked with this method before and when he saw how migrant workers were unable to rent a house or room in Tema and instead moved to Ashaiman, the neighbouring slum, he incorporated the same concept in Tema.

However, not without question. He considered state-run large-scale operations more appropriate as these allowed better monitoring of

21 DA Newsletter, November 1963, P. 16, Constantinos A. Doxiadis Archives.
22 'A crash programme for the construction of barrack-type dwelling units for workers in Ashaiman Village, Tema', Memorandum August 1966, Constantinos A. Doxiadis Archives.
23 Ghana Reports July-December 1960 Vol 9, Report 16: 13, Constantinos A. Doxiadis Archives.
24 Estimates from the 1960s indicated about 15% of the inhabitants in this middle class. Ghana Reports July-December 1960 Vol 9, Report 16, Constantinos A. Doxiadis Archives
25 See: Harris, R. (1988) 'Silence of the Experts, Aided Self-help Housing 1939-1954', Habitat International, Vol 22, No 2, June. Pp. 165-198.

26 DA Newsletter, April 1963, P. 10, Constantinos A. Doxiadis Archives.
27 DIARY-GHA 2 DOXIADIS C A 15.5.61, REF. 24414, P. 4, Constantinos A. Doxiadis Archives.
28 DA Newsletter, May 1963, P.21, Constantinos A. Doxiadis Archives.

construction time, quantity and coherence to architectural style. The shortage of affordable dwellings in the long term needed to be obtained by the continued improvement of construction techniques, technological facilities and staff training on the basis of the outcomes of the experiments in Community IV. In the short term, however, he accepted the need for residents 'to share responsibilities with the government in the construction of low-income houses'.[26]

During his previous trips across the region, Doxiadis had come to realise several things with regard to existing housing habits. He had seen how primitive the villages were, with bumpy dirt roads, goats, street vendors, and naked children fetching water from the well. People lived in huts that —in Doxiadis's words— were scattered about randomly, without showing any comprehension of land property.[27] This led him to conclude that the planning of Tema had to include an incremental growth strategy for this demographic, a phased planning that would allow the rational organisation of organic growth over an extended period.

The Firm Foundations Programme was a consequence of that insight: a sites and services scheme that was used in Community IX to build 272 dwellings in 1963.[28] Individual plots were provided with water, sewage and electricity, foundations, and a ground floor slab. The dwellers were given a simple plan so they could build their house with their own labour and materials, but in accordance with the existing zoning and building regulations. By sticking to strict regulations, a coherent streetscape emerged, even though the housing was self-built.

After the coup: privatisation

The CIA-backed coup that ousted Nkrumah in 1966 was bad news for Tema: it was not finished by far. Community IV had just been completed and Community V was under construction. Nkrumah's considerable investments in the realisation of his pet project suddenly ceased and his national policy of social modernisation came to an end. The first act of the new military regime lead by Joseph Ankrah was to shut down construction in Tema.

It was impossible to realise the Ghanaian welfare state without Nkrumah's governmental support and the same was true of Tema. The healthy financial situation that existed for the Tema Development Corporation (TDC) under Nkrumah, with the government initiating, organising and paying for urban planning and housing, was gone forever. Third parties, mostly private, went on to realise the remaining housing. They built numerous villas in Community VI, close to the lagoon and designated as a high-income area. The pace of construction in Tema slowed down, production became more one-sided and the careful composition of architecture and public space was lost. Successive governments, some of them right wing and others socialist, sometimes military and then again civilian, reformulated the housing policy over and over again until finally, in the 1990s, a private sector-oriented policy prevailed.

This did not happen without difficulties. Ever since the 1970s, the IMF and the World Bank had been charting the course of Ghana's economic development, as a condition for loans. This led to the privatisation of the state-owned companies Nkrumah had founded.[29] To Tema, this liberalisation policy meant that government grants to the TDC that were still ongoing were cut. To tap into alternative sources of income, TDC decided to sell off social housing as well as plots of land for middle class self-building purposes.

At that time, Tema already had countless urban problems — problems that are bigger than ever today and, with hindsight, foretold a typical African mix of planned and informal urban development. Houses were overcrowded, with up to ten people sharing a single room. Due to the pressure on public space, every available bit of pavement, every square and street corner was being used for construction. On the outskirts of the city, that same overcrowding led to the emergence of slums, self-built huts and workshops.

Serious problems arose in the 1980s. The dwellings in the oldest Communities were of course no longer new and needed maintenance. But the extremely low rents yielded an income that was too low to pay for the upkeep of either the properties or the living environment. Rents were low to keep the housing affordable, but also due to a political lack of will to raise them. Politicians had systematically withheld their consent for necessary but unpopular rent increases.[30]

There were a few other factors that aggravated the situation. An administrative reorganisation left the TDC with less influence and less money to spend. As in any New Town, authorities established a democratic body and structure in Tema once the city had reached a certain size. This happened incrementally, until Tema became an independent municipality in 1990, governed by the Tema Metropolitan Assembly (TMA). The TMA not only took over many of the TDC's tasks, but also withdrew the funding the TDC received for the construction and maintenance of infrastructure, with predictable consequences.

Owing to the continued devaluation of the Ghanaian currency in the 1980s, the rental income decreased dramatically until the rents at one time amounted to no more than 2% of the price of similar dwellings on the open market.[31] As a result, the occupancy rate of the dwellings rose to 100% and residents were disinclined to move out: after all, tenants lived virtually for free. Many people also saw the cheap housing as a profitable source of income and rented out dwellings or rooms at market prices.

Meanwhile, the population of Tema grew by some 2.8% annually, achieving the milestone of 100,000 inhabitants in 1985. A growing number of private developers and institutional parties bought land from the TDC to build houses, but they never managed to make them affordable for the people with the lowest incomes. This fed the uncontrolled growth of informal settlements.

29 www.modernghana.com/news/224262/1/tema-is-decaying-slowly.html 'Tema is Decaying Slowly', 19 May 2009.

30 Asabere, P., The Demise of Rent-controlled Public Housing Programmes of Ghana: The Story of the Tema Development Corporation, Urban Studies 2007, No 44, P. 1921.

31 Idem

Tema was nevertheless in its prime in the 1980s; it was a popular settlement location and had a good reputation, 'the pride of the nation. It became the destination of young school leavers who sought a living at the sprawling main harbour, the adjoining fishing harbour and the numerous factories the city could boast of. Those were the days Tema was vibrating with activity throughout the day and night, with big buses of the various companies ferrying their workers to and from work on their shifts.'[32]

In 1994, the acceptance of three strategies put forward by the IMF and the World Bank consolidated the trend towards privatisation. In the first place, participation in affordable housing by the private sector was to be encouraged. In addition, it was decided that the dwellings in the first Communities were to be sold to residents. Finally, the TDC was expected to start a special 'Site and Services' programme.[33] At first sight, this sounds similar to the Firm Foundations Programme from the 1960s and involved plots that the TDC provided with water, sewage and electricity and subsequently issued to residents so they could realise their own homes. The TDC programme was different in the sense that rather than being aimed at providing the poorest residents with dwellings, it was meant to provide the TDC with new capital through the sale of building plots to middle class homeowners.

The sites and services scheme was successful and, using this strategy, three Communities were built in a few years. As a private company, the TDC received income from the land sales that were part of the programme. Later communities, like Community XX, consist mainly of villas and detached houses, well equipped and protected, but without any kind of public space or amenities. The owners of these houses are often retirees and foreigners or belong to the diaspora of Ghanaians that amassed their capital abroad: more than 55% of all newly built homes are sold to Ghanaian expats that live abroad.[34]

In these neighbourhoods, only a benevolent eye can still discern the outlines of Doxiadis's masterplan. Their structure comprises only streets for car traffic. There are no squares, centres or other communal spaces. The finer points of the earlier Communities' design are wholly absent here. The unity-in-diversity of the architectural setup that Doxiadis so valued has been replaced by a motley collection of individual palaces.

Clearly, the sites and services programme was also not able to facilitate housing for those with lower incomes profitably or even cost-effectively. Every attempt by the sector to realise social housing failed: at their completion, the dwellings were found too expensive and only suitable for the middle incomes.

That meant that the shortage of affordable dwellings persisted, as did overcrowding and subletting; houses were maximally extended, topped up and built-on, and most gardens were sacrificed and built over as well. Conflicts with the traditional chiefs of the villages Teshi, Nungua and Labadi, whose land the TDC had bought, remained unresolved. In order

32 'Tema is Decaying Slowly', 19 May 2009, www.modernghana.com/news/224262/1/tema-is-decaying-slowly.html.

33 Acquah,W.K. (2001) Urban Development Problems of Ghana. The Case of Tema, Lund University, www.lth.se/fileadmin/hdm/alumni/papers/ad2001/ad2001-07.pdf.

34 www.timeincnewsgroupcustompub.com/sections/100726_Ghana.pdf.

to share in the benefits of urban development, they continued to sell land, but without services: as a result, vast residential areas devoid of paved roads, sanitation, water, electricity, sewers or drainage emerged. During the economic crisis, some of the tenant farmers who worked big farms around Tema also decided to divide their land and illegally sublet residential plots. This is how large areas consisting of shabby informal settlements grew on the fringes of Tema.

Over the past decade, moreover, informalisation has advanced from the inside out: the old parts of the city, especially Communities I and II, are now completely run down and overcrowded; public amenities such as street lighting, water supply and sewers have been neglected and are out of order. Tema has entered a new phase, one in which the New Town is in need of renovation.

Mega-region and national planning

The mushrooming city puts a lot of pressure on the area. Doxiadis's seemingly radical vision from the 1960s, which anticipated that the entire Accra-Tema zone would turn into a single urban area, has long since materialised. Accra and Tema have grown together, though not based on the infrastructural grid that Doxiadis recommended. Without good roads, the area is nothing but a chain of slums and self-organised settlements, everything covered by a thick crust of commercial kiosks and stalls on either side of the bumpy two-lane roads, a traffic nightmare that turns the mere 20 km that separate Accra from Tema into an hours-long adventure.

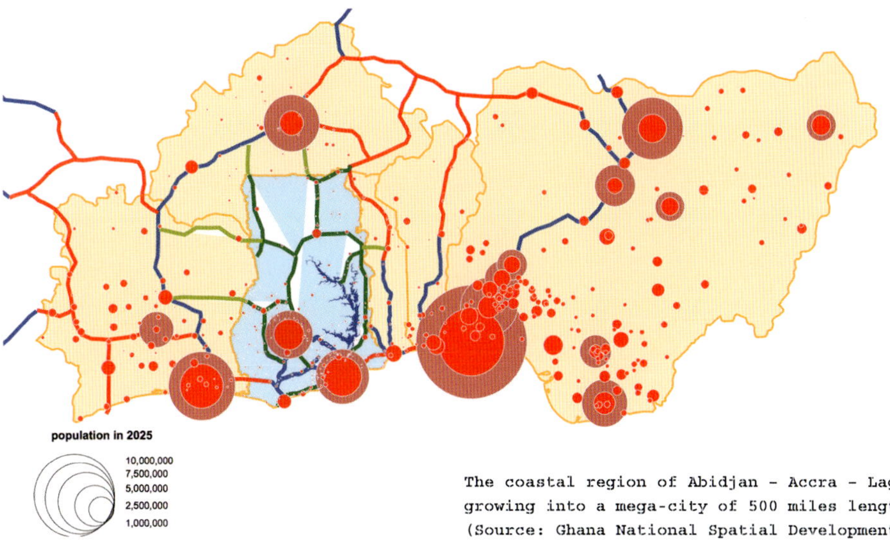

The coastal region of Abidjan - Accra - Lagos, growing into a mega-city of 500 miles length. (Source: Ghana National Spatial Development Framework (2015-2035). Volume II: Overall Spatial Development Strategy, Government of Ghana 2015)

But it is not only this stretch of the coast which is urbanising quickly: the entire West-African coast from Abidjan in Ivory Coast up to Lagos, Nigeria is becoming one continuous urban mega-region: 'Here and there already,

the continent's biggest cities are spawning enormous urban corridors that are spilling over borders and creating vigorous new economic zones that are outstripping the ability of weak and plodding central governments to manage or even retain their hold on them.'[35]
The national policies in the five countries of this mega-region (Ivory Coast, Ghana, Togo, Benin, Nigeria) are now anticipating the economic power that will accommodate this growth by means of new international infrastructure: the Trans West-African highway is currently being planned, paralleled by a railroad.

Ghana is one of the forerunners in Africa when it comes to national spatial planning: in 2013 it launched a 'National Urban Policy', 'the first comprehensive urban governance framework in the country's history'.[36] The document is a comprehensive programme of measures to deal with rapid urbanisation. More than half of all Ghanaians already lived in cities in that year (at the time of independence that was 30%[37]), and 'the country's urban population is expected to double between 2000 and 2025'.[38] Moreover, some 51% of urban residents live in slums.[39]
When the country became independent in 1957, it had a population of 6.7 million and it now houses almost four times that number (24.6 million people in 2010), expected to grow to 34.7 million in 2035.[40] And while in 1960 491,000 people lived in the Accra region, this number had risen to almost 5.8 million in 2010 and the government expects its population to be almost doubled by 2035, to 11.1 million inhabitants.[41]

In the National Spatial Development Framework that was published in 2015, a wide and varied set of instruments is presented, ranging from growth poles and corridors, spatially targeted investments like special economic zones, informal settlement upgrading projects and local economic development programmes.[42] A number of mega-projects are also planned for the near future, including two international airports, three new harbours, international roads and railways, a green infrastructure network and agricultural growth corridor, urban food sheds and alternative energy projects. And although in general the strategy is to promote existing urban settlements and discourage new (small) ones, a new Airport City is envisaged in the centre of the triangle Accra-Kumasi-Takoradi, to combine international air traffic with an economic hub and a city of 500,000.[43] All this will be financed thanks to a formidable increase of GDP, which is expected to double in the period to 2025 and after that will double once more in the decade up to 2035.[44]

The Accra City Region, of which Tema is one of the districts, is one of the three most urbanised areas in Ghana and therefore also a focus of the National Planning Policy. Centrally located in the West African coastal mega-region, the city is a magnet for investments. Its population grew at a staggering 3.54 and 3.92% annually between 2000 and 2010.[45] But while the population is growing, the density is declining, and the city is sprawling.[46] Therefore the government aims to contain the city and increase its density.
Just east of Tema a new city, Ningo Pram Pram, is being planned for

35 www.theatlantic.com/international/archive/2013/07/how-africas-new-urban-centers-are-shifting-its-old-colonial-boundaries/277425
36 'Ghana launches first-ever National Urban Policy', www.citiesalliance.org/node/3748
37 National Urban Policy Framework, Ministry of Local Government and Rural Government, May 2012, P. 3, www.giz.de/en/downloads/giz2012-en-national-urban-policy-framework.pdf
38 'Ghana launches first-ever National Urban Policy', www.citiesalliance.org/node/3748
39 'Ghana launches first-ever National Urban Policy', www.citiesalliance.org/node/3748
40 National Urban Policy Framework, Ministry of Local Government and Rural Government, May 2012, P. 13, www.giz.de/en/downloads/giz2012-en-national-urban-policy-framework.pdf
41 Ghana National Spatial Development Framework (2015-2035), Executive Summary, Table 4.2, Pp. 4-35. www.ghana.gov.gh/index.php/about-ghana/regions/greater-accra
42 Ghana National Spatial Development Framework (2015-2035), Executive Summary, Ministry of Land and Natural Resources, Ministry of Environment, Science, Technology and Innovation, Town and Country Planning Department, National Development Planning Commission, Febr. 2015. www.ghanalap.gov.gh/files/NSDF-Final-Report-EXECSUM-Vol-III-Final-Edition-TAC.pdf
43 For an explanation of the Airport City concept, see: www.aerotropolis.com/files/AirportCities_TheEvolution.pdf
44 Ghana National Spatial Development Framework (2015-2035), Executive Summary, Figure 6.1, Pp. 6-53
45 Idem
46 Between 1985 and 2000, Accra's overall density decreased at the annual rate of 3.2% and between 2000 and 2010 it decreased at 5.8% per annum.

1 million inhabitants. The innovative grid design for this city, based on flexibility, the possibility for organic growth and the safeguarding of a green and water network for sustainability and safety reasons, is developed in cooperation with UN-Habitat, who state: 'This National Priority Planned City Extension would represent an international example of sustainable urban development in West Africa, positioning Ghana as a national champion in addressing fast urbanisation challenges.'[47]

47 'UN-Habitat and partners hold forum on extension of Accra', unhabitat.org/un-habitat-and-partners-hold-forum-on-extension-of-accra/

48 thechronicle.com.gh/redevelopment-of-tema-to-begin-november/ 9 October 2012.

Urban renewal

In Tema, the density of the first built Communities is not declining, but rather increasing. The oldest parts of the city, Communities I to IV, have become seriously overcrowded over the past decade and have partly deteriorated into slums owing to the continued population growth and the lack of maintenance and new social housing.[48]
Whereas the dwellings in Community IV were meant to house 5.5 residents, they accommodated 8.6 people in 2000; in the resettlement village Tema Manhean there are 12.3 inhabitants per dwelling and in neighbouring Ashaiman up to 15.[49]

Rendering of the new apartment blocks in between the Fry & Drew flats from the 1950s, in Community I. (Source: Tema Development Corporation)

The same blocks being built. (Photo: M. Provoost, 2016)

In 2010, the TDC had plans drawn up for the restructuring of some of the oldest areas in Tema. By 2015, the first new buildings were realised in Community I, where new residential towers, designed by the TDC and constructed by a Chinese contractor, have arisen in between Fry and Drew's apartment blocks from the 1950s, introducing densification and high-rise building as starting points for Tema's urban renewal. This strategy is not only necessitated by the great need for housing, but especially by financial considerations: the construction of a new public service infrastructure (water, power and sewer) is only affordable if housing density is increased. The public service system is in urgent need of renovation: the sewer system is in ruins and the water and electricity systems are in a state of disrepair.

At first sight it looks as if the urban renewal is taking place within the framework of the original masterplan, consisting only of densification and the realisation of parts of Doxiadis's plan that were never completed. Nkrumah's government financed and built the original plan, but political and economic conditions have changed drastically since

Overpopulation in Community I.
(Photo: M. Provoost, 2015)

49 Lyssens, M. (2011-2012) Dwelling Transformations in Community 4, Tema, Ghana, Master thesis KU Leuven. Pp. 28-29.

50 Lyssens, M. (2011-2012) Dwelling transformations in community 4, Tema, Ghana, Master thesis KU Leuven. P. 27.

then. Within the context of a privatised TDC and given the effects of a globalised economy — which affects both housing demand (by expats) and housing construction (by Chinese parties) in Tema – simply completing the old masterplan is not enough. That is why in 2010, the TDC commissioned Accra-based office The Consortium, to revise the masterplan, in which they focused on the city centre and on Community IV.

In the original Doxiadis plan, the city centre consisted of two connected areas: the location on the site of the former Tema-village, adjacent to the harbour, and the main axis which connects the centre to the highway in the North. The latter was designed as Tema's transport hub and central business district (CBD) with banks, offices, shops and other city functions. Although in the 1960s, several banks and a hotel were built in the CBD, the few scattered blocks amid the wastelands never managed to form a city centre. The new centre plan designed by The Consortium in 2010 is awaiting implementation, but its financing is hardly guaranteed as it depends on funding from USAid and the World Bank.[50] Given the unrealistic character of the plan and the many outdated urban planning ideas that inspired it, the fact that it may fail to materialise is hardly regrettable.

The central axis (Hospital Road) did not grow into the city centre Doxiadis anticipated, either. More than anything, it is in use as a spatially

Community I just after completion in the 1950s. (Photo: M. Hirst)

dimensioned thoroughfare with undefined flanks, busy and chaotic traffic and a few haphazardly scattered facilities. It is not the dense and dynamic extension of the city centre as was meant to be and needs rethinking.

Community IV has been designated by TDC as the first urban renewal area to set a new spatial and business standard for Tema's spatial development. To that end, the area comprising the Kaiser flats has been appointed a pilot project. Originally built for Kaiser's (European) employees, the flats were later rented out to Ghanaians. Again, the rent was insufficient to allow maintenance and authorities declared four blocks of flats unfit to live in due to their poor constructional condition as early as 1993.[51] However, squatters subsequently moved into some of the flats and they are currently used very differently than originally planned: the garages are in use as workshops or shops, the dwellings on the ground floor have been developed into hairdressers or kiosks and chickens are kept in the communal courtyard. It is a lively community, but the buildings are dilapidated. The residents have lost all their court cases against demolition and displacement and the TDC redevelopment plan, in which a Chinese investor is participating, is ready for implementation. However, some of the residents made use of 'the right to buy' long ago and are therefore legal owners of their flats. This further complicates matters and means that the TDC needs to buy out these residents, who are well aware of the value of their property.

51 Joseph Ayitio, Kwadwo Ohene Sarfoh, 'Nkrumah's Flagship and the Dilemma of Ghana's Urban and Housing Future', www.urbanafrica.net/urban-voices/9733, 13 October 2014.

Selling kitchen equipment, parking trucks, and banking in the centre of Tema. (Photo: M. Provoost 2015)

52 'Ghana Looks Forward to Stronger Ties With China: FM', allafrica.com/stories/201507071062.html.
53 Attenkah, R. (2014) 'Ghana: TDC to Commence Redevelopment of Tema Soon', 3 December, allafrica.com/stories/201412240888.html.
54 Interview of the author with Emmanuel Adjeteh (Chairman of the board, TDC) and Joe Abbey (CEO TDC), February 2015.

In the involvement of Chinese parties, another Nkrumah legacy is visible: the relations with China he initiated in 1960. After 55 years, this relationship is intense and thriving, and both exports and imports to China are increasing.[52] Many of the old state industries have changed into Chinese hands and Chinese private and state companies constructed much of the infrastructure, such as highways and the recent Bui Dam in northwest Ghana. Now the Chinese are also playing an increasingly important role in building the urban renewal projects.

The plot in Community IV is ideally located along the central axis of Tema and near the unofficial city centre in Community I, which has developed into a lively area with a busy daily market. With the run-down flats demolished, the construction of a new mixed-use complex aims to demonstrate the potential and the positive sides of densification. Simultaneously, the new buildings are supposed to demonstrate the best way to develop the central axis and set an example for the other vacant or underused locations along the axis.

The plan, designed in 2010 by The Consortium/Design Associates consists of high residential buildings, a shopping mall, a theatre and auditorium and parking facilities in a dated design that is emphatically not in keeping with modernist Tema. Nevertheless, TDC hopefully anticipates a high iconic value and sees this project as a model for the redevelopment of the whole of Tema, one they even think they can export to other parts of Ghana.[53] It is a new spatial and business model, therefore, that transcends the city boundaries of Tema.

A high-rise city for the middle classes

Tema's challenges and ambitions for the future show that its development still parallels that of its Western contemporaries, the New Towns in the UK, the Netherlands or Scandinavia. Tema, too, struggles with the fact that it never amounted to much more than a dormitory town that lacks entertainment, restaurants and metropolitan functions. The TDC believes that: 'Tema is less urban than Doxiadis meant it to be: it should become a real urban settlement, a complete city.'[54] This ambition echoes the current desires of the post-war Western European New Towns, where the urban renewal of New Towns also centres on the creation of 'a complete city'. To remain attractive, the often homogeneous housing stock has to become more versatile and the city needs more urban facilities. Like any other New Town, Tema is adding a theatre, a cinema and other entertainment venues to come up to the standard of a traditional, complete city. And again, like in other New Towns, it is the open space, the parks and the sports fields that are the first to be sacrificed and built over because, like low-hanging fruit, they are easy to pick and use for densification.
The limitations Tema encounters during its pursuit of renewal are not unique, either: in Western Europe, the financial and institutional frameworks that led to the building of the post-war neighbourhoods and

New Towns of the welfare state in the 1960s disappeared as well. Here, too, housing associations and government agencies that organised the construction of housing and the planning of cities were privatised in the 1980s and 1990s. Consequently, social housing made way for middle class dwellings. In this respect, too, Tema is beginning to resemble the Western New Towns, in this case due to the global trend of privatising government agencies. Of course, the challenges Tema faces are bigger and more complicated than those of its Western counterparts, especially due to the large income differences and the absence of an economic model to build for the largest group of people, those with the lowest incomes.

The most topical question is how TDC —as a privatised agency— can develop a new business model now that the old one has run its course. The income the sites & services programme generated for years dried up when all of the Communities on the land reserved for the city in 1952 had been built. The TDC ran out of undeveloped land.
The ambitions of TDC are those of an expanding company: there is an active lobby to lift the separation of powers between the TMA and the TDC. The separation, established in 1974, led to confusing situations with negative consequences to the living environment and to the power of the TDC. While the TDC is constructing the infrastructure, the TMA is responsible for its maintenance; the TDC draws up spatial plans and guidelines, but the TMA issues the building permits. In short, the two organisations compete with each other and this leads to confusion and inefficiency.

Financially, the TDC is now doing quite well again, as the organisation has made huge profits over the past years.[55] However, the lower income brackets do not share in the benefits and as before, hardly any houses are built for them. The small stock of social housing built to resettle residents from Tema's restructuring areas is located far outside Tema, in Kpone. Tema is changing into a middle class city, something architect Emmanuel Adjetey, long time resident of Tema and presently Chairman of the Board of TDC, also regrets. As he explains, 'the high cost of financing estate development have seen the low income earners being left out of house ownership schemes. Exorbitant interest on commercial loans for housing have seen offshore customers and non-resident Ghanaians becoming the determinants of rent rates on housing in the country'.[56]

Tema is fortunate because it can build on a good spatial and organisational structure that is still proving its usefulness. Starting from this position, the city can develop adjustments that address its current condition. Today, Tema is part of a densely built-over region and can no longer pass for a separate city. Inevitably, moreover, planners have to be aware of the connections between the physical, economic and programmatic structure of Tema and that of Ashaiman, between the planned and the self-organised city that form an indistinguishable economic and social entity.

From a low-rise city amidst the trees, surrounded by green lagoon oases, Tema is changing into a high-rise city for the middle classes, surrounded

55 'Mr. Emmanuel Oko Adjetey, Chairman of the Board of Directors of TDC, disclosed that the corporation generated a gross income of GH¢39.7 million, showing a growth of 37.5% over GH¢29.9 million (excluding revaluation gains) generated in 2012' in: Attenkah, R. (2014) 'Ghana: TDC to Commence Redevelopment of Tema Soon', 3 December, allafrica.com/stories/201412240888.html.

56 Ocloo, D.R. (2014) 'TDC takes possession of four block apartments within the Kaiser Flats', Graphic Online, 5 December, graphic.com.gh/news/general-news/34955-tdc-takes-possession-of-four-block-apartments-within-the-kaiser-flats.html.

by informal settlements. Formerly open spaces are built over. The clumps of trees along the roads and the parks as well as the big lagoons are first neglected; then they become filthy and finally, when it is difficult to see their value anymore, they are built over. Tema is becoming less recognisable as a social city, a beacon of Nkrumah's socialism, a pioneering place for modern Ghana, with the open urban design that symbolised a new society. This ambition has been abandoned.

As urbanisation speeds up, economic growth, climate refugees and a high birth rate ensure an influx of residents to the entire coastal zone. Tema is slowly becoming one of the rare planned parts of the 500-mile long mega-region starting at Abidjan and extending to Lagos. Thus Ecumenopolis, the global city that Doxiadis envisioned in the 1960s, is actually materialising today.

Applying the 10 principles of the Manual

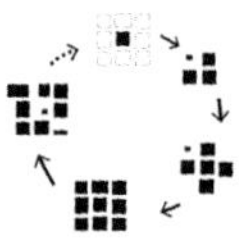

Planning is an ongoing process

After the masterplan for Tema was revised and detailed several times in the 1960s, there have been no major updates or integral changes in 50 years. Certain parts of the original plan which have never fully materialised, for example the city centre, have been the subject of new (unrealised) proposals. A new integral vision for Tema, taking into account recent regional demographic and socio-economic developments, has not been made.

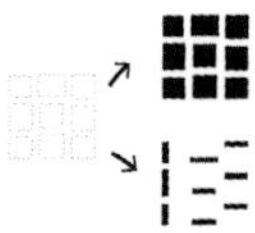

Plan for adaptivity

The grid of the urban plan, aiming to provide a spatial framework for incremental infill and building, has proved to be a proper instrument to guide the growth of the city, up until recently, when the original Communities were completed. The growth and expansion that was foreseen in the original masterplan by extending the grid to the north was prevented, a.o. by the unplanned, spontaneous urbanisation in the region. The grid also makes redevelopment easier; as long as the main lines of the grid are being respected, many different developments are possible within the Communities.

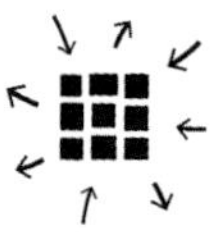

No New Town is an island

Tema's planning process shows a close relation with the planning of the region; an awareness and anticipation of developments in the region over time. Ghana has a strong national policy for spatial planning and this is an essential instrument to deal with large scale urbanisation. Tema has become part of the mega-region along the coast of West-Africa and its urban development should be seen in this perspective.

Use no cut and paste universal model

Tema is the opposite of this principle: the city is an almost universal model developed by Doxiadis and applied with slight adaptations in many different countries in the developing world. Its modernistic principles show in the rigid zoning of programmes, the abundance of infrastructure and open space, and the modernist housing typologies. The concentration of all employment in one big industrial terrain was favoured instead of mixing it with the housing Communities. Small scale and informal economy was forgotten and ultimately introduced by the residents themselves.

Embrace new ideas
Tema boasts several technological innovations: it was the first city in Africa that introduced electricity, water, sewage, private bathrooms and street lighting. Social innovations include neighbourhood services like schools, churches and community services that provided the opportunity for community building, emancipation and personal development. Every Community included a church, a community centre, a cinema and health centres, facilities that together shape a regulating and pedagogical system to achieve a democratic, open society.

Infrastructure and mobility for all, from the start
Tema was built with a good internal infrastructure network and connected with Accra by the highway and the train. However, as the present traffic chaos shows, provisions for public transport are not sufficient or even dilapidated. The train doesn't run anymore. Private trotro's perform the only bus services. There are insufficient provisions for bicycles and pedestrians. They need to be provided for in the urban plan, not just cars.

Use a blue-green infrastructure as the central framework
On both sides of Tema, lagoons are being protected by the international Ramsar Convention on wetlands. However, maintenance is insufficient and the lagoons are polluted. Water management in the urban areas of Tema is also insufficient, with regular floods as result. The original internal green network of trees and green spaces in the Communities has been compromised due to bad maintenance and illegal land use.

Incorporate local cultural heritage(s)
Local culture was not so much an inspiration for the original masterplanners. Housing typologies favoured the western, nuclear family, while Tema residents still often lived as extended families or rented out rooms, causing overcrowding and other problems. However, because of the abundance of open space the inhabitants of Tema have been able to adapt their houses and Tema has developed into an African city despite its European roots. In the 1960s a tabula rasa approach was seen as the preferred option. We have since learned that the creation of a tabula rasa means also the destruction of the existing landscape, village and/or social structure. In the present urban renewal schemes in Tema, economic motives have led to discarding these lessons.

Combine top-down and bottom-up
The development of Tema shows the importance of the right organisation and 'design' of the institutions. Building and developing the city on the one hand and maintaining it on the other hand are equally important. By separating the two in different institutions (TDC and TMA), many organisational and financial problems arose in Tema. Cooperation between the organisations or concentration of responsibilities into one organisation is necessary to streamline this process. While Tema is definitely a top-down project, there are lower income neighbourhoods realised as sites & services projects, with houses (partially) built by residents themselves. They are a successful part of the masterplan and have developed into attractive areas.

New Towns need diversity
The masterplan provided for a range of incomes, from blue collar workers to upper class. However, Tema was only inclusive as long as the political will, policies and funding existed. After Nkrumah, it proved that social housing is not viable on a commercial basis. The lack of affordable housing created large informal settlements around Tema with a low quality of life. Presently, with the regeneration of Tema, the difference in living standards among the Communities in Tema and the surrounding areas is being exacerbated. This inequality is also increasing at regional scale, making differences more visible as they become more acute.

Mitchell's Plain: The Translation of a British Urban Planning Model to South Africa's Apartheid New Town

Anne Sophie Erdl

The British New Town model is one of the most powerful models that has influenced the planning and development of New Towns since the 1950s. Planners, engineers, and urban policy officials from all over the world have carried out large-scale developments according to this model to contain metropolitan growth by concentrating the population in new cities and towns.[1]

Developed at a time when international planning practises in the postcolonial world expanded and diversified, this model not only influenced the construction of New Towns in the global North, but also in the postcolonial world.[2] It diffused through multiple channels, including education for foreign planners in the UK, the work of British consultants abroad, agencies promoting British planning abroad, and international conferences.[3] This transfer lead to the development of New Towns based on the model in former British colonies such as Sri Lanka, India, South Africa, and Ghana, but also in other countries such as Brazil, whereby these country's planning structures and cultures were shaped profoundly.[4] However, as with every building, design or planning model, the British New Town model originates from specific cultural values, unique historical experiences, geographies, and ideological beliefs.[5] Accordingly, the transfer of the model was challenged by local economic, cultural, and political conditions different from those faced in the UK, such as more rapid urbanisation, lower financial recourses, and different political systems.[6]

This challenged transfer can be exemplified by the case of South Africa. Apartheid, the institutionalised racial segregation and discrimination against non-white South Africans, largely determined the country's planning system from 1949 until 1994. During this period, urbanisation was controlled by policies that legally required the segregation of each race into separate areas, which caused the development of many New Towns and townships for non-white citizens, which were influenced by the British New Town model.[7] This was, however, originally built up

1 Levine, B. M. (1983) 'British New Town Planning: A Wave of the Future or a Ripple across the Atlantic'. *Journal of Legislation* 10.1, P. 12. See also: Provoost, M. (2014) 'Exporting New Towns. The Welfare City in Africa'. In Swenarton, M., Avermaete, T. and Van den Heuvel, D. (eds.), *Architecture and the welfare state*. London: Routledge.

2 Levine, B. M. (1983) ibid.

3 Ward, S. (2010) 'Transnational Planners in a Postcolonial World'. In Healey, P. and R. Upton (eds.) *Crossing borders: international exchange and planning practices*. London and New York: Routledge.

4 Ward S. (2010). See also: Leao Rego, R. (2010) 'Traveling ideas: British Town & Country Planning Models and the transformation of Brazilian tropical hinterlands'. Paper presented to the 14th IPHS Conference, 12-15 July, Istanbul, Turkey.

5 King, A. D. (1980) 'Exporting planning: the colonial and neo-colonial experience'. In: Cherry, G. E. (ed.), *Shaping an urban world*, Vol. 2. London: Mansell.

6 King, A. D. (1980).

7 Provoost, M. (2015) 'The Openheid State. From closed to open society in Cape Town'. In M. Provoost (ed.), *Cape Town Densification as a cure for a segregated city*. Rotterdam: Nai010. See also: Watson, V. (1993) 'Regeneration of the Apartheid city'. Paper presented to the Vision of Cape Town conference, 7-8 October, Cape Town.

on egalitarian ideals of social justice and within a democracy that values opportunities for personal development, emancipation and social progress for all; ideals and values that are reflected in the model's principles. Thus, the model completely contradicted South Africa's political ideology and spatial planning system of discrimination and segregation but was 'applied' nevertheless. Today, most of these South African New Towns are characterised by poverty, unemployment, crime, and overcrowding; a development that raises the question how the model was actually contextualised, and what the consequences of this process are. This question is the focus of this essay.[8] It provides a historical review of the development of Mitchell's Plain, a New Town in Cape Town's Metropolitan Area built in the late 1970 and thereby focuses on the consequences resulting from translating[9] a British planning model into a South African context and underlines the challenges faced by many South African New Towns and townships.

To do so, this essay draws on urban policy mobility research, which aims to better understand how and why cities are produced in and through cross-scale circulations, transnational relationships and movements.[10] One feature of this field discerns that mobile urban policies and models rarely travel as complete 'packages' but that they 'move in bits and pieces (…) and they therefore "arrive" not as replicas but as policies already-in-transformation' creating new forms of spatial development.[11] Hence, the resulting dynamic in the policymaking process is not a simple emulation and linear replication across sites, but a more complex process of nonlinear reproduction in which policies mutate, morph and thereby create new urbanities, urban policies, and models.[12] This argument is closely linked to Robinson's view of cities as 'ordinary cities' in the context of postcolonial urban theory.[13] She proposes a cosmopolitan perspective on urban theory by focusing intently on the essential character of cities as sites of difference, thereby highlighting the equivalent standing of all urban centres across the North-South divide. According to Robinson, the concept of modernity needs to be dislocated and reconfigured, as it is associated with the global North. Instead of regarding the circulation of modernity to countries outside the West as 'imitative' leading to 'alternative modernities', Robinson argues that an appropriation of modernity takes places. Following this reasoning, the circulation and translation of, for example, urban planning models lead to new, different urbanities instead of altered versions of the 'original' model.[14]

The translation process & the British New Town model characteristics

In order to examine the localisation of the model in the case of Mitchell's Plain in depth, an analytical framework consisting of the concept of the 'translation process' and the characteristics of the British New Town model, is used in this essay. Derived from Social and Technology studies, the concept of the translation process argues that once models travel, they are de-territorialised from their original setting and re-territorialized

8 This essay is based on Erdl, A.S. (2018) 'Localizing Mobile Planning Models: The translation of the British New Town Model into South Africa's urban planning practices'. (Unpublished master thesis) Utrecht University, Utrecht, The Netherlands. See also: Monstadt, J. and Erdl, A.S. (2018) 'Localizing Mobile Planning Models: The translation of the British New Town Model into South Africa's urban planning practices'. Manuscript submitted for publication.

9 The term 'translation' refers here to the process of how urban models actually become adopted and inserted into a new context.

10 Jacobs, J. M. (2012) 'Urban geographies I: Still thinking cities relationally'. Progress in Human Geography, 36.3, Pp. 412-422.

11 Peck, J. and Theodore, N. (2010) 'Mobilizing policy: Models, methods, and mutations'. Geoforum, 41.2. P. 170.

12 Ibid.

13 Robinson, J. (2006) Ordinary cities: between modernity and development. London: Routledge.

14 Robinson, J. (2006).

in new settings.[15] The working of models presuppose methods and techniques that consist of 'embodied knowledge' that does not travel with the objectified model and neither do institutions required for the model to work. Therefore, as the model enters into a new setting with a different institutional set-up and infrastructure, it changes because it needs to be adopted, appropriated, and altered to connected to these new circumstances.[16] Four different forms of translation can be discerned following Monstadt and Schramm: (1) adaptation: the alteration of the existing planning legislations and technologies to comply with the circulating ideals; (2) appropriation: the adjustment of the circulating ideal to accommodate the available urban planning practices which remain basically unchanged; (3) hybridization: the creation of something new by combining elements of the new ideal or model with the existing one; (4) refusal: the rejection of the travelling ideals and a persistence of the already existing planning ideals.[17]

The New Town's general characteristics as defined in the British New Towns Act of 1946 can be summarised as follows: With respect to the socio-economic structure, the New Towns would be as 'self-contained' as possible, in that sufficient homes and facilities were to be provided to enable the residents to work and live within the New Town.[18] Furthermore, the model aimed to create socially balanced communities, thereby bringing all income groups and people with different backgrounds together. Concerning the towns' sizes and densities, the Act recommended housing 30,000 to 50,000 people in low-density configurations. The New Towns' design would follow a list of broad principles including:

- The neighbourhood unit concept as a means of creating a sense of community: Housing is built around community facilities, particularly schools, embedded within cells defined by superblocks.
- The functional zoning of industrial and residential areas to separate housing from industry (with its polluting noise, smells and traffic), but easy transit between the two would be provided by pedestrians and transit links.
- A pedestrian-friendly town centre and covered shopping malls to allow a safe and pleasant shopping experience and emphasise public space and social life.
- Separated pedestrian and vehicles networks, allowing people to move freely and safely: corridors, underpasses or overpasses make it unnecessary for pedestrians to cross busy roads and allow motorized transport to move more rapidly.
- Integrated green infrastructure networks into the town's fabric along transport corridors and through parks, 'green wedges', and verges, separating neighbourhoods and transport modes.
- Spaces for social and community development located within a short walking distance of homes, using multi-functional spaces and facilities.
- A mix of housing types for different income groups in one neighbourhood to create socially balanced communities.[19]

15 Behrends, A., Park, S. J., and Rottenburg, R. (2014) 'Travelling models: introducing an analytical concept to globalisation studies'. In: Behrends, A., Park, S. J., and Rottenburg, R. ((eds.), Travelling models in African conflict management: translating technologies of social ordering. Leiden and Boston: Brill.
16 Rottenburg, R. (2009) Far-fetched facts: a parable of development aid. Cambridge: MIT Press.
17 Monstadt, J. and Schramm, S. (2017) 'Toward the Networked City? Translating Technological ideals and Planning Models in Water and Sanitation Systems in Dar es Salaam'. International Journal of Urban and Regional Research 41.1. Pp. 104-125.
18 Town and Country Planning Association (2014) 'New Towns and Garden Cities – Lessons for Tomorrow, Stage 1: An Introduction to the UK's New Towns and Garden Cities'. London: TCPA.
19 Town and Country Planning Association (2014).

A historical review of Mitchell's Plain in the next section reflects on the development of this particular town by focusing on these New Town model principles. The analytical framework described above is used to analyse the translation of the UK model to the context of Mitchell's Plain.[20] Finally, the question is asked: what are the resulting effects of this translation process?

Mitchell's Plain – the South African apartheid New Town

Mitchell's Plain is a New Town situated 27km southeast of the central business district of Cape Town in the Cape Flats, a large area of wind-blown, flat land, covered predominantly by sand. First thoughts were devoted to its construction by the Cape Town City Council in the late 1960s as housing for the so-called 'coloured population' was urgently needed.[21] This shortage was predominantly a result of the implementation of the Groups Areas Act of 1966 and its consequential forced resettlement of Cape Town's coloured communities from the central areas of the inner city of Cape Town such as District Six, Claremont, Wynberg, Monwbray and Newlands.[22] On top of that, Cape Town experienced large-scale migration of coloured people to the city that was encouraged

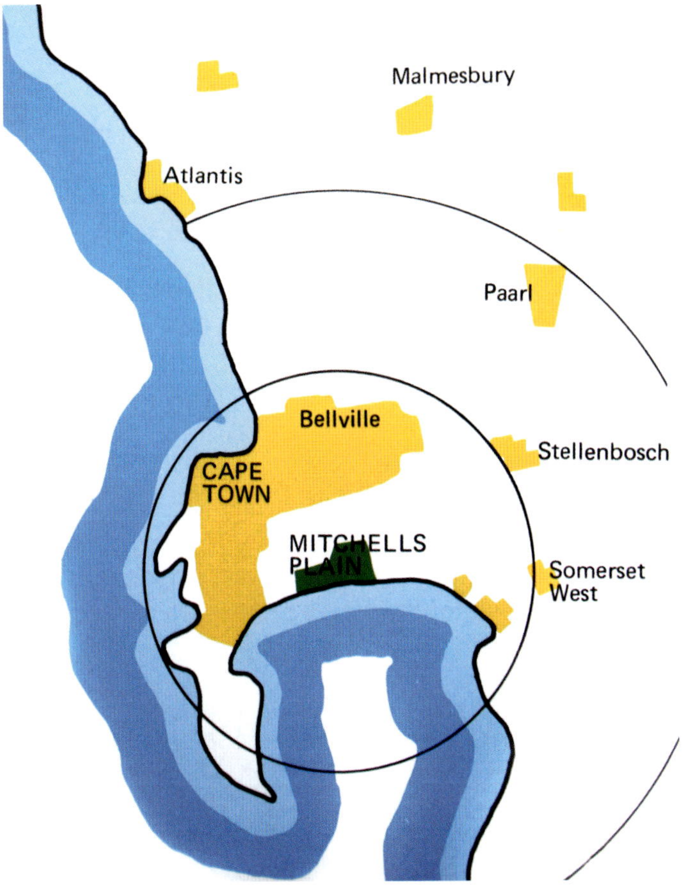

The Metropolitan Area of Cape Town (Source: Brand, J. Building a New Town, City Engineer's Department, Cape Town)

20 The analysis is informed by qualitative data collected through empirical research conducted from September 2017 to January 2018, which includes interviews held with South African academics, contemporary witnesses, representatives of local and provincial government and local municipal planners. In addition, countless official city and state documents, grey literature, newspaper articles and pictures found in archives were assessed, and site observations were performed to examine the present situation.

21 'Coloured' refers to a person of mixed European ("white") and African ("black") or Asian ancestry, as officially defined by the South African government from 1950 to 1991 See: Mabin, D. (1977) 'The development of Mitchell's Plain'. Paper presented at the Conference of Institute of Housing Management. September 1977, Durban.

22 Mabin, D. (1977). See also: Madell, C. (2016) 'A historical account of the impact of land use planning in the Western Cape – elusive spatial and economic integration and inclusiveness'. In: Western Cape Government (ed.) Land use planning law reform in the western cape: the road to transformation. Cape Town: Western Cape Government.

by industrialization and the Coloured Labour Preference Area Act of 1955, which worsened the housing shortage.[23] In addition, the poverty and perceived 'lawlessness' of the coloured population was seen as a problem by the local authorities, as unrest in coloured townships increased in the 1970s and became more linked to the growing resistance found in black townships.[24]

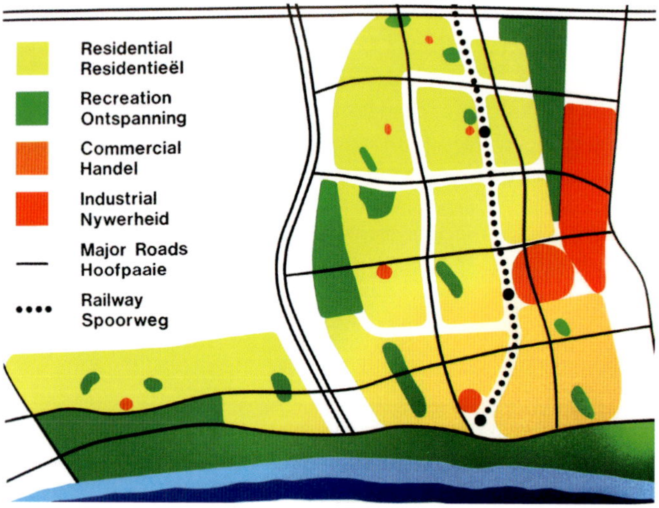

'Development Guide Plan / Ontwikkeling Gidsplan' of Mitchell's Plain (Source: The City of Cape Town: Planning Unit Mitchell's Plain)

A solution to the housing shortage and 'social problems' was believed to be found in the development of a New Town. In 1974, after the central government gave its permission, the City of Cape Town started planning the town, which when completed in 1984 would have a population of 250,000 coloured residents.[25] The ultimate goal was to allow homeownership and to provide a complete, improved residential environment, instead of only erecting a specific number of housing units without community amenities that 'reinforced the self-perpetuating nature of poverty' (as done previously in places like Bonteheuwl, Manenberg and Hanover Park).[26] This, it was hoped, would encourage upward social mobility, create community interest, increase the levels of economic welfare and productivity and reduce poverty.[27] The social structure envisioned was that of a coloured middle class. The administrative delivery was in the hands of the Cape Town City's Engineering department, in co-operation with the national Department of Community Development, which financed the project in the forms of subsidised loans to the Cape Town City Council.[28] A special section within the municipal Engineering Department was set up to oversee the project in 1975. This new section, the Planning and Design Unit, consisted of a multi-disciplinary team of specialists, including civil engineers, architects, planners, urban designers, and sociologists, of which five had been educated in the UK.[29]

The construction of the New Town started in 1975 and the first residents moved in a year later. A 31 km^2 piece of land was divided into 10 suburban

23 Brand, J. (1979) 'Building a New Town'. Cape Town: City Engineer's Department. See also: Morris, S.S. (1972) 'Good Hope: a first report on the development of Mitchell's Plain'. Cape Town: City Engineer's Department.

24 Brand, J. (1979) Op. cit. P. 22.

25 Ibid.

26 Ibid. P. 3

27 Ibid.

28 Deacon, J. (1979) 'Mitchell's Plain: An investment in the people'. Brochure, Information Service of South Africa, Pretoria.

29 Interview 2 (2017).

30 Mabin, D. (1977) Op. cit. P. 20.

31 Deacon, J. (1979) Op. cit. P. 26.

A typical neighbourhood lay-out in Mitchell's Plain. (Source: The City of Cape Town: Planning Unit Mitchell's Plain)

communities shaped by a hierarchical road grid system, a railway line, and natural features.[30] The road network divided the superblocks into units of approximately 2,000 families, based around a high school, primary schools, and a range of local facilities. These units were designed as classic neighbourhood units with a road hierarchy. To create an ease of movement for the inhabitants, the planners implemented separate pedestrian and vehicle networks. Pedestrian networks often included pathways and playgrounds linking quiet cul-de sacs, which were placed in relation to green spaces and community facilities to form a safe pedestrian circulation system. Traffic was restricted to widely-spaced arterial roads.[31] In addition, a railway line connecting Mitchell's Plain to the suburban railway system was opened in 1980. An open, green space system running north-south through the suburbs on both sides of the railway line formed an integrated green infrastructure network in the town and linked the primary schools and all the community facilities. Moreover, the Engineering Department realised the construction of a wide range

Residential unit of Mitchell's Plain in the late 1970's portraying the cul-de-sacs, green public spaces, pedestrian allies and limited access road. (Source: The Planning Unit of the City of Cape Town)

Two story town houses in Mitchell's Plain in the late 1970s. (Source: The Planning Unit of the City of Cape Town)

32 Brand, J. (1977) Op. cit. P. 22.
33 Van de Spuy, A. (1977) 'Mitchell's Plain Town Centre Outline Repost'. Cape Town: City Engineer's Department.
34 Brand, D. (1977) Op. cit. P. 22.
35 Interview 2 (2017).
36 Deacon, J. (1979) Op. cit. P. 26.
37 Mabin, D. (1977) Op. cit. P. 20.

of additional facilities, equipping each neighbourhood with a number of schools, children's play parks, sport fields, and a suburban centre including a community centre, and other municipal service facilities.[32] Some sites for churches and similar religious and welfare facilities were reserved for development. A town centre with a pedestrian shopping street was opened in 1980 in the geographical centre of the town and was envisaged as the major commercial, administrative, and cultural centre.[33] Throughout Mitchell's Plain, 70 different housing types were offered for sale to create communities and influence the formation of social groups, however, this architectural diversity was not intended to create a social balance of income groups as the town was envisioned purely for a middle class.[34] A few years later, council-housing dwellings were added on the east side of town in 1982 due to high political pressure for more affordable housing.[35]

In regard to the socio-economic profile of the New Town, the City Council envisaged a self-sufficient town that could provide all civic amenities and facilities to support its population. However, this vision did not include sufficient employment opportunities within the New Town.[36] The central government planning authorities discouraged industrial development near Mitchell's Plain in favour of work opportunities being created in Atlantis, another New Town 50 km to the north of Cape Town's CBD, which was designated as a growth point as part of the industrial decentralization policy. Mitchell's Plain did not qualify as a growth point because it was considered to be located too close to Cape Town and Atlantis.[37] Consequently, the only work opportunities within

Mitchell's Plain in the late 1970s. (Source: The Planning Unit of the City of Cape Town)

A street in Mitchell's Plain in the late 1970s. (Source: The Planning Unit of the City of Cape Town)

Mitchell's Plain would be generated through the commercial sector and light manufacturing activities, for which a few sites were zoned. In addition, the planners referred to two industrial areas bordering the development, Philippi and Ronde, which would provide work.[38]

38 Interview 2 (2017).

In 1983, massive construction contracts issued by the City Council ended, and private sector development started, which in a way marks the end of Mitchell's Plain's main development phase.[39] From the mid-1980s onwards, Mitchell's Plain became a site of political resistance against the apartheid regime, as the political and economic crisis that had begun to escalate in the mid-1970s, intensified on a national scale.[40] One of South Africa's major anti-apartheid organisations, The United Democratic Front, was founded in Mitchell's Plain in 1983, and throughout the 1980s rallies, civic and militant campaigns, and street battles characterised the town. As a reaction, the apartheid regime applied strict security measures, with barricades put up at entrance and exit points to prevent "unauthorized people" from entering the town.[41]

39 City Engineer's Department (1985) 'The history of Mitchell's Plain'. Cape Town: City Engineer's Department.
40 Dewar, D., Watson, V., Bassios, A., and Dewar, N. (1990) 'The structure and form of metropolitan Cape Town: Its origins, influences and performance'. Urban Problems Research Unit Working Paper 45. Cape Town: University of Cape Town.
41 Interview 4 (2017).
42 Ibid.
43 Interview 1 & 4 (2017).

Phasing and population sizes of the neighbourhoods of Mitchell's Plain (Source: The City of Cape Town: Planning Unit Mitchell's Plain)

The economic crisis also hit Mitchell's Plain. With the end of apartheid in 1991 and the following years of political transition, socio-economic tensions increased. By the late 1990s major areas of the New Town had deteriorated, and poverty, gangs, and drug abuse became prevalent in Mitchell's Plain.[42] Today, Mitchell's Plain houses around 300,000 residents of which 90 percent identify themselves as coloured, nine percent as black, and one percent as Asian or Indian. The socio-economic problems have not improved throughout the years. About 48 percent of the households live below the poverty line and crime and gang activity is still endemic in the area.[43]

The translation process

Having reviewed Mitchell's Plain development history, it becomes evident that the translation process of the British model created tensions and conflicts as the context of apartheid reflected in the vision for Mitchell's Plain was contradicting the original model's social values. In this section, this will be explained with reference to the characteristics of the model listed earlier, and the concepts used in the analytical framework.

Considering the socio-economic aspiration of British New Towns to create socially-balanced communities, it is clear that this characteristic was rejected by decision-makers involved with the design and implementation of Mitchell's Plain. In order to fit the British model (established in a social-democratic welfare state), to South Africa's political ideology of apartheid, the model's values and principles of social justice, equality, and opportunity for all had to be discarded. Segregation and the separation of 'races' dominated the urban planning practices at the time and thus the town was restricted to one ethnicity and one income group. The rental houses added later for the low-income groups are segregated from the rest of Mitchell's Plain and therefore did not contribute to creating socially-balanced communities. On the other hand, the socio-economic characteristic of 'self-containment' (referring to creating mixed-use communities for living and working), was partially applied in Mitchell's Plain. It had to be adjusted to accommodate the national planning legislations of decentralization that forbid the facilitation of work opportunities such as industrial sites in Mitchell's Plain, whereas the aspect of providing civic amenities and facilities was pursued. Regarding the design characteristics, five out of seven were adopted, namely the neighbourhood unit, the pedestrian-friendly town centre, the separated pedestrian and vehicle networks, the integrated green infrastructure network and the spaces for community and social development. This is due to the fact that the British model's motive of improving people's quality of life through the provision of a better built environment was in line with the Cape Town's planners' vision of upward social mobility achieved by improved surroundings. The design characteristics of zoning for industrial and residential areas, and the mix of housing typologies reflecting different income groups, were rejected.

Having considered the translation of each characteristic of the British New Town Model, it becomes clear that the model's translation as a whole was not a simple cut and paste, but rather a complex selective process. It was guided by South Africa's politics of industrial decentralization and most notably by the apartheid ideology of segregation, which contradicted the values embedded in the model. Consequently, in order to fit the model to the vision of creating a mono-ethnic, middle class town with an 'uplifting' residential environment, the socialistic features of the model were removed by changing or omitting certain characteristics, while adding others. This process therefore can be summarised as an appropriation of the model which created a new, local New Town model.

The consequences

Considering the situation in Mitchell's Plain today, forty years after its official opening, some consequences of the translation process of the New Town model have become apparent. From a *socio-economic perspective*, Mitchell's Plain is a large dormitory town, almost entirely dependent upon economic activities in other parts of the Cape Town metropolitan area, particularly the central business district. This is undoubtedly a result of the rejection of the self-containment characteristic, which included the omission of facilities that generate work opportunities. This has led to one-way commuting patterns creating congestion and overcrowded and expensive public transport, in addition to high unemployment rates.[44] In 2006, only 43 percent of the working age population of Mitchell's Plain were employed, a number which has only decreased in recent years.[45] Moreover, an astonishing 40 – 60 percent of the disposable income of Mitchell's Plain residents goes to public transport.[46] The municipality's strategy to conquer these problems has been to establish more work opportunities within Mitchell's Plain by attracting investment into the town and the adjacent areas. However, so far this initiative has met with

44 Interview 3 (2017).

45 Interview 3 & 4 (2017).

46 Ibid.

Shipping container converted into a barbershop situated in the backyard of a house facing a wide, limited access road (super channel) in Mitchell's Plain. (Photo: A. Erdl, 2017)

minor success, as many investors still perceive Mitchell's Plain to be a risky investment location due to continuing crime and drug problems. Furthermore, a national urban renewal programme upgraded the town centre in 2003 aiming to attract more commercial activities but had little success due to the establishment of a big shopping mall developed by the private sector on the northern outskirts of the town.[47]

In regard to the *social structure* of Mitchell's Plain, we can observe a very segregated and fragmented town, mainly caused by the refusal to create socially-balanced communities. Throughout the years, each neighbourhood developed differently, as some housing designs turned out to be more resilient toward the changing environment than others, and thus became more valuable over time.[48] This has led to a segregation of residents with similar income levels, cultural and racial backgrounds, and other demographic characteristics within neighbourhoods, which has created very homogenous, sterile environments and little exchange among residents. This is seen as problematic by the City Council, especially because many neighbourhoods are characterised by extreme, concentrated poverty, which is associated with negative social effects (higher crime, decreased mental and physical health), and lower economic prospects (both for current residents and their children over their lifetimes).[49] To readdress this segregation and concentration of poverty, the City of Cape Town is trying to attract investment to the area and especially more affluent families to create a greater mix of income groups. Unfortunately, the adopted neighbourhood unit concept further exacerbates segregation with its inward orientation and limited entrances

47 Interview 1 (2017).

48 Interview 1 (2017).

49 Interview 1 & 4 (2017).

Front yard of a house occupied by an illegal kiosk. (Photo: A. Erdl, 2017)

to the neighbourhoods. In Britain, this design element was used with the intention to bring people from different backgrounds together and create communities. Through the appropriation of the New Town model in Mitchell's Plain, the neighbourhood unit contributes to the complete opposite of that. This shows that the failure to include one element of the model (in this case, the socially-balanced communities), has an effect on the function of another component: the neighbourhood unit.

Considering the *cityscape*, plots of decayed, vacant land, unmaintained public green space, playgrounds, and civic amenities characterise Mitchell's Plain. The Cape Flat's summers with their low rainfall and strong winds, in addition to deep sand, make it very difficult to grow any vegetation other than fynbos.[50] Nevertheless, the planners adopted the model's design characteristic of a generous green infrastructure network, which derives from a different geographical setting with a completely different climate. This has resulted in low quality and high maintenance costs for the open spaces, which the City has never been able to bear.[51] The same accounts for the adaptation of providing spaces for social and community development. Many of the plots initially reserved for community facilities have remained undeveloped and the facilities built have not been maintained due to the local authority's financial constraints.[52] This indicates that local geographic and economic conditions were not carefully considered. Consequently, instead of a built environment that enables social 'uplifting', most public space in Mitchell's Plain is now a setting for crime and social disorder. In order to address this challenge, the city is considering re-zoning public spaces into smaller

50 Brand, J. (1979) Op. cit. P. 22. Fynbos refers to a treeless vegetation type associated with the Cape region similar to heathland.

51 Interview I (2017).

52 Interview I & 5 (2017).

Wide arterial road and walled housing facing it. (Photo: A. Erdl, 2017)

parcels to make them available to the private market. A study by the City conducted in 2016 assessed all open spaces in Mitchell's Plain, and indicated which ones can be subdivided to promote densification and employment opportunities.[53]

Furthermore, the cityscape is characterised by considerable appropriations by its residents throughout the years. Due to evolving crime issues, today, the vast majority of housing units has been completely fenced and walled off. This has led to walled pedestrian alleyways that do not allow for surveillance and therefore have been increasingly perceived as safety risks. Residents' initiatives have successfully promoted and realised the closing of many of those passages.

As a consequence of these appropriations and of the general low car ownership amongst Mitchell's Plain's residents, pedestrian flows have changed. Contrary to plans, people now use the limited access routes originally designed for cars.[54] These more concentrated pedestrian flows are seen as an opportunity by informal traders and small-scale enterprises who occupy spaces along the superblock channels (with limited access routes), and on major intersections. Through this appropriation of the rigid, mono-functional design, the streets have now turned into actual urban roads.[55]

Today, Mitchell's Plain is a large dormitory town segregated along economic lines and characterised by few job opportunities, a decayed built environment, poverty and crime. This situation reflects the long-term perspective of the town's translation experience as a combination of the socio-economic and political developments of Cape Town, and the British New Town model's appropriation on this site.

53 Interview 1 (2017).

54 Interview 1 & 4 (2017).

55 Interview 1 & 4 (2017).

Conclusion

The historical review of Mitchell's Plain reveals that during the process of being inserted into a new context, the British New Town model was appropriated and thereby a new, unique urban planning model was created. The social-democratic characteristics of the British model did not coincide with the local political setting of apartheid in South Africa. Consequently, the social ambitions of this model were rejected, while the formal aspects were adopted. This had devastating effects for the residents of Mitchell's Plain, because the translation process caused the complete opposite of what was originally intended by the creators of the British planning ideal. It turned from enabling to confining.

From a more general perspective, the study shows that the New Town model, as any other planning model, is a system comprising of a set of related components that work together in a particular environment. Changing or leaving out one element of the system affects other components and ultimately the working of the model as a whole. Decoupling the system from its local context and placing it into a new one has also been shown to affect the functioning of the model. Thus, as the long-term perspective of the translation processes in the case Mitchell's Plain shows, the consequences of these changes can hardly be foreseen, making the transfer of planning models a risky endeavour that can have serious effects. That is why we need a more critical outlook on the process of transferring urban planning models from one context to another: planning practices need to be more bilateral and culturally nuanced.[56] Ultimately, planning must respond to the particular context within which it is practiced and needs to recognise and be informed by the particular personality and regionalism of any area; that is the relationship between physiography, climate, flora and fauna, history, culture, economy, lifestyle, and feeling of identity which form the qualitative character of that area and which make it different from any other area.

In addition, the study indicates that the transfer of planning ideas and models is not a simple copy or repetition of what happened elsewhere. Instead, this case study provides evidence for the creation of a new New Town Model. As illustrated, the British model derives from specific values and variables, and had to be translated to connect to the new site to which it was transferred. Since every site is different, the outcomes of this translation vary from locale and domain. Therefore, this study supports Robinson's (2006) argument that circulations of modernity to countries outside the west are not acts of 'imitation' creating 'alternative modernities', but rather acts of re-invention, which create new urban modernities. From this perspective, African New Towns can no longer be interpreted as abnormal cases of European models, but as contextual translations to specific places.

56 Also see: Monstadt, J. and Schramm, S. (2017) 'Toward the Networked City? Translating Technological ideals and Planning Models in Water and Sanitation Systems in Dar es Salaam'. International Journal of Urban and Regional Research 41.1. Pp. 104-125.

As part of the research I conducted five interviews with (former) designers, managers and councillors of both Mitchell's Plain and Atlantis. They requested to maintain anonymous. Therefore they are referred to by their profession. List of interviews:

1 - Urban Designer Mitchell's Plain, Planning and Building Development Management City of Cape Town, November 2017

2 - Former Director of Planning Services, Planning Unit Mitchell's Plain, December 2017

3 - Urban Planner Atlantis, Planning and Building Development Management City of Cape Town, November 2017

4 - Ward Councillor Mitchell's Plain, City of Cape Town, December 2017

5 - District Manager: Mitchell's Plain, Planning and Building Development Management City of Cape Town, November 2017

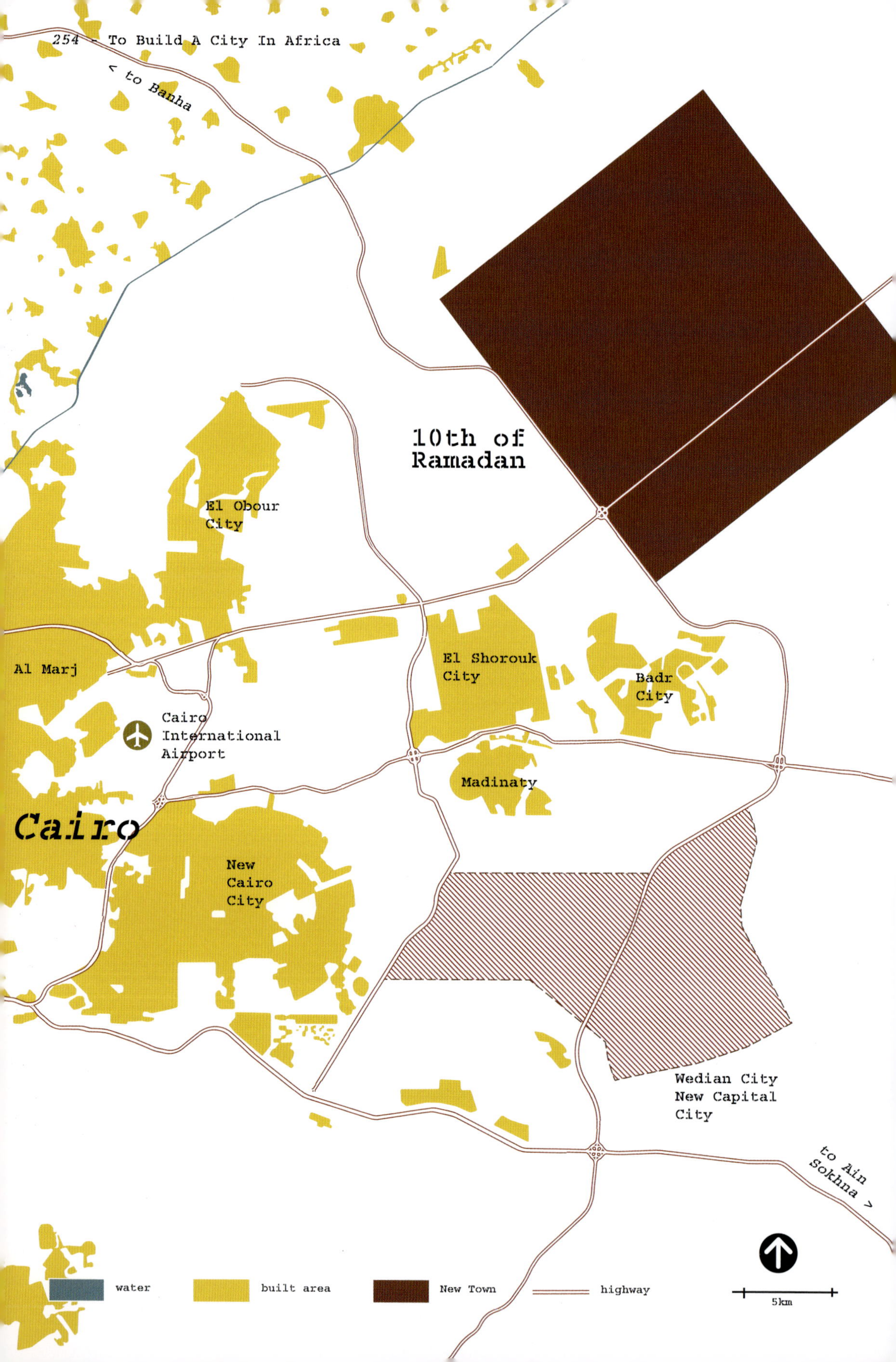

< to Banha
10th of Ramadan
El Obour City
El Shorouk City
Badr City
Al Marj
Cairo International Airport
Madinaty
Cairo
New Cairo City
Wedian City New Capital City
to Ain Sokhna >
water
built area
New Town
highway
5km

CASE STUDY

10th of Ramadan, Egypt

'If you build it, will they come?'

To conquer the desert

Seen from the sky, Egypt is a vast, dust coloured land with a narrow green 'Y' yawning open at the Mediterranean Sea and sliding south into Lake Nasser. Despite being a huge country, about 95% of Egyptians live on just five per cent of its land: inside the borders of the fertile Nile Valley. It's a statistic that is often repeated because it immediately conveys the pattern of human occupation that has characterised this country for thousands of years. Slowly at first, then more quickly in the decades after the Second World War, this precious green land has been eaten up by urban growth. In 1974, everything changed when an idea that had been taking shape in the national consciousness for a few decades was finally put into policy: Egypt would 'conquer the desert' and redistribute its burgeoning population across the white sands of the Sahara.

It is logical that Egyptians would see the desert as a sort of challenge: a Saharan version of the United States' nineteenth century 'Manifest Destiny' to move west, no matter how punishing the consequences. Beginning with the 1956 Cairo masterplan, the idea of urban development in the desert began to form part of the national narrative.[1] The 1956 plan announced six industry-based satellite cities to be built around greater Cairo. Only one, however, was actually constructed: the satellite city of Helwan. In 1969, a new Cairo masterplan called for four new satellite cities and strict limits on Cairo's growth: after the capital reached an anticipated 9.5 million inhabitants, all future growth would be redirected to the planned New Towns. But like its predecessor, this plan also failed to materialise.

A few years later, in the heady days following Egypt's victory in the 1973 Arab-Israeli Jom Kippoer War, President Anwar Sadat presented his October Working Paper.[2] The Paper detailed his continued commitment to socialism but simultaneously introduced his 'Open Door' economic policy, figuratively opening the door to private sector, foreign and domestic investment. This was largely seen as a reversal of former

1 Stewart, D. (1996). Cities in the Desert: The Egyptian New-Town Program. Annals of the Association of American Geographers,86: (3), 459-480.

2 Sadat, A. (April 1974) The October Working Paper. Cairo: Ministry of Information, State Information Service.

President Gamal Nasser's Soviet-friendly socialist economic policies. The Paper helped consolidate state support for desert New Towns, envisioning their redistribution of urban nodes and incentives to industry as a key aspect of Egypt's future growth and development. A modernised economic plan, coupled with an exciting opportunity for Egyptian planners created new cities and towns that would redefine Egypt's urban organisation and usher in a more modern era.

As the Open Door policy quickly took effect, international attention from companies looking to expand into Egypt began to grow.[3] Faced with this new popularity, the Egyptian government decided that all future international industry should be located outside of existing cities, in new industrial centres. This meant that the first New Town, 10th of Ramadan, would have to accommodate the 'increasing demands from international firms for industrial sites near Cairo. The government 'felt' that this influx of new business should not add to the overpopulation and congestion in Cairo but rather should form the basis of a self-sufficient new city.'[4] The Ministry of Housing and Reconstruction's Terms of Reference outlined the government's goals for the New Town: 'to increase national and regional income; to provide opportunities for relief of population pressures in Cairo; to increase the industrial base of the country; and to diversify and improve employment opportunities.'[5] In short, the Egyptian New Town programme was created first and foremost because the Egyptian government needed somewhere to house the international industries that were knocking on their door. In this sense, the entire programme can be read as a direct result of Sadat's liberalising policies. Just three years after his Paper, President Sadat announced the construction of 10th of Ramadan in the desert between Cairo and Ismailiya: the first of many Egyptian New Towns.

Named for the date that marked the beginning of the 19-day Arab-Israeli War in 1973, the establishment of 10th of Ramadan was a populist move by an increasingly unpopular President Sadat. As his Open Door policies began to create a new class of rich entrepreneurs, importers and business(wo)men, the improvements that had been expected by the average Egyptian didn't materialise. Rampant unemployment and poverty continued unabated. Inflation, high prices and competition from foreign imports were the main results that most Egyptians saw from Sadat's policies. Violent food riots rocked the country the same year 10th of Ramadan was announced, tensions were high in rural communities and labour unions were getting restless. Against this increasingly desperate backdrop, 10th of Ramadan was offered as a grand-scale solution that would provide one 100,000 jobs and half a million homes.

Another two years passed in a flurry of administrative and financial mayhem, until in 1979, the New Urban Communities Authority (NUCA) was established within the Ministry of Housing and Reconstruction (now MHUUD).[6] NUCA was granted the right to declare special development zones on desert land, all of which was (and remains) owned by the state. 'Furthermore,' writes economist and urban planner David Sims, who has

3 This policy was meant to attract Foreign Direct Investment and accommodate it through New Towns. In a way, this approach can be read as a foreshadowing of similar situations elsewhere in Africa today.

4 Arab Republic of Egypt Ministry of Housing and Reconstruction (September 1974) *Terms of Reference for the Industrial Area and Associated City Master Plan Study*. P. 1.

5 Arab Republic of Egypt Ministry of Housing and Reconstruction (September 1974). Op. cit. P. 2.

6 The Ministry of Housing and Reconstruction is now called the Ministry of Housing, Utilities and Urban Development (MHUUD).

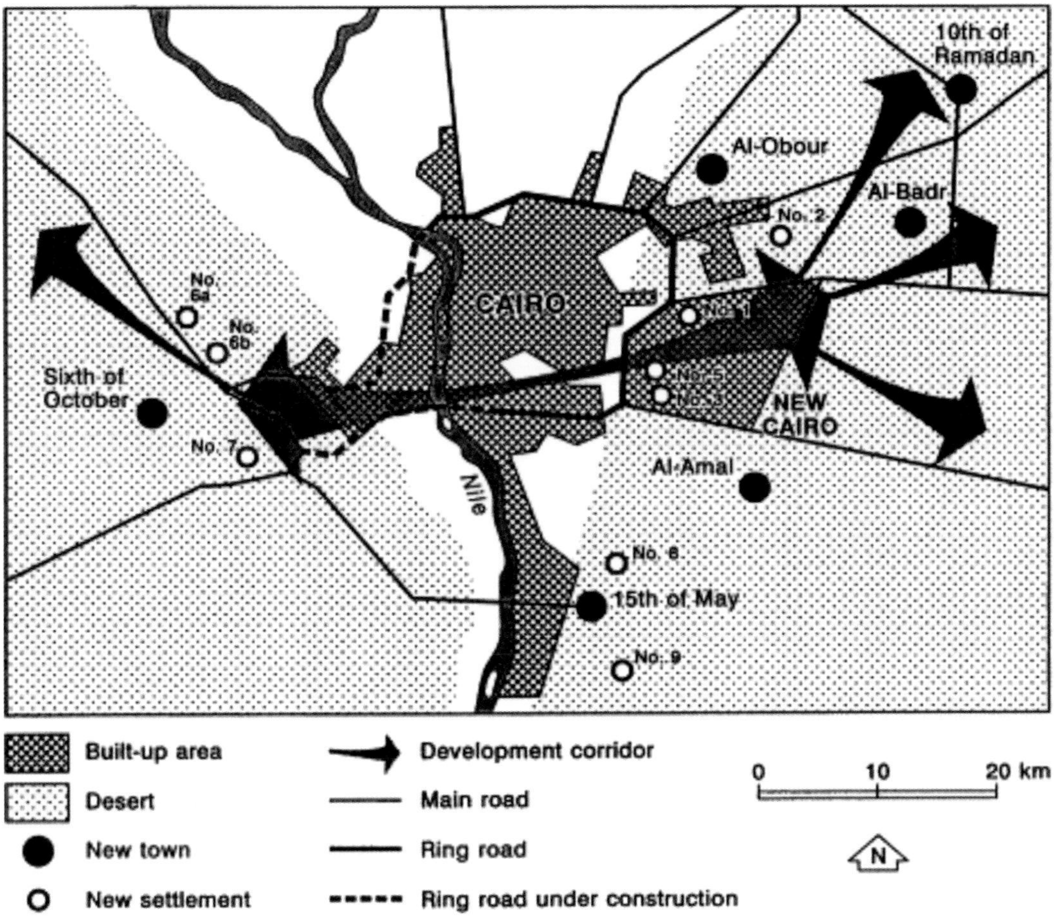

The 1969/1970 masterplan for Cairo by the Ministry of Housing proposed a polynuclear approach through development of four New Towns: 6th of October, Al Badr, El Obour, and a West Bank project which was never built. The masterplan was never executed, but the three proposed New Towns were eventually carried over into 1983 masterplan. (Source: Sutton, K. and Fahmi, W. (2001) Cairo's urban growth and strategic masterplans in the light of Egypt's 1996 population census results. Cities Vol 18, Iss 3. Pp. 135-149.)

studied Egyptian New Towns extensively: 'the [same] law gave NUCA the right to develop and sell lands within these special zones and retain these revenues to finance further development. Such a right over lands was unique, something neither govern-orates nor ministries enjoyed.'[7] Within months, NUCA became the most powerful urban planning body in Egypt.

Forty-one New Towns

Following this bold start and the subsequent planning approval of five additional New Towns (Sixth of October, El-Sadat, El-Obour, 15th of May, and New Domiat), the 1983 masterplan for Cairo was developed with input from French consultants and imagined an additional 10 'New Settlements' to provide housing for 900,000 residents, although these were never realised as planned.[8]

7 Sims goes on to write that after maturing, NUCA New Towns should revert to the same form of municipal administration as other Egyptian towns and cities. As of 2018, not a single New Town has passed out of NUCA's hands. Sims, D. (2012) Understanding Cairo: The Logic of a City Out of Control. Cairo: The American University in Cairo Press. P. 77.

8 The 1983 Master Plan was developed by the Ministry of Development and Construction, the GOPP, and in consultation with the IUERIF Institute

Egypt's cities, especially informal settlements, are quickly expanding into limited agriculture land. (Photo: R. Keeton, 2016)

The quick succession of scrapped masterplans between 1956 and 1983 was primarily a result of Cairo's rapid growth in the second half of the twentieth century. Plans anticipated population numbers that seemed reasonable, only to be outpaced by actual growth statistics that verged on the fantastical. What drove greater Cairo's enormous increase from 4.9 million in 1960 to more than 18 million in 2016?[9] Part of the answer is Egypt's high fertility rate. In Cairo and surrounding areas, most of the population growth has been from natural repopulation.[10] Combined with falling infant mortality rates and increasing life expectancies, higher birth rates are projected to continue driving population numbers up in the foreseeable future.

The increase is not, as one might expect, from significant rural-to-urban migration. In fact, Egypt has one of the lowest rates of rural-to-urban migration in the world. Unlike most African countries, the proportion of urban Egyptians to rural Egyptians has remained steady since 1976.[11] Timothy Mitchell, Professor of Middle Eastern Studies at Columbia University, points to rural Egyptians' *proximity to density* in the form of widespread small towns and villages that provide accessible services to even the most remotely placed citizens as an explanation for this phenomenon.[12] In striking contrast to the continuously rehashed narrative of almost all Egyptians crowded into Cairo and Alexandria, Mitchell presents a more nuanced imagery of interconnectedness among rich networks of small urban nodes.

and OTUI, two French consultancy firms. See: El-Sawy, K., et al (2016) 'Detection of Land Use and Land Cover Changes for New Cairo Area, Using Remote Sensing and GIS', International Journal of Science and Research (IJSR), Vol 5 (2): 1186.

9 Estimates vary; these numbers come from CAPMAS, the Egyptian Central Agency for Public Mobilisation and Statistics. See: www.capmas.gov.eg/

10 After a steady decline over half a century, average fertility rates began climbing again around 2005. From an all-time low of 2.8 children per woman, Egyptian women now give birth to an average of 3.5 children. See: www.economist.com/news/middle-east-and-africa/21653623-challenge-egypts-rising-fecundity-too-fertile-crescent

In the years following the announcement of 10th of Ramadan in 1977, the character and focus of Egyptian urban planning transformed many times. The path was not smooth: Egyptian scholars, planners and even government employees debated the new communities from the moment they were first proposed. Critique of their size, ambitions for growth, lack of social integration and general wastefulness, alongside all the studies, evaluations and monitoring done over the last 40 years could fill a library. Professor of Housing Nasamat Abdel-Kader and Professor of Urban Design Sayed Ettouney have been following the New Towns since the 1970s. Their reports repeatedly call into question these same aspects of the New Towns, while defending the original ambitions that drove NUCA to become the most proficient New Town authority on the continent. Abdel-Kader and Ettouney write: 'New Communities were thought of as an effective solution to the problems of rapid encroachment of agricultural land, deteriorating urban fabric, and low-quality living. It represented a serious endeavour and a heavy undertaking in a developing context burdened by challenging priorities and limited resources.'[13]

Egypt's New Towns project is as ambitious as any planning programme in the world, outstripping even China and India's fast-paced New Town development by envisioning bustling cities in an almost lunar desert landscape. As of 2018, there are 41 New Towns (planned or built), under NUCA's authority. Out of about 96.3 million Egyptians, NUCA claims that 7 million live in the New Towns—about 13.5% of the population.[14] As Sims writes in *Egypt's Desert Dreams: Development or Disaster?*, 'the government has devoted so much of its attention (and resources) to the desert dream that is has, in many respects, neglected the Valley and left it to its own devices… The new towns programme has, since the late 1970s, represented for the government the only vehicle for Egypt's urban development, in spite of its abysmal track record. Existing towns and cities have been left to smoulder, and informal urban areas have grown and grown.'[15] In light of this critique, 10th of Ramadan has become, comparatively, one of NUCA's success stories, attracting both industry and more than half a million residents over the last four decades. As such, there are a number of aspects of this New Town that deserve closer examination. The first, without question, is the urban plan itself.

City in the sand

When you drive from Cairo to 10th of Ramadan, the trip is defined by a series of quick transitions. Blink, and the cosmopolitan density of downtown Cairo gives way to a forest of towering informal housing. The road winds through mid-rise concrete and brick apartment buildings that look solid, but are notorious for collapsing. Another blink and the pyramids of Giza are suddenly behind you. Finally, the highway has room to breathe and agricultural land spreads out below you. If you turn away for a minute, you will miss the line where lush date palms and green cotton plants become desert sand. Another blink, and you have passed New Cairo, the gleaming, most expensive New Town in Egypt, and the poshest place you could choose to live. An hour or so after you leave

11 The urban population was 43.8% of the entire Egyptian population in 1976. As of the 2017 census, it was in fact a tiny bit lower: 42.5%. See CAPMAS: www.capmas.gov.eg/Pages/StaticPages.aspx?page_id=5035.

12 Mitchell, T. (2014) 'Foreword', in: Sims, D. Egypt's Desert Dreams: Development or Disaster? Cairo: The American University in Cairo Press. P. xx.

13 Abdel-Kader, N. and Ettouney, S. (September 2013) Rethinking New Communities Development – with Reference to Egypt's 40 Years Experience. Paper presented at the 39th World Congress on Housing Science, Milan.

14 CAPMAS census data available at: www.capmas.gov.eg/Pages/StaticPages.aspx?page_id=5035. NUCA data available at: www.newcities.gov.eg/english/aboutUs/achievments/default.aspx

15 Sims, D. (2014) Egypt's Desert Dreams: Development or Disaster? Cairo: The American University in Cairo Press. P. 294.

Public housing blocks.
(Photo: R. Keeton, 2016)

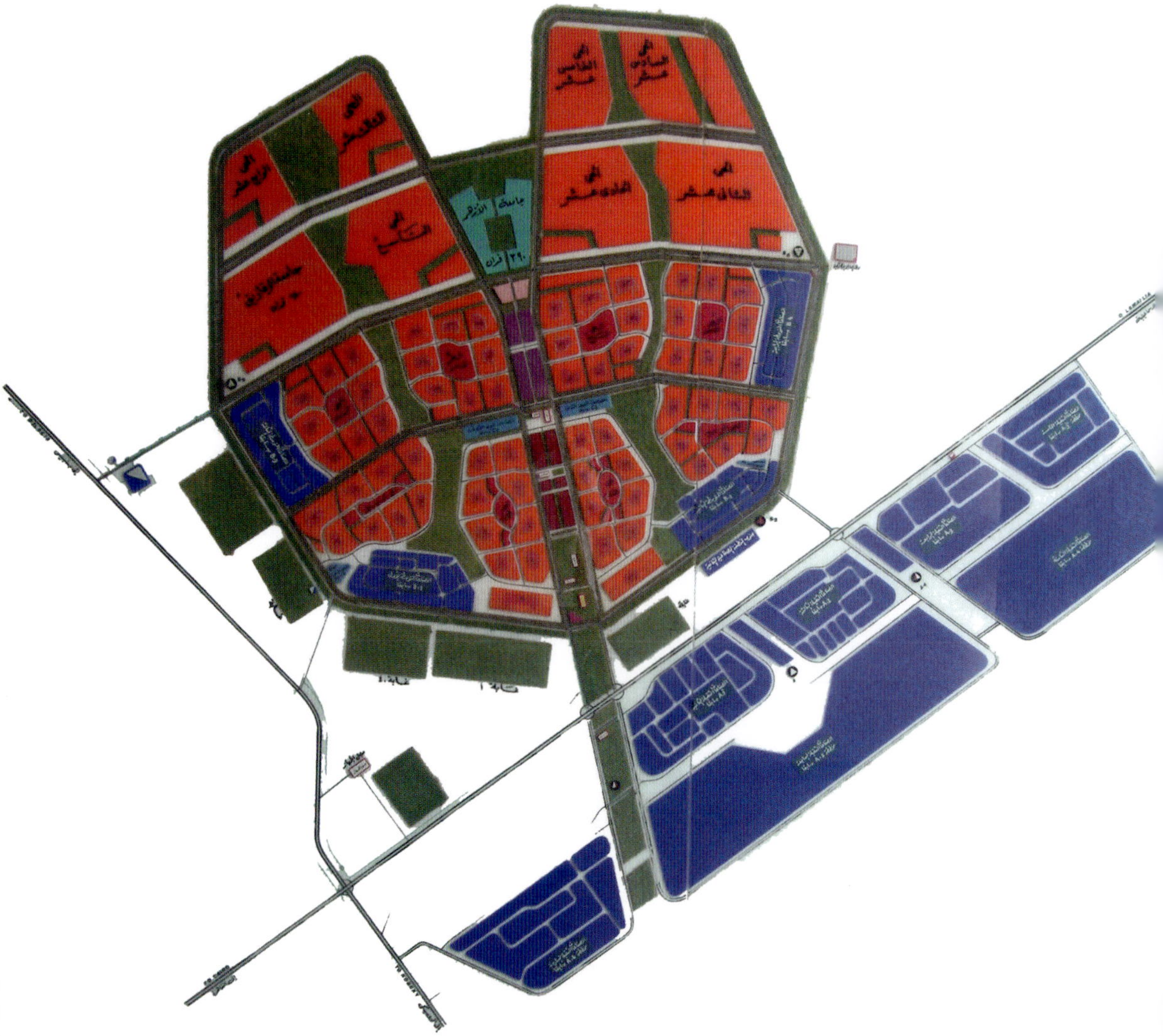

The masterplan of 10th of Ramadan seperates residential and commercial areas from the huge industrial part to the southeast. Some light industry is also located within the main part of the New Town. (Source: NUCA)

the crowded heart of Cairo, you approach a large sign announcing 10th of Ramadan. Before entering the city, you pass a stretch of industrial warehouses and factories that continues into the distance. Turning left off Ismailia Desert Road onto Abu Bakr El Sedeek Street you pass a series of roundabouts and your speed slows. El Sedeek Street is the central axis of 10th of Ramadan, and its commercial core.

Although the masterplan depicts the city as a diamond in the desert, in reality the unfinished city appears to fade out from south to north, as though the desert were already reclaiming this forty-year struggle, rather than the other way around. Things here change fast, however: every year the New Town is filled in with more apartment blocks and villas. A white and brown landscape is the backdrop to an endless strip of sand-coloured apartment blocks marching along the horizon. Huge open spaces, flagged for future development but currently home to wandering packs of dogs, allow for impressive vistas of this half-built city. According to NUCA, 650,000 residents live here in prefab housing blocks with very little variation, with a few gated villas making for a slight change of pace.[16] Having officially surpassed its initial target of 500,000, NUCA raised the current population target to 2.1 million for 2023.[17]

The original feasibility studies and plans for 10th of Ramadan were made by an international team led by Shawky-Zeitoun, an Egyptian engineering firm, and SWECO, a Swedish engineering firm. Both were commissioned by the Egyptian government. Mustafa Shawky and Salah Zeitoun were educated in the United States during the 1940s and have been described as 'ardent vectors' of modernism.[18] Modernist principles and influences like Constantinos Doxiadis and the French *villes nouvelles* would later become visible in the prefab construction, phased masterplan and functional zoning.[19] Industry is located far from residential areas. Commercial and office areas are strictly segregated from residential areas. Following the masterplan, housing and more detailed designs were produced by COPA, an Egyptian architecture firm that replaced Shawky-Zeitoun in 1977.[20]

The total planned area encompasses a massive 300 km^2 within the shape of a rotated square. At the northern corner, a smaller square within the first square contains all civic and residential functions, while industry and agriculture are located along the southern edges. Inside the smaller square, the shape of a tulip is symmetrically bisected by a central spine that lengthens over time as the city expands. The mixed-use functions which the masterplan imagined here were commercial and offices, service and administrative areas, as well as recreation and entertainment. This principle of growth and extension as the basic element in the urban plan was clearly based on Doxiadis' Ekistics, offering an alternative for the urban growth experienced in Cairo and other large cities, in which the centre would inevitably become clogged and pressured.

Inside the tulip-shape, 16 residential boroughs would be constructed in four consecutive phases over time. The first phase consisted of four boroughs, each made up of 8-9 clearly defined neighbourhoods. Each neighbourhood unit was designed with its own service centre, a school, and a mosque within walking distance. The neighbourhood units are connected by six-lane roads that facilitate the large distances and are buffered with strips of landscaping. However, a lack of affordable public transport makes movement within the sprawling New Town difficult for anyone without access to a car.

The southern and western edges of the city are ringed by neatly divided agricultural fields. The agriculture extends north to an irrigation channel from Timsah Lake, on the Suez Canal. Throughout Egypt, agricultural production is mostly practiced by small-scale commercial operations rather than subsistence farmers. In this part of the country, crops like cotton, sugar beets, potatoes, onions, and cereals are popular choices.

16 See: www.newcities.gov.eg/english/New_Communities/Ramadan/default.aspx

17 The NUCA's habit of increasing population targets in New Towns is a key part of its business model. The NUCA website also enumerates the public buildings in 10th of Ramadan: 37 schools, 14 hospitals and health centres, 38 commercial services, 33 social buildings, 3 church[es], 5 mosques, 2 communication centres, 73 public service [administrative buildings]'. See: www.newcities.gov.eg/english/New_Communities/Ramadan/default.aspx

18 See: Volait, M. (September 2006) 'Mediating and domesticating modernity in Egypt: uncovering some forgotten pages'. in: Docomomo Journal, special issue Modern architecture in the Middle East, #35. Pp. 30-35.

19 10th of Ramadan's designers followed the well-known hierarchical model of New Towns developed in Europe, but on a scale that matched the demographic growth of Egypt. Today, 10th of Ramadan's target population of 2.1 million is at least 10 times bigger than most European New Towns, which usually don't exceed 50-70,000 inhabitants.

20 In January, 1979, the University of Cairo jointly hosted a conference on core housing and sites and services with the Massachusetts Institute of Technology (MIT). The conference was organised in collaboration with the Egyptian Ministries of Housing and Development and New Communities, who felt there was a lack of expertise on these (then) innovative housing techniques. COPA architect Ismail Reda contributed a presentation on the core housing project at 10th of Ramadan.

2019 GoogleEarth

commercial
residential
industry
public green
agriculture
unknown
1km

School children pose in one of the sprawling open spaces of 10th of Ramadan. (Photo: R. Keeton, 2016)

Industries —of every scale and type— are mostly concentrated along the massive 15km-long strip at the southeastern edge of the diamond shape, across the Ismailia Desert Road. This 45 km^2 zone is home to both international companies and local businesses, including plastics, paper, medical supplies, garment factories and manufacturing. Many of the businesses are family-owned and operated. Egyptian factory owners flocked to the New Town in the late 1970s when the government offered attractive incentives to move their businesses there. As an autonomous city, 10th of Ramadan is entirely dependent on the industrial belt that forms its economic base. It is, in fact, the largest industrial zone in Egypt. Workers commuting from rural areas who supply the manpower for these industries make up some half of the industrial employees.[21] Those who actually do live in the New Town often live in employer-provided rest houses, shared flats, or in dormitories within the factory itself.[22] Factory managers, supervisors and owners live in the New Town, but most low-level industrial employees are brought in daily by private buses from surrounding villages. Each factory has its own fleet of buses, and it is common practice for a business to 'adopt' a village, employing extended families and establishing strong connections over generations. According to a production manager at a garment factory, village women work in the factories for an average of just three years, between ages 18 – 22, or until they get married.[23]

Almost all NUCA New Towns are designed with extremely low densities of about 50-70 persons per hectare, with up to 60% of the land reserved for public space and roads.[24] Compare this density to Cairo's 1000 persons per hectare in some of the older neighbourhoods, and up to 2000

21 In his comprehensive study on workers in 10th of Ramadan, political scientist Jochen Möller cites a number of reasons for the commuting workers' resistance to living in 10th of Ramadan. The first, is the relatively high cost of living. The second, is the lack of social ties in the New Town. Möller writes: 'The modernity of 10th of Ramadan City seems to enhance feelings of alienation for people coming from a traditional rural background.' See: Möller, J. (1998) 'Working and living in 10th of Ramadan City: The Perspective of Workers in Small Industries'. In: Travailleurs et industrie à l'heure des réformes économiques. No. 33. Pp. 67-80. Available online here: ema.revues.org/1575#tocto2n9

22 Ibid.

23 Interview with the author 12 December 2015.

persons per hectare in the informal community of Mashiet Nasser, and the rationale behind the New Town's 'quiet' atmosphere quickly becomes obvious. Housing is mostly sand-coloured and unapologetically bare. Graffiti often covers the ground floor façades, fading out at the reach of the street artist's arm. Residential neighbourhoods show a repetition of identical concrete social housing estates, and consist of uniform walk-up apartment flats with units of varying size. The city also has some areas with individual plot developments, which exhibit more variation. Recently, private villas and gated communities have started popping up in the newer sections of the city.

It's not a beautiful place. Even in the mild days of December, the sun beats down and seems to bleach everything; colours are muted and green things struggle for life. Public squares and playgrounds are dusty brown, rather than the vibrant jade in the highly-irrigated spaces along the central axis, Abu Bakr El Sedeek Street. Still, the joy of public life is evident here. Schoolchildren wander between home and their lessons, stopping at shops for a soda or kushari, a local street food. Women move in small groups, running errands collectively or gathering children from school. It is a working-class culture and residents take pride in their town with the defensiveness of an underdog. They know what cosmopolitan Cairenes think of 10th of Ramadan: that it is a blue-collar city without culture or finesse. On the street, residents will tell you how much they appreciate the 'open space', 'quietness' and 'good organisation' of the New Town. The availability of public space—from a planning perspective—is indeed one of 10th of Ramadan's strong points. Every district has an open space of considerable size, although the quality of this space is often less than what might be desired: vast expanses of sand characterise most of the open areas.

Even though downtown Cairo is only an hour away by car (46 km), for the residents of 10th of Ramadan, the capital city may as well be on the other side of the Sahara. It is an autonomous New Town in a way that very few satellite cities ever truly become. This is partly because of its distance, but also due in large part to the agricultural backgrounds of many residents. Since 1977, the city has attracted residents mainly from surrounding rural areas and small villages along the Upper Nile as far south as Aswan. In the 1970s and 1980s, men came for jobs and brought their families with them. Today, there are second- and third-generations living in 10th of Ramadan. Holidays are usually spent at family compounds far to the south, rather than in Cairo.[25]

Intention versus implementation

10th of Ramadan was meant as a city with affordable housing. To this end, a 'sites-and-services' approach was combined with core housing in parts of the city. The new approach was intended to make the resulting public housing as affordable as possible—in line with NUCA's socialist mission. The problems with this process soon became apparent: 'a lack of cheap building materials, an insufficiency of basic services (e.g. water and

24 See: Golia, M. (2004) Cairo: City of Sand. London: Reaktion Books. Pp. 17-18. And: Sims, D. (2012). Op. cit. P. 171.

25 From his interviews with 104 workers in small industries in 10th of Ramadan in 1998, Jochen Möller concluded: 'More than 50% of these workers share flats or stay in "rest houses" - flats provided by their employer (*istiraha*). Some even live in the factory where they work. Those living in 10th of Ramadan City without family members and/or spouse consider their dwelling a mere "work residence", as their social activities concentrate on their original hometown, where they return every weekend. The workers often state their intent to return "home" if they find work there.' Möller, J. (1998) 'Working and living in 10th of Ramadan City', Égypte/Monde Arabe, Vol 33: 67-80. Interviews with industrial workers by the author in 2016 reflected similar attitudes.

This patriarch (seated, first from right) came to 10th of Ramadan from a village in southern Egypt for employment in the late 1970s. He has owned this garage since 1979 and the sons are now responsible for managing the business. (Photo: R. Keeton, 2016)

Staying alive in the Sahara

From an ecological standpoint, desert New Towns have some obvious challenges. 10th of Ramadan is no exception. Accessible only by car, private minibus or bus, movement to, from, and within the New Town requires massive amounts of (state-subsidised) fuel. Notorious traffic jams clogging the highway between 10th of Ramadan and central Cairo compound the problem. Plans for public transport options have been on and off the table for the 40 years since 10th of Ramadan was first proposed. Currently, a railway from 10th of Ramadan to Cairo is under construction; fully constructed, financed, operated and maintained by private sector companies. When completed, the 104 km railway line expansion will connect the New Town to the national railway network and finally provide passenger services to north Cairo, with the possibility of an extension to the city of Belbais.

Affordable public transport between Cairo and 10th of Ramadan may induce significant changes. While most residents currently remain in the New Town or travel to surrounding rural areas, an efficient connection with the capital could potentially shift both the demographic structure of the New Town as well as its capacity as a viable housing alternative for 'overcrowded' Cairo. This would, for the first time, help 10th of Ramadan meet one of its original objectives, namely, to redistribute population overspill from Cairo.

The bus station in 10th of Ramadan is located in the centre of the city, and surrounded by a bustling commercial area. Buses currently provide the main mode of transportation between the New Town and Cairo, although the new railway connection may change that. (Photo: R. Keeton, 2016)

In addition to transportation challenges, 10th of Ramadan's food and water security depends on smart use of existing resources. Resources that, at a national scale, are limited and erratically available. Food security in Egypt is a question of purchasing power at the household level, and because Egypt imports more than half of its wheat, it is vulnerable to fluctuations in global food prices as well as exchange rates.[34] Egypt has typically relied on food assistance programmes and subsidies to assuage urban food insecurity, with varying degrees of success. As in many countries, it is the poor who depend most on cereals to provide a higher percentage of their daily calories, which means that they are the most affected by rising grain prices. This was made evident during the Arab Spring, which was partially triggered by increasing bread prices.

Water security is an equally pressing issue. At the national scale, Egypt is almost completely reliant on rainfall and the Nile. The entire country has been facing a serious water shortage since the 1990s.[35] In 2014, both the UN and the Egyptian Ministry of Water Resources and Irrigation said that the country would be confronted with 'absolute water scarcity' as soon as 2025 if population growth continues as projected.[36] When the taps stop running, water trucks bring drinking water to villages and towns without other options. Water trucks, of course, are more expensive than civic water. Water scarcity is also closely related to food security, because it is needed for irrigation, and an increasing population means increasing demand for agricultural products.

34 In May 2013, the World Food Programme published a report stating that, 'While the highest poverty rates remain in rural Upper Egypt (51.5% of the population against a national average of 25.2%), significant pockets of poverty and food insecurity are emerging in urban areas, where poverty increased by nearly 40% between 2009 and 2011. In population terms, Greater Cairo (Cairo, Qualoubia and Giza) has an even larger number of poor people (approximately 3.8 million) than the poorest govern-orates in Upper Egypt.' World Food Programme (May

A groundwater aquifer gives 10th of Ramadan independence from the Nile, but also makes the city vulnerable to groundwater pollution. Unfortunately, a study from 2012 detected chemical inorganic, biological, organic and bacteriological pollutants in all 31 groundwater samples it tested.[37] Despite having independent wastewater networks, the wastewater from both residential and industrial areas are combined before being discharged at the treatment plant. Industrial wastewater makes up between 55-80% of the water to be treated.[38] According to a study from 2011, the three (unlined) oxidation ponds on the eastern edge of 10th of Ramadan haven't been appropriately maintained since their construction, and are blatantly unable to treat the wastewater to permissible standards.[39] Separating the industrial and residential wastewater would allow for more efficient treatment, as well as the possibility for re-using treated water for landscaping and irrigation.

Finance and governance in the New Urban Communities

In early 2018 Egypt began emerging from a deep financial crisis and growth is expected to continue through 2019.[40] Increased revenue from tourism, the Suez Canal and remittances have supported recent economic growth. At 9.9% in 2018, unemployment is the lowest it has been since before the 2011 revolution.[41] Still, Egypt has long been dependent on foreign aid to balance the books, and this continues despite a positive short term outlook.[42] Nearly 30% of Egypt's annual budget is coming from soft loans and aid packages.[43] This money is then redistributed in the form of government subsidies for everything from bread and other commodities to housing and gasoline. This stop-gap solution, combined with a heavy-handed military government, has so far been enough to thwart the kind of public outrage seen in 2011.

While tensions have clearly eased since then, Egypt's new communities have a history of 40 years, allowing us to examine an evolution of financing approaches. When NUCA was first established in 1979, the first-generation New Towns were industrial in character, with mostly working-class housing, neighbourhood schools and mosques, some higher learning institutes and colleges, but somewhat limited recreational facilities and amenities. These weren't cultural centres, they were industrial cores. As such, their financing was dependent on state-subsidised public housing and NUCA's access to cheap—almost free—desert land. Their working-class ambitions were visible in the simple, concrete housing blocks. 10th of Ramadan attracted industry initially through a combination of 10-year tax breaks and 10 years without customs duties on imports. Higher wages than elsewhere in the country raised residents' average income above the national average. Foreign industries were all but required to set up shop in 10th of Ramadan until the other industrial New Towns were completed, and the city continues to enjoy the benefits of this short-lived monopoly.[44]

In the 1990s, there was a radical shift in policy after a major upheaval took place in the Egyptian cabinet. President Hosni Mubarak signed

2013) *The Status of Poverty and Food Security in Egypt: Analysis and Policy Recommendations (preliminary report)*. Pp. 6, 7. Available online at: documents.wfp.org/stellent/groups/public/documents/ena/wfp257467.pdf

35 The 2014 report *Water Scarcity in Egypt* defines the terms 'water scarcity' and 'absolute water scarcity': 'Egypt has reached a state where the quantity of water available is imposing limits on its national economic development. As indication of scarcity in absolute terms, often the threshold value of 1000 m^3 / capita/year, is used. Egypt has passed that threshold already in nineties. As a threshold of absolute scarcity 500 m^3 / ca/yr is used, this will be evident with population predictions for 2025 which will bring Egypt down to 500 m^3 /ca/yr.' See: Egyptian Ministry of Water Resources and Irrigation (February 2014) *Water Scarcity in Egypt*. Cairo. P. 1. Available online at: www.mfa.gov.eg/SiteCollectionDocuments/Egypt%20Water%20Resources%20Paper_2014.pdf

36 Ibid.

37 El-Sayed, M.H., et. al. (2012) 'Hydro-geochemistry and Pollution Problems in 10th of Ramadan City, East El-Delta, Egypt'. In: *Journal of Applied Sciences Research*, 8(4). P. 1971.

38 Atimtay, A. and Sikdar, S., Eds. (2011) *Security of Industrial Water Supply and Management*. Dordrecht: Springer. P. 211. See also: El-Sayed, M.H., et. al. (2012). Op. cit. Pp. 1959 – 1972.

39 Atimtay, A. and Sikdar, S. (2011). Op. cit. P. 213.

40 See: www.focus-economics.com/countries/egypt

41 These statistics have been reported by CAPMAS. Available online at: www.tradingeconomics.com/egypt/unemployment-rate

42 The United States delivers 1.6 billion USD annually, most of it earmarked for the Egyptian military. See: Najjar, F. (2017) 'Why US aid to Egypt is never under threat.' Al Jazeera. Available

structural adjustment agreements with the International Monetary Fund and World Bank in 1991. Those agreements led to the cabinet reshuffling from 1994 to 1996 that resulted in leadership that continued to liberalise the economy by driving privatisation forward, deregulating the trade sector and increasing competition.[45] In this context, NUCA began selling huge tracts of subdivided and serviced land to private developers at below market value. The new policy proved more profitable for NUCA, who became, and remains, one of the government's most reliable income-generating agencies. The shift also signalled the advent of gated communities and more upscale residential options in the New Towns, along with more luxurious leisure facilities. The face of the New Towns changed: while 10th of Ramadan remained middle class, the so-called 'second generation new communities' (as exemplified by Sheikh Zayed City) were becoming enclaves for wealthy Cairenes eager to escape the 'chaos' of the capital. This model has all but overtaken the social-housing focus of the previous generation.

In addition to NUCA's income from private development, the Egyptian government continues to pour huge amounts of public funding into the New Towns. Infrastructure is put in place before land is sold, including water treatment facilities and water access, sewerage, roads, public spaces and lighting, as well as public buildings. The NUCA budget for fiscal year 2015-2016 was 28 billion EGP (1.6 billion USD)—nearly five per cent of expected revenue for the entire country.[46]

One result of pouring a seemingly endless amount of public funding into the Egyptian New Towns has been the redirecting of funds *away* from older urban areas that are very much in need of both general maintenance and comprehensive planning solutions. This effective turning away from the existing city in thrall to the New Town is something we see repeated again and again worldwide. In the case of the Egyptian New Towns, it has meant that while downtown Cairo and Alexandria are crumbling, with no large-scale renovation or upgrading plans, money is poured into construction of additional infrastructure and housing in areas far from the densely populated centres. An integrated, systemic approach to the existing urban environments would be a much more effective use of funds.

After three sweeping changes in the years since the 2011 revolution that ousted Hosni Mubarak, Egypt is currently ruled by a military government led by President Abdel Fattah el-Sisi. In many ways, the current regime is considered more brutal and controlling than the Mubarak government; in today's Egypt, there is little potential for political negotiation. Challenges to this power do exist, but are necessarily limited by the government's harsh reactionary approach. Many activists use social media and blogging to spread their messages. There is a strong legacy of youth activism and dissent in Egypt, despite—or perhaps in direct response to—the government's attempt to smother it. Since 2011, civic engagement appears to be on the rise.[47]

at: www.aljazeera.com/news/2017/10/aid-egypt-threat-171002093316209.html See also: Plumer, B. 'The US gives Egypt $1.5 billion a year in aid. Here's what it does.' In: The Washington Post, July 9, 2013. See: www.washingtonpost.com/news/wonk/wp/2013/07/09/the-u-s-gives-egypt-1-5-billion-a-year-in-aid-heres-what-it-does/ Saudi Arabia promised an $8 billion aid package in early 2016, and the Gulf states collectively offered a $12.5 billion relief package in 2015. See: english.alarabiya.net/en/business/economy/2015/03/13/Saudi-announces-4-billion-aid-package-to-Egypt.html And: www.al-monitor.com/pulse/originals/2016/03/egypt-saudi-arabia-aid-military-cooperation-disagreement.html

43 See: www.cfr.org/egypt/egypts-solvency-crisis/p32729?cid=ppc-Google-grant-egypts_solvency_crisis&gclid=COuYovXDtswCFdiZGwod7tgEdA

44 The tax benefits enticed both foreign and domestic industries, and there are currently about 2000 factories operating in 10th of Ramadan. Another 1000 are 'under construction', according to NUCA. See: www.newcities.gov.eg/english/New_Communities/Ramadan/default.aspx

45 See: www.aljazeera.com/indepth/opinion/2012/03/201232784226830522.html

46 Revenue for the 2015 / 2016 fiscal year is expected to be EGP 622.2 billion according to the budget ratified by President Sisi in July 2015. According to NUCA's website, total public investments in 10th of Ramadan stand at 12.8 billion Egyptian pounds, ($1.4 billion USD).

47 Activist actions before the revolution helped pave the way and inspire many of the current movements for justice. Among them, 'Two incidents brought together social media and rising discontent in a potent moment that triggered an uprising against the Mubarak regime. The first was

One of the New Town's characteristic large open spaces. (Photo: R. Keeton, 2016)

the death of Khaled Said, a young Alexandrian who was beaten to death by police officers in broad daylight, in apparent revenge for posting a video on Youtube that showed the officers dividing up a drug bust. Public opinion was stirred by Wael Ghonim's fervent Facebook group "We Are All Khaled Said". Ghonim used social media to forge a virtual public space, one where Khaled Said's death was not just one more evidence of police predatory behavior towards the people. More significantly, Khaled Said became symbolic of the myriad forms of oppression that Egyptians experienced on a daily basis.' See: Stroud, S. and Ibrahim, B. (2011) Youth Activism and Public Space in Egypt. Cairo: The American University in Cairo. P. 8.

Conclusion

Although most of what has been written about Egyptian New Towns in general, and 10th of Ramadan in particular, tends to focus on what doesn't work, there are lessons to be found both in the New Town's well-documented failures and rather less celebrated successes. One of those is its proven ability to attract and accommodate international industry and foreign capital. The New Town is also overwhelmingly popular with residents, many of them now second- or third-generation locals. On the street, residents repeatedly point to 10th of Ramadan's large, safe, open spaces, general cleanliness, and the well-irrigated greenery. All these aspects owe their existence to the New Town's rigorous urban management. In older Egyptian cities, one finds uncollected piles of trash, farm animals (and their waste) plodding along the streets, potholes and unpaved sections of road, and an endless stream of people, everywhere. It takes a specific lens to see such complexity as beautiful. In contrast, 10th of Ramadan succeeds in providing an environment that is organised, controlled, quiet, and clean. It has set itself up in opposition to the older cities, defining itself as modern and new, and thus appealing to the values of the Egyptian middle class.

Strict management also has its disadvantages. Somewhat bewilderingly, NUCA runs 10th of Ramadan much more rigidly than other New Towns. While waste management, administrative issues and public services are efficiently organised, this also means that any appropriation of public space is not tolerated and informal activities are quickly terminated. NUCA's uncompromising land-use regulations make the street vending and small kiosks that mark every corner of Cairo punishable by fine in 10th of Ramadan, and make it difficult to find spaces for small businesses to operate. This in turn limits the opportunities for small and medium enterprises, on which so many Egyptians depend for their livelihood. Moreover, the low density of the city contrasts markedly with the continuous stream of pedestrians in older cities, and this lack of clientele can put serious strain on small business owners.

Those small business owners and employees are almost entirely from the agricultural areas surrounding the New Town or south along the Upper Nile. As a result, 10th of Ramadan effectively functions as a focal point for internal migration within Egypt, rather than the magnet for Cairo's urban overspill that it was intended to be. Efficient public transport links to Cairo and Ismailya could change this, but for now, the New Town does not meet its goal of redistributing Cairenes from the capital.

The social challenges of life in a New Town should also not be underestimated. 10th of Ramadan has been more successful than many of the other New Towns, but it still struggles to attract new residents. The strong familial networks and community support systems that have evolved over generations in older villages, towns and cities are simply nonexistent in the New Town. The value of these connections can hardly be overstated, especially within the more rural farming communities. People depend on each other for both financial and social support during difficult times. They find work and other opportunities through their extensive networks. Without this lifeline, a New Town can be alienating and lonely. As one first-generation garage owner put it: 'the first few years here were the hardest thing I've ever done. No friends, no big family, nobody to rely on but ourselves.'[48]

For 10th of Ramadan, the most critical issue is that housing is still completely unaffordable to the average Egyptian worker. The industrial workers for whom the New Town was originally planned, will likely never call 10th of Ramadan home. The daily bussing ritual is now so well ingrained that it has become accepted practice; commutes of up to two hours each way are considered normal. This discrepancy between housing costs and local incomes continues to slow the New Town's growth. Although 10th of Ramadan *has* overtaken its original target population, it will have to quadruple in size to meet the revised target of 2.1 million. A recent report by the GOPP actually lists the inability of new cities to attract population as one of Egypt's main challenges in complying with UN-Habitat's New Urban Agenda: 'The statistics showed that new cities attracted 1.5 million people (17.6%) of the targeted population size until 2017, which is 8.5 million people, due to weak services and attraction elements.'[49] The report goes on to reflect critically on Egyptian planning in general, stating: 'the comprehensive planning approach leaves no room for adaptation or responsiveness to economic and political changes internationally and regionally. Furthermore, this approach does not allow local units to be flexible nor to make the planning decisions suitable to their relevant local context.'[50]

With so many challenges, what is it that keeps NUCA building more New Towns? At such great expense and with such little real public demand? According to Sims, the answer may lie in the fact that the Egyptian New Towns programme is now simply too big to fail: 'Once such a headlong… scheme had gained momentum, it became nearly impossible to relent. There were just too many cheerleaders for desert development, too many interests intertwined in this development, and too many client groups to satisfy.'[51] The NUCA programme also gives the government something concrete to splash across state media, claiming that it has done its job by building so many new homes and thus reinforcing its perceived value to the average citizen. The current New Town programme does all of these things, as well as supplying luxury housing to an Egyptian upper class eager to escape the throng of downtown.

It would be naïve to expect any planned city to develop exactly as planned. Some are more popular than expected, some never meet projected targets. All of this unpredictability is a result of the complicated background: political and institutional intrigue, shifting economic priorities and dependencies, social and cultural norms or aversions. Unlike most of the other examples in this book, 10th of Ramadan now has the benefit of four decades of experience, and it has become clear that there is too much pressure from competing interests to ever allow this New Town to become the workers' paradise it was intended to be. Instead, 10th of

48 Interview with the author, December 2015.

49 GOPP (2017) Issues and Challenges for a New Urban Agenda. Cairo: GOPP. P. 28. Available at: gopp.gov.eg/wp-content/uploads/2017/07/Chapter-2.pdf

50 GOPP (2017) Op. cit. P. 31.

51 Sims (2014). Op. cit. Pp. 297-298.

Ramadan fills a gap in the Egyptian housing market and supplies jobs for hundreds of thousands of employees. In this, and the subsequent boost to the economy, the New Town has been undeniably successful.

Sheep graze in public space around standard 5-story public housing blocks. (Photo: R. Keeton, 2016)

Applying the 10 principles of the Manual

Planning is an ongoing process
As of 2018, the Egyptian New Town building programme is responsible for plans for 41 New Towns, 22 of which have been (partially) built. It is likely the most ambitious New Town building programme in the world. However, as 10th of Ramadan clearly illustrates, New Towns are seen by development authorities as a package to be delivered. Feedback from designers and planners is unwelcome, and often ignored. The system is not nimble enough to effectively incorporate discoveries made during planning and implementation. There are many planners at the GOPP and NUCA itself who are aware of the programme's failings, but change will not come until it becomes political will.

Plan for adaptivity
10th of Ramadan was designed to grow in accordance with the ambitious targets made by NUCA. This growth has slowly materialised, but rather than redevelop the plans to reflect reality, NUCA has insisted on maintaining its projections for future growth. A more flexible approach could examine 10th of Ramadan as it exists today and, based on historical growth patterns and realistic projections, rethink the New Town within existing boundaries and focus on densification rather than expansion.

No New Town is an island
10th of Ramadan may be one of the most striking examples of a truly autonomous New Town. Because of its distance from Cairo and dependency on local industries, jobs are abundant in 10th of Ramadan and facilities and amenities are considered adequate. Workers from rural villages commuting to and from the New Town, however, face the same challenges seen in other satellite New Towns.

Use no cut-and-paste universal model
Although 10th of Ramadan is not a cut and paste urban design, it takes much of its inspiration from the international modern planning ideology. Using this underlying layer to better effect could be done by increasing densities, allowing for more mixed programming, and encouraging the informal sector rather than regulating against it.

Embrace new ideas
10th of Ramadan was undoubtedly an experimental New Town. At the time of its creation, the New Town represented a huge departure from previous Egyptian urban planning projects, and initiated the country's turn towards privatisation, foreign investment and increased industrial activity. Although low-cost housing experiments within the New Town largely failed, there are lessons to be drawn from those examples.

Infrastructure and mobility for all, from the start
10th of Ramadan has an efficient road network and infrastructures are relatively well-maintained. Strict regulations against popular forms of public transport (such as the tuk tuk), however, limit movement for a large group of people. Access to Cairo's metro network could greatly improve the New Town's connection to the capital. The huge scale of the development also limits the walkability of the New Town.

Use a blue-green infrastructure as the central framework
Blue-green infrastructure in the desert exists in the form of both oases and underground water aquifers. During the site selection phase, however, neither of these opportunities was taken into account. Today, continuing environmental degradation from industries in 10th of Ramadan is an ongoing problem that attracts very little attention. Runoff from industries leaches directly into the desert and groundwater supplies. 10th of Ramadan is extremely vulnerable to climate change threats in the form of salt water intruding into underground reservoirs, less overall rainfall, and increased weather variability. Food and water security will be major concerns.

Incorporate local cultural heritage(s)
10th of Ramadan is located in the desert, and according to author David Sims, this context was interpreted by planners as a tabula rasa. Of course, no place is ever a tabula rasa and the planning team's failure to take this into account can be read back in the lack of passive cooling at the architectural scale, and mistaken analysis of target residents. A more nuanced reading of architectural styles in local villages and social constructs of local villagers could have benefited the plan.

Combine top-down and bottom-up
Although grassroots organisations appear to be growing and gaining strength, 10th of Ramadan remains extremely top-down in terms of governance and administration through NUCA. More room should be made to increase public participation and respond more effectively to the changing needs of local residents.

New Towns need diversity
As in many Egyptian New Towns, 10th of Ramadan fails to attract its stated target population. Housing that was intended for low-income groups is now inhabited by what can be called the Egyptian middle class. This is a problem we see repeatedly throughout the world. Smart low-cost housing with designs based on local assessments must be supported by housing policy that provides a legal framework for renting, as well as ownership.

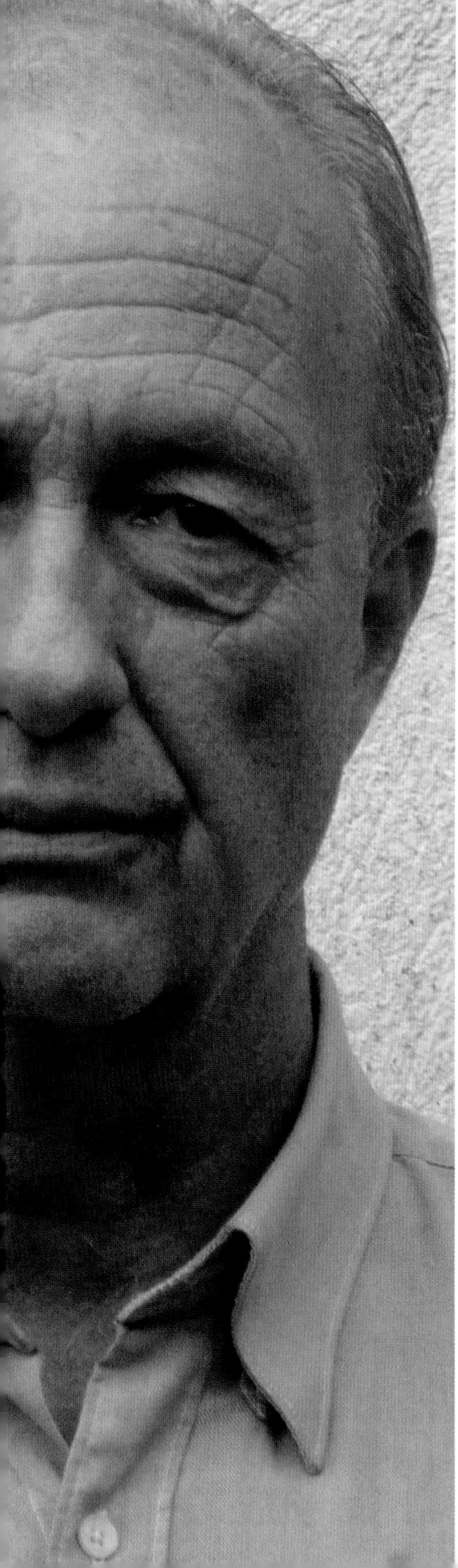

David Sims, Economist and Urban Planner

Economist and urban planner David Sims has been based in Cairo since 1974. An expert on contemporary urbanisation processes in Egypt and in developing countries in general, he is the author of both *Understanding Cairo: The Logic of a City out of Control* and *Egypt's Desert Dreams: Development or Disaster?* Both books explore the Egyptian government's preoccupation with urban development in the desert and the evolution of this desire to 'conquer the desert'.

Sims has been vocal in his critique of the Egyptian New Town programme, calling it, 'part of the manufacture of hope'.[1] In his account, the Egyptian government has used the New Town programme since 1977 to assuage citizens' frustrations with their ineffectual urban management and problematic development strategies. In the new preface to the paperback version of Egypt's Desert Dreams (2018), Sims concludes: 'A serious consequence of this obsession for wholesale desert development is that the challenges and opportunities found in rest of Egypt, where over 95 percent of the people actually live (and will remain), can be conveniently ignored. Not only is the Old Egypt starved for even crumbs of the annual budget, but the government's spatial approaches to it seem limited to nonsensical talk about de-population and de-densification in order to reshape what is left into some image of a modernist Egypt that never arrives. The over-the-top promotion of desert projects and of how these will miraculously solve Egypt's many ills (you name it: excessive population growth, national food security, housing crises, anti-social behavior, even terrorism), allows an easy out, a way of continuing to ignore the ills and problems of the Old Lands.'[2]

In the following interview, we discuss the current state of affairs and future perspectives for the largest New Town programme in the African continent, and perhaps the world. This interview has been edited and condensed for clarity.

Rachel Keeton (RK): Cairo is currently home to 21 million people, and its population is expected to double by 2050. In your latest book, Egypt's Desert Dreams, **you write that according to the 2006 CAPMAS census, the New Towns housed less than 800,000 people throughout Egypt, and only some 600,000 in the New Towns around Cairo—casting doubt on their usefulness as a tool to combat overcrowding. Have things changed in the last decade? And if so, what has driven that change?**

David Sims (DS): In 2006 the 8 New Towns around Cairo (6th of October, New Cairo, Sheikh Zayed, Badr, Ubour, 15 May, Tenth of Ramadan, and Shorouk) had a total population of 601,000. By 2017 this total was 1,298,000 meaning a doubling over 10.5 years. Sounds impressive, except that during the same period Greater Cairo grew by at over 5 million (to 21.2 million, up from 16 million), meaning these New Towns only absorbed at best 14 percent of this growth. In other words, 84 percent of the metropolis's growth went into the existing city – mainly in the massive informal areas.

The government (in particular the New Urban Communities Authority (NUCA)) and private developers would like you to believe that the New Towns are booming and so are their populations. Especially those towns around Cairo. And in terms of high-end residential projects (gated communities and villa/garden apartment suburbs), office space, malls, private schools and universities, and leisure attractions, certainly there has been a tremendous amount of construction since 2006. This also applies to social and middle class housing built by the government. But there is no way to gauge how successful these developments are. This is because few projects in New Cairo or Sixth of October (or other New Towns around Egypt) are operational. Most are still under construction, with (at best), a first phase having opened. More and more projects are just at the groundbreaking stage, and even more seem to be stalled. Everyone speculates on land and building. Most of the unit sales are made on paper (off-plan) to middle class and rich Egyptians (especially those working in the Gulf). Practically no one is in a hurry to live in these units, and this helps explain the extremely high vacancy rates in New Towns. For example, a NUCA official recently claimed that over 2.5 million housing units have so far been built in the 20-some New Towns all over Egypt. Yet the total 2017 population of all these New Towns does not exceed 1.7 million persons, meaning that there are on average only 0.8 persons per housing unit!

RK: Egypt's new capital is designed by the American architecture firm SOM and planned for about 7 million people at an estimated cost of $45 billion, 50km east of Cairo. You were skeptical about this project when it was first announced in March 2015. Since then, Egyptian state media has reported that a deal was made with China State Construction Engineering Corp. worth 15 billion USD, and road construction (by the army's engineering authority) has started. Phase I (including government offices, ministries, a residential area with 25,000+ housing units and a large

1 See: www.aucpress.com/t-enewsletter-DavidSims-February2015.aspx?.

2 Sims, D. (2018) Egypt's Desert Dreams: Development or Disaster? **2nd Edition. Cairo: AUC Press. P. 68.**

park), is scheduled to be completed in time for President Abdel-Fattah El-Sisi's re-election campaign. What does this urgency tell us about the relationship between politics and New Town construction in Egypt?
DS: Yes, the talk about—and reported agreements on—projects for the new administrative capital have increased and even accelerated. Politically, the new capital can be seen as one, perhaps the most important, of the president's mega-projects, through which he can confirm his legitimacy as the leader of Egypt's renaissance. Not a day goes by without mention of mega-projects: all huge, all in the desert, and all very modern and hi-tech. There is very little (if any) criticism of the costs or real benefits or simple feasibility of any of these mega-projects. From a political standpoint, it is interesting that the management of the new capital, through a recently formed state company, is half run by NUCA and half by the army (and chaired by a major general). The army is also to remain owner of all the land. Thus the blending of military and civilian interests in matters of state-led development is being solidified.

RK: Project websites claim that the new capital will have 100+ neighbourhoods designed at 'medium and high' densities, although they do not elaborate. They also suggest that 'extensive' public transport links will connect the new capital to the existing city. Those qualities would be a departure from the existing New Towns, where average densities are very low and public transport is problematic. It seems like someone is finally learning from the experience of the last forty years. Or is that all a PR game?
DS: It seems to be largely a PR game. But we don't know for sure since there are lots of project pronouncements for the new administrative capital, but few details about planning and layouts, except those generated by private developers for particular sites. Even an up-to-date map of plans for the first phase is not publicly available. My guess is that, with NUCA and the General Organization of Physical Planning (GOPP) being very non-transparent masterplanners, the same low-density approach found in the other New Towns will predominate in the new capital. Add to this the fact that, as in the other New Towns, massive land allocations are made pell-mell, and that projects on these huge parcels take years or even decades to mature (if ever). That same massive urban sprawl and half-finished urban landscape will characterise the new capital. I visited the new capital site in September 2016. There was very little to see apart from two gigantic roads under construction to link the site with New Cairo to the east. Each is designed to be 120 meters wide; enough for 15 lanes of traffic each way. So much for human scale development. Only one building project could be seen, still at the skeleton stage.
In 2018, things have progressed a lot more: the government is moving ahead with one housing district and breaking ground for a second, and with lots of roads. Some 15 ministry buildings plus the new parliament and cabinet buildings are well along, as is the presidential palace. A huge mosque and 'the largest church in Egypt' figure prominently in the media. The first gated communities are beginning to take shape

RK: It is clear that Cairo needs more low-income housing, but it continues to build for the high-income market. With high vacancy rates in most New Towns, can you discuss the government's 'requirement' that private

developers build social housing and why this doesn't appear to work? Does Egypt need a new definition for social housing to make it accessible to the very poor?

DS: The Ministry of Housing is rushing ahead with its One Million Unit social housing programme, almost all of which is located in the New Towns or in desert land in the governorates (almost always in remote areas where modest families cannot find work or livelihoods and therefore cannot survive). Most units are 90 m^2 apartments that are 'affordable' only with massive direct and indirect subsidies. This is another mega-project, and it follows from many previous government housing projects. In fact, one could say the target is more the loyal, regular salary earning lower/middle class than those in need. And as with former public housing programmes, these units (which are only now being delivered to beneficiary families) are likely to remain vacant for years, since families speculate too. That government housing doesn't provide solutions for the majority has been said for years, but the government is deaf to any critiques.

RK: Why is there such resistance to urban regeneration or planned urban extensions? Why the need to build complete satellite cities that have proven, repeatedly, to be unpopular and financially unsound?

DS: The simple answer is that satellite towns are all located on empty public land (which can, these days, turn a nice profit). Not only are there no land acquisition costs, but the messiness and hassles of urban regeneration is something the state knows nothing about and would like to avoid.

RK: The Egyptian New Town narrative and the 'conquest of the desert' imperative started under Nasser and became a reality after Sadat announced 10th of Ramadan in 1977. New Town construction has continued under Mubarak, Morsi and el-Sisi, but shifted slightly under each new government. What are the biggest changes you see under the current administration?

DS: In the el-Sisi period the conquest of the desert narrative remains the same, with the same design parameters, but even more grandiose. Maybe the main difference is the heightened role of the army.

RK: Egypt has a 37 percent urban home ownership rate—relatively low despite recent changes to mortgage models. Does this number have more to do with the fact that most Egyptians simply cannot afford to buy real estate, or does it reflect a cultural resistance to long term financing and associated interest rates?

DS: The high level of rental tenancy is partly due to holdovers from the old fixed rental system. Now, especially in the informal areas, renting is the only solution for families without equity. The mortgage system in Egypt—now over 15 years old—has never worked, mainly because of the high interest rates and lack of clear titles. Cultural adversity towards debt, plus a healthy suspicion of private real estate developers, are also reasons.

RK: It might surprise some readers that rural-to-urban migration is not a big part of Egypt's most recent urbanisation, but rather repopulation is driving urban growth (Egypt's fertility rate is 2.9; higher than the

replacement rate of 2.1). And although informal settlements only began to be built after WWII, more than 70 percent of Cairenes now live in informal settlements. Can you tell us a bit about how housing dynamics have shifted in recent decades and what role the New Towns in play in this?
DS: Informal housing is the only affordable solution for urban Egyptians (cheap, well-located, accessible, mixed use, with many informal business opportunities). In the New Towns housing is very expensive, remote, and sterile.

RK: In both of your books on Cairo and the surrounding region, you have explained in detail the problems that result from NUCA's current strategy. What suggestions would you make for increasing the livability of the New Towns that are already built? How could the government increase their popularity? Or should there be an entirely different goal at this point?
DS: Many have said that you must have a kind of urban regeneration in the New Towns that increases density and allows more mixed use, and even the government is toying with the idea of allowing increased building heights. But at the same time, more and more land in the New Towns is being allocated to privately-built compounds (which generates lots of revenues to NUCA through land sales), repeating and exacerbating low-density sprawl. And, as a result, making more exclusive cities.

RK: The 'public housing' built in the New Towns has been accessible for middle- and high-income groups, but has never succeeded in matching the needs and capabilities of low-income groups. The informal market has answered this need in Cairo, but the strict building regulations in New Towns have prevented the growth of informal settlements. What would happen if low-income groups were allowed to self-build in New Towns?
DS: Ha! There was the Ibni-beitak programme from 2007-2012, but it was so badly managed, so rigid, so low-density, and so remotely located, that even the government admits it was a failure. Only if high-density mixed-use residential areas with good and cheap public transport were allowed in New Towns, with lots of commercial and other job-creating activities, could they become attractive to lower income groups. But this would negate the idea that the New Towns represent the modern, organised face of the new Egypt.

RK: Have the New Towns increased spatial segregation and resistance to mixed-income developments? In our research, residents interviewed in Sixth of October and Sheikh Zayed were resistant to plans for a new metro line linking the New Towns to central Cairo because this would encourage 'the wrong kind of people' to settle there by making public transport an option. Are we seeing a new classism as a direct result of the last two decades' gated communities and enclaves?
DS: Yes, spatial segregation continues and is even accelerating, especially in Sixth of October, Sheikh Zayed, and New Cairo. This is partly due to the economics of land sales, where the highest prices (and thus revenue to NUCA and the state) come from upscale developments and compounds.

RK: One of the original goals of the New Towns programme was to alleviate the housing crisis in the 1970s. In the government's 2030 Sustainable Development Strategy, this ongoing crisis is still framed as a question of supply quantity, rather than affordability. What needs to change to in order to reframe this discussion?
DS: This will not happen without a complete change of mindset both in government and among most professionals, and I don't see any hint of this.

RK: Property speculation has benefitted the government, and NUCA in particular, as the largest urban landholder in the country, after the army. This being the case, are we going to see NUCA continue to sell off land to private developers in exchange for short term profits or is the threat of a real estate bubble beginning to enter public debate? Has there been any substantial discussion of tax reform or initiatives that would slow speculation?
DS: One can predict more of the same, especially from NUCA, who now can boast that it turns a handy profit. (In fact, the government claims that most infrastructure and public spaces in the new administrative capital are being financed through land sales.) Is there a bubble? Yes, but it seems that the demand for speculative investment on the part of high-income Egyptian society will continue, and land and bricks are the main ticket, especially in inflationary and devaluation times. If, at some point, an external shock were to make real estate prices falter, this could lead to some collapse of the bubble. But little of speculative investment is based on loans (mainly it is family capital), so don't expect a cascade of sales and a real bubble bursting.

RK: What is the biggest hurdle to a major re-evaluation of NUCA's strategies? Experts at the GOPP, urban planners, and local academics all recognise the same issues we've discussed here; none of this is news to Egyptians who have some knowledge of the situation. So why don't things change?
DS: Well, it's politics. NUCA and GOPP have a total non-transparent monopoly on policy, and they are immune to criticism. In fact, they have many cheerleaders, since much of the planning and architecture profession rely on them (or the developers that work with them) for their bread and butter. And it should be added that many of these same professionals have extensive business dealings in the Gulf, where modernistic glitz (that the New Towns are trying to mimic) is the order of the day.

Tema Manhean (1952), Ghana. (Photo: M. Provoost, 2018)

Dodoma (1973), Tanzania. (Photo: A. Pronkhorst, 2009)

Sheikh Zayed (1995), Egypt. (Photo: R. Keeton, 2016)

Tatu City (2010), Kenya. (Photo: S. Rots, 2017)

Appolonia City (2012), Ghana. (Photo: M. Provoost, 2013)

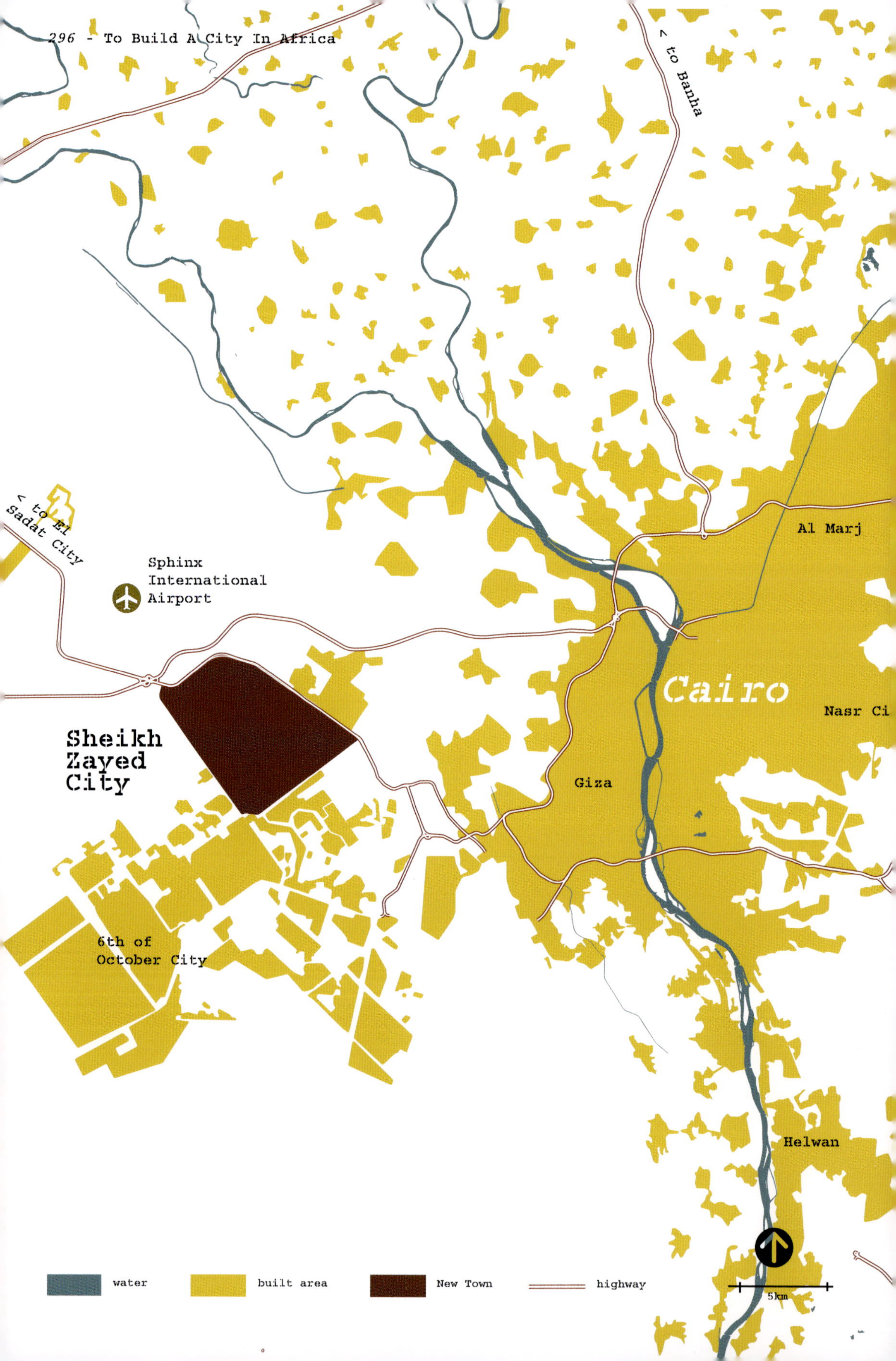
< to Banha
< to El Sadat City
Sphinx International Airport
Al Marj
Cairo
Nasr Ci
Sheikh Zayed City
Giza
6th of October City
Helwan
water
built area
New Town
highway
5km

CASE STUDY

Sheikh Zayed City, Egypt

'Who has the right to a planned city?'

As elaborated earlier in this book in the case study of 10th of Ramadan, Egypt is a large country with its population crowded into the thin slice of inhabitable land along the Nile River. Located at the northeast corner of the African continent, Egypt is also a geographical and social link between northern Africa and the Middle East. Sheikh Zayed City, a New Town 38 kilometres west of downtown Cairo, is a manifestation of this linkage. Named for Zayed bin Sultan Al Nahyan (1918-2004), emir of Abu Dhabi and president of the United Arab Emirates, the New Town was financed primarily by the Abu Dhabi Fund for Development (ADFD) at Sheikh Zayed's directive.[1] In 1994, this foreign grant came at a moment when the entire Egyptian New Town programme was shifting from a focus on social housing and industry to a new model based primarily on private sub-development. Sheikh Zayed City, like all Egyptian New Towns, was established under the management of the New Urban Communities Authority (NUCA). NUCA, a branch of the Ministry of Housing, Utilities, and Urban Development, is responsible for site selection, all related infrastructure, construction of public housing and services, and land sales in the New Towns.[2]

While 10th of Ramadan is considered part of Egypt's first generation of New Towns (1977-1982), Sheikh Zayed is part of the second generation (1982-2000). The generational divide refers to substantial changes in NUCA's approach to New Town construction. As discussed elsewhere in this book, the first generation of New Towns were seen as a means of decentralising urban amenities and redistributing Cairo's booming population. The first New Towns were state projects with subsidised

1 The ADFD financed the 735 million AED (200 million USD) project at the personal behest of Sheikh Zayed. Another Sheikh Zayed City was funded by the ADFD and constructed in Palestine in 1999. A third planned city, Zayed Town, Bahrain (2001), was also financed by, and named in honour of Zayed bin Sultan Al Nahyan.

2 Egyptian New Towns (also known as 'new communities'), fall under the control of NUCA and are administered by local development authorities (*jihaz tanmiya*). They are the exception to the rule. All other existing cities are managed by the Ministry of Local Development and Governors. The asserted aim is that New Towns should be moved into the remit of the Ministry of Local Development and Governors after reaching maturity, and thereafter be treated as any 'normal' city or town. As of writing, not a single New Town has yet moved out from under NUCA's management. See: The World Bank (2008) *Arab Republic of Egypt Urban Sector Update*. Washington DC: The World Bank. P. 55.

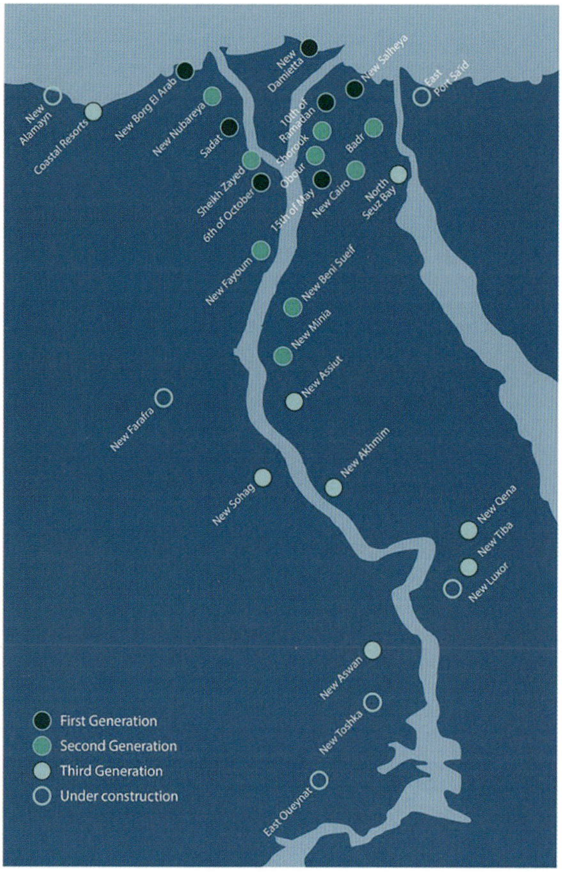

Egyptian New Towns up to 2015. (Source: Tadamun (www.tadamun.co/2015/12/31/egypts-new-cities-neither-just-efficient/?lang=en#.XGwV5s9KhE4)

housing and diverse facilities, including large industrial zones and attractive economic policies. This generation exhibits a clear focus on average Egyptians and a careful balance of employment opportunities with residential developments.

Second generation Egyptian New Towns were located around Greater Cairo and include El-Shorouk City, Badr, El-Obour City, and Sheikh Zayed City. This generation came into being at a time when neoliberal ideology was just beginning to permeate Egyptian politics. After slow economic growth in the early half of the 1990s, the latter half of the decade saw increased growth rates that were a result of economic liberalisation, greater competition within markets and controlled inflation.[3] This economic growth was coupled with a growing demand for the perceived security of gated communities and compounds. As Rana Almatarneh, Assistant Professor of Architecture at Ahliyya Amman University, writes: 'gated communities appeared [in Egypt] in the 1980s as a consequence of socio-cultural and economic restructuring… Gated housing communities have increasingly become a profitable segment in the real estate market and also provide a new marketing angle for developers offering security, status/privilege, and lifestyle.'[4] Sheikh Zayed City became one of the first New Towns in which gated compounds were built.

Against the changing economic backdrop, a new Minister of New Communities was appointed: Mohamed Ibrahim Suleiman. In contrast to his predecessor, Suleiman applied a markedly capitalist approach to his management of NUCA.[5] This change in leadership had immediate consequences for the next generation of New Towns. Established in 1995, Sheikh Zayed City was one of the first to be impacted by the changed policies. Although it was originally planned to be a mixed-income city, Sheikh Zayed City quickly transformed as NUCA discovered the profit-making potential of land sales to private developers. Sheikh Zayed City therefore represents a major shift in Egyptian New Town development, with private developers replacing individual buyers as primary investors. As a result, what was intended to be a real reflection of Egyptian society has instead become synonymous with an aspirational lifestyle of brand consciousness.

Following the second generation, the third generation of New Towns (2000 – 2018) reflected a renewed commitment to satellite cities, located at distances ranging from 2 - 18 km from existing cities. Presently, the fourth generation of the extensive Egyptian New Town programme is

3 See: El-Laithy, H., Lokshin, M., and Banjeri, A. (2003) Poverty and Economic Growth in Egypt: 1995-2000. World Bank Policy Research Working Paper 3068.

4 Almatarneh, R.T. (2013), 'Choices and changes in the housing market and community preferences: Reasons for the emergence of gated communities in Egypt: A case study of the Greater Cairo Region, Egypt.' Ain Shams Engineering Journal Volume 4, Issue 3, September 2013, P. 564. DOI: 10.1016/j.asej.2012.11.003.

5 Suleiman was found guilty of 'squandering public funds' by selling

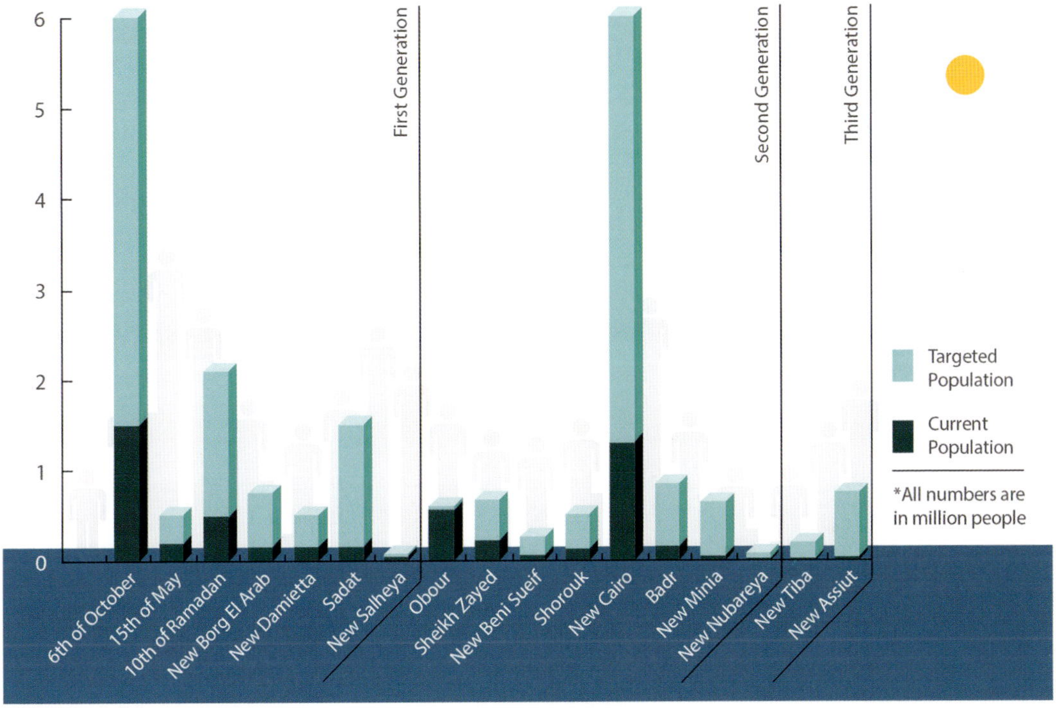

Current populations and targets, up to 2015. (Source: Tadamun (www.tadamun.co/2015/12/31/egypts-new-cities-neither-just-efficient/?lang=en#.XGwV5s9KhE4)

already underway. In September 2018, Prime Minister Mostafa Madbouly announced that the Ministry of Housing and Urban Development will construct 20 additional New Towns in the near future.[6] Collectively, the 20 new cities should house 30 million residents and will be spread throughout Egypt. In short, the New Town building boom does not show signs of stopping. What is unclear is whether this fourth generation will maintain the practices that have led to extreme levels of spatial segregation as evidenced by Sheikh Zayed City, or whether they will learn from the experiences of four decades of New Town construction in Egypt.

Current challenges in Sheikh Zayed City

In 1996, as construction at Sheikh Zayed City was underway, President Hosni Mubarak addressed Parliament and declared firmly, 'Leaving the narrow (Nile) valley and fanning out, in a planned and organised manner, throughout the country, has become an unavoidable necessity. In view of these facts, the conquest of the desert is no longer a slogan or dream but a necessity dictated by the spiralling population growth. What is required is not a token exodus into the desert but a complete reconsideration of the distribution of population throughout the country.'[7] This announcement cemented the future of the New Town programme, and clarified its aims. The New Towns around Cairo would act like magnets: pulling residents from the crowded capital and keeping them firmly rooted in the new urban cores with attractive landscaping, abundant space, and a coherent narrative. Only, it hasn't quite worked out that way.

state-owned land in New Towns for below-market prices in 2012. After first successfully appealing a five-year sentence in 2015, Suleiman was sentenced to three years in jail in September 2015.

6 The newly-announced New Towns include the New Administrative Capital, which is planned for 6.5 million residents, as well as an extension to Sheikh Zayed City, although details are scarce. See: Egypt Today staff. 'Egypt to construct 20 fourth-generation New Towns'. Egypt Today. 10 September 2018. Online: www.egypttoday.com/Article/2/57378/Egypt-to-construct-20-fourth-generation-cities.

7 Originally reported in Al Ahram Weekly, 14-20 November 1997. P. 2. Quoted in: The World Bank (2008) Arab

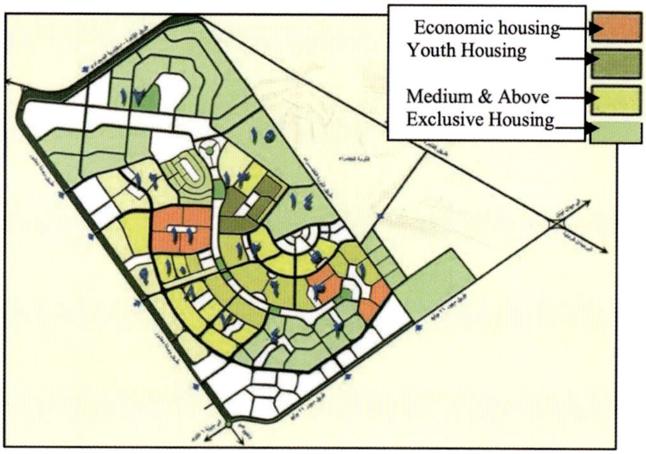

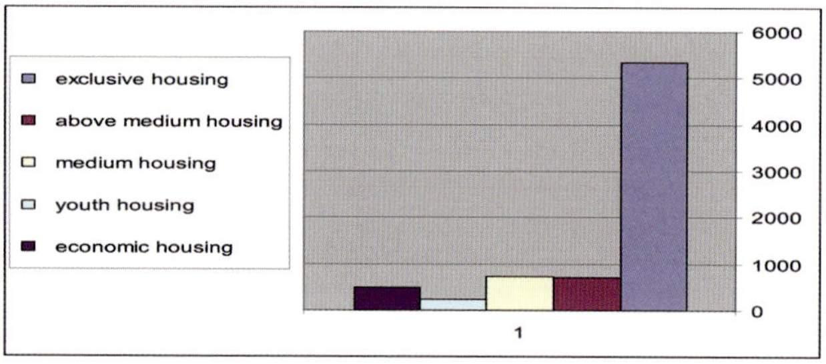

Housing and targeted income groups in Sheikh Zayed City. (Source: Metwally, M. and Abdalla, S.S. (n.d.) 'Impact of gated communities on the urban development of new cities in Egypt.' Cairo: Center of Planning and Architectural Studies (CPAS))

The most common critique of Egyptian New Towns, as echoed in both popular media and academic literature, and acknowledged by the Ministry of Housing, is that they have not succeeded in attracting sufficient residents; their intended function as tools to decentralise the capital city has therefore not yet been achieved. In the case of Sheikh Zayed, NUCA reports that the current population is 330,000 inhabitants, while the target is 675,000.[8]

Authors Rick Hagazy and Wael Moustafa usefully summarise other common critiques.[9] Two challenges apply specifically to Sheikh Zayed City. The first is: 'New Towns have been developed through typical processes, with little consideration of location dynamics, target beneficiaries, the economic underpinning of New Towns, and effective market incentives.'[10] In the case of Sheik Zayed City, the critique can be further broken down into two acute shortcomings: 1) a failure to maintain the original goal of the project as a tool to redistribute accessible housing and thereby decentralise Cairo, and 2) a mismatch between housing, employment, and service provision within the New Town.

Simply put, the majority of housing in Sheikh Zayed is too expensive for most Egyptians. The government acknowledges this problem and has made various attempts to rectify the situation in recent years, including investment benefits for private developers to encourage development of affordable housing. However, 'the private sector's cheapest housing unit stands at $13,946, which outweighs the actual purchase power of the lower incomes; therefore developers do not supply homes to this income group and rather target high-end buyers.'[11] Luxury housing accommodates 71 percent of the city's residents while low-income housing accounts for 15 percent.[12]

The mismatch between housing, employment, and service provision stems from the fact that almost all employment in the New Town targets formal employees with high levels of education. Residents of gated compounds have access to internal shops, clinics and other amenities, as well as the upscale *plazas* (outdoor shopping malls), accessible only by car. Low-income housing residents must rely on limited public transport options to reach more affordable options in nearby 6th of October

Republic of Egypt Urban Sector Update. Washington DC: The World Bank. P. 55.

8 See: www.newcities.gov.eg/english/New_Communities/Zayed/default.aspx. Notably, the Egyptian Central Agency for Public Mobilization and Statistics (CAPMAS) reports very different numbers: just 90,997 residents in Sheikh Zayed City according to the 2017 census. Data from Central Agency for Public Mobilization and Statistics (CAPMAS), Egypt. Online: Thomas Brinkhoff: City Population, www.citypopulation.de.

9 Hegazym I.R., and Moustafa, W.S. (2013) 'Toward revitalization of New

Public housing in Sheikh Zayed. (Photo: R. Keeton, 2016)

or downtown Cairo. The gaping divide between these two groups of residents was most recently illustrated by demonstrations outside of the NUCA-office in Sheikh Zayed in October 2016. Assmaa Abdel Fattah, a protesting resident, was quoted as saying: 'Our demands are quite normal; we wish to live in an integrated city with full services. Most of us are waiting for services such as shops, pharmacies, and schools to serve the population who've just moved to this rather remote area.'[13]

The second challenge pointed out by Hagazi and Mustafa is: 'Many private sector developers hurried to develop up-market sites without regard for market demand, leading many schemes to fail.'[14] This applies to Sheikh Zayed's later phases and the numerous gated compounds that now characterise the New Town. Although some of these compounds are considered the most attractive areas to live in the Greater Cairo Region, there are also many villas in states of dilapidation or unfinished construction. In Egypt, it is common practice for developers to self-finance the first stages of residential construction, giving buyers a physical frame to see and touch before they buy. However, layers of graffiti, security guards employed to live on-site and protect inactive construction sites, and other indicators suggest that many of these stately homes have remained uninhabited for years. This implies a further complication, that not only do private developers lean towards expensive enclave development without full consideration of the market, but that individual buyers also purchase housing in these areas as a speculative investment rather than to meet their immediate housing needs; a state of affairs that

Towns in Egypt case study: Sixth of October. International Journal of Sustainable Built Environment Vol. 2 Iss 1. June 2013. Pp. 10 – 18. DOI: 10.1016/j.ijsbe.2013.07.002.

10 The other challenges listed by Hegazym and Moustafa are: (2) 'Creating new towns is an expensive endeavour, since all basic infrastructures must be provided from scratch. (3) The new towns over-rely on governmental investments, and their continued development will require even greater budgetary commitments. (4) In some cases proper soil and other studies were not undertaken, and designated lands could not be developed… (5) Although the new communities law envisioned the eventual handing over of new towns to the respective local government authorities, this has not occurred, because either (1) local authorities are perceived as not having

An unfinished villa sits empty in Sheikh Zayed city. (Photo: R. Keeton, 2016)

the management capacities to maintain the high standards of the new towns, or (2) because local authorities cannot assume the service debts and liabilities associated with these new towns. (7) Many new towns, especially those with industrial areas, are experiencing severe environmental problems. (8) Despite various studies conducted to inform the choice of the new locations, there remains a lack of clarity about the constraints, potentials, and opportunities of the environmental and physical characteristics of the selected sites…' See: Hegazym I.R., and Moustafa, W.S. (2013) Op. cit. P. 14.

11 Khaled, F. (2018) 'A Good Year for Real Estate'. Egypt Today. Online: www.egypttoday.com/Article/3/39037/A-Good-Year-for-Real-Estate.

12 For a detailed analysis of the breakdown of housing supply in Sheikh Zayed, see: Metwally, M. and Abdalla,

has contributed to Egypt's ongoing housing deficit. What remains unclear, due to a lack of reliable data, is the extent to which to the uninhabited houses are bought for speculation (and thus an economic success story for developers, despite high vacancy rates), or whether developers are losing money on these large-scale projects.

Egyptian housing crisis then and now

In 1995, Egypt was in the middle of a deep housing crisis that began around 1981. During this time, *ashwa'yat* (informal settlements) in Cairo grew as public housing projects were moved to the New Towns.[15] The multiplication of *ashwa'yat* within Cairo was a response to the government's lack of understanding of conditions necessary to support low income communities. In general, the urban poor resisted moving to the remote New Towns, preferring the advantages of existing social networks, geographic proximity to employment, and 'the strength of private redistribution systems'.[16]

In the early 1980s, economic policies introduced by President Anwar Sadat opened real estate to private developers, but those same developers primarily focused on construction of luxury dwellings, which were more profitable. At the same time, Egyptian agricultural production faced new international competition as a result of the open markets, which caused massive rural-to-urban migration as farming families moved

Ashwa'yat multiply along the raised highways through Cairo. (Photo: R. Keeton, 2016)

to large cities in search of more stable income.[17] That influx exacerbated the existing housing crisis and the state's response was an attempt to meet housing demand by offering public housing projects in New Towns such as the Mubarak Youth Housing Program (MYHP), which is discussed later in this chapter. The housing crisis was further aggravated by the disconnect between rising housing prices and stable wages — a disconnect that continues today. Between President Sadat's death in 1981 and 1994 the price of a square meter of land tripled, with incomes remaining nearly steady.[18]

In 1992, Egypt experienced an earthquake that left 50,000 Cairenes homeless and more than 500 dead. Experts pointed to poor construction as the main cause of the widespread destruction.[19] That disaster may also have stoked middle-class disillusionment with the congested capital city. As a result, Cairenes with money began looking elsewhere for real estate investments. Private developers noted the shifting preferences. As the housing crisis simmered, new land legislation permitted the Egyptian state to transfer desert land to private ownership for the first time. As Petra Kuppinger writes: 'In the fast scramble for land that followed in the 1990s, developers secured considerable stretches of prime real estate at relative proximity to Cairo.'[20]

The plan for Sheikh Zayed thus came at a time when new neoliberal policies were clashing with a public outcry for subsidised housing. By 1996, NUCA was well aware of the urgent need for affordable housing in the

S.S. (nd) 'Impact of Gated Communities on the Urban Development of New Cities in Egypt'. Online: www.cpas-egypt.com/pdf/Sahar%20Soliman/English/04%20IMPACT%20OF%20GATED%20COMMUNITIES%20ON%20THE%20URBAN.pdf.

13 Al-Aees, S. (2016) 'Social housing unit owners demonstrate in front of NUCA for once again failing to respond to demands.' Daily News Egypt. 24 October 2016.

14 Hegazym I.R., and Moustafa, W.S. (2013) Op. cit. P. 14.

15 In Egypt, the quality of life in different *ashwa'yat* ranges across a broad spectrum from the vulnerable position of families without access to services, schools, or a social safety net to stable, working class families and professionals living in apartments that simply happen to have been built without permission. Both are

Greater Cairo Region. The initial design for Sheikh Zayed was therefore intended to accommodate low- and middle-income families and included several (subsidised) public housing projects.[21] However, the plans were altered over time for the benefit of upper-middle and elite groups.

The housing crisis led to the current situation in which there is no affordable housing available in Cairo for the average citizen to rent.[22] As a result, unregulated housing continues to multiply, and every available space is appropriated for residential use. Flat roofs become occupied, basement spaces are transformed into housing and young couples or families crowd into parents' homes. Meanwhile, in an ironic twist, housing in Sheikh Zayed City sits unfinished and uninhabited.

In addition to the unavailability of adequate housing, there are also difficulties in terms of accessing home financing loans. As in other parts of the continent, the Egyptian real estate market is largely a cash market. Although mortgages have been available since 2001, the mortgage system is inefficient and there is cultural resistance to long-term loans. Interest rates (currently around 14.5 percent) are seen as doubling the total cost of the investment over time. As a result, only 37 percent of the Egyptian population legally owns a home.[23] When compared with other African countries, that percentage may seem high, but in comparison to the rest of the world it is quite low: China, for example, has the highest home ownership rate in the world, at 90 percent (2014), while the European Union home ownership average is 66 percent (2016).[24] What the numbers tell us is that the housing that is available in Egypt simply doesn't match the purchasing power of most Egyptians – or it becomes inaccessible because of formal bureaucratic requirements.[25]

A recent estimate in the newspaper Egypt Today puts the current housing shortage at 3.5 million, while the number of Egyptians lacking adequate housing is estimated to be as high as 16 million. While there is a clear need for improved housing, the same article goes on to report that there are currently 5.6 million vacant dwelling units across the country. 'But', it concludes, 'these properties are beyond the purchasing power of low and middle-income classes.'[26] An official from the Egyptian Centre for Housing Rights (ECHR) neatly sums up the paradoxical housing crisis as, 'dwellers without dwellings and dwellings without dwellers'.[27]

Urban design and public space

As a visitor coming from Cairo, the first impression of Sheikh Zayed is one of absence: no urban cacophony, no pedestrians. The second impression is fragmentation. Walls painted in earthy tones seal off gated compounds and luxury plazas. Driving around, the city feels most like a collection of inaccessible islands rather than a coherent whole. Signs for international franchises like Starbucks, Baskin-Robbins, and Costa Coffee speak to the place's 'world class' aspirations. Billboards for new gated communities advertise variations on the themes of privacy, privilege, and exclusivity.[28] But getting a good feel for the New Town is difficult. Driving along

considered *ashwa'yat*, or slums and both are considered by the government to be undesirable.

16 Abouelmagd, D., Kesteloot, C., and Corijn, E. (2013) 'Housing Projects for Low-income Groups and Modes of Economic Integration: A Comparative Study in Greater Cairo.' Tijdschrift voor Economische en Sociale Geografie. Vol. 104, No. 4. P. 456. DOI: 10.1111/tesg.12026.

17 In general, Egypt has much lower rates of rural-urban migration than other African countries. However, this moment in time saw uncharacteristically high migration as a result of the introduction of international agricultural products into the Egyptian market.

18 'The price of a square meter of land [rose] from LE 99 [5.60 USD] to between LE 250 and LE 300 for the lowest-priced units, with the typical rise in wages not matching these inflated rates.' See: Fahmi, W., Sutton, K. (2008) 'Greater Cairo's housing crisis: Contested spaces from inner city areas to new communities'. Cities, Volume 25, Issue 5, Pages 277-297. DOI: 10.1016/j.cities.2008.06.001.

19 El-Sayed, A., Arvidsson, R. & Kulhánek, O. (1998) 'The 1992 Cairo earthquake: A case study of a small destructive event'. Journal of Seismology, 2: 293. DOI: 10.1023/A:1009717023043.

20 Kuppinger, P. (2004) 'Exclusive Greenery: new gated communities in Cairo.' City & Society, Vol. 16. P. 43. DOI: 10.1525/city.2004.16.2.35.

21 Argued in: Metwally, M. and Abdalla, S.S. (nd) Op. cit.

22 See for instance: Ibrahim, F.N. and Ibrahim, B. (2003) Egypt: An Economic Geography. New York: I.B. Tauris. P. 217.

23 See: hofinet.org/countries/country.aspx?regionID=5&id=51.

24 See: tradingeconomics.com/country-list/home-ownership-rate?continent=g20.

International franchise restaurants and shops at a plaza in Sheikh Zayed. An armed guard determines who qualifies for entrance in this semi-pubic space. (Photo: R. Keeton, 2016)

well-maintained main roads provides a view of the type of glassy office towers and mid-rise commercial areas one might expect to encounter anywhere in the world. But entering residential areas is confusing. Public housing areas exude an atmosphere of general neglect, while gated compounds present only a glimpse of greenery over the top of high-security fences. Residential roadsides are strewn with garbage, in contrast to the immaculate landscaping inside gated compounds. The differences in urban management between public space and private space are strikingly visible.

The built-up part of Sheikh Zayed City is shaped like a rhombus with four slightly irregular sides, each delineated by a main road. The 26th of July Corridor directly connects the southeast edge of the New Town with downtown Cairo. Along the southwest edge, Waslet Dashour Road divides Sheikh Zayed City from surrounding desert and the neighbouring New Town of 6th of October.

A large, triangular tract of land along the northeast edge of the built-up area is protected agricultural land, where irrigated fields produce grapes, oranges, lettuce, artichokes, onions and strawberries. The agricultural land is organised by an orthogonal grid placed at 45 degrees. Most of the urban area is confined to a tilted rectangular area, although new developments have been creeping into both the agricultural and desert areas along the northeast border.

A curvilinear form organising the urban plan looks like a fishhook dangling at 45 degrees off centre within the rectangular area. This curved main

25 Villas in Sheikh Zayed are currently priced around 13,850 EGP (774 USD) per meter. Apartments go for about half of that: 7,400 EGP (413 USD) per meter. See: egypt.aqarmap.com/en/neighborhood/cairo/el-sheikh-zayed-city/. International conversion rate of 1 EGP = 0.0558499 USD valid on 8 October 2018.

26 Khaled, F. (2018) Op. cit.

27 Fahmi, W. and Sutton, K. (2008) 'Greater Cairo's housing crisis: contested spaces from inner city areas to new communities'. Cities Vol. 25 Iss 5. October 2008. Pp. 277-297. DOI: 10.1016/j.cities.2008.06.001.

28 In her analysis of marketing materials from gated compounds in Egyptian New Towns, Almatarneh identifies a number of social factors

2018 GoogleEarth

residential low income
residential middle income
residential high income
educational
public green
agriculture
administrative
1km

Inside the gated compound Zayed 2000, carefully-tended landscaping creates a contrast with the barren ground in public spaces. (Photo: R. Keeton, 2016)

that dominate the advertising texts: Some indicative phrases from the marketing material include: '"You'll get to meet people who are wonderfully accommodating and friendly", "Meet new friends,"' "Old town spirit of friendliness," "People here tend to socialize together more," and "Community that gives you a strong sense of place". Certain real estate developers made explicit reference to homogeneity in the text of the marketing material. Phrases in the materials include "comfort of folks who are at the same place in life as you are", "meet others just like you", and "people of similar lifestyles".' See: Altmatarneh, R. (2013) Op. cit. P. 569.

axis informs the arrangement of 20 districts with rounded corners. Each district offers at least one mosque, market and service core, and is further divided into four neighbourhoods. Districts are peppered with private, gated compounds of varying sizes where vigilant guards check identity cards before allowing access. Once inside, gated compounds are characterised by a mix of villas, mid-rise apartments, and row houses. Curving streets slow traffic. Compounds are well-irrigated, with green spaces, golf courses, and even artificial lakes. Most compounds are organised in radial or curvilinear compositions. Al Rabwa, one of the most luxurious compounds, features dead-end cul-de-sacs arranged around a golf course. Many of the villas have private pools.

Before any of these homes were here, the first phase of Sheikh Zayed City began with two areas, the first consisting of six districts, the second area of five districts. Together they were planned to house 250,000 residents, provide a 1000 ha. greenbelt, and industrial areas. In Phase Two (1998), the two areas were combined, and much of the greenbelt was replaced with housing, decreasing it in size to about 100 ha. Industry was moved to 6th of October's industrial area. Phase Three (2003) added a large tract of land south of the adjacent agricultural area, earmarked for exclusive housing development.

Two decades later, huge tracts of land are still unbuilt, awaiting development. Despite these wide open spaces, in practice, the public realm in Sheikh Zayed is limited to the main roads. At the entrances to open shopping plazas, armed guards turn away groups of street children,

Open space awaits development in Sheikh Zayed. (Photo: R. Keeton, 2016)

allowing access only to those who look like they 'belong' in these semi-private spaces for commerce, restaurants and international chain stores. Inside gated compounds, private community centres, health services and other amenities replace the need for mixed-use development at the neighbourhood scale. In public housing areas, however, this creates a real lack of urban amenities.

One notable exception is the imposing Hyper One supermarket located at the turnoff to Sheikh Zayed City. Surrounded on three sides by a massive parking lot, the supermarket is more like an American Walmart or French Carrefour, offering not only groceries by also home goods, furniture, and even a play area for children. Hyper One has become such a focal point in Sheikh Zayed that the parking lot is now also used as an unofficial transportation hub. Buses, microbuses and shared taxis (*serfis*) continually collect and drop off riders at this informal gateway to the city. Located at the southeast corner of the New Town, the Hyper One parking lot is one of the few options for residents in need of public transportation; taxis don't drive into the New Town unless they are called in advance, and less formal transport options, such as the ubiquitous three-wheeled *tuktuks*, are regulated against.

Opened in 2005, ten years after construction began in Sheikh Zayed City, the Hyper One has become successful in part because it was the earliest commercial centre in this relatively remote area. It continues to function as one of the primary locations in Sheikh Zayed, supported by the transportation streams, and an adjacent mosque, with a shared

Economic housing areas do not offer a sufficient mix of urban amenities and facilities. (Photo: R. Keeton, 2016)

parking terrain. The mosque has extended Hyper One's popularity, enabling families or friends to connect Friday prayers to Friday shopping and socialising.

Many residents of the New Town experience Hyper One and the plazas as public space, but in reality they are privately owned enterprises, with accompanying rules and regulations. High quality public space is difficult to find in Sheikh Zayed, but for most of the residents this doesn't seem to be much of an issue. Residents of gated compounds have access to amenities that sufficiently address their day-to-day needs. In general, it is only the residents of public housing that criticise the lack of services.

Public housing

Private space that functions as 'public' space was not a part of the original plans for Sheikh Zayed City. NUCA originally built 9,938 public housing units, of which about half were intended for medium- and low-income groups and half classified as 'youth' or starter housing.[29] There was a clear intention to mix economic groups and target the lower end of the housing spectrum. Subsequent phases of development followed, and as NUCA began selling large pieces of land within Sheikh Zayed City, private developers quickly took the lead in housing construction. As of writing, the private sector has built 58,000 units (nearly all within the confines of gated communities), and continues to build more.[30] Many of the public housing apartments originally intended for low-income residents have since been privately upgraded, and now attract mostly upper middle class residents.

Luxury residential housing with gardens covers 2,157 hectares, or 71 percent of the total residential areas, and is entirely built by private developers.[31] NUCA is responsible for public housing in the New Town, and 587 hectares are occupied by 'middle and high middle classes' (mixed public and private), while 198 hectares are devoted to 'economic housing', and 97 hectares are indicated as 'youth housing' (both are considered public housing).[32]

'Economic housing', is instantly recognisable as five-story housing blocks with four apartments on each level, finished in cement plaster. Individual units range in size from 63m^2 to 79m^2.[33] Economic housing is provided with 'a very basic internal finish including cement floor tiles, coat-painted for walls, halfway ceramic tile walls for bathrooms and kitchens, mosaic tiles for kitchen and bathroom floors.'[34]

'Youth housing' indicates public housing that is intended for people between the ages of 25 and 40. Youth housing units are generally of a better quality than economic housing, and provided as turnkey residences. The Mubarak Youth Housing Program (MYHP) was started with the intention to provide more attractive housing options for young couples and families in lower income groups. The project was initiated by the Agency for Youth Housing in NUCA and ran from 1996 to 2004. In total,

29 Youth housing refers to a specific form of social housing designated for Egyptians meeting certain income requirements (i.e. a family's income must be less than 3000 EGP per month (337 USD)). See: Fahmi, W.S. (2008) 'The Right to the City: Stakeholder Perspectives of Greater Cairo Metropolitan Communities'. In: Jenks, M., Kozak, D., and Takkanon, P., World Cities and Urban Form: Fragmented, Polycentric, Sustainable? Abingdon: Routledge. P. 281.

30 See: www.newcities.gov.eg/english/New_Communities/Zayed/default.aspx

31 Metwally and Abdalla (nd) Op. cit. P. 5.

32 Ibid.

33 Wahba, S. (2007) Op. cit. P. 23.

34 Ibid.

about 70,000 housing units were built as part of the MYHP, as well as infrastructure and parking lots. About 80 percent of the MYHP units were built in 15 different New Towns around Cairo.[35]

In Sheikh Zayed City there are 5,199 MYHP dwelling units (each 70m2) with capacity for 16,400 inhabitants.[36] The caveat that buyers must have formal employment precludes people earning their income from unregistered or informal employment from applying for this type of housing.

The MYHP units are relatively remote in an area with few job opportunities. Most residents continue to work in downtown Cairo or in 6th of October.[37] Because of Sheikh Zayed's lack of public transport, that usually requires a commute (partially) dependent on private transportation. Car ownership in this part of town is less prevalent than in gated communities.[38]

The lack of sufficient urban amenities and facilities compounds the problem for many occupants of public housing. In Sheikh Zayed City, residents of the MYHP project 'have low access to the informal economy or having a second job. They still make part of their shopping in the consumption markets in their place of origin. In the redistribution sphere, there is a general problem of quality and shortage of educational and medical services.'[39]

MYHP was initiated as part of the government-subsidised housing programme that preceded the National Housing Programme (NHP), which spanned 2005-2012. Although well-intentioned, it is now generally agreed that neither programme succeeded in suppling accessible, affordable housing to the lowest income groups.[40] In fact, it is clear that the urban poor prefer to live in *ashwa'yat* that are more centrally located.[41] This has to do with the inaccessibility (in terms of both housing and mobility) of New Towns in general and Sheikh Zayed City specifically. It also reflects the limited social networks in the New Towns, as opposed to the extended family and other support networks often present in informal housing areas. As Abouelmagd et. al. conclude, 'The location of the public housing projects in distant and poorly connected new cities, the selection of inhabitants according to political motives and the deterrence of informal networks and activities are the reasons why the informal settlements are preferable to the [public housing] projects in the eyes of the poor.'[42]

Eventually, the programme was put to a stop. In their financial analysis of the MYHP, the World Bank concluded that the project had not met its objectives, stating: 'Extensive direct and indirect subsidies reaching close to 75 percent of total development cost and the reliance on sale proceeds of land in new urban communities to partly finance the programme are unsustainable and greatly reduce the ability to scale up.'[43] The authors point to the expensive infrastructure design needed to support the public housing as one major contributor to the project costs.[44] The MYHP housing in Sheikh Zayed has since taken on an entirely new life, with

35 Wahba, S. (2007) 'Arab Republic of Egypt: Analysis of Housing Supply Mechanisms, Final Note'. Report Number: 41180. P. 25.

36 See: Abouelmagd, D., Kesteloot, C. and Corijn, E. (2013), P. 466. And: Wahba, S. (2007) Op. cit. P. 26.

37 See: Abouelmagd, D., Kesteloot, C. and Corijn, E. (2013).

38 CAPMAS reports 9.4 million registered cars in Egypt at the end of 2016. In 2016, the World Bank reported the population of Egypt as 95.69 million. That indicates a nationwide car ownership level of roughly ten percent, which may serve as an indication of the mobility challenges many lower-income residents in Sheikh Zayed City currently face. See: english.ahram.org.eg/NewsContent/1/64/270451/Egypt/Politics-/-million-licensed-vehicles-in-Egypt-CAPMAS.aspx

39 Abouelmagd, D., Kesteloot, C., and Corijn, E. (2013) Op. cit. P. 472.

40 USAID's 2008 Housing Study for Urban Egypt supplies a useful, if slightly outdated, reference for income groups. In this study, USAID identifies five quintiles, breaking urban Egyptians into five earning groups, each comprising roughly twenty percent of the total urban population. The first quintile is identified as 'extremely poor' and includes people earning up to 600 LE (34 USD) per month. The second quintile, identified as 'poor', includes urban residents earning between 600 and 800 LE (up to 45 USD) per month. The National Housing Programme identified low-income groups as the target beneficiaries of the project, however, the housing that was constructed was financially accessible only to middle-income groups. USAID (2008) Housing Study for Urban Egypt

41 As Yahia Shawkat writes: 'In effect, this meant the exclusion of the bottom 32 percent of earners (most of the second quintile and all of the first quintile) from all but 8 percent

owners increasingly renting space to students of the Sheikh Zayed campus of Cairo University. Income from rent then supports life elsewhere for some of the original beneficiaries of the MYHP programme, reinforcing a familiar cycle where housing intended for low-income groups moves into the hands of the middle class.

Gated communities in Sheikh Zayed

Gated communities began to gain popularity in the United States in the 1970s in connection with 'white flight' or the retreat of middle-class white people from urban centres. This was driven largely by the social unrest and political conflict of the 1960s, when cities such as New York, Chicago, Los Angeles, Washington DC and Detroit became the backdrop for race riots and subsequent military interventions. The trend quickly spread throughout the world. Capitalising on the fear of violence, developers offered gated communities and privatised 'public' spaces as a stable alternative to the unpredictability of the urban core. That same narrative of fear and security has since been used effectively in cities around the world, particularly those with high degrees of inequality such as Sao Paulo, Johannesburg, Jakarta, and Cairo, among others. Focusing on her work in Sao Paulo, Teresa Caldeira has even gone so far as to conclude that the dramatic increase in gated communities can be read as a threat to the very structure of democratic society.[45]

But opinions vary. In public discourse and private conversations, the Egyptian New Towns, and Sheikh Zayed in particular, are continuously —and positively— presented as diametrically opposed to Cairo. Cairo is 'dirty, overcrowded, unsafe, polluted'; Sheikh Zayed is 'clean, quiet, well-organised, and safe'. The comparison is repeated to the point that it has become gospel for most residents of the New Town. One business manager (female, age 35) remarked on Sheikh Zayed's superiority to Cairo, noting the well-maintained roads, cleanliness, 'decent malls', and 'good supermarkets'. 'You feel free,' she concluded: 'There's no smell. Cairo smells like pigs.'[46] A marketing manager (male, age 37) offered one explanation for his happiness in Sheikh Zayed: 'Because you don't see any shabby people.'[47] Other residents noted the green spaces within Sheikh Zayed compounds, repeatedly contrasting this lushness with the dusty 'chaos' of Cairo.

Notably, many of those interviewed were satisfied with Sheikh Zayed City's lack of public transport, indicating that the proposed metro connection to downtown would bring 'the wrong kind of people' to Sheikh Zayed City and remarking on nearby 6th of October's '*tuktuk* (unregulated three-wheeled mini-taxis) problem'.[48] The kind of blatant classism expressed here is further reflected in the widespread desire to live in areas of strong social cohesion and homogeneity.[49] While academics and the New Urban Agenda talk about inclusivity as a necessity for good city-making, there is heavy resistance on the ground in Egypt and many other places. The question for planners becomes: how to integrate diverse groups who have no desire to live together?

of the units of the implemented NHP. With this, the only affordable options were the *Awla bel-Re'aya* scheme... and the *Igar* family unit schemes... However, access to these units was limited as the *Awla bel-Re'aya* were small units of 42 m^2 and are not family units. Rather, they are intended for retired couples or widows who would normally be living off a very modest pension. The other Igar scheme units (an acceptable family size of 63 m^2) were not available in all governorates and represented only 3 percent of the implemented NHP.' Shawkat, Y. "Mubarak's Promise. Social justice and the National Housing Programme: affordable homes or political gain?", Égypte/Monde arabe, Troisième série, Ville et révolution en Égypte, 203-233. See also: Abouelmagd, D., Kesteloot, C. and Corijn, E. (2013).

42 Ibid.

43 Ibid.

44 'One particular problem is that the planning and design standards for off- and on-site infrastructure delivery in these schemes tends to be high, especially in terms of road width, provisions for parking, etc. In addition, water and sanitation comprise 40% of the cost of off- and on-site service delivery. This is broken down as follows: the water supply network's share of total cost is 5%, the share of the water purification station is 10%, that of the sewerage network is 8%, and the sewage treatment plant is 17%.' The World Bank (2007) Op. cit. P. 24.

45 Caldeira, T. (2001). City of Walls: Crime, Segregation, and Citizenship in Sao Paulo. Berkeley: University of California Press.

46 Interviews have been anonymised at the request of the interviewees. Interview with the author December 2015.

47 Interview with the author December 2015.

Gated compounds first appeared in Egypt along the Mediterranean coast in the 1980s. These were quickly followed by gated compounds and (gated) resort communities along the Red Sea coastline, and the Sinai Peninsula. Rana Almatarneh argues that Egyptian gated compounds can be read as a return to traditional urban patterns of fragmented and socially homogenous spaces. 'Moreover, the spatial seclusion of social groups in the cities of the Arab world is not a new phenomenon. Urban studies on pre-modern towns depict the socio-spatial and material fragmentation of urban patterns in small and distinct quarters as one of the most typical characteristics of Arab cities.'[50] The author goes on to draw parallels between the sanctuary from the public realm that Arab houses and courtyards have traditionally evoked, and the enclosed collective space of the gated compound. 'In contrast with [fortified] European cities of the Middle Ages, cities in the Arab world have seen many conflicts *intra muros*. Therefore, the residential quarters, which were often accessible through only a single gate that could easily be barred and defended, offered protection that the city's central authorities did not always assure.'[51]

48 One exception came from a Vodafone employee (female, age 24) who welcomed the idea of a metro connection to Cairo as 'amazing'. All other interviewees, most of them residents of gated compounds, were universally opposed to the idea. Interview with the author December 2015.

A billboard in 6th of October advertises amenities in a new residential development. (Photo: R. Keeton, 2016)

Other authors, such as Dona Stewart and David Sims, have drawn connections between gated communities in the United States and gated compounds in Egypt, but these authors also insist on the specificity of the Egyptian gated compound as a particular response to a historical moment further specified by socio-cultural, geographic, political and economic contexts. Addressing the manner in which these gated compounds are marketed, Petra Kuppinger points out that, 'advertisements [for gated compounds in Egyptian New Towns] in obvious textual references and pictures, and subtle manners, using specific subtexts or locally available euphemisms, address specifically Cairene fears, concerns or demands.'[52]

It is no coincidence, then, that NUCA has managed its New Towns with much stricter enforcement of regulations than Cairo or other Egyptian cities. Sheikh Zayed City does not allow for (architectural representations of) the informal economy such as kiosks, appropriative uses of public space, commercial uses of residential space, or privately managed transport options (such as minibuses or *tuktuks*). Instead, the New Town adamantly forces informal processes to the unregulated edges.

In contrast to the vibrancy of downtown Cairo, the lack of these urban actors gives the New Town a somewhat sterile aspect that most inhabitants seem to appreciate. Residential streets are quiet and empty. No one walks in Sheikh Zayed, as distances are far and walking would

49 For elaboration on class divisions in Egyptian society see: Joel Beinin (2009) 'Workers' Protest in Egypt: Neo-liberalism and Class Struggle in 21st Century'. Social Movement Studies. 8:4, 449-454. DOI: 10.1080/14742830903234320. And: Sabea, H. (2014).

'Still Waiting: Labor, Revolution, and the Struggle for Social Justice in Egypt'. International Labor and Working-Class History. 86, 178-182. DOI:10.1017/S0147547914000222. And: Joya, A. (2017) 'Neoliberalism, the State and Economic Policy Outcomes in the Post-Arab Uprisings: The Case of Egypt'. Mediterranean Politics. 22:3, 339-361. DOI: 10.1080/13629395.2016.1219182.

50 Altmatarneh, R. (2013) Op. cit. P. 566.

51 Ibid.

52 Kuppinger, P. (2004) 'Exclusive Greenery: new gated communities in Cairo'. City & Society, Vol. 16. P. 37. DOI:10.1525/city.2004.16.2.35

53 Interview by the author December 2015.

54 See: www.dailynewsegypt.com/2015/05/13/weekly-average-salary-reached-egp-806-in-2014-capmas/.

55 www.al-rabwa.com/Villas.htm.

imply that one cannot afford a car. A male resident (22) of the Zayed 2000 compound recalls his parents' reasons for moving there in the 1990s: 'They liked that it was a quiet place, outside of the city. We could have a bigger house there, so that was better for us. We already knew that our lives would still be in Cairo; all our activities would be in Cairo. Even after twelve years, there is no interaction with our neighbours, there's no social activity inside the gated community.'[53]

Gated compounds function as semi-autonomous areas, with private security, special regulations and rules enforced by the managing authority. The more than fifty compounds in Sheikh Zayed City vary in terms of their relative luxuriousness, but all of them are of course out of range for the average Egyptian.[54] One of the original compounds, Al-Rabwa, offers the most complete list of amenities, including a school, shopping mall, mosque, golf course and club, medical services and 24-hour security. The compound includes 970 villas, designed according to 12 different plans, ranging in size from 220 to 637 m^2. The entire compound is encircled by a 10m wide horse track.[55]

Reflecting on his personal experience of growing up in Al-Rabwa, a student at the American University in Cairo writes,

> 'I recall the early promotional literature promising an international school, a mall, a health club, a golf course, all situated within an idyllic green setting… Many of the buyers who purchased homes in the 1990s believed that they were buying an investment "for the children", or perhaps a home to use as a weekend getaway.
> Like most compounds, Al-Rabwa is highly secured. There are several dozen security guards who man the entry points and conduct patrols… They are

One of the many guards' shelters inside a gated compound. (Photo: R. Keeton, 2016)

> working-class men who come in on a company bus, and work in rotating eight-hour shifts. The guards are anonymous fixtures in this suburban setting. For example, while there is always a security guard in the kiosk near my house, the guards are always changing, thus preventing the possibility of becoming familiar with them.'[56]

Omar's reflection underlines the distinction between the homeowners in Al-Rabwa and the guards employed to protect them. Claims of increased security are often one of the major selling points for gated compounds. In an effort to better articulate the pull factors used in advertisements for gated compounds in the Greater Cairo Region, Almatarneh identifies a number of references that are repeatedly used in marketing materials for gated compounds around Cairo. She breaks these down into their prevalence among affordable, moderate and high-end gated compounds, but across the board there is repeated reference to five distinguishable factors: friends, sense of community, community activities, meeting places, and homogeneity. All terms related to these concepts are used more frequently in the high-end gated compounds. As Almatarneh states: 'Certain real estate developers made explicit reference to homogeneity in the text of the marketing material. Phrases in the materials include, "comfort of folks who are at the same place in life as you are", "meet others just like you", and "people of similar lifestyle".'[57]

Conclusion

Sheikh Zayed City is a result of the combination of both global and distinctly Cairene influences. At the global scale, we can trace the trend towards gated communities as a popular (upper) middle-class housing solution that began in the United States and became popular in Egyptian resorts in the 1980s before finding its way into New Towns in the 1990s. We can also connect the spread of neoliberal policy that characterised many countries in the early 1990s to the simultaneous deregulation of land policy in Egypt. The proliferation of private developers was in response to this new market for large-scale development and the state's offer of cheap land in New Towns such as Sheikh Zayed City. The resulting construction boom eventually overtook NUCA's original plans for a mixed-income development, with the result that Sheikh Zayed is now predominantly a city of gated communities targeting the elite.

While it may be a natural instinct to want to live in an area surrounded by peers, gated compounds remain physically isolated spaces, creating inaccessible enclaves within a city. In Sheikh Zayed, three-quarters of the city are walled-off. So-called 'public spaces' are in actuality private spaces. In effect, this creates two very different spatial experiences for two groups of residents: the wealthy and the poor. A resident of a gated community enjoys access to medical, social, recreational, and commercial facilities within the compound, as well as access to a private car, and unchallenged access to shopping plazas. A resident of a public housing project does not have comparable amenities in their immediate environment, and may have only limited access to a car. As a result, a

56 cairobserver.com/post/136876563764/sheikh-zayed-city-mehwar-hyper-one-and-life-on#.WnGsp2aZNE4.

57 Almatarneh, R.T. (2013). Op. cit. P. 569.

58 World Bank (2017) P. 119.

59 cairobserver.com/post/136876563764/sheikh-zayed-city-mehwar-hyper-one-and-life-on#.WnGsp2aZNE4.

resident with less spending power may travel longer in a less efficient manner in order to purchase goods and services.

This disavowal of lower income groups and the services they require may eventually backfire. According to the World Bank, 'Land use regulations, zoning, and building regulations are some of the most valuable tools for governments to guide development and promote liveability. Yet certain interventions in urban land markets can negatively affect affordability and access to serviced land if they are not benchmarked against what the local population can afford to pay. Evidence from around the world indicates that inappropriate minimum standards actually increase informal development, even on formally titled land.'[58]

The Egyptian government must do more to address the gap between supply and demand that created and prolongs the current housing crisis. Even youth housing and other forms of public housing are inaccessible for the very poor and those reliant on informal economies. Because of Sheikh Zayed's lack of appropriate housing and its strictly-enforced building regulations, the lowest income groups are forced to remain in rural communities or in Cairo's labyrinthine *ashwa'yat*, where the basic amenities of water, electricity, safety and public services are insufficient.

Writing for Cairo Observer, a controversial blog documenting architectural and urban issues in the capital city, a student of the American University at Cairo reflects: 'When I first visited Sheikh Zayed City in 1998 to see our new home under construction, it was in the middle of nowhere. I was struck by the sense of distance, and the vast emptiness of the surroundings. Today, Sheikh Zayed City is a much busier place. Empty desert has given way to chic shopping spaces and villas. Once empty streets are now congested with vehicular traffic on a daily basis. This transformation, which occurred in a few, short years, has been nothing short of spectacular.'[59] This offers a positive view of the New Town and also reminds us of a universal truth: New Towns take time to mature.

In the Greater Cairo Region there is already a short historical progression of Cairene elite moving —however hesitantly as first— to newly planned areas at the periphery of the existing city. We can see this with Heliopolis, a New Town from 1905 that is now considered a desirable, central neighbourhood, and also with large planned suburbs like Maadi (1905) and Mohandessin (1950s). When Sheikh Zayed eventually meets its target population, it may be a very different city than the one we see now. As Cairo continues to grow and engulf the desert edge, Sheikh Zayed may be absorbed as one more upscale neighbourhood. Without the obscuring power of distance, the enclave effect that so many residents currently value may become a spectre of a distant past.

Applying the 10 principles of the Manual

Planning is an ongoing process

Sheikh Zayed City has changed considerably between its first phase implementation and the city that currently stands. While this process usually ensures more diversity and the natural incorporation of unregulated practices, in this case it has resulted in a New Town that provides ample leisure and recreational facilities for those in middle- and high-income groups, while disregarding the needs of low-income groups. This disparity can also be seen in the lack of public transportation options. As Sheikh Zayed continues to grow, more affordable housing options and more truly public facilities can make this New Town a more inclusive, vibrant and liveable city, but it will require constant rethinking of the current situation. At the moment, Sheikh Zayed City feels more like an unfinished project than an evolving city.

Plan for adaptivity

Very little adaptivity is planned into Sheikh Zayed City. Rather than an integrated approach that addresses local needs and alternative scenarios, it appears that NUCA sells land to private developers with only limited regulation. That has led to a situation with two groups of inhabitants who experience two different cities. Adaptivity speaks to both social and environmental issues, and for this New Town both aspects must be addressed urgently. For Sheikh Zayed City to become more adaptive, NUCA and local leaders must examine citizens' requirements at multiple levels and with both short-term and long-term solutions.

No New Town is an island

Unlike most other New Towns in this book, Egyptian New Towns are part of a comprehensive national spatial planning approach and locations have been decided upon in the context of various national spatial policies. Egypt is one of the few African countries that has this planning tradition. Still, we see difficulties in Sheikh Zayed because of the lack of integrated public transportation. Located 38 kilometres from downtown Cairo, Sheikh Zayed City currently supports a number of large-scale employers, but primarily functions as a bedroom community. Commuters travel daily between the New Town and neighbouring 6th of October or Cairo.
Although most residents we spoke with expressed resistance to the idea, the proposed metro line to downtown Cairo would increase Sheikh Zayed's connectivity by reducing travel times and costs. Furthermore, the establishment of open markets or commercial facilities aimed at lower-income residents would reduce their need to travel outside of the city in order to find affordable groceries. Other accessible transportation options such as better bus connections within the New Town and car-sharing could also improve the connectivity.

Use no cut-and-paste universal model

Sheikh Zayed City is visibly influenced by two planning models: gated communities in the style of American suburbs, and a public housing typology that has been prevalent in Egypt since the 1970s. Both models could be seriously questioned. More inclusive models and new ways of mixing income groups could encourage social cohesion rather than contributing to (self-) segregation. Taking a hard look at what is happening on the ground can be a way for planners to begin reconsidering how to address this New Town's specific needs and adapt their plans to those requirements.

Embrace new ideas

In the 1990s, Sheikh Zayed City was one of the first Egyptian New Towns to incorporate gated compounds. With the benefit of hindsight, this experiment has proven social and financially problematic.
It was not as profitable as expected because NUCA often sold land at below market prices and found it difficult to recoup infrastructural costs. In the future, NUCA might look to current best practices around the world that better integrate housing for all groups and supply appropriate urban amenities.

Infrastructure and mobility for all, from the start

Roads, electricity, sewage, and water networks in Sheikh Zayed are well-organised and functional. Mobility is problematic for low-income groups because the design of the city is based on the premise of private car ownership. It is not too late, however, to strengthen existing transportation systems and add additional options both within the New Town and at the regional scale.

Use a blue-green infrastructure as the central framework

Sheikh Zayed City is located 142m above sea level. Extensive use of irrigation keeps some (gated) areas of the New Town vibrantly green, but the majority of the New Town is powdered in the same sand that extends thousands of kilometres south across the Sahara. This blatant denial of existing environmental conditions is taken even further with golf courses, swimming pools and manmade lakes — which must be refilled regularly due to evaporation.
Water shortages, outages, and increasing water prices indicate that the Egyptian government is aware that this approach is not sustainable. It is not clear whether that will have any effect on the New Town's physical structure.

Incorporate local cultural heritage(s)

Sheikh Zayed City was largely built according to the global expression of a specific 'lifestyle', informed by private cars, gated compounds, and elegant shopping centres. However, the rich architectural heritage of nearby desert communities was not incorporated in plans, nor was traditional family life. As a result, parts of Sheikh Zayed feel placeless: their generic style recalls similar typologies from Brazil to South Africa.

Combine top-down and bottom-up

Residents in Sheikh Zayed City are not accustomed to organising grassroots initiatives or collective action. One way forward could be for NUCA to extend an outreach programme to citizens, to facilitate productive debate between NUCA and residents, and use that as a tool to slowly improve the quality of life in Sheikh Zayed City.

New Towns need diversity

Sheikh Zayed City is a high-income city in a middle-income country. Despite this majority, some middle- and low-income residents still call it home. It is urgent that this New Town finds a way to better integrate these groups in order to achieve a more inclusive and cohesive future for everyone.

Domestic workers arrive to start their work at a villa in Sheikh Zayed. (Photo: R. Keeton, 2016)

Preston Mendenhall, Developer and Executive Vice President of Rendeavour

With more than 12,000 hectares in their portfolio as of 2018, Rendeavour is currently the largest urban land developer in Africa. Rendeavour uses a New Town development model to create new urban areas within 10-30km of existing large cities. Over a 20-year development timeline, Rendeavour aims to create mixed-income integrated live, work, play communities, which reduce the burdens of urbanisation on heavily congested nearby city centres. Unlike most other developers, Rendeavour maintains management of the New Towns it develops, effectively creating a new form of private governance. In this interview, we discuss Rendeavour's approach to long-term development in Africa with Preston Mendenhall, Executive Vice President of Rendeavour.

Rachel Keeton (RK): One imagines that Rendeavour's initial interest in Africa was related to political stability, sustained economic growth and the growing middle class. Some critics, including experts at the African Centre for Cities, have questioned the composition of this 'middle class', claiming that in reality it only applies to about six percent of the African population. Is it a viable model to build for such a small percentage, or does Rendeavour build in anticipation of a new middle class?

Preston Mendenhall (PM): Too many 'experts' take a short-term view of the evolution of middle classes in emerging markets. There were plenty of naysayers when we began investing in Central & Eastern Europe in the 1990s, but 25 years later those regions have vibrant middle classes and economies. Our investments in urban development in Africa are long term. We have a 20-25 year investment horizon. Africa is the fastest urbanising region in the world; Sub-Saharan African countries consistently experience high GDP growth, even in commodities down cycles; and by 2050 one in every four people on the planet will be African.

Many international audiences find it hard to believe, but for the last 15 years Africa has been one of the fastest growing regions globally, with the world's most rapidly improving health statistics, school enrolment, governance and conflict reduction. Economic growth in Africa has averaged nearly six percent over the last 15 years. Six of the ten fastest growing economies in the past decade are African with the same being projected for the coming decade. The resurgence is broadly based: economic growth has accelerated in 27 of Africa's 30 largest countries.

Africans are also better educated than ever before. Literacy rates among the young now exceed 70 percent almost everywhere. Primary school enrolment rates are steadily approaching those in emerging Asia. The rise in secondary school enrolment has been even faster: an increase of more than 50 percent in just eight years from 2000.

Life expectancy is also improving rapidly. Since 2000, life expectancy has increased by as much as 42 percent and the 15 countries globally with the largest percentage increase in life expectation have all been African. Annual malaria deaths across Africa have fallen by more than 60 percent just since 2000 and new HIV infections are down 40 percent over the same period.

Not surprisingly, the collapse in global commodity prices and slower global growth have also affected Africa. However, the balance of the evidence strongly suggests that Africa's rise has been due to structural factors not commodity prices. For example, during the recent commodity boom, IMF data showed that natural resource endowments and geography had not been decisive factors in explaining the growth take-off. Moreover, Africa is consistently out-performing other developing economies (excluding China), and that gap has been maintained during the recent commodity downturn. The IMF predicts that Africa will be the second-fastest growing region in the world between 2016 and 2020.

What's driving all of these positive trends? There is a virtuous cycle between improved governance and improved economic performance, and it is likely to continue in most countries in the region.

RK: Rendeavour currently has urban developments underway in Kenya, Ghana, Nigeria, Zambia, and the Democratic Republic of Congo. What common denominators made these countries attractive and where does Rendeavour plan to expand next?
PM: Rendeavour takes many factors into consideration when evaluating a country. The key points are current or likely future trends in urbanisation, economic growth and political pluralism. We maintain a geographically diverse portfolio, because the emerging markets in which we operate sometimes face challenges, and by operating in multiple countries we can shift resources to other projects if one slows down.

RK: Who are the investors behind Rendeavour?
PM: Rendeavour was founded by Stephen Jennings, a long-time emerging markets investor who lived and worked in Central & Eastern Europe for 20 years. He began to invest in Africa in 2005. Rendeavour's shareholders are from the United States, New Zealand, Norway and the United Kingdom. They have all lived and worked in emerging markets for decades.

RK: What have been some of the major stumbling blocks or challenges as Rendeavour's portfolio has grown? What lessons have been learned from these experiences?
PM: Projects of the size and scale of ours face challenges all over the world. In our case, they range from the need to improve investment legislation to land records. We have learned a lot of lessons along the way, the most crucial of which is that we are investing for decades, not just a few years. In addition, we have learned that urban developments in Africa can only succeed if they are market driven. Developers can provide a masterplan and a framework for development, but then they need to let the market dictate what is built first.

RK: What is the governance structure for Rendeavour's New Towns? What is the relationship with local municipalities?
PM: We are building private municipalities whose governance is a combination of operating companies owned by Rendeavour and property owners' associations. At the same time, we have strong ties to local municipalities, because some services will be integrated with theirs.

RK: Rendeavour recently announced that SOM will be designing its new mixed-use development in Jigna, (Abuja, Nigeria). SOM is also responsible for designing the CBD in Tatu City (Nairobi, Kenya). How does Rendeavour choose planners and architects for its projects and how much does Rendeavour define the programme (housing, commercial, public space, etc.) in the project brief? How do you define the quality of a development?
PM: We have worked with a number of masterplanners on our projects, and they are chosen through our procurement process, which takes into account their experience, cost and commitment to our markets. Our brief to them, in basic terms, is for 2,500-acre mixed-use, mixed-income urban developments that are flexible enough to accommodate the changing economic needs of emerging markets.

RK: You led a business matchmaking tour in April 2017 to find American exporters and service providers to partner with Rendeavour. A related press release explained: 'Rendeavour's commercial mission is to "Buy American" for its projects… and increase American exports to sub-Saharan Africa and bi-lateral trade in key sectors.' Why is the American market a focus for Rendeavour?
PM: We have U.S. shareholders in our projects, and for that reason we are committed to attracting American suppliers and service providers to our projects. Similarly, we have held business matchmaking events with Norwegian and British companies, as well as companies with no connection to our shareholder base. As long-term investors in Africa, we recognise the need for international expertise and capacity building in these markets, and are committed to facilitating the entry of new products and services that can accelerate development, improve quality and build local capacity.

RK: The complexity of land ownership issues seems to prove that land is the ultimate commodity in Africa. Rendeavour's approach of first buying land to ensure clean property titles makes perfect sense in this context. How does Rendeavour choose greenfield sites for development and how does it go about solving land ownership puzzles?
PM: We adapt to the land ownership model of our markets. In some cases, we have bought land outright. In others, we have partners. For example, in Ghana land is either under government or tribal ownership, so for our developments there we have joint ventures with tribal stools. In Nigeria, we have one partnership with a private land owner, and another with the Lagos State Government.

RK: At the regional scale, one of Rendeavour's stated ambitions is to decentralise (and decongest) single node urban networks by bringing jobs, industry and residential areas to satellite cities. Our experience is that inadequate housing and jobs leads to commuting in one direction, while good housing and a lack of jobs leads to commuting in the other direction. Not providing low-income housing close to jobs leads to the same outcome. In what ways is Rendeavour attempting to combat the need for commuting?
PM: Our cities are planned to be mixed-use, with residential, retail, commercial, education, healthcare and other services and amenities within the development. Over time, as the cities reach maturity, there will be less and less need for commuting.

RK: Obviously Rendeavour is a private company that must make a profit. Targeting Africa's growing middle class market seems like a logical long-term strategy. However, we have repeatedly seen 'middle class' New Towns in Africa flanked by informal settlements because of the complex dependencies between these income groups. Has there been any thought put in to how Rendeavour might deal with this reality in advance by planning for it rather than responding as an afterthought?
PM: We are not only targeting the middle class. A mixed-income city must offer the full range of housing stock, and that is what we plan to do. In Tatu City, our flagship development near Nairobi, we already have 2,400 units

of affordable housing under development, over 4,000 units of middle class housing under development, and 500 high end residential homes under development. To address the issue of informal settlements, our goal is to ensure there is adequate affordable housing for workers at our developments. In addition, we invest in existing local communities around our developments, offering skills training to qualify them for a variety of jobs at our developments.

RK: At the urban scale, Tatu City will be a 'mixed-income, mixed-use' development. What range of incomes does that include? Are there units available for low-income or social housing? Will those units also be accessible for the very poor?
PM: Tatu City is built for a range of urban incomes, from affordable to high end. When we look at an eventual 100,000+ population at project maturity, we believe that about 15 percent will be lower income, 15 percent will be upper income, and the rest – 70 percent – will be a range of middle class homeowners. When building within 15-25 km of an urban centre, we are not targeting rural poor. Nonetheless, the affordable housing units are an extremely important part of reducing housing deficits in our markets.

RK: A main challenge for many New Towns (and a main ambition of the New Urban Agenda), is to avoid spatial segregation and urban enclaves. How does Rendeavour approach this issue?
PM: Our developments are large scale. You can't put a fence around 2,500 acres. They are open cities which will have a variety of housing, retail and commercial space. Yes, within 2,500 acres you may have a high-end estate with a security wall, but this too is integrated into a masterplan that envisions all parts of the community interacting physically and economically.

RK: Rendeavour's target buyer appears to be a middle-class professional with a family. Most of its developments feature single-family homes on private lots with access by car. Public transport is an essential component of successful New Towns. How do you promote or incorporate public transport in your developments?
PM: This is not the case. Rendeavour developments include medium and high-density residential buildings, which rise to eight floors and above. While some of our early developments are geared toward middle class professionals with families, this is due to current demand, and it is not a statement about the coming decades of development. With partners like SOM, we are already making plans for future public transport hubs – and limited private car access – that would be considered unrealistic today, but they won't be in 10 years. This will allow for public transport and accommodation of the thousands of day visitors to our developments. We are also planning for driverless cars, which will allow us to reduce parking spaces and improve pedestrian experiences.

RK: What is Rendeavour's long-term management strategy for these New Towns? What will Rendeavour's involvement look like after the developments are built and sold? How will you guarantee the quality or services in the long term?
PM: Rendeavour has established operating companies to manage the provision of everything from power and ICT to the upkeep of public spaces. Rendeavour

and its partners will have sold or developed the land in our projects, but we will continue to provide services and maintain facilities.

RK: Rendeavour clearly appears to be invested in Africa for the long term. What is your personal vision of Africa's urban future? How do you think the continent will look in 20 years?

PM: We forget that in until the mid-1970s it was Asia that was considered the over-populated, politically incompetent, war-riven basket case beset by ethnic conflict, malnutrition, disease and illiteracy, all complicated by poorly drawn borders. With the exception of Japan, per capita income in Asia hovered near a paltry 400 USD.

Africa is already following Asia's growth trajectory over the last 40 years. The evidence of this is in the figures presented above. There will be winners and losers in this process. There will be some surprises. We at Rendeavour are excited to be part of this economic and social transformation.

South Atlantic Ocean
Luanda
Aeroporto Internacional 4 de Fevereiro
to Matubas >
to Catete >
KILAMBA
Aeroporto Internacional de Angola
to Caboledo >
water
built area
New Town
highway
5km

CASE STUDY

Kilamba, Angola

'If it worked there, will it also work here?'

Angola lies in southwestern Africa with 1600 km of coastline along the South Atlantic Ocean. It is flanked by the Democratic Republic of the Congo to the north, Zambia to the east, and Namibia to the south. The geographic area now known as Angola was originally home to Bantu people, ruled by kingdoms including the Ndongo, Imbangala and the powerful Kongo. At its height, the Kongo Kingdom ruled the territory from the Congo River in the north to the Kwanza River in the south. The Kongo governed the area from the 1390s until the monarchy was forced into vassalage in 1891 and then abolished in 1914, following war with Portuguese colonisers. From 1914, Portugal governed the occupied area until Angolan independence in 1975 ended nearly five centuries of Portuguese influence.

Angola is characterised by a wide belt of coastal plains bounded by a range of mountains and hills extending from north to south, parallel to the coast. East of the mountains, a central plateau covered by dry savanna grassland extends across much of the country. Numerous rivers flow down from the central plateau across the coastal plains and west towards the Atlantic Ocean. The extensive Okavanga river system also begins in the plateau (known in Angola as the Rio Cubango), flowing southeast and converging in the Okavanga basin in Botswana. The northern part of the country is covered in rainforest. Only four percent of the land is arable, which partially accounts for Angola's reliance on imported foodstuffs, although agriculture is considered to have enormous potential for development.[1]

The capital city of Luanda has a hot, semi-arid climate, and is kept dryer than more inland areas by the Benguela current that sweeps north along the coast from the tip of South Africa. When the Benguela Current is weak, rainfall in Luanda can increase dramatically, as in March 2017 when a month's worth of rain flooded the capital over a period of just 24 hours.[2]

1 World Bank (2014) 'Angola: Arable Land (% of Land Area)'. Online: tradingeconomics.com/angola/arable-land-percent-of-land-area-wb-data.html.
2 Al Jazeera (2017) 'Angola Floods Kill 11; Cause Widespread Destruction'. Online: www.aljazeera.com/news/2017/03/angola-floods-kill-11-widespread-destruciton-170324084831333.html.

Luanda in the 17th century. (Source: Vingboons, J. 'D Stadt Loandas Pauli' Map of Loanda St. Paolo/Luanda, Angola, 1665. Kaartcollectie Buitenland Leupe, Nederlands Nationaal Archief)

Established in 1575, Luanda's historic centre is typical of a Portuguese colonial city. Located about three-quarters of the way north along the Angolan coast, the city's *baixa* (downtown) curves around Luanda Bay and spreads from this central core to cover a semi-circular area of 113 km^2. The main road network is more or less radial, originating from the central baixa and extending along the coast as well as into the interior. The colonial city is organised according to a modified grid that curves in response to the underlying topography.

Luanda developed over the twentieth century in accordance with a number of masterplans, notably those developed by Portuguese planners and architects Vasco Vieira da Costa and Fernão Simões de Carvalho, both of whom worked at the office of Le Corbusier at different times, and were influenced by his radical planning approach. In 1948, Da Costa was responsible for an elaboration of the *Urbanization Plan for the City of Luanda* designed seven years earlier by fellow Portuguese architects and urbanists Etienne de Groër and D. Moreira da Silva.[3] Da Costa's elaborated proposal envisioned five satellite cities for about 50,000 residents each, placed in a ring around the periphery of Luanda at a distance of 6 km from the existing city centre.[4] The plan was quickly deemed insufficient to match the rapid population growth after the end of the second World War, and the satellite cities were never built.[5] Two decades later, in the early 1960s, Fernão Simões de Carvalho drew an alternative masterplan for the city that rejected satellite cities in favour of redeveloped neighbourhood units and a reorganisation of the city centre.

3 Nunes Silva, C., ed. (2015) Urban Planning in Lusophone Countries. Ashgate: Farnham. P. 70.
4 Viegas, S.L. (2012) 'Urbanization in Luanda: Geopolitical Framework. A socio-territorial analysis'. Sao Paulo: 15th International Planning History Society Conference.
5 Ibid.

Like its predecessors, this plan was also never implemented, but some of the ideas 'paved the way for the international expression of an integrative overseas Portuguese policy'.[6]

Portuguese influence on Angolan urbanisation was mainly focused in Luanda and continued until independence in 1975. From 1975 to 2002 the country was embroiled in a violent civil war and experienced very little planned growth, as elaborated in the next section. Since the end of the war in 2002, the idea of redistributing urban services in the form of satellite cities has taken on renewed interest. In post-war Angola, the national government initiated state-led housing projects that include rehabilitation of existing infrastructures and the delivery of more than 100,000 new housing units.[7] This housing has taken various forms, including 'social housing' townships like Zango, Panguila, Sapú and Projecto Morar. The most widely publicised project, however, has undoubtedly been Kilamba. Criticised by international media as a 'Chinese Ghost Town' shortly after completion, this new city south of Luanda deserves a closer look.[8]

Chinese flagship project

On 15 January 1975, a quiet, cobblestoned fishing village on the southern coast of Portugal was witness to the death rattle of colonialism in Africa. Angola was one of the last African countries to declare independence, with only Seychelles and Djibouti becoming independent later. On that day in 1975, an agreement was signed affirming Angolan independence would begin ten months later — exactly four hundred years after the establishment of Luanda by Portuguese traders.[9] Between January and October of that year, a mass exodus of 300,000 people flooded out of Angola in the general direction of Portugal, taking with it much of the expertise on Angolan governance and planning.[10] Conflicts among the three Angolan nationalist movements steadily increased in violence as independence drew closer. When the power vacuum officially opened on 11 November, uncertainty and riots escalated to outright war. For the next twenty-seven years, a tripartite civil war ravaged the country, leaving an estimated one and a half million people dead, and a nation traumatised by battle.

Because the war raged mostly in small towns and villages that were vulnerable to ranging militias, it also created a massive housing shortage in the country's capital city as people swarmed to the relative safety offered by Luanda.[11] During the years of bloody conflict, however, construction halted as all efforts focused on the war machine. Between the first days of war in 1975 and the peace treaty in April 2002, Luanda grew nearly tenfold from a city of about 600,000 residents to more than five million.[12] The combination of this huge rural-to-urban migration and the prolonged absence of any new housing development created conditions that led to large scale expansion of *musseques*[13] (informal settlements) that have since grown to house an estimated 75 percent of Luanda's population.[14]

6 Viegas, S.L. Op. cit. P. 4.

7 Croese, S. (2017) State-led Housing Delivery as an Instrument of Developmental Patrimonialism: The Case of Post-war Angola. African Affairs Vol 116, Iss 462. Pp. 80-100.

8 Redvers, L. (2012) 'Angola's Chinese-built Ghost Town.' BBC. Online: www.bbc.com/news/world-africa-18646243.

9 Angola officially declared independence on 11 November 1975.

10 The Economist (1975) Flight from Angola. The Economist: 16 August 1975. Online at: www.economist.com/node/12079340.

11 In a 2016 interview with the author, Mayor Israel Marques put this housing shortage at 2 million. In 2008, the African Development Bank placed the shortage at 800,000 units—or roughly 4 million residents without access to adequate housing in Luanda. See: AFDB/OECD (2008) African Economic Outlook 2007/2008. Paris: OECD Publishing. P. 135.

12 The 1970 census identified 561,145 residents living in the province of Luanda, however, censuses were not taken between 1970 and 2014, so the data for 1975 and 2002 remains an estimate. See: Direccao dos Servicos de Estatistica (1971) Populacao de Angola. Recenseada em 1970, segundo os distritos e os concelhos ou circunscricoes: Apuramento provisorio. Luanda: Direccao dos Servicos de Estatistica. The 2014 census reported 6.9 million residents in the province of Luanda See: INE (2016). Censo 2014: Recenseamento Geral da População e Habitação: Resultados Definitivos. Luanda: Instituto Nacional de Estatística.

13 The *musseques* (unregulated housing areas) of Angola are characterised by well-defined individual identities and it is extremely simplifying to consider them as a homogenous group. The government of Angola's most recent approach to *musseque* redevelopment has been to remove residents from

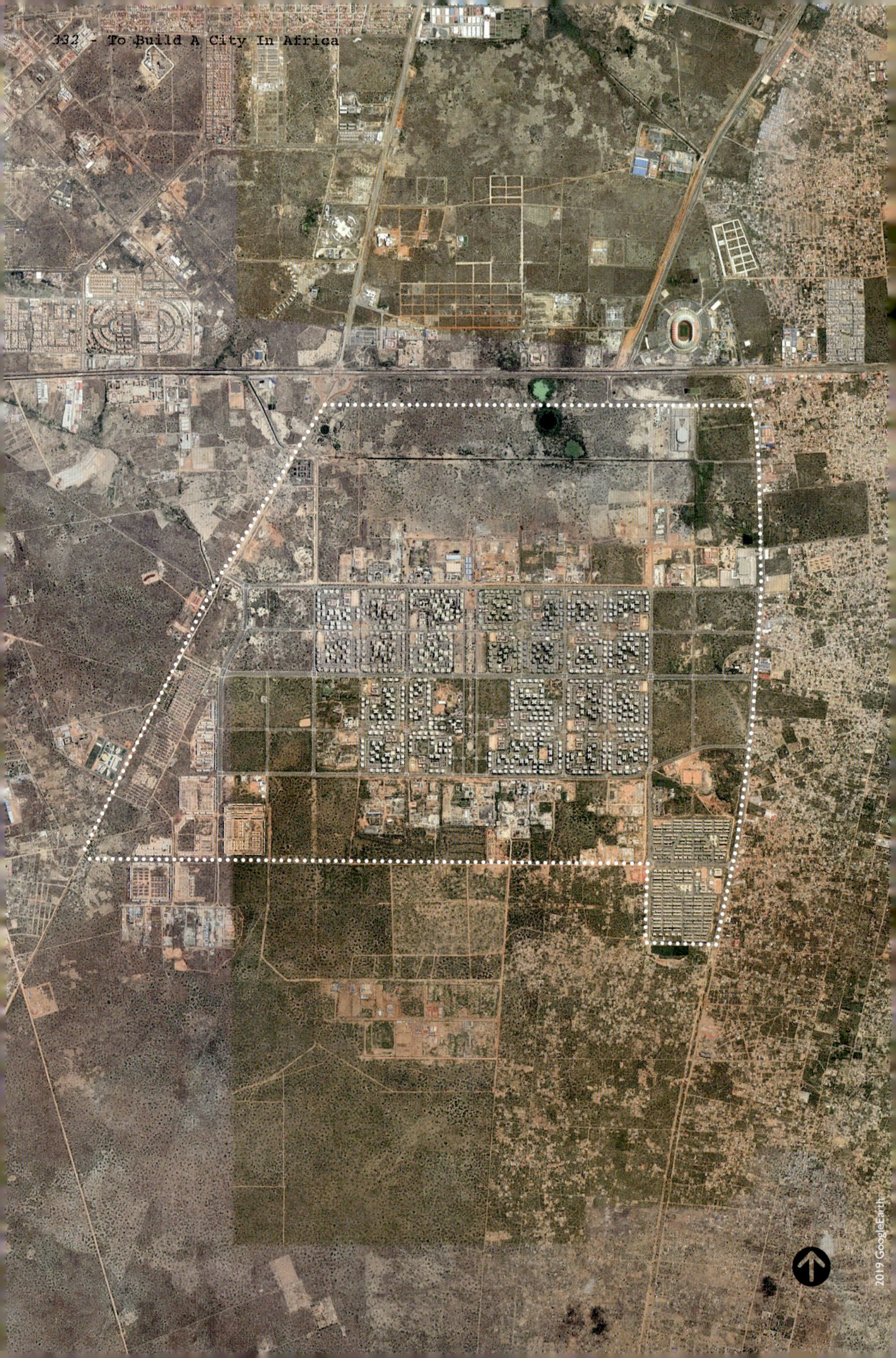
2019 GoogleEarth

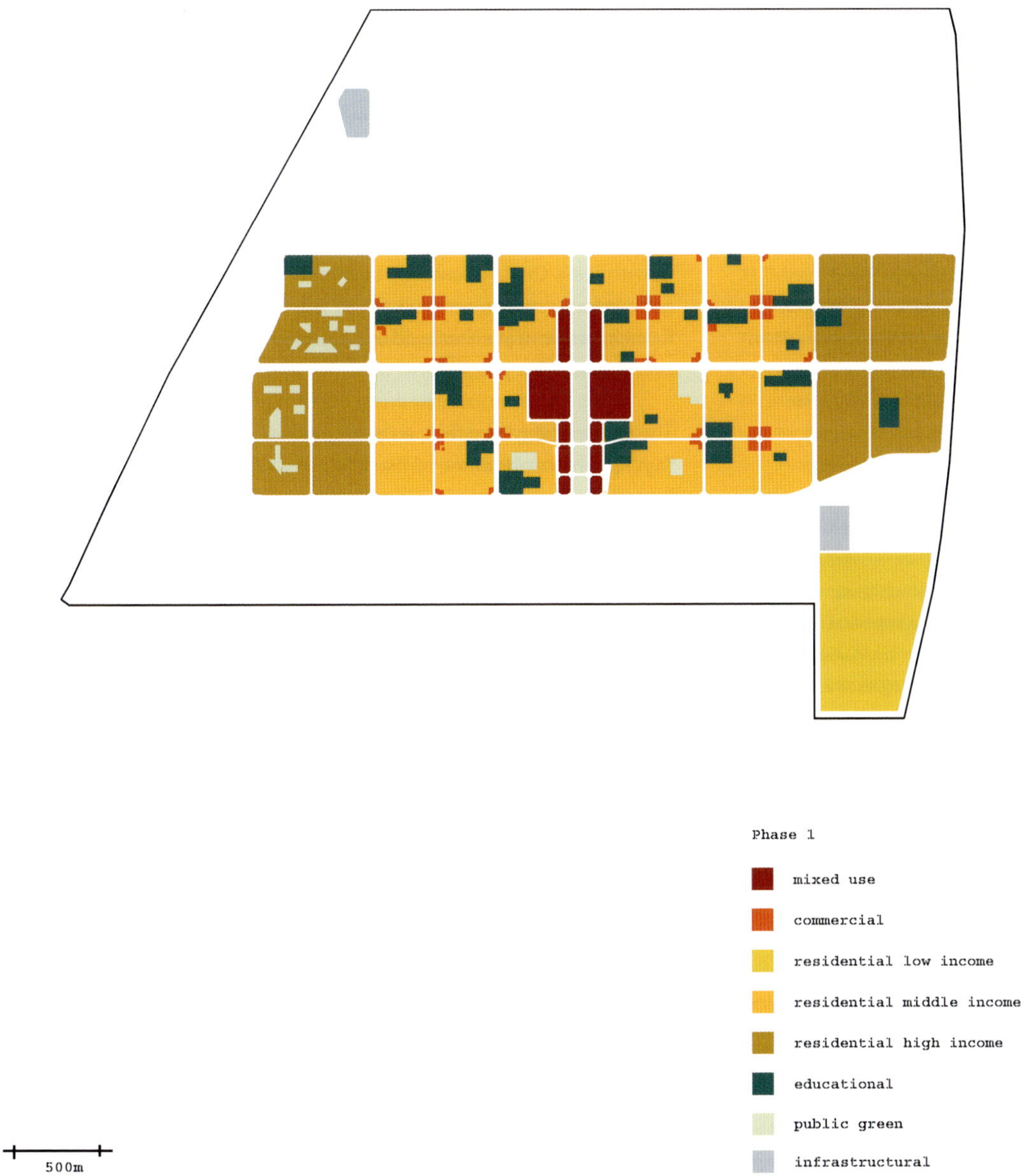
Phase 1
mixed use
commercial
residential low income
residential middle income
residential high income
educational
public green
infrastructural
500m

interview with Allan Cain, Director of Development Workshop, 12 January 2016.

24 Author's interview with Antonio Gameiro, National Advisor on urbanism and housing policy, on January 14 2016.

25 Steenkamp, A.C. (2008) Space, power and the body - the civil and uncivil as represented in the Voortrekker Monument and the Native Township Model. Delft: TU Delft.

26 Gastrow, C. (2013) 'Zango: Plans Unravel.' UrbanAfrica.net. Online: www.urbanafrica.net/news/zango-plans-unravel/.

27 See: World Bank, Angola. Online: data.worldbank.org/country/angola, and World Inequality Database, Angola. Online: wid.world/country/angola/.

28 The Centre for African Housing Finance (CAHF) provides a useful explanation of housing finance in Kilamba: 'In 2009, the Angolan government created a Housing Development Fund (FFH) (Decree 54/09 of 2009) to support the financing of social housing for low income households. However, the portfolio of the FFH remains limited to the provision of subsidised loans for public servants in state housing projects, such as the new city of Kilamba. Loans are extended for 30 years with a three percent interest rate. To facilitate access to other prospective inhabitants, in 2013 the government launched subsidised rent-to-buy schemes through Sonangol Imobiliária e Propriedade (SONIP), the real estate arm of the national oil company, to those with formal employment, a national identity card and a tax payer card. Apartments in these projects were initially priced between US$125,000 and US$200,000 a unit. These schemes reduced apartment prices to US$80,000 for a three bedroom apartment through twenty-year mortgages with a three percent interest rate and monthly payments of US$390. This brought

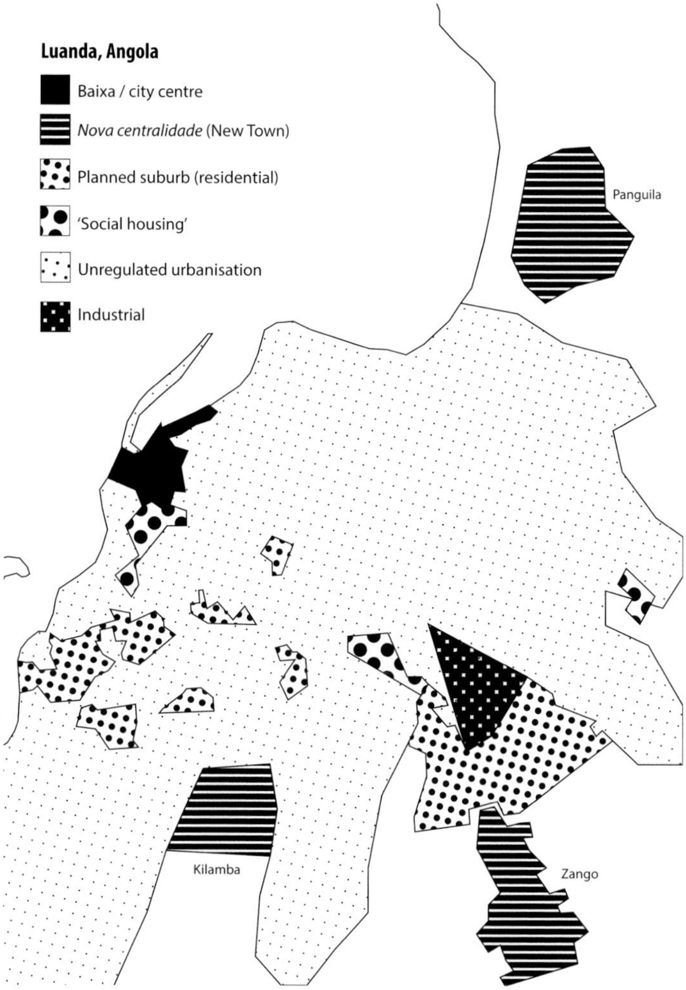

Spatial developments around Luanda: Kilamba, Cacuaco, Zango, Km 4, Capari/Sequele, Dundo and Cabinda, under National Urbanisation and Housing Programme. (Source: R. Keeton, based on works by Chloe Buire and Development Workshop)

contrast, such personalisation is impossible in Kilamba's high rise flats—in fact, it was explicitly designed to prevent it. Instead of flat roofs that could be occupied illegally, designers chose for gabled roofs. Instead of apartments that could be finished with materials of varying cost, designers specified the finishing of every flat. Instead of allowing for a range of interior organisational options, only three apartment types were offered.

Although it was originally presented to the public as 'social housing', Kilamba's property prices clearly indicate that it was aimed at middle class buyers. Angola's GDP per capita for 2017 was 3,484 USD, with annual incomes averaging around 10,000 USD.[27] Kilamba's intended function was to help regulate prices in Angola's strained housing market. The main problem with 'social housing', in Angola however, is that access to social housing has yet to be regulated and defined by national legislation.[28] In August 2010, the President raised the maximum price for social housing from 50,000 to 60,000 USD — an amount that is completely out of reach for most Angolans.[29] The lack of an accessible mortgage system has also had widespread ramifications on the housing market. A mortgage loan from Standard Bank, for example, currently comes with an interest rate of 24.5 percent, and at the personal discretion of a loan officer—making housing finance all but inaccessible to the vast majority of Angolans.[30]

When Phase I of Kilamba was completed in early 2011, there was no mortgage system in place to allow potential residents to buy properties. As a result, only the 5,000 handpicked public servants with housing financed through the government were able to move in. 5,000 residents in a city meant for 100,000 certainly looks bleak, and in July 2012, the BBC's Louise Redvers reported on 'Angola's Chinese-Built Ghost Town' with film footage of empty streets.[31] *Business Insider* and *The Daily Mail* quickly recycled the striking images.[32] In November 2012, CNN's David McKenzie reported on a, 'Chinese-built Angolan city feels like a ghost town'.[33] The story gained traction internationally, playing on western paranoia related to collaboration between China and African countries. By 2017 the dated narrative had become accepted truth, perpetuated in books like *Atlas Obscura: An Explorer's Guide to the World's Hidden Wonders*, and *The Lonely Planet Kids Travel Book: Mind-Blowing Stuff on Every Country in the World*.[34]

In 2012 multiple international media outlets critiqued Kilamba as a "Ghost Town". (Source: Youtube)

Despite this international saga of homes without occupants, by 2014 Kilamba was actually facing a very different situation. The year before, state media outlet ANGOP announced that all available Kilamba apartments had sold out, with 40,000 residents living in the New Town, and waiting lists for future buyers.[35] The story on the ground transformed from one of empty apartments to a much more complicated narrative that questioned the lack of transparency in the housing sales process. It became widely suspected that apartments in Kilamba were being awarded based on personal connections to power.[36] Kilamba was becoming one of the most sought after addresses in the country. What changed during that year? According to researcher Chloe Buire, the answer has everything to do with housing prices and access to housing finance: 'In February 2013, President dos Santos ordered that the apartments be made affordable and the state-backed mortgage scheme open to all Angolans. When the smallest unit (T3) dropped in price from US$125,000 to US$70,000, Kilamba suddenly became Luanda's most accessible property market. Hundreds of applicants queued for days outside the offices of SONIP.'[37]

The first mayor of Kilamba, Israel Marques, was personally appointed by Dos Santos to oversee the start of the New Town. In an interview with Marques in 2016, he reported steady growth, claiming that Kilamba was 97 percent occupied with about 100,000 residents. 'BBC, CNN, they all

ownership within the reach of early career professionals and mid-level civil servants earning over US$1,500 a month. However, government housing projects still remain unaffordable for low income households.' See: housingfinanceafrica.org/countries/angola/.

29 Croese, S. (2012) One Million Houses? Chinese Engagement in Angola's National Reconstruction. In: Power, M. and Alves, A.C. (Eds.) China & Angola, a Marriage of Convenience? Cape Town: Pambazuka Press. Pp. 138-140.

30 According to the Centre for African Housing Finance, 'In 2011, only 2.2 percent of Angolans above the age of 15 had an outstanding mortgage at a financial institution.' See: Housing Finance in Angola: Overview. Online: housingfinanceafrica.org/countries/angola/. The state also offers a mortgage programme for public servants at 3 percent interest. See: Author's interview with Antonio Gameiro, National Advisor on urbanism and housing policy, on 14 January 2016.

31 Redvers, L. (2012) 'Angola's Chinese-built Ghost Town'. BBC. Online: www.bbc.com/news/world-africa-18646243.

32 Badkar, M. (2012) 'Check out the

The neighbourhood of KK5000 offers affordable housing in Kilamba, but few amenities or services. (Photo: R. Keeton, 2017)

Mayor Israel Marques. (Photo: R. Keeton, 2016)

came during the time after the opening when we were trying to figure out how to sell the apartments without access to bank mortgages. They never came back.'[38]

After the first phase of Kilamba was completed, the government instructed Sonangol Imobiliária e Properties Lda. (SONIP, a subsidiary of state oil giant Sonangol), to build an extension to the project with more affordable housing.[39] The new 76.15 ha extension was added at Kilamba's south-eastern edge. Known as KK5000, the area includes housing for about 30,000 residents. The five story apartment blocks have only one apartment typology: 5,000 three-bedroom apartments (T3). In September 2018, a T3 flat in KK5000 was listed for 8,000,000 AOA (27,6000 USD).[40] KK5000 offers the same urban infrastructures as Kilamba, with efficient road access, electricity and street lighting, clean drinking water supply, drainage, sewage, and a telecommunications network. The area includes two kindergartens, a primary school, and secondary school. However, no commercial or mixed use areas enliven this residential district, and aside from educational facilities, urban amenities are non-existent. According to Marques, 'You go there, you will be shocked. The quality of design is so bad… KK5000 looks like a military camp. I always say, "this is going to be my headache"...Of course, your life is your connections, not just a house... Here in Kilamba, we are taking a risk with KK5000. [Residents of KK5000] have to travel too far for shops or any services.'[41]

If Kilamba's final phase is completed according to plan, it will eventually house 750,000 residents. By the time it is completed the surrounding area may have a completely different character: in 2015, minister of State Edeltrudes Costa announced the General Metropolitan Master Plan (PDGL) for Luanda Province. The new masterplan shows a proposed commercial and business area north of the New Town, a massive change that would provide Kilamba with the urban amenities it will need to become a vibrant city.

massive Chinese-built ghost town in the middle of Angola'. Business Insider. **Online:** www.businessinsider.com/chinese-built-ghost-town-kilamba-angola-2012-7?international=true&r=US&IR=T, and Daily Mail Reporter (2012) 'Why has China built a ghost town in Africa?' Daily Mail. **Online:** www.dailymail.co.uk/news/article-2168507/Footage-shows-brand-new-Angolan-city-designed-500-000-lying-empty.html.

33 McKenzie, D. (2012) 'Chinese-built Angola city feels like a ghost town'. CNN. **Online:** www.youtube.com/watch?v=V8HyDGCNxpo.

34 Foer, J., Thuras, D., and Morten, E. (2016) Atlas Obscura: An Explorer's Guide to the World's Hidden Wonders. New York: Workman Publishing Co., Inc. P. 213. and Lonely Planet Kids (2015) The Lonely Planet Kids Travel Book: Mind-Blowing Stuff on Every Country in the World. New York: Lonely Planet. P. 133.

35 'Kilamba City Flats Sold Out.' ANGOP Agencia Angola Press, 4 September 2013. Online: www.angop.ao/angola/en_us/noticias/sociedade/2013/8/36/Kilamba-City-flats-sold-out,9a874ce7-f6fa-4f25-b35a-9d888d4c07d4.html.

36 Onishi, N. (2017) 'Angola's Corrupt Building Boom: "Like Opening a Window and Throwing Out Money"'. New York Times. 24 June 2017. Online: www.nytimes.com/2017/06/24/world/africa/angola-luanda-jose-eduardo-dos-santos.html.

37 Buire, C. (2015) "View of Suburban Luanda: Banishing the Ghosts from Kilamba". Africa Research Institute, 2 September 2015. Online: www.africaresearchinstitute.org/blog/views-of-suburban-luanda-banishing-the-ghosts-from-kilamba/.

38 Interview Marques 2016

39 SONIP was replaced in 2014 by state real estate company IMOGESTIN, who took over management and property sales.

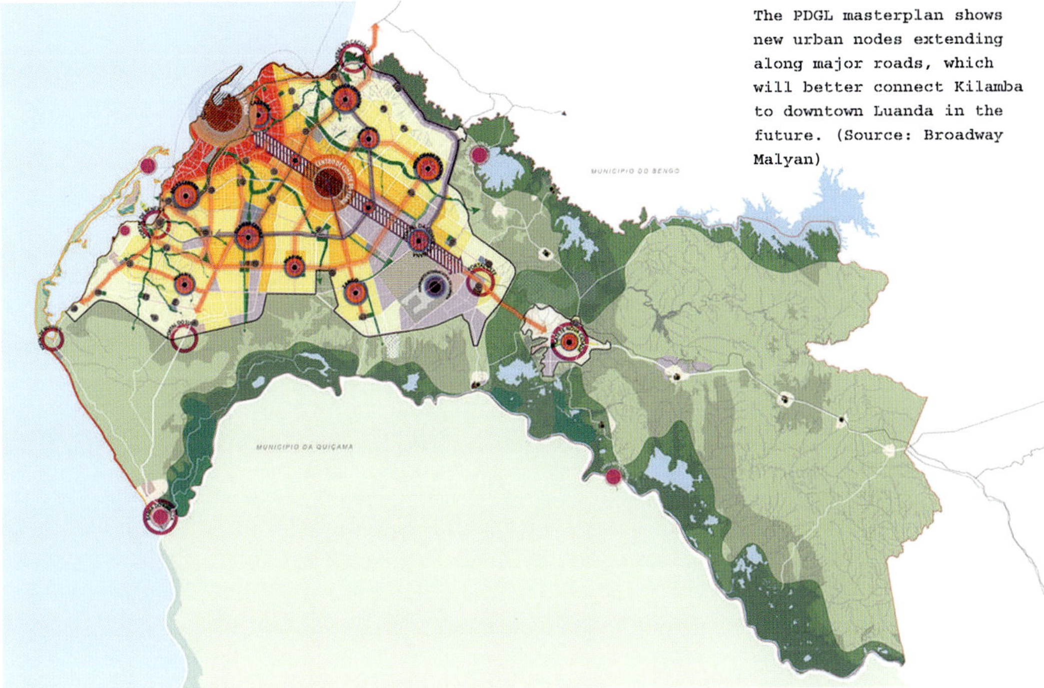

The PDGL masterplan shows new urban nodes extending along major roads, which will better connect Kilamba to downtown Luanda in the future. (Source: Broadway Malyan)

The Chinese city in Africa

In Kilamba, the strict deployment of the grid at the scale of the superblock is problematic: the model provides a strong organisational framework, but stops short of integrating this structure with more human-scale development. As a planning tool, the grid plan was introduced in many parts of Africa under European colonisers, particularly the French. Prior to this, however, the grid plan was also used in some ancient African urban planning projects, most notably in the Senegalese heartland (Senegambian royal capitals such as Kahone, Maka and Daikhao, as well as the clerical cities of Pire and Koki), and ancient Egypt.[42] In China, the grid pattern has also been used in urban planning for millennia. In addition to this traditional link to the grid, contemporary Chinese planning models show the influence of the modernist CIAM-principles as laid down in the *The Athens Charter* (1933). In fact, according to author Duanfang Lu, *The Athens Charter* has had a profound influence on Chinese urban planning since the 1980s.[43] Specifically, *The Athens Charter*'s call for 'highrise apartments placed at wide distances apart [to] liberate ground for large open spaces' can be read back in contemporary Chinese planning models.[44] Soviet planning principles also inform contemporary Chinese urban planning.[45] Both models advocate for a functionalist approach, with clear divisions among urban functions, rational organisation and heavy road infrastructure.

Although the Chinese grid model and its infill of apartment towers is an unfamiliar typology in Africa, Angolan planners and architects recognise the value of this efficient model, while still questioning its application in

40 Flats listed for sale at www.olx.co.ao/imoveis-casas/apartamento-casa-a-venda/q-kk5000/. Converted at a rate of 1 AOA = 0.00345947 USD, valid on 24 September 2018.

41 Interview Marques, 2016.

42 Silva, C.N. (Ed.), Urban Planning in Sub-Saharan Africa: Colonial and Post-Colonial Planning Cultures. New York: Routledge, 2015.

43 Lu, D. (2006) Remaking Chinese Urban Form: Modernity, Scarcity and Space, 1949 – 2005. New York: Routledge. P. 94.

44 Congress Internationaux d'Architecture moderne (1933) The Athens Charter. Trans J. Tyrwhitt. Boston: The Library of the Graduate School of Design, Harvard University, 1946.

45 Lu, D. (2006) Op. cit. P. 94.

Aerial view of Kilamba.
(Source: CITIC, 2015)

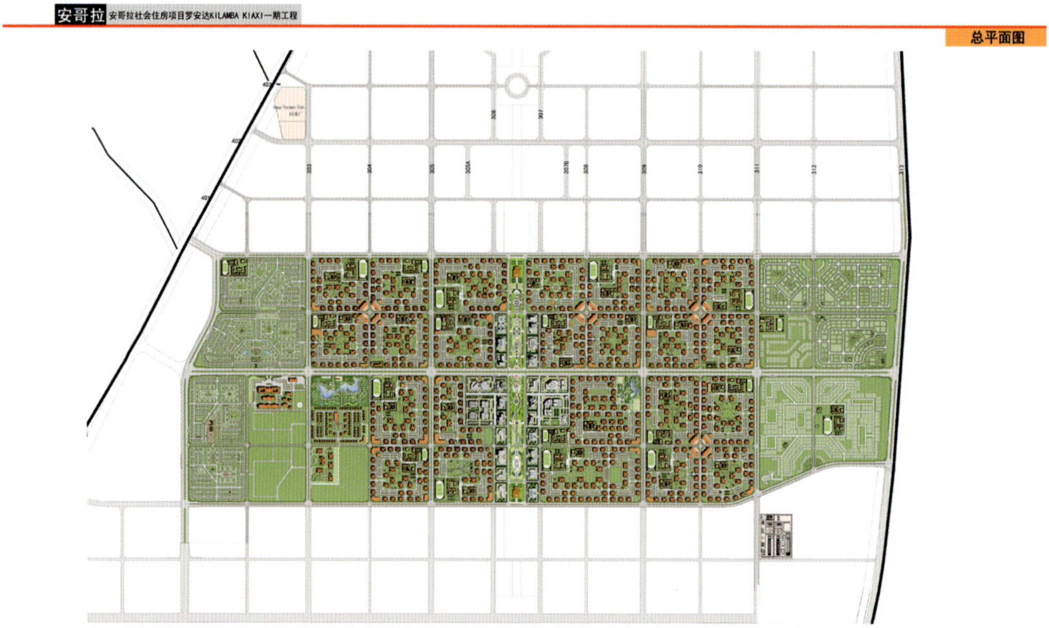

The masterplan followed by CITIC reflects standard Chinese urban planning principles. (Source: CITIC, 2016)

this context. As Antonio Gameiro, National Advisor on urbanism and housing policy and a professor of urban planning revealed: 'The politicians didn't like the idea of verticalising in the beginning [of Kilamba]. But infrastructure in places like Zango [township] is so expensive. When we started thinking of new cities, some people said, "we are Africans, we don't want to live like this, we want to have our chickens, our backyard." And I said no, this the way to go. It's cheaper in terms of infrastructure.' …[However,] Kilamba doesn't yet have much mixed use, but that will come. Maybe for the second phase of Kilamba there can be some change. Something that responds more to the context".[46]

According to Ma Baowen, Regional Division of Africa Vice President at CITIC, the first step for Kilamba was a demographic analysis and forecast for population growth — a standard starting point for most Chinese urban planning projects.[47] The first phase was designed to accommodate 160,000 residents, with future plans for a total population of 750,000 (Phases II and III). Technical infrastructures, such as water treatment facilities and electricity were based on these numbers.

Chinese urban planning employs a standard area of land use for each inhabitant (varying from 60 to 120 m^2 per person) and uses this number to determine the final area required for a new urban plan.[48] In Kilamba, the result is a project that appears very technical, very controlled, and very Chinese. That would be unremarkable for a suburb of Shanghai, but for an Angolan city flanked by the bustling, multi-layered and cosmopolitan Luanda, there is a sense of displacement, as if one has been teleported out of Angola by crossing the freshly paved road that delimits the New Town. Designed by Chinese architects in China according to Chinese planning principles, built with Chinese machinery and materials shipped from China

46 Interview Gameiro 2016

47 Interview Ma Baowen 2016

48 Many of the standards related to urban land use are set out in the Chinese national planning document 'Standards for Urban Use and Construction' (*Chengshi jianshe yongdi fenlei yu guihua jianshe yongdi biaozhun*), which, according to author Remi Curien, 'plays a key role in urban planning. This figure is approximately 100 m^2 per person, though it can vary from 60 to 120 m^2 per person depending on the size and characteristics of the city.' Curien, R. (2014) Chinese Urban Planning, China Perspectives No. 2014/3. P. 27.

in 15,000 sea containers, Kilamba provides an insight into the export of a streamlined urban planning process.[49]

The New Town also reveals the planners' conviction of the universal applicability of their approach.[50] With all eventualities quantified, there is little room for consideration of the messy ways in which people actually conduct their lives. Numbers become the rationale for every design decision. Creativity, innovation or informality within this system become unpredictable variables that are too costly to consider. According to Allen Cain, an advisor for the project and Director of Development Workshop, a research group based in Luanda for more than three decades, 'the first consultation with Angolan planners (including myself) happened after plans had been prepared in China. To be blunt, the consultation with Angolan planners happened after the fact. I think the people who participated in that first consultation (all heads of departments and experienced planners), all knew it was a consultation meant to legitimise the process. A thesis that we have been defending is that the more appropriate model for urbanisation here in Angola is in-situ upgrading, a pro-poor approach, and transformation of slums.'[51]

Services and comfort

Kilamba follows the hyper-functionalist urban planning principles that have become standard Chinese practice. Cartographic analysis of the masterplan reveals a hierarchical grid that informs the road system, with street widths of 20, 40 and 60 m. Commercial functions are located on the 40 m wide streets, with larger setbacks from the 60 m roads to protect pedestrians from faster traffic. The 20 m roads are mostly within residential blocks. Every street is lined with sidewalks, and intersections have pedestrian crosswalks and traffic lights. Large orthogonal blocks are split into mono-functional areas, with public services (such as education and health facilities) applied evenly across the plan, corresponding directly to residential numbers. Dispersed among the superblocks are 24 kindergartens, nine elementary schools, and eight junior schools.[52] There are two transformer stations that power the 710 buildings, with reserve capacity for further expansion. Water is pumped in from the Kwanza River, 15 km away, and treated locally to World Health Organisation standards (although it is still recommended to boil the water before drinking). The sewage treatment plant has a capacity of 35,000 tons per day.[53]

Housing and infrastructure were delivered first, and a visit in 2016 revealed that many commercial and business spaces were not yet occupied. A few cafés, banks and other amenities were in use and appeared popular with residents. The potential for a bustling urban atmosphere was there, but not yet crystallised. At the time, residents were mostly traveling outside of Kilamba to obtain the goods necessary to support daily life and the result was a city of wide streets that felt languid and sparse.

49 Interview Ma Baowen 2016

50 During the construction process, CITIC made a considerable effort to train Angolan foremen at a rate of one Chinese to five locals. The establishment of a scholarship-based vocational school that has graduated 500 students per year has also been a contribution to local capacity-building.

51 Interview with Allen Cain, 2016.

52 The schools are free, as public education in Angola is compulsory for eight years beginning at age seven. There are, however, school-related fees and identification requirements that make access to education problematic for some groups.

53 Interview Ma Baowen 2016

View of Kilamba apartments.
(Photo: R. Keeton, 2016)

Apartment 110 m^2

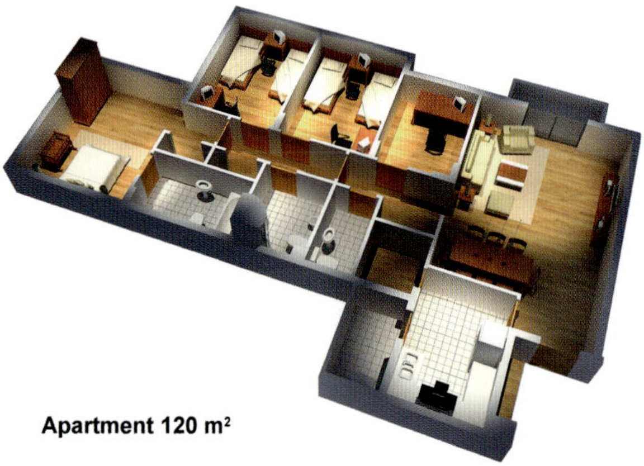

Apartment 120 m^2

Apartment 150 m^2

Apartment typologies.
(Source: CITIC, 2016)

The architecture in Kilamba is familiar to anyone with experience in China. Mid-rise apartment blocks stuccoed in light shades march along in strict formation. The roofs of these buildings are pink, yellow, green, blue, and white, giving rise to the New Town's alternative name: Rainbow City. Interiors are finished in high quality materials straight from China: aluminium door and window frames, polished tile floors and taupe-coloured drywall. Each apartment has a corresponding parking space, and almost all are in use. There are three layout options for apartments: 110, 120, and 150 m^2. This is larger than typical Chinese apartment sizes and a nod to Angola's high fertility rate—one of the only concessions to contextual specificities discernible in the masterplan. In Angola, families have an average of six children, and that number was the basis for the large apartment sizes. But Kilamba, like almost all contemporary African New Towns, has mostly attracted young, highly educated families—and almost none with more than two children.[54]
Some people associate this discrepancy with the higher income group, but according to Marques the demographics will likely change over time: ageing grandparents will fill empty bedrooms, children will marry and remain in their parents' apartments, or families will have more children as time goes by.
Kilamba is, more than anything else, a city of condominiums: privately owned apartments with shared common spaces. This is a housing organisation concept that is wholly foreign to the Angolan context. Residents have never before contributed to a lighting bill for collective spaces. They've never gathered on Saturdays to plant geraniums in the shared plant beds. They've never, perhaps, had to take their trash down an elevator to put it in the underground waste collection point. Learning to live differently in this New Town is part of the social cost, but one that is readily embraced by residents who are tired of the unpredictability of service provision in Luanda.

This is probably the main factor behind Kilamba's popularity. Residents in Kilamba have clean water, reliable electricity, new infrastructure, and a responsive—if underfunded—urban management team. Wherever else one might choose to live in Angola, power outages, traffic jams and poorly treated water are the norms. Kilamba is unique. With its large, modern

54 Interview Marques 2016

apartments, it appeals to a group of Angolans that is upwardly mobile but without many options.

Thinking green in the Rainbow City

It has become a familiar truism that environmental sustainability is a luxury of the wealthy. The highly technical approach taken by designers in Kilamba upholds this axiom. As Ma Baowen revealed: 'CITIC wanted to include solar powered water heating, but the idea was scrapped by the owner as being too expensive. We have reserved a socket in each house to install a solar panel, but it doesn't come with the unit. We will continue to suggest to the owners to put in more ecologically friendly systems, but the costs are often prohibitive.'[55]

Zooming out to a regional scale, Kilamba represents an increasingly common approach in New Town design that deals with the physical parameters of a site and leaves edge conditions unconsidered. Within the city, land has been appropriately graded and sits 100 m above sea level. The site slopes gradually about 10 m downhill from south to north. Adjacent to Kilamba, on its eastern flank, an informal settlement has grown up with the New Town since 2012. This community sits on ungraded land and has no street paving or drainage system. As a result, heavy rains periodically cause property damage, loss of lives and environmental degradation.

Although this is a logical way of dealing with property limits, it can also be read as a missed opportunity to address the increasingly frequent natural disasters plaguing Luanda and its surrounding region. Just since 2015, flooding in Angola has resulted in the deaths of hundreds and the displacement of tens of thousands.[56] The (flash) floods are the result of heavy rains and overflowing rivers. According to Cain, 'The succession of floods may be attributable to a combination of factors including the increasing climatic variability, the concentration of people with limited coping abilities in low-lying areas, environmental changes induced by settlement in vulnerable zones, and the removal of natural vegetation in upstream river basins.'[57]

Floods cause immediate damage and loss of life, but in Luanda and surrounding areas poor water management also results in long term public health issues such as cholera, malaria and yellow fever. 'Ponds of standing, stagnant water occur in some flatter areas more distant from the coast, in the *municipios* of Cazenga, Viana and Kilamba Kiaxi, after heavy rains. Clay soils predominate in these flat areas, whereas sandy soils through which water drains more rapidly occur closer to the coast.'[58] When flooding occurs in low-lying areas near Kilamba, the sharply defined edges of the development won't protect it from air-borne health threats.

Article 24 of the original Angolan constitution asserts the right of all citizens to live in 'a healthy and unpolluted environment', and

55 Interview Ma Baowen 2016

56 January 2017: 1800 households displaced. April 2016: 19 dead, 800 households displaced. March 2016: 50 dead, 182 households displaced. January 2016: 10,000 displaced. April 2015: 500 displaced. March 2015: 62 dead, 1770 households displaced. See: floodlist.com/tag/angola.

57 Cain, A. (2015) Climate Change and Land Markets in Coastal Cities of Angola. Washington DC: The World Bank. P. 3.

58 Cain, A. (2015) op. cit. P.8.

acknowledges the state's responsibility 'to protect the environment and national species of flora and fauna throughout the national territory and maintain ecological balance.'[59] However, the enforcement of these assertions remains limited and unpredictable. There is an opportunity here to show greater commitment to the value of natural landscapes and their contribution to high-quality urban environments.

A country of musseques

According to a survey done in 2008-9, 90.9 percent of the Angolan urban population lived in 'inadequate conditions' at that time.[60] In the decade since this survey, the national government has claimed the provision of housing as one of its main priorities. However, they have not been able to keep pace with the rapid urbanisation facing Luanda and other large cities, and as a result, unregulated housing construction in the form of *musseques* has become widespread. Development Workshop estimates that roughly three quarters (75 percent) of Luanda's housing provision is still 'informal' or unregulated, and these areas are most vulnerable to the threats posed by climate changes.[61]

The *musseque* that abuts Kilamba's eastern boundary has developed in tandem with the New Town and exchanges between the two areas are manifold and intensive, economic as well as social. Spatially, however, the four-lane road dividing the areas embodies a clear division between legal tenure and urban services on one side, and illegal tenure and the absence of basis services in the adjacent informal community. The spatial divide accentuates the physical advantages of formal planning, no matter

59 Constitution of Angola 1975 Online: en.wikisource.org/wiki/Constitution_of_Angola_(1975).

60 INE (2010) Inquerito Integrado sobre o Bem Estar da Populacao 2008-2009: Principais Resultados Definitivos. Luanda: Instituto Nacional de Estatística.

61 Cain, A. (2010) Research and practice as advocacy tools to influence Angola's land policies. In: Environment & Urbanization Vol 22(2): 505–522.

Streetview of 'musseque' (informal community) across from Kilamba. (Photo: R. Keeton, 2016)

its urban form: efficient drainage and sewage that reduces the impact of flooding and associated health risks; asphalt roads that increase access and have the capacity to support public transport networks; availability of potable water and in-house sanitation systems that eliminate health and safety risks; reliable electricity that supports access to lighting, digital systems, refrigeration, etc.; and legally recognised tenure that cannot be subjected to forced eviction. These advantages are brought into sharp focus when contrasted with the insecurities of life in the *musseque*.

Conclusion

To consider Kilamba's spatial challenges is to realise that formal planning offers residents many benefits: safety from flooding, reliable urban services, internal social cohesion, and (the perception of) safety. In this case, however, it also drives the growth of an adjacent informal settlement with no access to Kilamba's services and compounds existing classism by increasing the visibility of existing inequalities.

While the urban plan of Kilamba can be read as a series of direct responses to quantifiable data, an alternative approach might be a closer examination of both the *baixa* and *musseques*—and what their (self-)organisation can teach future planners about alternative land management, local social networks, existing interdependencies and different ways of moving through life.

Before it can become a vibrant city, Kilamba needs more diversity, more urban amenities and more integration between existing formal and informal systems. These things take time, and Kilamba is very young. Still, Kilamba already succeeds in many ways, by efficiently providing quality housing, infrastructure, and services to 100,000 residents. As it grows and changes there may be ways to stretch these clear benefits into adjacent areas, and thereby achieve a more socially inclusive and environmentally sustainable urban future.

Applying the 10 principles of the Manual

Planning is an ongoing process
One of Kilamba's key challenges has been good urban management since CITIC stepped out of this role in 2017. With the current organisation for urban administration processes, this will continue to be a challenge. The municipal government does not have the financial or manpower capacity to effectively manage and maintain the city. As we have already seen, this will continue to erode the New Town's image (and physical state) unless alternative management processes are explored. It is crucial that local government continues to monitor, evaluate, and reconsider Kilamba, rather than accepting the New Town as a completed project. That change in mindset can be the key to a sustainable and inclusive future.

Plan for adaptivity
Kilamba has a number of attributes that could be useful to future adaptation. Perhaps most promising is the grid organisation of both streets and utility infrastructures that could be extended to surrounding areas as well as subdivided to increase densities and facilitate more diverse urbanisation patterns.
Residents' committees in Kilamba have assumed increasing power since the rent strikes of 2016, and this may signal an increase in participatory governance and municipal decision-making processes. Their insights and ambitions can give the local government insight into necessary changes.

No New Town is an island.

Kilamba fails to adequately take into account its surrounding context from both social and environmental perspectives. This presents a missed opportunity for the New Town, and facilitates the growth of unserviced musseques along its borders. Although the surrounding area is likely to urbanise in the coming years, Kilamba currently functions as a suburban satellite to Luanda, with most of its working residents commuting to the baixa daily. 'Public' transport connections in the form of candonguerios (private mini-buses) are limited and inefficient.

Use no cut-and-paste universal model

Kilamba falls into the trap of embracing a one-size-fits-all model. Chinese planners designed the city based on quantifiable data with extremely limited input from local experts. The results of this process are visible in the urban management challenges the New Town continues to face, as well as the social adaptation challenges faced by residents (cooking on balconies, trash thrown from windows, poor care of shared spaces, and the inability to repair broken elements (elevators, lighting, etc.) imported from China).

Embrace new ideas

Kilamba can be understood as an experimental New Town in the sense that it is the first entire city imported from China into Africa. Although the circumstances that brought it into being were unusual and unlikely to be repeated, there are lessons to be drawn from what has worked well in this New Town: namely, the efficient provision of basic urban services.

Infrastructure and mobility for all, from the start

In the Angolan context, Kilamba does an exceptional job of providing urban services and high-quality infrastructures. It falls short of its potential, however, by prioritising cars as the main mode of transportation and relying on the baixa as the main source of employment, leisure and commerce for its residents. This may change with the new masterplan for Luanda that proposes a large mixed-use node north of Kilamba.

Use a blue-green infrastructure as the central framework

Kilamba's masterplan does not actively acknowledge the natural landscape nor does it take a forward-looking approach to the effects of climate change and climate variability. Kilamba is 10 km from the Atlantic coast, and only 100 m above sea level. Deadly floods in Angola leave thousands of people homeless every year, and anticipated sea level rise could cause massive migrations away from the central urban core. Kilamba's current plan does not take these eventualities into account.
Climate change projections for Angola indicate a temperature rise and decrease in rainfall, both of which will affect agricultural production. However, Kilamba makes no attempt to acknowledge local food security or health issues stemming from climate change. These are areas where there is room for great improvement. The towers in Kilamba could easily be adapted to anticipate flooding, while the massive open spaces could be zoned for use as urban agriculture production sites. Kilamba could also benefit from more sensitive consideration of its waste management and the exploration of renewable energy production.

Incorporate local cultural heritage(s)

Local cultural heritage was not considered before or during the planning process for Kilamba. That is evident in the lack of local historical analysis, and lack of participation from either Angolan professionals or potential residents during the planning process. This has become a weakness for the New Town as residents have struggled to adapt to the specificities of life in mid-rise condos such as shared common spaces and monthly fees. It has, however, presented an experiment in above-average-density housing from which lessons can be drawn.

Combine top-down and bottom-up

The Angolan national government exerts strong control over its cities. For this reason, real change in the sense of more inclusive housing legislation will have to come from the Ministry of Urbanism and Housing. Within its borders, however, Kilamba's urban management team could explore regulations that embrace a more inclusive and participatory approach when possible.

New Towns need diversity

Kilamba remains an exclusive New Town. This is due largely to housing prices, but also to existing legislation that inhibits the formal banking sector's ability to offer loans for housing mortgages. The absence of a land cadastre further handicaps the growth of the formal housing sector, effectively limiting residents in Kilamba to a small percentage of the population; thereby excluding 75 percent of the population without access to legal tenure. The three housing types offered within Kilamba further limit the diversity of potential residents. Because of its towers-in-the-park typology, however, Kilamba has the space to potentially rethink the masterplan and alter regulations to allow for more varied housing stock. At the national level, the Ministry of Urbanism and Housing (MINUH) could facilitate this by reconsidering existing housing legislation to legally acknowledge incremental tenure and so-called 'good faith occupation'. Kilamba municipal authorities could also reduce the current spatial segregation between the New Town and its surroundings by changing regulations that penalise the spatial components of the informal economy and instead incorporating these kiosks, minibuses and markets into the New Town in ways that benefit local residents and enrich the public realm.

Public park in Kilamba.
(Photo: R. Keeton, 2016)

Israel Marques, Mayor of Cidade do Kilamba, Angola

In July 2011, just after the official opening of Ciudade do Kilamba, a New Town outside of Luanda, President of Angola José Eduardo dos Santos personally appointed Israel Marques as mayor of the new city. Mr. Marques was asked to manage a city with no inhabitants, no commercial activities, and a growing reputation in international media as a 'Chinese Ghost Town in Africa'. Turns out, those were the golden days. As he puts it: 'In the beginning it was easy, before we had residents'.

Rachel Keeton (RK): The masterplan for Kilamba looks extremely Chinese; to the point that it almost feels like we are actually in China. I understand it was developed in China by a team of architects and planners from CITIC. Which changes did the Angolan team working on Kilamba suggest as context-specific alterations to the proposed masterplan?
Israel Marques (IM): The main changes we made to the masterplan were the shops. We knew a city this large needed commercial developments to support it. We took the Chinese planners to Nova Vida [a nearby planned residential development] to learn from it. We realised that people did complete renovations before they moved into the new apartments they had bought, because of bad materials and poor quality finishes. We said for Kilamba we'd rather have good quality finishing materials and it has worked: only one percent of the residents here have changed the tiles or the kitchen. Maybe even less, and that is because the quality is high.
Another thing we looked at was the size. The houses in Nova Vida were too small. There were 'bedrooms' where you couldn't fit a bed. So in Kilamba we made the living spaces comfortable sizes. The average family size in Angola is eight people. For Kilamba, our reference was six family members. But we realise now that it's even less. For one reason: the majority of our residents are young people. The average household here only has two kids.

From a planning perspective, we thought about playgrounds, sidewalks everywhere, drainage, everything. But in terms of amenities the planners only included schools and kindergartens, not a hospital or cultural facilities. Housing was the priority. In order to have other things, they would have had to have less housing. So we had to compromise on some things. Even to have a supervisory committee for 710 buildings was not easy. Each block had one or two subcontractors. You have to prioritise issues with a project this big. We followed the construction for three years, and then the government was worried about management of the city and I was asked to stay involved.

RK: So despite their uniqueness in the Angolan context, the tower housing blocks and gridded, hierarchical streets were not considered problematic?

IM: Some people were worried, so it was advertised, and we made a check to see how many people were interested. We got 80,000 potential buyers on open day, so we knew there was a market.

But it's true that the politicians didn't like the idea of verticalising in the beginning. But if you look at less dense urban models, infrastructure in places like Zango [a nearby township] is so expensive. When we started thinking of new cities, some people said, 'we are Africans, we don't want to live like this, we want to have our chickens, our backyard.' And I said, no, this the way to go: it's so much cheaper in terms of infrastructure. There was obviously a market for it: it only took us 10 days to sell 50,000 apartments. The government allocated 5000 units to civil servants before that. We started selling, and we had people sleeping in queues. We had to shut down after ten days and say: no more apartments. Some people had to be put on the waiting list.

RK: Many people in Angola earn a lot of money—also in the informal sector, but isn't it true that Kilamba is only financially available to about 10 percent of the population? That makes it a very exclusive community in a country where about 80 percent of the urban population lives on $100 - $300 USD per month.

IM: I wouldn't say that Kilamba is upper class. We have a mix of people here. Some apartments will shock you: they have no furniture at all and residents live in very bad conditions. We have a social programme financed by our administration to include kids in the kindergartens, and sometimes neighbours report to us and we have to go and see the families. We have a mix of incomes groups. At the beginning, we found one family selling ice creams made from baobob tree fruit in their apartment. And we said, 'come on, you cannot do that; we are going to close this operation down'. But then we saw the reality of the family and we knew if we closed down their business we would ruin them, so we let them continue doing that, but we helped them to make a deal with the canteens in the schools, to make and sell the ice creams there instead of in the home.

To be clear, though, it's not cheap: minimum rent in dollars is something like $500 - $600 USD per month. But with the exchange rate, residents now pay 30 percent less. The top tier is 150m2, five bedrooms, in the beginning it cost around $800 - $900 USD per month. Now they pay $520 USD with the exchange rate. After 30 years, they will own the apartment.

We have some people who are very low-income because the government allotted 5000 units to government civil servants in the beginning. Each department selected the workers that they thought should benefit from the opportunity. We also have veterans of war; the government provides for those people and family members, but they have kids. The idea from the beginning was not to create a segregated city. We wanted to put all the social classes together. At the end of the day, we can say that people are learning a lot from each other. Everyone is improving.

RK: It's clear to me as I walk through the city that this is an exceptional place for Angola, but it also appears to have very familiar problems with urban management. There is trash that needs to be collected, grass that needs mowing. What is the biggest challenge in terms of providing day-to-day management?
IM: The fact that there are so many players in Kilamba makes things difficult: IGTI, Imogestin, our administration, the gabinete, and the national government. The decentralised responsibility and management is one of the biggest challenges. The initial idea was to establish a management that should be completely independent. The municipality should be able to collect money from the residents to maintain the city.
In the beginning, it was easy, before we had residents. For two years, no one collected rent from the shops or from the residents. We were here the whole time. We could have collected that and used a percentage to reinvest in the management of the city. But each party wants the best piece of the cake. In fact, the municipality is the one who sees the problems, and should be able to deal with those problems with our own resources. People don't understand that. We have more than 300 shops in Kilamba. We have said from the beginning that we should get the rent from those to help maintain the city. Then we could charge less to the residents. If we managed to control these shops we could provide more services, more business. For this to be changed, we need a political decision from the presidential level.

RK: Have there been any lessons learned from your experience with Kilamba that could be applied to future urban planning projects in Angola?
IM: There have been lessons from Kilamba, certainly. After we finished Phase I, the government instructed Sonip to build Phase II. They started building 5000 apartments [KK5000]. If you go there, you will be shocked. The quality of design is so bad. The idea was to provide a cheaper house. But that shouldn't mean you have a bad design. CITIC said they would do the design, but change the finish materials to reduce the price. But now KK5000 looks like a military camp. I always say, 'this is going to be my headache'. Bad design. What can we do?
Of course, your life is your connections, not just a house. Here in the centre, we are lucky we have these shops. If we didn't have shops and cafés and schools, it would be bad. Here in Kilamba, we are taking a risk with KK5000. People who live there have to travel too far for shops and services.

RK: Just after Kilamba was opened in 2012, you had a flood of reporters coming in and writing articles calling the New Town a 'ghost town'. They came during a critical period after construction was finished, but before the Angolan government had developed any kind of mortgage programme

that would allow residents to finance property. Like in most countries, very few people here can afford to buy a home outright, so what those reporters saw was actually a pretty strange moment for the city. When I speak with people in Luanda today, everyone gets this gleam in their eye when I mention Kilamba. It's like the promised land now. Everyone wants to live here.

IM: BBC, CNN, they all came during the time after the opening when we were trying to figure out how to sell the apartments without access to bank mortgages. They never came back. If they would come back now, they would see that we are 97 percent occupied and we have 100,000 residents. When Kilamba Phase II and III are fully constructed, we will have 500,000 residents. We have a life here that you don't find in other parts of Luanda: people sit at sidewalk cafés and watch football games projected on screens in the evenings. It's vibrant. It's a life that people actually like.

In Kilamba, you are not allowed to have a generator. We rely on the power company, and we don't have problems: because we pay our bills. And the power company knows this, so they don't turn it off. Everyone has a prepaid meter. Everyone has access to drinking water. Those services are what makes Kilamba attractive. Where else in Angola can you find a house with reliable access to clean water and electricity? It doesn't exist.

Appolonia (2012), Ghana. (Photo: M. Provoost, 2018)

Kilamba (2008), Angola. (Source: CITIC, 2015)

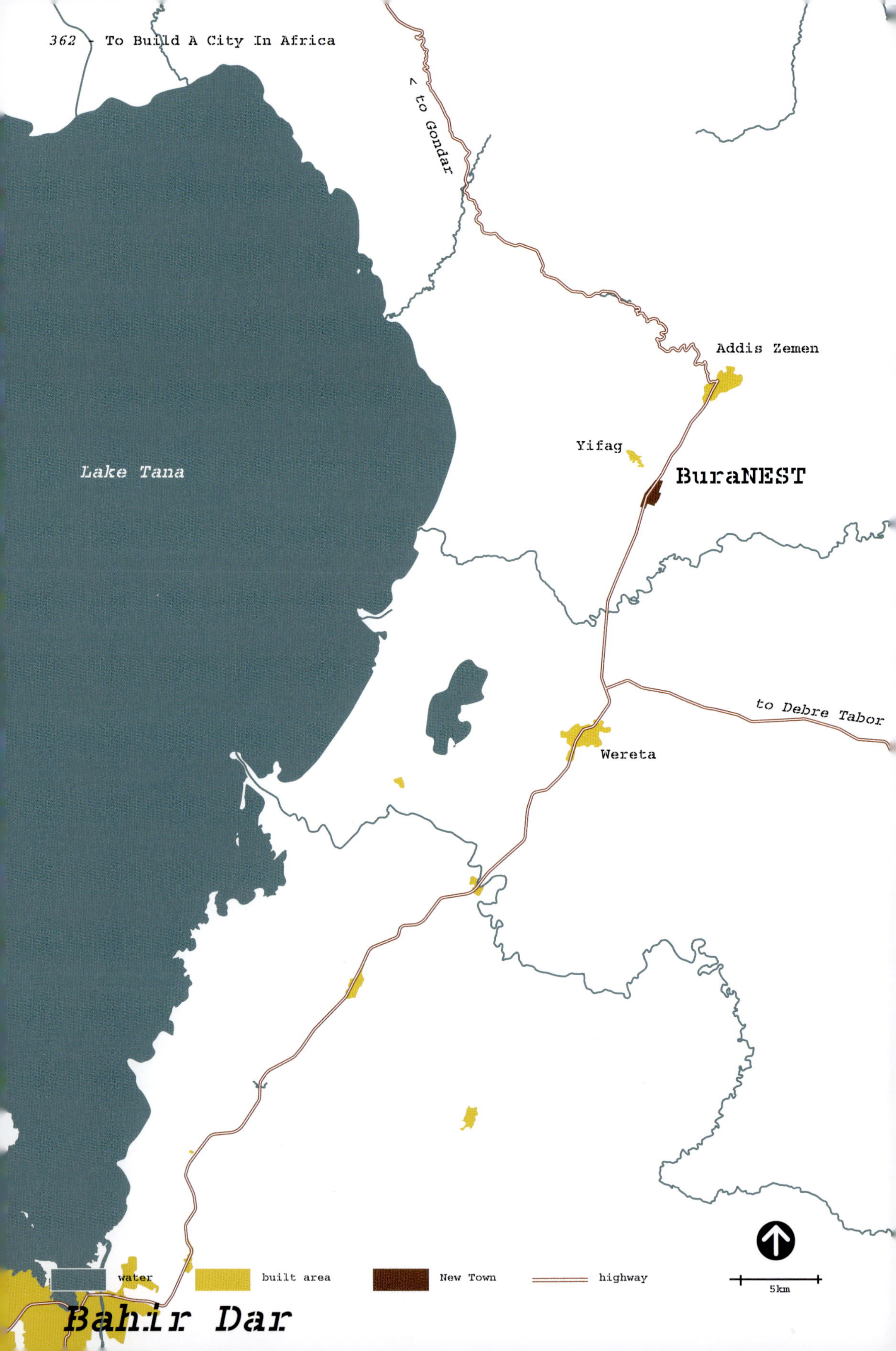

< to Gondar
Addis Zemen
Yifag
BuraNEST
Lake Tana
to Debre Tabor
Wereta
water
built area
New Town
highway
5km
Bahir Dar

CASE STUDY

BuraNEST, Ethiopia

'For whom do you plan?'

Ethiopia lies in the Horn of Africa. Landlocked by Eritrea, Djibouti and Somalia to the northeast, the country shares western borders with Sudan, South Sudan, and Kenya to the south. The landscape is diverse, ranging from jungles to mountains, plateaus, and fertile plains. River systems cut through the country, flowing in all directions: towards endorheic basins, the Indian Ocean, and the Mediterranean Sea. Some rivers originate deep in the Ethiopian Highlands, the largest range of mountains in Africa. Ethiopia's extensive drainage systems irrigate the fertile agricultural fields maintained by roughly 80% of the population.[1]
Lake Tana, the source of the Blue Nile and home to island monasteries from the tenth century, lies 560 kilometres northwest of Addis Ababa. At the southern shore of the lake is Bahir Dar, a city of about 600,000 people and administrative capital of the Amhara region. The area has a tropical savannah climate, with intense dry and wet seasons. Average temperatures are warm, usually between 25°C and 30°C during the day, with chilly nights. The landscape offers panoramic views of gently undulating hills and plains, while the Simien Mountains rise like a wall across the horizon.

1 The World Bank and The United Nations Population Division's World Urbanisation Prospects both estimate Ethiopia's urban population to be 20% (2017). See: data.worldbank.org/indicator/SP.URB.TOTL.IN.ZS.

Traditional 'Dancing houses' in Bura Kebele. (This photo and all other photos in this case study: R. Keeton, 2017)

Following the two-lane road to Gondar north, out of Bahir Dar, farming communities momentarily materialise on both sides of the road: individual family houses that appear strikingly similar from the exterior. The rectangular houses are constructed from vertical eucalyptus wood held in place by horizontal braces at roughly 50 cm intervals. Most houses have

Future residents of BuraNEST sit inside their current home. The skillfully adobed interior is typical of the Amhara region.

either small windows, or none at all. All houses are roofed in sheets of corrugated iron, which must be replaced every five years or so. A lack of diagonal bracing has led to the common occurrence of 'dancing houses': houses leaning at terrifying angles and facing imminent collapse.

Local homes are spacious from the inside: two doors placed symmetrically at the front and back ensure adequate daylight and air circulation. These doors open into a main room, which generally takes up two-thirds of the house and is used for cooking, eating, talking and the events of daily life. The remaining third may be divided into two bedrooms, or a bedroom and storage area. At night, livestock sleep in the main room, a small indication of the close bond between farmers and their livestock. Most houses appear wooden from the exterior, but are fully, and artfully adobed in a mixture of mud and hay from the interior. Smooth walls jut out into built-in seating areas and sink back into recessed shelving. Movable furniture is often limited to beds.

These rectangular houses are referred to locally as 'modern houses' and seen as an improvement on traditional round houses, or *tukuls*. *Tukuls* can still be seen intermittently in the landscape, but they are becoming much less common in this area. Circular *tukuls* are generally smaller, and have thatched roofs rather than corrugated iron sheets. They are also clad in vertical eucalyptus sticks. The architectural aspiration towards modern materials and design thus seems tempered by a deep appreciation for traditional building techniques and proven methods.

The turnoff to BuraNEST is marked by a small hand-painted sign.

Continuing north, the scenes outside shift back and forth between small, brightly coloured towns, and achingly beautiful open landscapes. Children play outside, and farmers drive cattle along the road. Women carry yellow five gallon jugs back and forth to communal hand-pump wells. Maize gives way to rice fields and grazing land. The bucolic setting is painted in shades of green and brown, with the bright sunlight casting shadows in heavy contrast. A sharp right turn 72 km from Bahir Dar is marked by a hand-painted blue and white sign: 'Amhara Model Town BuraNEST Laboratory'. Asphalt gives way to a packed dirt road. This is BuraNEST.

Rural and urban development in Ethiopia

BuraNEST is the name of NESTown Group's first model town. The NESTown (New Ethiopian Sustainable Town) concept is an urban development strategy based on four E's: Education, Energy, Exchange and Ecology. BuraNEST is the first, and thus, a 'living experiment'. It is located at Bura, in the Amhara region, and so named for its site: Bura New Ethiopian Sustainable Town (BuraNEST). Following the project development at Bura, there are two other sites in Ethiopia that have expressed interest in becoming future NESTowns.[2]

The model is also being considered by partners of the Rural-to-Urban Transformation project, an ambitious plan to develop 8,000 New Towns in rural areas over the next 10 years. The plan was initiated by two powerful Ethiopians: Tsedeke Woldu, a developer, and Bereket Simon, a

2 One of these, Awra Amba, is an exceptional community founded by Zumra Nuru in 1972. The settlement has 570 current residents and practices complete gender equality and egalitarian distribution of goods. There is no religious belief system, but children are educated according to the 'Golden Rule', and older or unwell residents are cared for communally.

politician. That influential combination has enabled the project to pick up where a 2015 state plan for the development of 8,000 new rural centres left off. The development of rural locations is a key part of the national government's strategy to decentralise development by slowing rural depopulation and resulting urban growth.[3] Some studies have shown that rural to urban migration in Ethiopia is partially driven by erratic climate variation.[4] Subsistence farmers who depend on rain-fed agricultural production are sometimes forced to migrate to cities (whether permanently or temporarily) to diversify their incomes through other types of labour. With the intent to increase quality of life and economic and educational perspectives in the countryside, the new rural New Towns will offer schools, health centres, local government administration offices, new housing options, and alternative employment opportunities.

Ethiopia has been pushing for rural development since the adoption of the 1994 constitution, which anticipated an urban transformation based on autonomy and diversity of individual urban nodes.[5] More recently, since 2006, the national government has made it a priority to develop new affordable housing in existing cities, and plans to develop new urban centres in rural areas to stem the flow of migration that has put massive pressure on cities like Addis Ababa, Dire Dawa, and Bahir Dar. Housing deficits disproportionately affect lower-income groups, who are often forced to settle in inadequate housing with limited access to public services.[6]

Ethiopia's pro-active approach differs significantly from other examples presented in this book, and Ethiopia is one of the few African countries prioritising a systematic shift in internal migration flows. The country's strong economic growth over the last decade has translated into public investment projects and overall poverty reduction.[7] Recent public projects include ambitious public housing schemes in Addis Ababa[8], rural development and densification projects, and large-scale infrastructural projects like the Grand Ethiopian Renaissance Dam (GERD) that are expected to stimulate local development and job creation. These huge infrastructural works stand in sharp contrast to the small-scale, incremental intervention at Bura.[9]

Testing a New Town: BuraNEST laboratory

BuraNEST is conceived as a 'living experiment' —a test, in other words— of the ideas that inform it. Those ideas were elaborated by a small group of architecture and planning academics from Ethiopia and Switzerland. The project began in 2007 after a guest lecture on urban capacity building by Professor Emeritus Franz Oswald (ETH Zurich) at Addis Ababa University. In discussions following the lecture, Oswald and Professor Fasil Giorgis (EiABC Addis Ababa University) saw the potential for developing rural centres that would provide the benefits of good planning to communities without access to basic infrastructure. Hilawi Yosef, Ethiopia's ambassador to Israel and a friend of Giorgis, became involved

3 See Gardner, T. '"Addis has run out of space": Ethiopia's radical redesign'. *The Guardian*. 4 December 2017. Available online: www.theguardian.com/cities/2017/dec/04/addis-ababa-ethiopia-redesign-housing-project.

4 See Hunnes D.E., 'Understanding Rural-to-Urban Migration in Ethiopia: Driving Factors, Analytical Frameworks, and Recommendations.' *Journal of Global Health Perspectives*. 2012 Aug 1. Edition 1.

5 See: Oswald, F. 'NESTOWN: New Ethiopian Sustainable Town; Notes on Urban Transformation and its Architecture in Ethiopia'. Cherenet, Z. and Sewnet, H., Eds. (2012) *Building Ethiopia: Sustainability and Innovation in Architecture and Design*. Addis Ababa: EiABC. P. 15.

6 See: Taher, M.T. and Ibrahim, A. (2014) 'Transformation of Slum and Squatter Settlements: A Way of Sustainable Living in Context of twenty-first Century Cities.' *American Journal of Civil Engineering and Architecture* 2.2: 70-76.

7 Ethiopia's economy has grown at a rate of about 10% annually for the last decade. See: 'Ethiopia Overview' The World Bank. 19 April 2018. Available online: www.worldbank.org/en/country/ethiopia/overview

8 The Integrated Housing Development Program (IHDP) initiated in Addis Ababa in 2006 is a state-subsidised housing programme meant to alleviate the city's acute housing shortage. Sustained political commitment to the project has resulted in the construction of more than 250,000 housing units to date. See: Gardner, T. '"Addis has run out of space": Ethiopia's radical redesign'. *The Guardian*. 4 December 2017. Available online: www.theguardian.com/cities/2017/dec/04/addis-ababa-ethiopia-redesign-housing-project.

9 Many of the large-scale infrastructure projects in Ethiopia have been delivered

A view of BuraNEST looking west towards the main road. Two unfinished Rainwater Units line the left side of the road, while traditional housing lines the right side. These will eventually be replaced by more multi-family Rainwater Units.

in the project as it started to take off. With strong political connections in Amhara, Yosef was instrumental in securing the Bura site for the project.[10] By 2010, a research fund was obtained, BuraNEST was inaugurated and a tree nursery was planted. Site plans and architectural prototypes were developed during a joint workshop in Singapore, and a *kebele* (ward) council vote on the masterplan in 2011 served as final approval.

BuraNEST is a New Town born from the reality that the vast majority of Ethiopians live in rural areas and practice (subsistence) agriculture. Initiated by Oswald, Giorgis, and Zegeye Cherenet (EiABC AAU), among others[11], BuraNEST is the brainchild of academics, rather than developers. According to Oswald, 'Our premise was: you work for the majority. The other 20% will find a way to live anyway.'[12] The project's academic background is apparent in its ambitions. Unlike other examples presented in this book, BuraNEST is based on an ideological Roadmap[13] that offers seven 'propositions' for the New Town:

- The town governs autonomously and acts with solidarity
- The town sustains itself by self-defined urban quality and self-sufficiency
- The town controls its metabolism and offers all basic urban activities
- The town lives from renewable resources and generates its own energy
- The town develops free exchange internally and externally
- The town educates as practice and laboratory
- The town has open institutions and gardens

by Chinese companies. In 2017, China was Ethiopia's biggest foreign investor and largest trading partner. See: Gray, A. 'Ethiopia is Africa's Fastest Growing Economy.' World Economic Forum. 4 May 2018. Available online: www.weforum.org/agenda/2018/05/ethiopia-africa-fastest-growing-economy/

10 Interview with Bizuayehu Jembere, 2017.

11 Other initiators include: Martin Grunder, Dieter Laepple, Surendra Kotecha, Corinne Keunzli, Rene Schaetti, Peter Schenker and Roland Walthert.

12 Interview with Franz Oswald, 2017.

13 For more elaboration on these propositions see: Oswald, F. (2015)

Mastewal Chane represents the local government as 'woreda' coordinator, and has been involved in the BuraNEST project since 2010. He stands beside a pump at the back façade of Rainwater Unit 2. Each family unit has a private pump, well, and a cistern for rainwater storage. Water from the cistern is used for irrigation and livestock.

From the beginning, Oswald and Giorgis had ambitious plans for participation from the local farming community, but faced skepticism from farmers. The initiators also questioned their own role, as Oswald says: 'Participation becomes a very difficult issue because it immediately provokes the question: *do they want what I can offer?* ... One has to have the courage to explicitly ask; to put that question in the centre of a discussion.'[14] As the project moved forward, the group quickly learned that the most effective way of involving the residents was simply to do everything together, so the residents would see the reasoning behind various activities. Working together and learning by doing, thus became a successful method of communication between initiators and the local community. Reflecting on those early days, Oswald concludes, 'If you want a project to be sustainable, one has to address these hidden dimensions, because if you cannot communicate clearly, how can you provide a service?'[15]

In the decade since the project started, the issue of communication has proved to be a constant challenge. Seminars, workshops, interviews and presentations were carried out repeatedly within the community. BuraNEST coordinator Mastewal Chane describes the participation process: 'We did presentations and workshops to convince the people. We also discussed in the church. We used many options. Eventually everyone understood. Gradually opinions are changing. So now the number of members of the Bura farmers' cooperative is increasing. More people want to join [the project].'[16]

Looking Back on a Radical Idea: the BuraNEST Cooperative Rural New Town, Amhara, Ethiopia. Architectural Digest Volume 85, Issue 4. July/August 2015. Pp. 114-119. NESTown Group also developed a Charter for Rural New Towns, that has since been ratified by the Amhara regional government.

14 Interview with Franz Oswald, 2017.

15 Ibid.

16 Interview with Mastewal Chane, 2017.

An urban plan and urban agriculture

The residents of Bura are farmers with limited education, but they have clear ideas of what a New Town should be, and for many of them, good infrastructure is the priority. One female head-of-household stated: 'A modern town should have electricity, water, and telephones. It should be convenient for the cultivation of vegetables and fruits. And a market is mandatory. In the future, I want to make the front of my house into a shop, a mini-market.'[17] Another beneficiary pointed to the need for secure tenure: 'A town should consist of legal ownership plans. In my view, that is vital. [There should also be] trade activities in Bura. It should be active. And have infrastructures like water, electricity, schools, and telephones.'[18]

An older farmer stressed that in addition to public services, effective urban management was key to a successful New Town: 'The town should conform to the planning criteria of the municipality. It should include basic infrastructure like electricity, water, schools, health and sanitary facilities… Management should be good. Managers should play a strong role and communicate better.'[19]

The planners and architects involved in the project share these views, and have incorporated most aspects into plans for BuraNEST. The urban plan has gone through a few iterations, but currently looks like a four-armed pinwheel, extending outwards toward the surrounding landscape. The Town Core, reserved for public (meeting) space, is defined by the intersection of the four arms, which align to axes traced from local churches.[20] These arms form a square around the Town Core, where a low stone ring encircles a slightly raised grassy area with one large shade tree[21] and two smaller trees adjacent to a stone platform. This is

17 Adugna is highly committed to the BuraNEST project. She also stated: 'I was introduced to the project six years ago, when I came here after my marriage. I want to live in a place with infrastructure, a modern house and integrated town agriculture (ITA). I was divorced a year ago because of my interest in BuraNEST. I want to live in the new project and own my house. Because of this, we divorced.' Author's interview with Adugna at BuraNEST, Ethiopia, on 16 November 2017.

18 Interview with Birhan Abegaz, 2017.

19 Interview with Gebeyehu Endale, 2017.

20 The area is intensely religious, and holy days are observed by church attendance and a break from hard labour.

A view of the Town Core from the first technical skills training centre. The circular raised platform is currently used for town meetings and public discussions. Three trees have been planted in memory of people who played important roles in BuraNEST's development. This public space will be at the centre of the future development.

2019 GoogleEarth

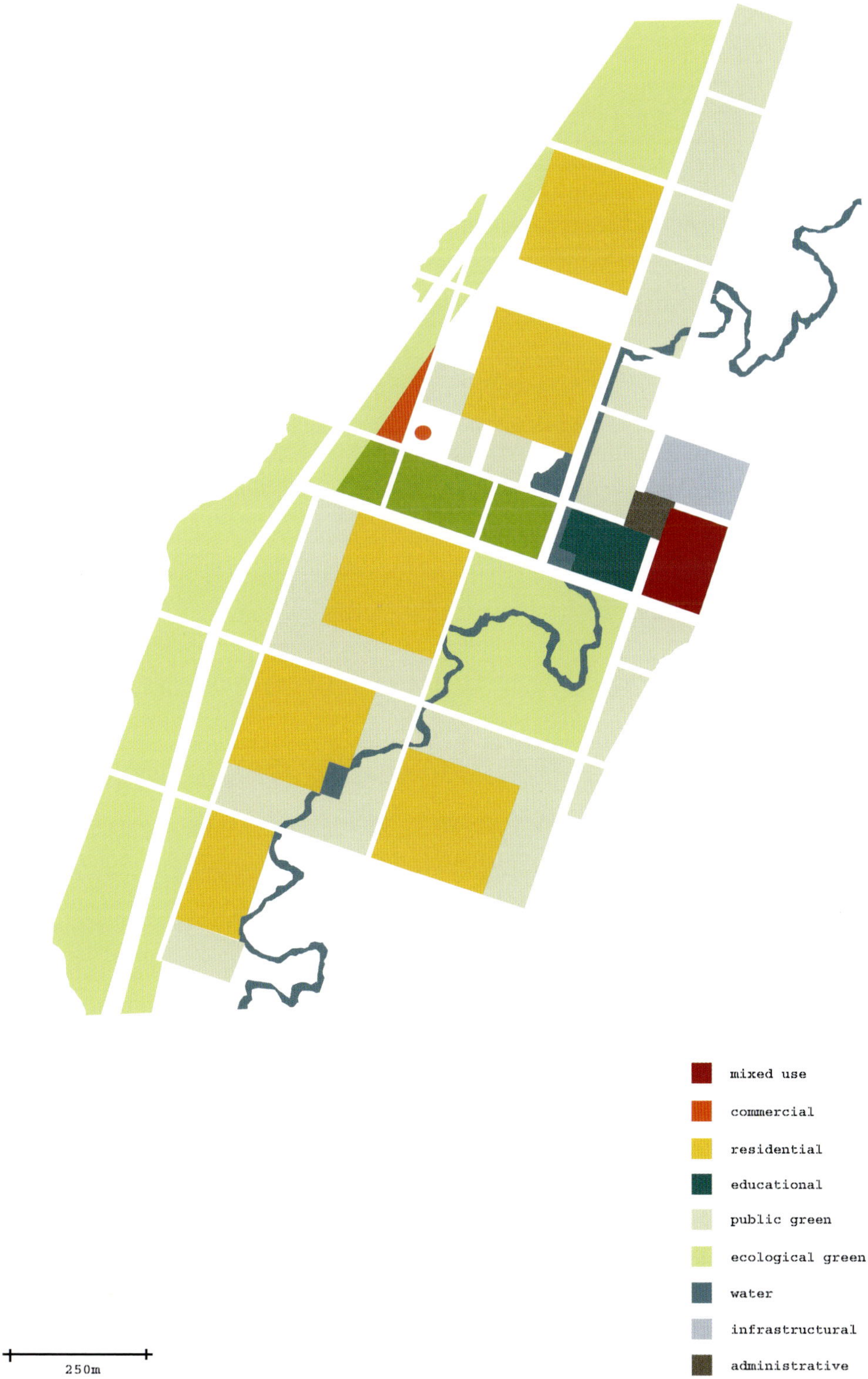
mixed use
commercial
residential
educational
public green
ecological green
water
infrastructural
administrative
250m

21 This tree was planted in memory of Peter Schenker, one of the initiators and leaders of the BuraNEST project.

22 Interview with Franz Oswald, 2017.

23 See: Oswald, F., Giorgis, F. and Stahli, B. (2016) Amhara Model Town. Bern/Addis Ababa: NESTown Group. P. 3.

the largest public space in BuraNEST and is used for formal meetings, announcements and other public events. The axes traced from the churches meet at the centre of four rectilinear blocks, called 'nuclei', that provide an orthogonal structural framework for the town that may expand, densify, and evolve over time. Oswald is adamant about the need for diverse programming in urban planning. According to him, 'a *town* is not created by building houses. It's a formal intention that allows for phases of development and transformations. A plan has to be there, and it has to allow for subdivision and allocation of land. That is incredibly important.'[22]

The BuraNEST Farmers' Training Centre provides continuing agricultural education for farmers, as well as ICT classes and other skills.

The model garden adjacent to the Farmers' Training Centre has already become a source of food and income for the Bura community. Permaculture planting methods are taught here, and residents practice their new skills in private gardens. Some farmers estimate that production has tripled since the new agricultural methods have been introduced.

In addition to informing the organising principles behind the project, the 4 E's mentioned earlier (Education, Energy, Exchange and Ecology) also inform the urban patterns.[23] In BuraNEST, each 'E' is represented spatially as a nucleus with a different programmatic function. Education (nucleus 1) is represented by a technical skills training centre, and adult education. Energy (nucleus 2) is conceived as renewable resources and transportation infrastructure. Exchange (nucleus 3) references the proposed market and communication. And Ecology (nucleus 4) is regarded as the natural landscape and resource cycles. The landscape is also considered as the primary structuring element for the plan.

The Education nucleus is the only fully constructed nucleus at the time of writing. The Bura Farmers' Training Centre is located within this 1.45 ha area, with a productive model garden taking up 70% of the total nucleus.[24] Rainwater cisterns flank the garden to the north and south, providing easy access to water.[25] Orange trees, guava trees, avocado trees, and mango trees are planted in orthogonal rows with tomatoes, peppers and other vegetables growing between the trees. Butterflies, rabbits and birds have all found this garden and it has become the pride of many locals who benefit both directly from the food produced here, and the profits from food sales. The training centre has been somewhat less successful, and although the classrooms and workshops are sporadically in use, they do not yet see the kind of daily traffic many people involved with the project would like.[26]

The Energy nucleus is also known as the town factory, with two large workshops and ample space for carpenters to work. There is a timber plantation for renewable building material, and there are plans to build guest rooms and more storage facilities here. The two Rainwater Units currently under construction are also part of this nucleus. This nucleus is further divided into 'closes', or residential neighbourhoods. One 'close' is conceived as 2.9 ha, or fifty-two households (6.5 Rainwater Units).[27] Looking around the site, BuraNEST's target population of 40,000 people sounds ambitious. However, the project's popularity has increased in direct relation to its construction: as the built forms have emerged, farmers from surrounding areas have progressively expressed more interest.

The Exchange nucleus is intended to be a large open market, with trees planted at triangular points to provide shade and spatial definition. The market not yet materialised, and farmers continue to trade in Yifag, a town some 15 km away, commonly reached by cart and donkey. According to plans, the market will eventually be situated next to small businesses, a coffee shop, bank and transport facilities.

The Ecology nucleus will offer communal recycling services, health care, a kindergarten, an elderly home and public administration offices. Communal land is currently farmed in this nucleus, and rice, cereals, maize, sorghum, field vegetables and dairy products are produced for the market. Brought together as a whole, the 4E concept provides a framework for careful consideration of the project's programmatic elements.

For both the Swiss and Ethiopian architects, working in rural Bura presented some surprising dilemmas. Protracted discussions and

24 For more details see the BuraNEST working drawing: BuFTC_Overview_2014_07_16.pdf

25 A new drip irrigation method introduced by local project partner ORDA was first introduced here, and will also be implemented in the gardens of Rainwater Unit residents.

26 These setbacks have been a recurring challenge for people involved with BuraNEST. The project's steering committee has 11 members, and the designers (known collectively as NESTown Group) have a non-voting membership. Other members include a number of governmental and non-governmental organisations: Organisation for Rehabilitation and Development in Amhara (ORDA), ARNS, BORLAU, Cooperative Promotion Agency (CPA), BOA, AWWA, TVED, MUDH, Libokemkem Woreda, Amhara Development Association (ADA), and Bahir Dar Univeristy (BDU). After decisions are made by the steering committee (which is expected to hold monthly meetings), new plans must be approved by the regional government. Less committed steering committee members, skipped meetings and bureaucratic requirements from the regional government have been known to delay implementation.

27 See BuraNEST working drawing: BuraNEST - close 1 for plot 10-04-2016-Model.pdf

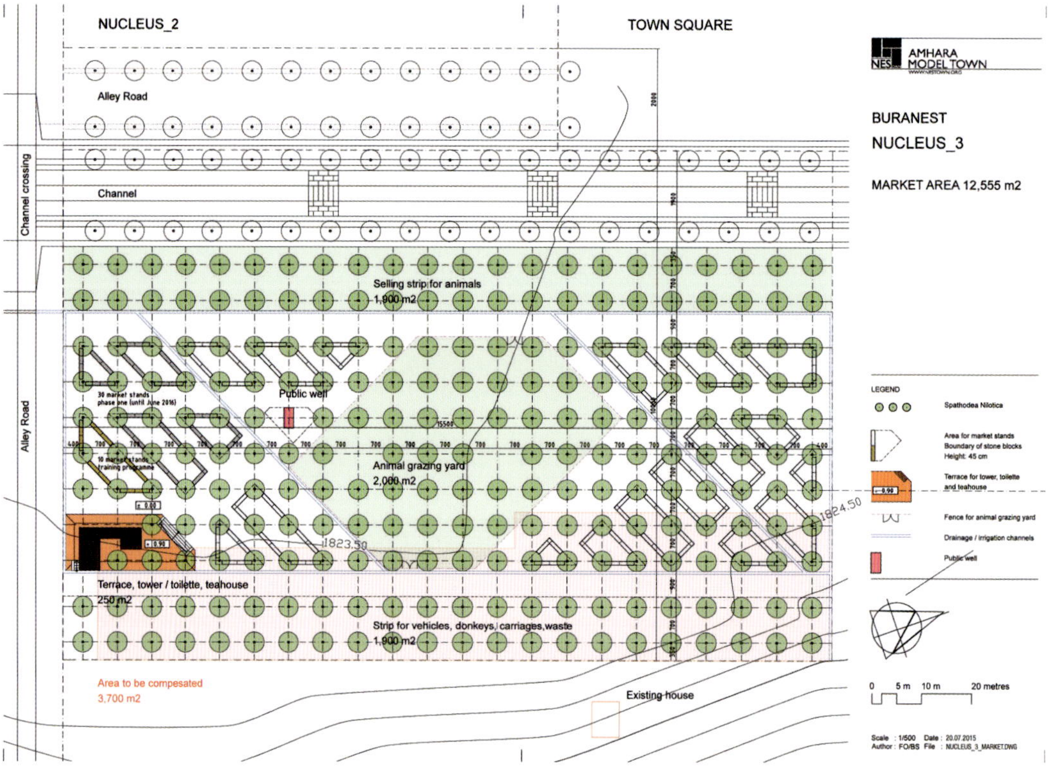

The Exchange nucleus (Nucleus 3) is planned as public space shaded by densely-planted trees to create a comfortable respite from the heat. This area is intended for use as a market, with stalls as well as areas for selling livestock and grazing. A small teahouse and public toilets will complement the exterior space. (Source: NESTown Group, 2018)

miscommunications between architects and residents contributed to project delays. Frustration on both sides has ebbed and flowed as the project has progressed, but now that the first residents are preparing to move in, the project is more popular than ever. Both residents and initiators expect that subsequent phases will move more quickly. As Oswald elaborates:

> Each of those '4 E's' presents choices. Those are planning choices that must be made after an evaluation of advantages and disadvantages. For example, when we made the choice to design water cisterns attached to individual houses instead of a single communal well, we did that knowing that the well had previously functioned as one of the only places where women and girls could come together and communicate freely without male influence. Traditionally, girls carry 20 L of water to the house every day. If I'm the father and I allow the girl to go to school, then who brings the water? If you want to have a certain gender equality, then I think we provided the possibility for equality with the individual cisterns. But those are choices, and the social impact is very real, and sometimes you have conflict between your values and the values of the local residents.[28]

In the end, the availability of water at each individual home has become a major selling point for the Rainwater Units. The process of winning hearts and minds, however, has been hard fought by project leaders.

28 Interview with Franz Oswald, 2017.

Rainwater Units

One Rainwater Unit is 360 m², composed of four individual housing units of 90 m² spread over two floors. As of 2018, two Units were nearly completion, but were not yet ready for inhabitants to move it. The designers are adamant about referring to the housing as Rainwater Units; in their view, the roofs serve the primary function of collecting rainwater: a more critical contribution to the project than simply sheltering people.[29] That concern for water is well-founded. The area faces increasing climate variability, with short wet seasons that are becoming wetter and long dry seasons that are becoming drier. The large roof expanse increases catchment capacity, and the ability to store the rainwater collected during the three-month wet season has already changed farmers' lives. Extra water means better irrigation and more crops. More crops yield more profits, and money allows access to life-improving tools like solar panels to charge mobile phones or books for schoolchildren.

Farmers seem less convinced about the need for two floors, however. Adugna, a divorced mother of three and future beneficiary of the project describes her early concerns: 'In the beginning, I was in doubt about the structure, but according to the engineers, they told us that the house can stay for a minimum of 15 years and we have been convinced by this. We intend to use the ground floor for living and dining and the upper floor for bedrooms. We might use the livestock stable for additional rooms.'[30]

29 According to Franz Oswald: 'we said that a house has to be a water resource. It is not primarily to protect people. It is a piece of infrastructure which provides water resources, a garden area, and individual and communal spaces. That function and the idea of a town centre are the two most important aspects of the NESTown model.' Interview with Franz Oswald, 2017.

30 Interview with Adugna, 2017.

A single Rainwater Unit is made up of eight housing units, each about 90m2. Eucalyptus wood construction is infilled with adobe bricks to provide insulation and privacy. The wood frame may be left open at the ceiling of the top floor to allow for air circulation and natural cooling. The massive shared roof is designed for maximum rainwater collection, which is then channeled into the four underground cisterns. (Source: NESTown Group, 2018)

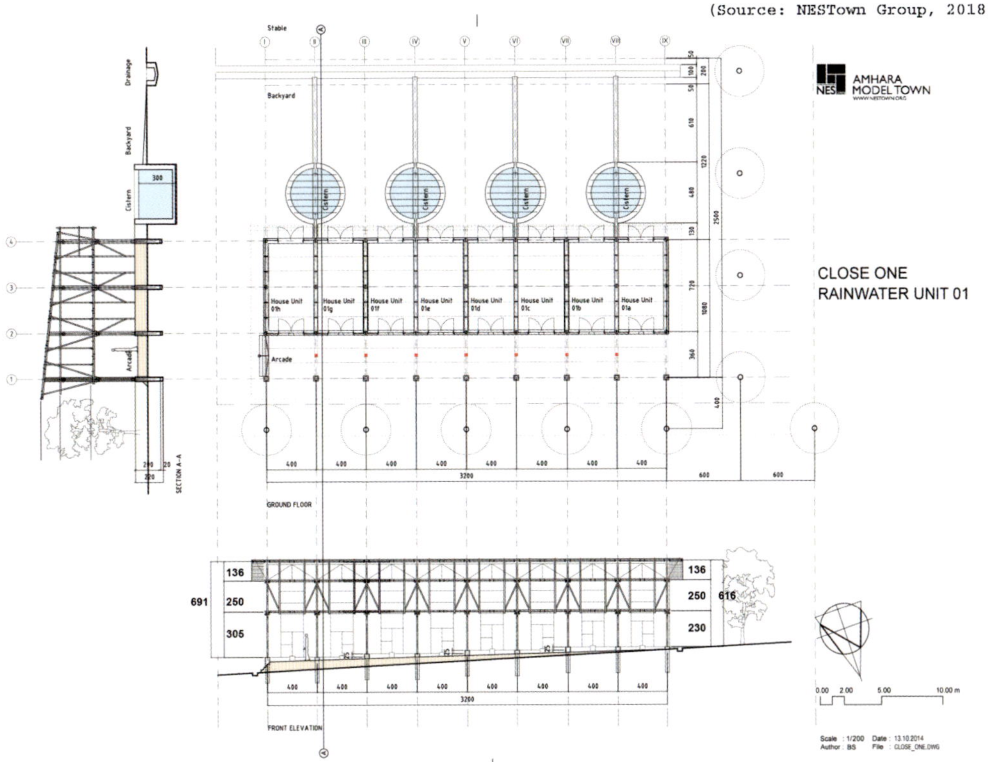

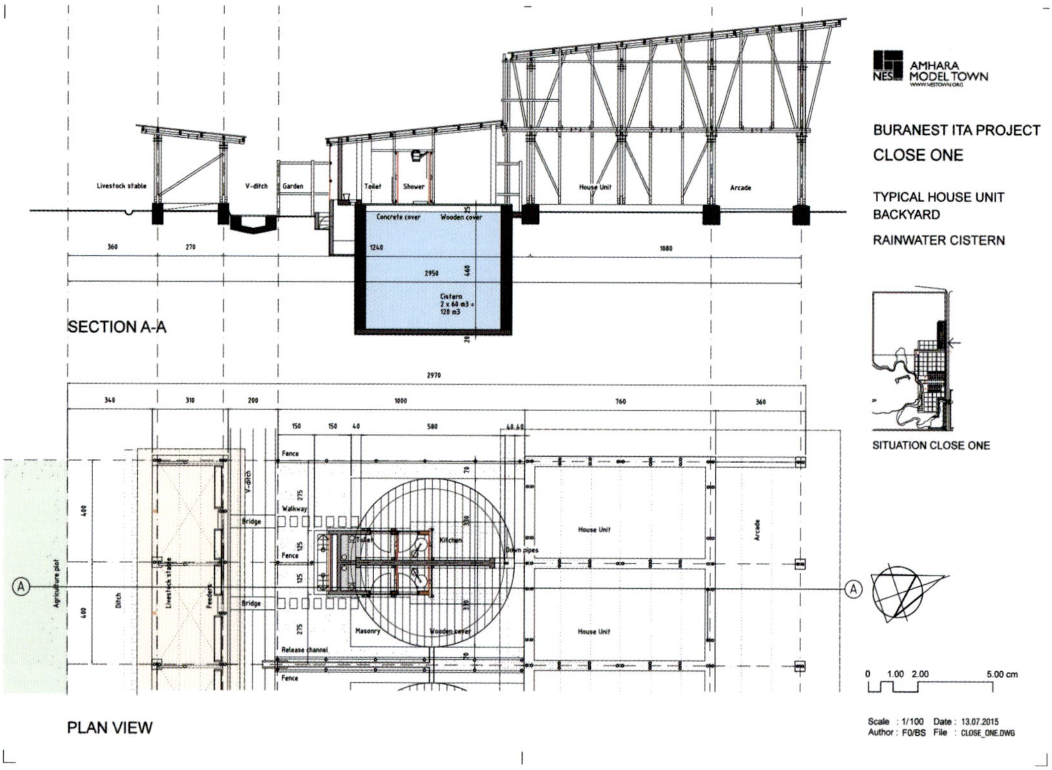

A section through one housing unit in a Rainwater Unit shows the relationship between living space facing the street, a private wet area with toilet, shower and kitchen above the cistern, and a small kitchen garden and drainage channel separating the home from the livestock stables. Some individuals already have plans to transform the stables into guest rooms, workshops, or other uses. One future resident suggested she would transform the ground floor of the house into a shop and use the livestock stable as a storage area. All of these transformations are allowed, as long as neighbouring residents do not object. (Source: NESTown Group, 2018)

Birhan Abegaz, another future beneficiary, echoes Adugna's sentiments: 'At first, when it was just the framing construction, we were in doubt: how can we stay there forever? But now that the [mud brick] walls are in place, we assume that it's going to be a strong house. This convinces us to stay there forever.'[31]

Informed by vernacular typologies and traditional building techniques, the Rainwater Unit frames are constructed from local eucalyptus wood, with adobe brick infill walls. Based on the results of a pilot Rainwater Unit design/build challenge in Bahir Dar[32], project architect Benjamin Stähli detailed a structural framework using prefabricated bracing (produced on site), concrete piling foundations that could bear the expansion and contraction of the earth during rainy and dry seasons, and wooden nail connections that would also expand and contract at a uniform rate. The ground floor is raised off the ground, with concrete and local stone used to support load-bearing columns. The two Rainwater Units on site as of writing are oriented to facilitate cooling by prevailing winds.

Each Rainwater Unit has four cisterns, divided in half by a concrete wall. Two individual housing units share a single 60,000 L water cistern, located underground at the rear of the building. PVC piping connects the v-shaped, water-collecting roof to the cistern. Above the underground cisterns, each home has a wet unit that consists of an open kitchen, a hand pump, a dry (compost) toilet and an enclosed showering area. The wet

31 Interview with Birhan Abegaz, 2017.
32 The Rainwater Units were designed by a group of Ethiopian and Swiss architects, and underwent multiple renditions before the current design

The wet cell with private water access, toilet, shower, and outdoor kitchen shown here is one of the biggest advantages of the new housing design. Current residents of Bura share communal latrines and wells. Both require long walks to and from local homes. Private access to these services will save residents both time and effort, and reduce safety risks associated with walking outside in the dark.

units are placed back-to-back, providing both privacy and efficient use of space. Currently, Bura residents use one communal hand-pump well and a single block of latrines. The improvements to sanitation and health offered by this design are apparent to all, as well as the time-saving convenience and safety of a private toilet for each family.

Behind the wet unit is a 28 m^2 livestock holding shed, followed by a 306 m^2 backyard garden with drip irrigation for each family. Each beneficiary family is also entitled to participate in an integrated town agriculture (ITA) pilot project to teach farmers new farming innovations with technical support from the Organization for Rehabilitation & Development in Amhara (ORDA), one of the project's steering committee members.

Multiple farmers indicated that the compact spatial arrangement of house, livestock and garden was a key advantage of the BuraNEST project. According to Abegaz: 'If done as planned, [BuraNEST] will bring a vital change to us. The house is modern. The ITA and the way the house is organised with the livestock and water harvesting and backyard garden will bring a vital change to our lives. We are currently using water from the river. We rent a water pump for agriculture. For drinking we use a nearby hand pump well. In my view, those things will be better facilitated in the new house.'[33] Project coordinator Chane, agrees: 'Our biggest achievement is that this is a new model for this area.[34] The organisation with housing, cistern, livestock and garden. They see how they can live in a different way now.'[35]

was settled upon. A prototype was built in Bahir Dar on the shores of Lake Tana in 2012, and acted as a show model to attract local (political) support.

33 Interview with Birhan Abegaz, 2017.

34 According to NESTown Deputy Coordinator Bizuayehu Jembere, the organisational model used at BuraNEST is inspired by a model used by Gurage people in southwest Ethiopia. Author's interview with Bizuayehu Jembere at Bahir Dar, Ethiopia, on 17 November 2017.

Kefyalew Hailu has been involved in the BuraNEST project from the beginning. He trains local residents to become registered carpenters and as their skill sets grow they are able to find work not only on the BuraNEST project, but also in surrounding areas. In this way, the project has not only brought new architecture to the area, but also new technical, agricultural and entrepreneurial skills to local residents.

The Rainwater Units currently under construction are built from the same plan, but the quality of construction is visibly superior in Rainwater Unit 2 — proof of the local construction crew's increasing confidence. Rainwater Unit 1 was built first, after construction crews had completed the Career Training Center, model house and warehouses in other nuclei. Rainwater Unit 1 is not quite finished, as of writing. Adobe bricks are laid in place by all-female teams of masons; a unique sight in the male-dominated Ethiopian construction industry. Bura women were interested in masonry work, and according to Chief Mason Tegaye Biadglign, local women have proved more patient and better-suited to the subtleties of adobe brick masonry than their male colleagues.[36]

A carpentry team of five local men completed construction of the eucalyptus framework on Rainwater Unit 1 in one year and twenty-four days, led by Chief Carpenter Kefyalew Hailu. Hailu also oversaw framing construction on Rainwater Unit 2, which was completed in just eighty days, an improvement resulting from the rapid skill development of the carpentry team. Traditional techniques such as wooden nails and complex joinery, which had been largely forgotten in this area, were re-introduced at BuraNEST. The skills developed on site as part of this 'living experiment' have already been transferred to surrounding areas as Bura masons and carpenters take on jobs and share their new talents.

New financing models for the New Town

The BuraNEST project is primarily financed through a cost-sharing agreement between NESTown Group and BIUD, the regional government authority responsible for implementation.[37] Other steering committee members have financed individual aspects of the project, such as ORDA and Green Ethiopia's support for the tree nursery, and ADA's support for the Career Training Center school building. Funding has also come from philanthropic Swiss partners including the Arthur Waser Foundation, Allgemeine Baugenossenschaft Zurich (ABZ), and the Tesfa Ilg Foundation, Zurich.

Farmers interested in joining the project must first become members of the farmers' cooperative. There are currently 80 members, 16 of which will be housed in Rainwater Unit 1 and 2.[38] Cooperatives are a new concept in this area, but the idea has been welcomed. A common financial model in Switzerland, the cooperative model was introduced by Swiss partners from the beginning as a way to increase access to finance, and support collective land ownership. Well-structured cooperatives strengthen the role of their participants, and largely prevent speculation. In Ethiopia, a legally organised collective society can also receive land formally from the government.[39]

35 Interview with Mastewal Chane, 2017.

36 Biadglign also indicated that it was more efficient to hire female masons because 'they ask for less money, so we can hire more of them.' See: Author's interview with Tegaye Biadglign at BuraNEST, Ethiopia, on 17 November 2017.

37 See: Oswald, F., Giorgis, F. and Stahli, B. (2016) Amhara Model Town. Bern/Addis Ababa: NESTown Group. P. 8.

Gebeyehu Endale was one of the first farmers to join the cooperative in 2013. He immediately saw the benefit of pooling resources, and continues to support the project. According to Endale, 'the BuraNEST model should definitely be repeated around the country. Cooperatives for farmers and carpenters are great opportunities created by BuraNEST.' See: Interview with author 15 January 2017.

Membership in the cooperative is the only way to buy a home in a Rainwater Unit. Membership fees are small, but individual families must save 15,000 ETB (550 USD) for a down payment to put their names on the waiting list for a Unit. If space in a Unit is available, the family may move in, and then has 10 years to pay off the remaining 56,000 ETB (2000 USD).[40] Farmers in the Amhara region earn about 7000 ETB (254 USD) per ha annually.[41] Farmers with more land are wealthier, and it is indeed these relatively high-earning farmers who are moving into the first Rainwater Units. Since construction began, poorer farmers have expressed more interest in the project, and requested more affordable housing types. At the time of writing, there was only one Rainwater Unit type available in BuraNEST, but project leaders were considering the demand for alternatives.

Limited access to housing credit puts constraints not only on individual farming families, but also on the construction of Rainwater Unit 3. According to project Coordinator Mastewal Chane, 'For me, my frustration is that you see now two Rainwater Units, and we don't have a credit institution who will invest for the third. We need a person who is responsible for finding credit institutions to contribute to the project… The Rainwater Units inspire people. We want to be able to house all the families who want to live here.'[42]

Although things have gone relatively smoothly for an international project with a complex governance structure, the project faces other financial threats, especially during the current transition period where responsibilities are shifting from the Swiss NESTown partners to the

38 Interview with Bizuayehu Jembere, 2017.

39 Interview with Franz Oswald, 2017.

40 These numbers correspond to a construction cost breakdown by Benjamin Stahli and Temesgen Atnafu 02/07/2016.

41 'Ethiopian Farmers See Incomes Increase by 300%' World Council. 18 August 2014. Available online: www.woccu.org/newsroom/releases/Ethiopian_Farmers_See_Incomes_Increase_by_300_

42 Interview with Mastewal Chane, 2017.

Ethiopian NESTown partners. Everyone involved in the project has been paid regularly until now, however, the carpenters and masons working on Rainwater Units 1 and 2 were not paid for the month of October 2017.[43] That kind of bureaucratic blip has been disheartening for many.

Governance in Bura

The federal government based in Addis Ababa oversees *kililoch* (regional states) who enjoy a high degree of autonomy. Within the nine regional states, zones, *woredas* (districts), and *kebeles* (wards) hold tiered administrative powers. BuraNEST is located in Amhara region, within the Libokumkum *woreda* and Bura *kebele*. Roughly 19 million people live in Amhara region, with 722 of those located within the Bura *kebele* (1.6 km^2).

Ethiopia is currently led by the Ethiopian People's Revolutionary Democratic Front (EPRDF), a political party that came to power democratically in 1991. The EPRDF currently holds all of the seats in parliament; effectively ruling without opposition. Public protest and low rumblings of dissent have increased in recent years, with government crackdowns increasing in response.

Ethnic resentment from residents of the Amhara and Oromo regions who feel unrepresented by the EPRDF has fuelled the conflict and came to a boiling point in 2015 under Prime Minister Haile Mmariam Desalegn. After protests and demonstrations related to land rights and political representation in 2015, Ethiopia imposed a state of emergency in October 2016, including 'sweeping restrictions on protests, social media, diaspora television and movement' as well as the ability for police forces to make arrests without warrants.[44] That state of emergency was lifted in August 2017, although, as Human Rights Watch points out: 'thousands remain in detention without charge, none of the protesters' underlying grievances have been addressed, and politically motivated trials of key opposition leaders, artists, journalists, and others continue.'[45]

Another state of emergency followed Desalegn's abrupt resignation in February 2018. Since April 2018, however, Ethiopia has seen major political reforms spearheaded by newly elected prime minister Abiy Ahmed. In contrast to his predecessor, Ahmed has lifted media bans, freed thousands of political prisoners, reached out to begin repairing relations with Eritrea, and generally inspired a sense of optimism despite Ethiopia's job shortage and growing inequality. Ahmed's Oromo ethnicity has also been seen as a harbinger of change. In June 2018 Ahmed lifted the state of emergency two months earlier than planned.

During BuraNEST's development, these events were playing out in the background. While Addis Ababa is far from Bura, political resentment was not difficult to find in Bahir Dar, the regional capital of Amhara where at least thirty peaceful protesters were killed by security forces on 7 August 2016.[46] These machinations and the fragile political situation were made evident in Bura by the regional government's unresponsiveness to land

43 Mastewal Chane: 'For the moment, we don't have budget for the carpenters and masons who are working. They haven't been paid for October. This must be solved. We are discussing how to solve it. That is crucial for the project to succeed.' Interview with Mastewal Chane, 2017.

44 See: Human Rights Watch timeline of Ethiopian Protests 2015-2016 (www.hrw.org/tag/ethiopian-protests).

45 See: Horne, F. State of Emergency Ends in Ethiopia: Government Should Use Reform, Not Force, to Avoid More Protests. 7 August 2017. Retrieved from: www.hrw.org/news/2017/08/07/state-emergency-ends-ethiopia, 29 November 2017.

46 This number (reported by Amnesty International) is disputed, and estimates vary from 12 – 70. Amnesty International also reported hundreds of arrests related to the protests in Bahir Dar. See: Amnesty International, Ethiopia: Dozens killed as police use excessive force against peaceful protesters. 8 August 2016. Retrieved from: www.amnesty.org/en/latest/news/2016/08/ethiopia-dozens-killed-as-police-use-excessive-force-against-peaceful-protesters/, on 29 November 2017.

compensation issues and other political roadblocks. As elsewhere in Africa, the issue of land ownership plays a pivotal role in the BuraNEST story. Historically, private land ownership is uncommon in Ethiopia. For 3,000 years, most of the country has functioned under a feudal system with royal and religious land owning elites. In 1975, the communist Derg regime introduced state ownership of all land and natural resources, and the government elected to power in 1991 has maintained state control until now. Rural farmers are given lifetime 'holding rights' (excluding the right to sell or buy), and are able to inherit land. Urban residents have a similar right to 99-year land leases.

The state's strict control of land makes supplying adequate compensation for farmers who must be relocated for development projects (as in the case of BuraNEST), difficult and complex — the states owns the land, but farming families with 'holding rights' may refuse to budge. Farmers at Bura were quick to indicate that the delays associated with land compensation at the regional government level were discouraging to potential participants in the project. Gebeyehu Endale, the first farmer to save enough for the required down payment at BuraNEST, shared related concerns: 'I have a threat of losing the land. The regional government might take the land because of the delay. We have a temporary land ownership certificate, but if this delay continues for years, there is a threat that the government might take the land.'[47] That lack of clarity has caused discord among some project participants who are making —by far— the largest investment of their lives.

47 Interview with Gebeyehu Endale, 2017.

48 See: Bewket, W. and Conway, D. (2007) A note on the temporal and spatial variability of rainfall in the drought-prone Amhara region of Ethiopia. International Journal of Climatology 27. Pp. 1467–1477.

Natural landscape and the New Town

Despite its picturesque beauty, BuraNEST faces urgent environmental challenges. The site spreads across both sides of the Chane River, a gentle stream with steep, five-meter-high banks in the dry season, and a roaring river spilling over those same banks and into Bura fields during the wet season. The dynamic nature of this Janus-faced water source is difficult to imagine, but parts of Bura can be completely cut off during especially heavy rains, rendering residents home-bound for months at a time. The riverbed excavations made as part of the initial phase of the project in 2012 have somewhat reduced the threat of floods. Excavations also created a dammed pool that serves livestock communally during dry seasons.

Bura is located in the same part of Ethiopia that was famously devastated by drought and famine in the 1980s. The Amhara region now experiences increasing rainfall variability, and is classified as 'drought-prone', two characteristics that increase the hardships faced by farming communities in this area.[48]

The Chane River looks inviting during the dry season, but swells over its banks during the rainy season.
Parts of Bura can become inaccessible for weeks at a time, which was part of the impetus for the regional government to construct a concrete bridge connecting the banks of the Chane for the first time.

49 Eucalyptus is a strong wood that grows quickly, making it suitable for construction use. However its oil is toxic to other plant species, limiting local biodiversity. Eucalyptus is an invasive species in Ethiopia. It was introduced from Australia by Emperor Menelik in the 1890s when timber was needed for the construction of a new capital at Addis Ababa.

Before the BuraNEST project, local farmers planted and harvested crops only once per year. The drip irrigation and integrated town agriculture (ITA) techniques introduced as part of BuraNEST now allows farmers to harvest three times per year. Three harvests will effectively triple farming incomes, and farmers see calculation as a convincing argument for change. Much of Bura is already cleared of trees and currently in use as farmland. Local farmers produce teff (a species of lovegrass used for *injera* pancakes), maize, wheat and rice. Cattle roam freely, grazing on fallow fields and keeping the landscape free of most small flora. Trees, however, are a critical component of BuraNEST. Project leaders incorporated trees from the beginning, and Oswald is convinced of their fundamental impact on the project: 'If you would ask me now what the first step should be when planning a New Town, I would say, "first plant a forest". A forest prevents erosion, which helps reduce flooding, it cleans groundwater and air, it provides free building material, and it is beautiful. If you want to plan a New Town, first plant a forest.'

After just five years, the eucalyptus[49] tree farm planted for construction material is thriving. A local guard is paid to discourage locals from over-harvesting lumber, and a large clearing in the gridded forest functions as a secondary public space for the community. The cool glade offers an intimate space for discussion and relief from the midday sun.

An additional forest of indigenous trees was planted at the main curve of the Chane River as a communal tree planting project—the project's very first action on the ground, before construction began elsewhere. The indigenous forest achieved several aims at one time, including bringing awareness of environmental issues to the community. The grevillea, nerium oleander, and acacia trees have since grown to provide spatial definition, a sustainable energy source, 'lungs' for the town, increased biodiversity, and erosion prevention.

In addition to the eucalyptus tree farm and indigenous forest, a tree nursery run by residents was started in 2012 and currently produces 75,000 seedlings during the months of June, July, and August. The seedlings are sold locally for communal profit.

Conclusion

Bura faces an uncertain future. Although only five buildings, a road, a bridge, and new road patterns have been implemented so far, the project has already brought great changes to the local community. Integrated town agriculture and new techniques have increased local productivity and incomes. New water management tools have reduced the threat of flooding and multiplied agricultural production. The architectural design of the Rainwater Units offers residents private sanitation facilities that are currently lacking. A new training centre has brought tools for employment to young men and women interested in construction, and the incorporation of traditional and new building techniques has inspired a reconsideration of the single architectural typology present in this

The traditional way of life in Bura may change as the BuraNEST project continues to develop. Many farmers welcome and embrace this change, envisioning a nearby future where good infrastructure supports commerce, education, and a lifestyle enriched with access to more urban services.

area. Those improvements have benefitted the Bura community and will continue to benefit local residents in the future.

There have also been challenges and setbacks associated with the project. Management has been a concern for farmers, perhaps primarily due to the complicated, top-down political structure that has created unnecessary delays and roadblocks. Closer to the project, BuraNEST's steering committee has 11 members —some local and some international— with varying levels of commitment, and this discrepancy is evident in the committee's infrequent meetings. Limited access to housing loans has also frustrated farming families interested in the project, but without adequate liquidity.

From a design perspective, the limited housing stock —only one model— precludes many families from joining the project. As Chane points out: 'This type of house is for rich farmers. Now the users are asking to have another type of house based on their income. So we need different housing models, or we should get the land out of the project [and sell homes on smaller plots], to make it cheaper. Other people have opposing ideas. In general, different options should be available.' Some locals doubted the structural integrity of a two-story building, and they thought attached housing might not offer enough privacy for the intimacies of family life. The architects also faced resistance to the use of local materials, which seemed strangely old-fashioned for such a groundbreaking design. The Rainwater Unit design has since been widely accepted, but another challenge that may play a role in BuraNEST's long-term success is its ability to support livelihoods other than farming. Rural Ethiopian youth appear largely disinterested in farming[50], and if there is no chance for education or self-development, they will move to cities with more opportunities. To combat this, the plans call for commercial areas, a new market and life-long learning facilities. They also leave flexibility for spatial usage — an attractive opening for entrepreneurs who may use ground floor space in a Rainwater Unit as a small shop or to provide a service.

The BuraNEST project offers many lessons for designers interested in rural development. For example, coming from a Swiss perspective, Oswald was struck by the unexpected intricacies of the project's progress:

> It was a very slow, very complex process. An example may help illustrate the difficulties that we had... We said from the beginning, 'this project must be built with local resources'. In this case, that meant either local timber or soil which you can press [into bricks]. It's too expensive to build with imported materials. We thought, 'people here have a life experience, a cultural experience, with these materials'. But this is an assumption. Because then you find out that in this particular culture, they've had civil wars for the past fifty years. Every generation had a civil war. Which means that all the know-how is gone. Nobody tells you that. You find out by going to see buildings that were beautifully built 100 years ago—complex joinery and wooden nails—and then you think, 'but why didn't they continue with that?'. And then you find out that since 1960 Ethiopia has had near-constant civil wars in certain areas. And that means that the younger generation cannot go and see what the older generation did, and learn why and how.[51]

The kind of 'learning-by-doing' approach described by Oswald puts the BuraNEST designers and future beneficiaries in the same position. Every day at BuraNEST becomes, as Oswald puts it: 'confrontation, collaboration, confrontation, collaboration.'[52] Eventually, BuraNEST's real contribution may be the hard lessons from this 'living experiment' that may facilitate implementation in future New Towns. If the Rural-to-Urban Transformation project initiated by Woldu and Simon moves forward, there may be 8,000 future Ethiopian New Towns that ultimately benefit from the roadblocks and design re-iterations that slowed progress at Bura.

In August 2017, the Association of Ethiopian Architects (AEA) presented NESTown with their annual design award. The New Town's designers appreciated the acknowledgment of their work, but Oswald was careful to differentiate between more traditional planning and the symbolic ideas that inform the NESTown approach and the BuraNEST project more specifically: 'The most important thing is to stick to the principle ideas. The design can be anything. [American architect] Louis Kahn made a beautiful differentiation between order and form. Order remains on a conceptually level, and form is physical, material. NESTown is defined by a clear pattern of associations, but they can take different forms, in different places, for different people. That's what makes this model different from

50 See: Sosina, B. and Stein, H. (2014) Are Rural Youth in Ethiopia Abandoning Agriculture? World Development. Volume 64, December 2014, Pp. 259-272.

51 Interview with Franz Oswald, 2017.

52 Ibid.

other New Towns… If people learn about this and interpret the ideas for themselves, then that's the idea. We want people to benefit from this.'[53]

53 Ibid.

As stated earlier, BuraNEST is based on seven 'propositions' that can also be read as the project's ultimate ambitions. BuraNEST's success in achieving these propositions can only be evaluated after the project evolves from 'living experiment' to actual town. The collaborations between Ethiopian and Swiss architects, funding bodies, training agencies and government authorities have proven to be fertile ground for new ideas, and new political commitments. But BuraNEST is at a transitional moment, and a crossroads. Currently, after seven years on the ground, only five buildings have been constructed and none of those are yet inhabited. What happens next will determine the long-term success of this innovative and ambitious project.

Applying the 10 principles of the Manual

Planning is an ongoing process BuraNEST is planned from a strong concept that focuses on complimentary programmatic elements (Energy, Education, Exchange, and Ecology) rather than a specific design. If they continue to be used as a strategy for development over time, those principles, or 'propositions', will enable the evolving New Town to grow in ways that make sense as the community changes over time. The community should also be able to re-evaluate the New Town's progress as specific moments, to determine whether the '4E's' remain relevant, or whether alternative develop trajectories may be more suitable.

Plan for adaptivity The '4E's' concept developed by the BuraNEST initiators allow for a certain amount of spatial flexibility. One threat to BuraNEST, however, has been land ownership and land compensation issues stemming from the regional government's lack of initiative. That threat has changed the project's timeline dramatically, and as a result, farmers (future beneficiaries) are voicing doubts about the project's continuation. BuraNEST project leaders must find a way to encourage continued development, whether that is through the design of alternative, cheaper housing options, or more focus on programmatic elements other than housing. The Ethiopian NESTown members must engage this transitional moment and use it to determine an approach that acknowledges the hard lessons of the last seven years. BuraNEST must prove it is adaptive enough to overcome stagnation.

No New Town is an island BuraNEST is 15 km from Yifag, the closest market town. This means that self-sufficiency will be an important aspect of the New Town's growth strategy. However, encouraging mutually beneficial relationships among BuraNEST, Yifag, and other surrounding communities will enable BuraNEST to grow in ways that attract residents.

Use no cut-and-paste universal model BuraNEST is considered a 'living experiment'. It is the first test of a concept that may be applied to 8,000 New Towns in the near future. But BuraNEST is not a design that will be re-used on another site. Rather, the NESTown model is a set of principles that prioritises Education, Energy, Exchange, and Ecology as the basic building blocks of new urban centres. When implemented, those elements will look different in different places.

Embrace new ideas The NESTown model is innovative in its clear move away from design-based urban planning towards conceptually driven development. The '4E's' that provide the framework for development in BuraNEST are innovative in that they are relevant to local life, but also ambitious enough that even at this early stage, the developments at BuraNEST have changed people's lives. If the BuraNEST experiment continues to grow, it will undoubtedly emphasise innovation within the Bura community and inspire others to follow suit.

Infrastructure and mobility for all, from the start The regional government built a packed dirt road and concrete bridge that connected the existing Bura community to the main road (Route 3) for the first time. Vehicular accessibility has already allowed for dramatic transformation such as riverbed excavations, importation of materials, and access for emergency vehicles. That accessibility may act as an important catalyst for the area as it continues to develop.

Use a blue-green infrastructure as the central framework

The natural landscape at Bura was taken as the primary structuring element for the New Town, and the environment plays a large role in this project. The Chane River weaves through the site, and part of the project has included excavations to reduce flooding. A new eucalyptus tree farm and indigenous forest have reduced erosion and improved local biodiversity. The model garden at the training centre provides fruits and vegetables, as well as hand-on lessons in new agricultural techniques. New water collection, storage, and irrigation methods allow farmers to harvest three times per year instead of relying on irregular rainfall. By improving existing conditions, BuraNEST offers residents an easier, safer, and more profitable quality of life.

Incorporate local cultural heritage(s)

The Bura community has a rich heritage of small scale farming and a specific vernacular architecture. Those elements have been closely considered and sensitively incorporated in the BuraNEST plan. The continuous communication with Bura residents through workshops, presentations, church meetings and interviews has given project coordinators deep insights into the dynamics of this community and their priorities.

Combine top-down and bottom-up

The BuraNEST project initiators have maintained a focus on clear and consistent communication between project leaders and local residents. That participatory approach has not been easy, or convenient; both project leaders and farmers have expressed frustrations. But the will to engage in meaningful discussions and exchange may show fruit in long-term local commitment to the project.

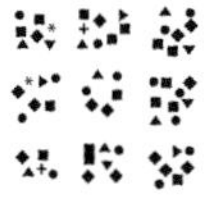

New Towns need diversity

Bura is currently a community of farmers who share an ethnicity, religion and livelihood. When it is completed, BuraNEST will offer residents new choices that encourage diversity: the ability to run a shop along the main road, or attend school in town, or sell products at the market. BuraNEST also offers an alternative architectural type to local residents; one that increases density and illustrates the benefits of compact development. BuraNEST can and should offer more alternatives in the future, and residents are already realising this, as they ask designers for cheaper housing options.

Ato Tsegaye Biadglign,
chief mason at BuraNEST,
is training local women in
masonry skills so that they
can later find employment

Fasil Giorghis and Zegeye Cherenet, members of the NESTown Group

For more than a decade, Ethiopia has achieved consistent economic growth in which the government is heavily involved. This involvement is primarily based on a sequence of national plans and programmes such as the Growth and Transformation Plan (GTP) for the years 2010/11 – 2014/15.[1] This document stated that, though the level of urbanisation in the country is low, there is an alarming increase in rural to urban migration. To mitigate the stress on existing urban areas, the GTP suggested to enhance living opportunities in rural towns. In addition to continued efforts toward developing existing cities, it also promoted the need to generate 'urban plans/maps' for 750 small towns.[2]

A test project for establishing new rural towns was initiated in 2008. In 2010, its implementation started, under the name BuraNEST in Bura kebele, Libokemkem woreda of the Amhara Regional State.[3] The planning, design, and implementation process was consulted by a consortium of local and international experts known as the NESTown Group.

BuraNEST is a striking case, where self-built initiatives are planned and organised within a governance structure whose instinctive disposition is top-down with firm regulations. This conversation by Anteneh Tesfaye Tola is with the local experts of the NESTown Group: Fasil Giorghis, chair of Conservation of Urban and Architectural Heritage, and Zegeye Cherenet, Head of Emerging Cities Lab (ECL), both at Addis Ababa University's EiABC[4]. This interview illustrates the contemporary challenges planners face in dealing with forming New Towns in emerging economies such as Ethiopia.

Anteneh Tesfaye Tola (ATT): Reflecting back on the genesis of the BuraNEST project, what were the initial inceptions? Who initiated it? What was the general idea behind it?
Fasil Giorghis (FG): The story starts with our dear friend Professor Franz Oswald who initially came to EiABC through the Engineering Capacity Building Program (ECBP) of the Ministry of Capacity Building. He was an expert helping us to reform the EiABC. During this time, he had the chance to travel around the country and make subsequent assessments. Through several discussions concerning Ethiopia's urbanisation he and some of his colleagues started talking about a new vision for New Towns as a means of directing Ethiopia's development towards a sustainable urban future. These discussions led to the formation of the NESTown group, which Zegeye and I joined at a later stage.
At the same time, the Amhara regional government was already contemplating forming New Towns. Their idea was to start with what they called 'kebele centres' and it was basically meant as an administrative centre. The plan was that people would converge to those kebele centres in search of public services, infrastructure, and the like. In their minds, the kebele centres were to become the magnets or the nuclei for the future New Towns.
The regional government was quite excited to further discuss our visions. They had the political will and some administrative ideas while we at the NESTown group, especially Franz Oswald and Peter Schenker, were already making plans. Of course, the next step was to find land. They selected the land based on their own criteria and that is how the realisation started.

Zegeye Cherenet (ZC): The background context, as well as some of the paradoxes within the context, are very important. One contextual issue is that the Ethiopian government was interested to initiate industrialisation and promoted the reformation of engineering education, which is why we have this ECBP. That is how high-level professionals such as Oswald were invited to consult with us.

The other context, a bit contradictory to the first one, was that there were less ideas within the government's policy framework towards urbanisation. This became a challenge in later stages. The other contextual reality at the time was that some NESTown group members, particularly Franz Oswald, were better able to articulate the issues we were all grappling with, because they were free from being entangled with the details of reality here. For instance, I was not as scared as they were back then about population growth, about subsistence farming and the basic economic trends in the country. But [as outsiders] they could see these big numbers which were at play and ask: 'where are all these millions of people going to be accommodated in a few years?'

ATT: Concerning the Amhara region's interest in initiating New Towns, what was the background of the political decision to transform kebeles into urban centres?

FG: Through prior agricultural development programmes, in rural Ethiopia the output and the income of farmers has increased. The region had to decide what to deliver to these farmers. They were thinking of making better houses to improve domestic life, but also understood that better infrastructure and services should be provided. In most parts of Ethiopia, farmers live in a very scattered fashion. You would find one extended family at one location and the next one would be a few kilometres away. They understood that it is practically impossible to provide adequate infrastructure, roads, electricity, and water, unless you form rural agglomerations.

During the Derg communist period (1974-1991) there was a time when the government ran a 'villagisation' programme. Farmers were forced to resettle and live in very dense settlements. This idea failed, and there is a stigma attached to it. On the other hand, they understood that they could not continue with the scattered settlements. The challenge was thus: how to institute the kebele centres through attractive and voluntary means?

ATT: How was Bura selected? It is between Bahir Dar and Gondar cities, how was it decided for the town to be situated on that specific location?

FG: The regional government chose it for four reasons. The first one is the proximity to a main road because, as a model town, it needed to be easily accessible for visitors. The second reason was that the farmers of this kebele had, in previous years, registered high degrees of productivity and success in their agriculture, and the project was to be an encouragement. The third reason was the presence of a river close by. The fourth and maybe subdued reasoning was that the site didn't need compensation payments to the farmers. But when the NESTown plan was ready and our team started investigating the soil conditions, hydrology, climate and so on, there were a few surprises, to say the least.

ZC: The site selected was not good enough. The area floods regularly. The ground is black cotton soil, so it is very difficult to build on. We asked if they could push the site a little bit further to the north but that could not happen because it is the property of a neighbouring kebele. We argued in vain that a town should not be handled by a single kebele, it should rather be an open structure for all. We were quite naïve about land administration and management processes in this country and how intricate they can become.

1 The sequence of national development plans included the Agricultural Development Led Industrialization (ADLI), the Sustainable Development and Poverty Reduction Program (SDPRP), the Plan for Accelerated and Sustained Development to End Poverty (PASDEP), and finally the Growth and Transformation Plan (GTP).

2 The Federal Democratic Republic of Ethiopia - The Second Growth and Transformation Plan (GTP II) (National Planning Commission, September 2015).

3 Kebele and woreda indicate the first and second smallest administrative units in the Ethiopian government structure, similar to a ward and a district.

4 Ethiopian Institute of Architecture, Building Construction and City Development (EiABC)

Even if the findings of our technical assessments were not supportive of the choice of the location, we could not change it because of the administrative processes. That was quite a lesson for us.

ATT: Can you elaborate on the built forms and spatial organisation of BuraNEST? Some buildings are, for example, double stories or shared buildings for multiple households. These are concepts that require changes in domestic lifestyles and sense of ownership.
FG: Customarily, when people move from a rural area to an urban one, they say goodbye to agriculture - usually reluctantly. But in NESTown, BuraNEST being the first model, agriculture is still there. The idea is that you can combine an urban lifestyle with agriculture. Their primary source of income would still be agriculture. The 4 E's of NESTown (Energy, Education, Exchange and Ecology) are thus an articulation of a community that produces, processes, exchanges, and enhances this cycle through applied education.

ZC: The real clash between our perception and the way people live and also the way things are managed continued in the particularities such as the design of houses. Because of the scarcity of land, particularly arable land, in the northern regions of Ethiopia, we decided at an embryotic level to economise the use of land and develop at a reasonably higher density so the urban footprint would be smaller and we could prioritise the use of land for agriculture.
In the future, we know that the market will reverse the value of land whether it is fertile or not. Building a house and renting it will become more profitable than producing vegetables on your land. But at this moment, one has to be conscious to conserve land. Thus, we had to build up: two stories, three stories.
One of the mottos that was formulated by the group was 'a town by the people for the people'. The idea was to equip the farmers with simple techniques, whereby they could build their town by themselves using the materials they can access easily from their vicinity. But the local material happened to be the fragile black cotton soil. Successive exploration led us to settling for a frame structure made up of unprocessed eucalyptus wood logs and the black cotton soil to be used as infill. There is an existing tradition of building with eucalyptus from a nearby forest but building more than a single story presented a technical challenge. I can say we were not content with the techniques we set up until Fasil came across some local techniques that advanced the building methodology.

FG: Yes, through an accidental conversation, the farmers informed me about a church elder in a nearby village who had experience building with the black cotton soil that expands when its wet and shrinks to almost half its size and cracks when dry. We employed this person, made him part of our team and he trained our staff to produce building blocks as infill. This indigenous knowledge came in handy to advance our technique.
We also call the dwellings Rainwater Units. The roof was designed to collect the abundant rainwater and there would be a cistern where water gets collected for each household. Wells would be built per two households for domestic use and backyard gardening. Water was an essential element in the

design of the house. At the block level, possible overflow would be collected and channeled to the river. This also, in a way, dictated the form of the houses. The absence of stone also forced us to use a special kind of foundation, almost like a pile footing going down using the corrugated iron sheet. At first a prototype house was built near Bahir Dar, a bigger city to the south of Bura. The purpose was that, if for some reason the prototype failed, we did not want to frustrate the future inhabitants and risk the loss of their faith in the project. We only took a few of them who had some experience in carpentry and construction, so they could experiment and learn with the guidance of professional carpenters and coordinators. We were relieved that it all worked out and to see that the eucalyptus structure, with some new construction details, could be applicable for multi-story building.

ATT: I can see that this project was a result of multiple interests and engagements; the local administration and regional government, local academics such as yourselves, expat personnel, and the community and their indigenous expertise. Looking back, how would you evaluate the level of engagement by the locals? How do you assess the bottom-up and top-down processes?

FG: I think it would be difficult for a community to have the initiative to build a New Town from the bottom-up. In areas of agrarian lifestyle with dominant rural structures and culture we as planners have to bring the issue of urbanisation to the centre. To transform a settlement into a dense urban setting requires help. You can translate that as top-down, maybe.

On the other hand, we had to convince the community and make sure they own whatever comes out of it. Initially it was not easy to convince farmers and local administrators. Nothing was forced. People had to vote whether they would like this town or not. There were multiple visits, discussions and explanations about every issue. The (then) regional president came and gave a speech to the inhabitants of Bura, where he said 'you deserve to have better houses', and that was good rhetoric. Broadly speaking, urbanisation does not come very easily to a rural society. It has to be nudged a bit by external agents such as the expertise we brought in. But we also needed to bring local institutions together, to participate in such a multifaceted project. We had to include the government bodies and NGOs and so on.

Without the participation of the local community nothing can happen. Ideas were probably top-down, but the realisation had to be local and participatory. That meant we needed to be open for discussion and very patient while constantly coming up with techniques to facilitate and innovate during the process.

ATT: Now let's come to the negotiations and confrontations relating to the definition of a 'town' in Ethiopian laws and regulations. How was Bura accepted as a town, considering the regulations that an area should be inhabited by at least 2000 inhabitants to be considered a town?

ZC: When it comes to New Towns, the complexity is extremely dense and difficult to navigate. In order to crack into this complex setup, first we had to pool all the stakeholders and decision makers together and ask for some exemptions or considerations. Not only land but in many subsequent decisions as well. The process had to create a regional level supervisory board and a local level town implementation committee. On the regional level, we had to pool together various governmental agencies and land management bodies. On the local level authorities and community members (including churches and elders) assembled as a body.

The communal land which we were supposed to build on was owned and used by the community as a whole. We were advised to form a cooperative model just to access the land. That was another layer whereby we had to create a new system.

Though the project is declared a model town, there was no budget from the government, and the farmers would not put money into it without understanding what it was. So the next challenge was securing seed money. Thanks to our partners from Switzerland, and with the help of ETH Zurich, we were able to channel research money.

ATT: Can you explain more about accessing finances and local money?

FG: Unfortunately, the Ethiopian banks do not engage in rural housing. When it comes to construction, they will only lend money with collateral, only for urban houses. This means that more than 80 percent of our population cannot access that system.

We had a difficult time because the BuraNEST houses were bigger than what farmers normally build and the water reservoir and other costs were also relatively higher. Even though we formed the cooperatives, the banks were very reluctant to engage with them. Finally, Abay Bank agreed to give some seed money but not as a loan. Their experts came, assessed, and concluded that the farmers cannot repay loans; maybe their system cannot evaluate the income of farmers. However, the board of the bank believed in the idea and its potential, so they gave us the money as a donation. It was not much, just half a million Ethiopian birr for the first few prototypes. This would be topped up by the additional funding raised by the cooperatives.

The other challenge was that the government was not investing. Their argument was that they cannot make an exception for just one kebele out of the 3,000 that were in the Amhara region. They only paid for the construction of a bridge over the river and some water channeling works to avoid flooding. For the rest, the town had to be self-reliant. NGOs such as Amhara Development Association (ADA) built the school, and the Organization for Rehabilitation and Development of Amhara (ORDA) helped with the town agriculture and training of farmers. Green Ethiopia and other Swiss NGOs helped with some other issues. We as the NESTown group were facilitating and bringing these groups together. We learned the hard way that we, as architects and planners, have to change our attitudes from straightforward technocrats into patient multi-taskers and moderators.

ATT: How much of a success was it? Of course, theoretically, we can learn a lot from it but as a physical entity how much of it was a success? What could be done differently? How do you assess BuraNEST as a project to be scaled-up?

FG: BuraNEST is a real-life experiment. Normally, as planners, we would make the plan, make some report and leave. In this case, we involved ourselves in the realisation. Little did we know we were going into very complex, deep waters. The lessons learned are many. Success or failure

depends on the point of view. It required a lot of inputs; aspects architects or planners usually do not consider important.
For the future, I think the preparedness of the state and the commitment and capacity of local government are extremely important. It would be naïve to say a kebele or woreda can realise a town. No, they neither have the knowhow nor the managerial capacity to handle it. If we are talking about New Towns, there needs to be a lot of restructuring of governance. There needs to be a separate ministry or agency that actually focuses on this matter. This cannot be an auxiliary task for another agency. Comprehensive collaboration among agencies is also vital. We have seen that the local state's engagement, and clarity of responsibility was really not up to the project's demands.
As a model, it is successful because people need to see an example. Building that model Rainwater Unit was an important demonstration to others who are interested. The Awra Amba community, which are already known to have organised themselves in their own organic way, have visited BuraNEST and are keen on adopting significant aspects of the model. Having it as a built form is significant to inspire more local initiatives, which I believe is very essential. We have seen how difficult a task it is to cultivate participation on a relatively abstract vision.

ZC: When it comes to measuring successes, it would require a long time to mature before rushing to evaluate it. BuraNEST is not yet a truly functioning town. In terms of results, there are some you can see on the ground. The natural environment has started healing; it is amazing when you compare it with earlier photographs of the land. Now you have all the trees growing up and giving fruits and this gives you hope that a town can also become a tool to improve the environment. Cities are always accused of being the problem of environmental degradation but one can also make a city into a tool for healing an environment. We planted more than 1.5 million seedlings and they have shown results not only on the site but also along the river and further upstream. With time, we hope the water flow can be more predictable and manageable. So in terms of the environment, it is a success.
In terms of exchange and education, trade diversification is necessary. In the Ethiopian context, the primary agenda is how farmers can transition or exit from their primary economic activity. So, how could a city contribute to this transition of a farmer becoming a value-adding industrial producer? In this sense, we have trade diversification as a central challenge. Since the beginning, if this is a town 'by the people for the people', it also has to become a platform for adapting new skills. We have been trying to train many farmers with different skills, creating cooperatives of carpenters, manufacturers, and so on. They are already certified and have started their own businesses. This is also a way of measuring success because some farmers have transitioned and trade has started to diversify.

ATT: After such an engagement, how do you see the role of architects and planners in forming New Towns and cities? Would it be sustainable to engage with the intensity with which you were involved in this project? Or should the practice itself change?
ZC: In the context of Ethiopia, I don't believe in these jackets that we put on in the name of professions as architects and planners. Generally, here in

Ethiopia, we lack a strong urban tradition. The multi-layered complexities of urbanisation, be it political or economic, nobody would understand it here because in its general sense we have a predominantly rural society. You can look at our political agendas, they are primarily about land and agriculture. I think we have to start changing education. Our experience in the project has brought us together with biologists, economists, lawyers, and so on. We were all in these straightjackets of professionalism and lack the transdisciplinary means to deal with the complexities of urbanisation. This means we have to revisit our education system and professional orders. If Africa has a chance to create better cities, it has to expose young people to the organic and complex realities of urbanisation before wearing the straitjackets of professionalism.

New Towns, Old Places: Four Lessons from Konza Techno City, Kenya

Femke van Noorloos & Diky Avianto

A new wave of African New Towns is on its way: large-scale utopian plans for masterplanned cities, often in public-private collaboration, abound across the continent. Although many of these ambitious plans are not yet realised, their effects are already appearing. While the UN-Habitat New Urban Agenda remains silent on the topic of New Towns, it clearly advocates for 'well-planned' solutions for rapid urban growth across Africa, and this matches the current landscape of large-scale, often top-down urban housing and infrastructure projects, including New Towns. Meanwhile inclusive urban development is also a key goal in the New Urban Agenda, as well as in Sustainable Development Goal 11, which deals with cities. The two policy documents refer to inclusiveness as a way of ensuring that different (particularly poor and marginalised or 'vulnerable') groups benefit from urban development and are included in decision-making. But what is needed to plan New Towns in a more inclusive manner, particularly among Africa's widespread diversity of social, spatial and economic circumstances?

This question must be viewed from multiple angles: while from-scratch planning and design can in theory offer new opportunities for inclusiveness, frequently mentioned problems that thwart inclusive development are: (1) the lack of accessibility and suitability of the new-built housing and services for a variety of groups (including the poor); (2) low accessibility and quantity/quality of newly created jobs and business opportunities; and (3) the issues of enclave development, socio-spatial segregation and governance fragmentation.[1] However, one key issue

1 For further reading on these issues see: Cirolia, L.R. (2014) '(W) Escaping the Challenges of the City: a Critique of Cape Town's Proposed Satellite Town', *Urban Forum* 25: 295-312. And: Grant, R. (2015) 'Sustainable African Urban Futures. Stocktaking and Critical Reflection on Proposed Urban Projects', *American Behavioral Scientist* 59(3): 294-310. Also: Murray, M.J. (2015) 'Waterfall City (Johannesburg): Privatized Urbanism in Extremis', *Environment & Planning* A 47 (3): 503-520. And: Moser, S. (2015) 'New cities: Old wine in new bottles?' *Dialogues in Human Geography* 5(1): 31-35. And: Watson, V. (2013) 'African urban fantasies: dreams or nightmares?' *Environment and Urbanization* 26 (1): 215-231. And: van Noorloos, F. and Kloosterboer, M. (2017) 'Africa's new cities: The contested future of urbanisation', *Urban Studies* 55(6): 1223-1241.

that is often overlooked is how to deal with pre-existing and surrounding populations of the spaces where New Towns are planned, their access and rights to resources such as land and water, and how they can benefit or lose from the wide array of new developments surrounding New Towns.

Against the background of increasing land scarcity and global struggles over land rights, this problem raises concern, particularly given the large-scale and enclave character of many of the recently planned and announced New Towns in Africa. Indeed, the scale of the projected urban visions is such that dramatic changes in land tenure and use can be expected. In this essay, based on a critical assessment of New Town projects, we argue for more attention to the insertion of the New Town into the pre-existing socio-spatial context and more respect for the rights of local inhabitants. We also draw some very preliminary lessons learnt so far from recent African New Towns, many of which are still on the drawing board.

Pre-existing resource rights

The challenge of inclusive planning while recognising pre-existing populations and resource rights starts with the issue of where New Towns are planned. Most African New Town plans are located in the peri-urban and suburban areas near existing (mainly capital) cities,[2] although there are also some examples of completely greenfield developments (e.g. the newly built capital of Equatorial Guinea), and of total inner city redevelopments or 'new cities within cities' (e.g. Addis Ababa and Kigali). While peri-urban New Town development seems at least preferable to inner city remaking from the point of view of preventing large-scale expulsions (although not from a compact city point of view), it is not problem-free. In reality, empty, unused or unclaimed land is extremely difficult to find, particularly around the largest cities which continue to grow. Instead, New Towns are often located on the rural-urban fringes, in particularly complex spaces with multiple intersecting land governance arrangements and diverse livelihoods; other towns are created on 'new land' reclaimed from water.[3]

The crux is in the frequent failure of states and private actors to recognise and adequately deal with customary and 'informal'[4] land, housing and resource rights as the *de facto* mode of tenure for a large part of African (peri-)urban dwellers. New Town projects managed by public-private partnerships or those led by international investors (including state-owned companies such as the Chinese ones) often rely on land being 'granted', 'leased' or 'freed' by the state, as for example in Konza Techno City, Kenya. However, the legitimacy of such actions is in many instances questionable, given long-standing customary land rights that risk being overruled. On the other hand, when land transactions are private-to-private and the landholdings are really largely unused, the process is less problematic at first sight (e.g. Tatu City near Nairobi, Waterfall City near Johannesburg[5]).[6] Nevertheless, even in those instances problems can occur.

2 Van Noorloos, F. and Kloosterboer, M. (2017).

3 Ibid.

4 The notion of informality is critically debated and all but straightforward, see for example: Roy, A. (2005) 'Urban Informality: Toward an Epistemology of Planning', *Journal of the American Planning Association* **71(2): 147-158.**

5 Murray, M. (2015).

6 Van Noorloos, F. and Kloosterboer, M. (2017).

Parallel to the danger of displacement that pre-existing villages may experience, there is also another interesting development around many planned New Towns: new migrants flock to the areas in anticipation of economic opportunities. They often form informal settlements around the borders of the projects. Hence these projects need to pay close attention to both pre-existing and new settlements around the New Towns, especially if they are regarded as informal. The governance dynamics of securing access to resources such as agricultural land, grazing land, and water by pre-existing and newly emerging surrounding populations (and land users), including the roles of different types of customary and other non-state authorities, need to be taken seriously.[7] New Towns with their all-encompassing character and modernisation agenda may reinforce the tendency to formalise and 'modernise' everything (e.g. 'clean the city' of street vendors, street hawkers, etc.), thereby intensifying different forms of displacement and exclusion.

7 This argument can be taken further and include 'informal' or diverse ways of economic and business activities: new town designers can take up the existing commerce of the area (e.g. food, handicrafts) to make more inclusive economic linkages. However, walling and other types of segregation that are often evident in Africa's current new city plans preclude these types of developments.

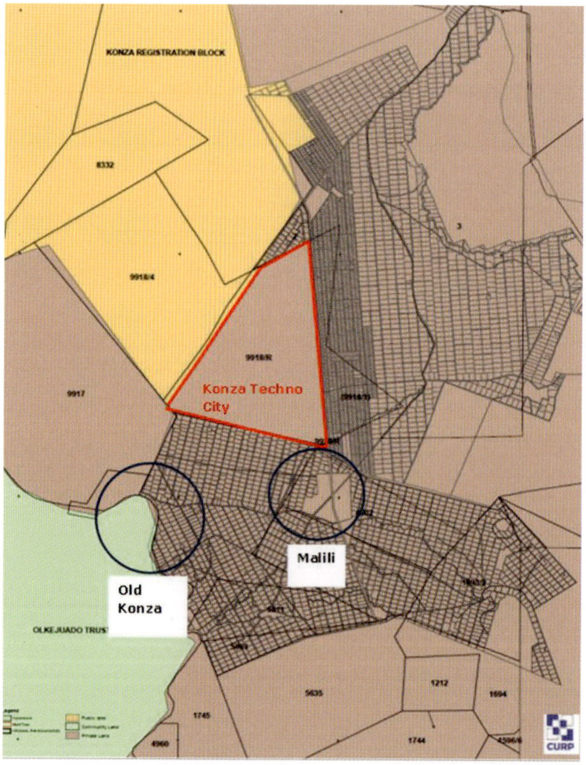

Land Tenure Situation (Source: Ministry of Lands, 2013. Modified by D. Avianto)

Four lessons

To take this discussion further, we have identified four important lessons to take into account how New Town planning can be more conscious of pre-existing and surrounding populations' rights and needs. These are partly based on a general view of current African New Towns, and illustrated with findings from empirical field research around Konza Techno City near Nairobi, Kenya. Konza is one example of an ambitious New Town plan managed by a Development Authority consisting of the Kenyan Ministry of Information and Communications in collaboration with a number of (mostly international) private developers.
It is part of the Kenya Vision 2030 national development strategy to spearhead the country into a middle-income status with Information and Communication Technology as a main service sector. In this picture, Konza Techno City, 60 km south of Nairobi, is a major flagship project aimed at developing the 'Silicon Valley of Kenya' (or 'Silicon Savannah') and a major ICT hub with 17,000 jobs and 200,000 residents. The project is holistic and multifunctionally planned, and will include housing, offices / work, a university, a hospital, schools, hotels, shopping, etc. However, it is suffering from delay and intra-governmental conflict, and has seen very little construction so far, although the newly installed government (2017) seems committed to continuing the project. Although most of the area to be developed is currently just grassland with a fence, land sales and speculation are ongoing. The national government leases the land (5,000 ha) to private developers for 99 years terms. The government bought the land in 2010-2011 from the representative of a privatised and subdivided former

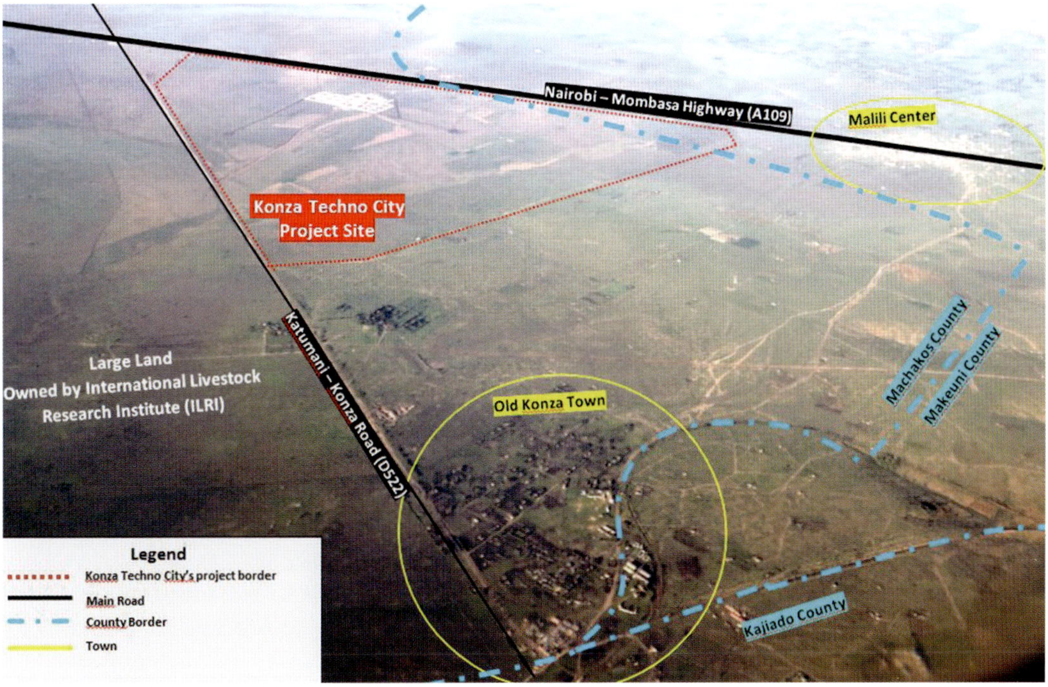

Konza Techno City and its surrounding (Source: D. Avianto, 2017)

group ranch, and the process has involved some conflict and fraud (there is still a court case ongoing),[8] but no major involuntary or unwanted displacements. However, the creation of a buffer zone around the project is another complex issue, leading to our first lesson.

1. The creation of buffer zones and land use regulations around the project can also lead to displacement and exclusion.

Around the 5,000 ha Konza Techno City project itself, a much larger buffer zone of 20,000 ha has been planned with the aim of keeping upcoming 'uncontrolled' informal and slum developments at a distance as they would become an 'eyesore' and discourage investors.[9] This reminds us of the colonial types of urban planning that used segregation in the form of *cordons sanitaires* or green buffer zones around the city, a form of segregation that was rationalised by those in power as a way to protect the city against infectious diseases.[10] Clearly an exclusionary idea in the first place, the buffer zone around Konza Techno City furthermore creates livelihood and land tenure insecurity for two communities present in the area: Old Konza and Malili.

The area, which was until recently very rural, is part of the arid and semi-arid lands (ASALs), where pastoralism is historically an important source of livelihoods. Malili or Malili Center used to be a group ranch under Kenya's group ranch policy, and its lands were subdivided among the members in 2006. The group ranch allocated land for a small commercial centre near the Nairobi – Mombasa highway, which is now the location of Malili Center. Around 2010 and 2011 there was slow growth, with

8 Johari, A. (2015) 'Kenya's Konza Techno City: Utopian Vision Meets Social Reality', Independent Study Project (ISP) Collection. Paper 2024.

9 Wapenaar, M. (2015) Formal Planning & Informal Settlement. The case of Konza Technology City, MSc thesis Universiteit van Amsterdam.

10 Bigon, L. (2012). 'A History of Urban Planning and Infectious Diseases: Colonial Senegal in the Early Twentieth Century'. Urban Studies Research 2012, DOI: 10.1155/2012/589758

11 Furthermore, it potentially creates governance conflicts between three involved county governments and federal government with the latter imposing its development planning on the first, thereby overruling existing spatial plans.

some structures such as shops and hotels. After the announcement of Konza Techno City in 2012, rapid development started, and the pieces of land were further subdivided and sold. Lots of newcomers from all over Kenya arrived, searching for job opportunities. The small town became more crowded and urbanised, with semi-permanent structures using iron sheets for both wall and roofing. The current population is estimated at 1,500 -2,000 residents. Malili developed rapidly devoid of planning and infrastructure provision. While subdivided plots initially had individual private ownership, rapid further subdivisions were not formalised, and an informal land buying and house rental market emerged, along with semi-permanent houses and buildings. Most inhabitants are recent migrants who arrived there less than 2 years ago. Currently the majority of people rent their houses, and the original shareholders of the group ranch mostly live elsewhere. Malili Centre is thus largely a residential and commercial town, with services such as shops, kiosks, hardware, food joints, water selling points, salons, small guest houses and roadside commerce. Most people's income is based on commercial activities and casual jobs.

Old Konza is a small town to the south of the Konza Techno City site. It was established in the 1970s when the first settlers came to this empty land and started farming and growing livestock in a collective manner. During that time, the land was owned by the government and people were considered squatters, but in the 1990s the government started giving out allotment letters of the land to each household. However, these letters do not provide particularly strong land tenure security, which is why people are still struggling to receive stronger types of ownership. Most inhabitants of Old Konza have lived there for a long time, between 10 and 30 years, and own their house. The housing structures are mostly permanent, and built with various materials such as iron sheets and bricks. Old Konza has not seen rapid development like in Malili, which is probably due to the further distance from the highway. Land use patterns and population have not changed much recently. Most people are farmers on their own lands and/or pastoralists. Old Konza also has a small market area with commercial activities such as shops, food joints, salons, etc.

The Konza Techno City buffer zone plans could endanger land rights and livelihoods in both towns. The first plan was to prohibit any land use in the zone; this subsequently changed to strict land use and construction regulations which are laid down by government in a comprehensive Local Physical Development Plan. Old Konza was assigned as a zone of 'modern agriculture' and Malili as a commercial and possibly residential zone. Inhabitants of both communities are largely uninformed about the buffer zone plans, and afraid their houses will be demolished as these do not fit the 'modern' image as laid down in the construction requirements.[11] Indeed, some informal structures have been assigned as 'to be demolished', but given project delays no further action has been taken.

As this example shows, careful evaluation of displacement effects should not only be based on direct project land, actual land leases or acquisition. It must also take into account that the creation of extra infrastructure

Malili - Buildings with X mark (soon to be demolished). (Source: D. Avianto, 2017)

Konza Techno City Project Fences. (Source: D. Avianto, 2017)

and buffer zones can fuel displacements, and new regulations (for example on land use) can create livelihood insecurity. In order to enhance inclusiveness it is imperative that surrounding populations, particularly those in conditions of informal land tenure and housing, are integrated into New Town planning with respect for their livelihoods.

Of course, the issue is more complex than outright displacement of long-term inhabitants: as explained above, Malili was in fact created by recent settlers as well as developers who arrived in the past 10 years with prospects of urbanisation and new opportunities. This was greatly enhanced by the New Town plans which have recently sparked land speculation.[12] Malili's rapid growth points to the complexity of controlling informality around New Towns.

2. Diverse, flexible and mobile livelihoods and land uses are at higher risk.

In assessing the impacts of large-scale urban and peri-urban plans on land use and resource rights, a limited focus on direct displacement or expulsion of sitting land users tends to overlook important land users and livelihoods dependent on the spaces in other ways.[13] Particular groups which are often overlooked are mobile and temporarily inhabiting groups such as pastoralists, who move their herds around in search of fresh pasture land and water. As outlined above, Old Konza consists of long-term (partly Maasai) inhabitants with pastoralist and agriculture-based livelihoods. They experienced a loss of grazing land when the Konza project site was fenced. They now risk more livelihood loss due to the

12 Mwau, B. (2013) 'The planned hatches the 'unplanned'', Living the City: Urban Africa. Available at: slumurbanism.wordpress.com/2013/08/02/the-planned-hatches-the-unplanned/.

13 Van Noorloos, F., Klaufus, C., and Steel, G. (2018). 'Critical Commentary: Land in urban debates: Unpacking the grab-development dichotomy'. Urban Studies, e-pub ahead of print, DOI: 10.1177/0042098018789019.

Masterplan Konza Tech City. (Source: www.shoparc.com)

possibility of changing zoning of their lands to 'commercial' in the future, as anticipated in the development plan.

In general, people with flexible and mobile livelihoods are among those groups that tend to go unrecognised when it comes to land rights. This also includes urban farmers that use diverse 'empty' spaces in and around the city to farm or access resources. As they often lack formal recognition of this *de facto* land use, land is easily taken away by the state (notwithstanding the increasing attention to urban agriculture in policy debates). In various instances, New Town planning or initial construction has shown to affect the livelihoods of (peri-)urban farmers. For example, this was the case and/or is envisioned in la Cité du Fleuve in Kinshasa;[14] the New Town projects in Khartoum;[15] and Beira in Mozambique.[16] In addition, the creation of artificial islands and large-scale water infrastructure related to New Towns (e.g. the sea wall of Lagos[17] near Eko Atlantic new city) can put fishers' livelihoods at risk.[18]

3. The mere planning of the project can already have an impact. The case of Konza Techno City, as well as many other New Towns, shows us that even if no real construction has happened yet, the mere existence of a New Town plan or idea already creates impacts.[19] Malili has experienced large-scale population growth and great land speculation, created by the promising opportunities of new infrastructures, employment and rising land prices around the New Town. This translates spatially into 'doughnut development' around Konza Techno City, with rapid settlement of people outside the fence in Malili, while the New

14 De Boeck, F. (2011) 'Inhabiting ocular ground: Kinshasa's future in the light of Congo's spectral urban politics', Cultural Anthropology 26(2): 263-286.
15 Zoomers, A., van Noorloos, F., Otsuki, K., Steel, G. and van Westen, G. (2017) 'The rush for land in an urbanizing world - from land grabbing towards developing safe, resilient and sustainable cities and landscapes', World Development 92: 242-252.
16 Murtah Shannon, 2018, pers.comm.
17 A sea wall to protect the coastline from flooding, promoted as the 'Great Wall of Lagos'.
18 See also De Boeck (2011).
19 For a more elaborate analysis of how New Towns are often speculative projects; in some cases creating a world city image and raising expectations of profit are the mere objective (hence fulfilled by only plans without the need for actual construction) rather than a by-product, see: Steel, G., Van

Main Entrance to Konza Techno City project. (Source: D. Avianto, 2017)

Noorloos, F. and Klaufus, C. (2017) 'The urban land debate in the global South: New avenues for research', Geoforum 83: 133–141.

20 Mwau, B. (2013).

21 Ibid.

22 Datta, A. (2015) 'New urban utopias of postcolonial India: 'Entrepreneurial urbanization' in Dholera smart city, Gujarat', Dialogues in Human Geography 5(1): 3-22. Goldman, M. (2011) 'Speculative urbanism and the making of the next world city', International Journal of Urban and Regional Research 35(3): 555-581. Van Noorloos, F. and Kloosterboer, M. (2017).

Town site itself is still an empty field. Paradoxically these settlers are now facing a heightened sense of land tenure insecurity as a result of the buffer zone, but also as a result of rapid land speculation and multiple claims on one plot.[20] In addition, there is a wide gap between people's high expectations of employment and services on the one hand[21] and the very volatile and insecure nature of many New Town plans on the other. This was also clear in Old Konza and Malili villages, where people's positive and aspirational perceptions of the project have gradually made way for scepticism due to delays and political problems.

4. High-level interests and rapid change cause problems for inclusiveness.

It is clear that current African New Towns are often backed by high economic and political interests; they are spectacular city-marketing projects, and the world city image they embody is supposed to attract investment as well as grant political power. In such situations governments (often as part of a development authority) tend to fast-track legal and regulatory procedures, including those related to land acquisition and resource use, thus posing a risk to land and resource rights such as fair compensation and expropriation procedures.[22]

In Konza Techno City, the central government clearly considered the project of national interest, and side-lined the relevant county governments in the process. Public participation and informed consultation of the inhabitants has hardly taken place. The speed of developments as soon as the green light was given probably left very little

Rendering of the transportation hub of Konza Tech City. (Source: www.shoparc.com)

room for this. Nevertheless, given the delays there may still be other opportunities and ways for the public to have a real say in their future.

Conclusion

Africa's upcoming New Towns must be viewed through a number of critical lenses. Without denying the importance of other key inclusivity issues such as accessibility and suitability of housing for the poor, this paper has focused on the often forgotten fact that New Towns are inserted into real places with pre-existing activities, humans, and livelihoods which start to change and co-evolve as soon as an idea for a New Town is elaborated. Against that backdrop, we have noted that the peri-urban spaces where many New Towns are planned, are hardly ever empty, and insertion of new structures in such peri-urban locations brings its own risk of displacement and loss of rights.

While the specific developments around Africa's individually planned New Towns remain idiosyncratic and unique, preliminary findings suggest that we should pay attention to four dynamics: first, the planning of buffer zones as a very exclusionary way of dealing with informal settlement around the projects; second, the often indirect and elusive types of displacement that can happen when the spaces are inhabited by mobile, temporary populations; third, the dynamics of change that are introduced from the initial announcement of a New Town project onwards, thus generating its own process of change independent of the realisation of the project; and fourth, the high-level interests behind the New Towns, which increase the risk of fast-tracking procedures and loss of rights.

Gareth Edwards, Associate Urban Designer and Planner at SOM

Skidmore, Owings & Merrill LLP (SOM) is one of the largest and most influential architecture, interior design, engineering, and urban planning firms in the world. Founded in 1936, the firm has long been active in the field of planning New Towns, the first of which was the well-known Oak Ridge New Town in Tennessee (1949). In recent years, SOM has been involved in the planning of King Abdullah Economic City, Saudi Arabia, the new capital of Egypt near Cairo, and numerous plans for cities in China, Indonesia, and Vietnam, among other places. In Africa, SOM has also been involved in designing four communities for Rendeavour, an international developer with a focus in Africa: Tatu City in Kenya, Jigna and Lekki in Nigeria, and Appolonia in Ghana.

Gareth Edwards is an associate urban designer and planner. Throughout his 12 years at SOM (London) he has worked on projects of a variety of scales and programmes worldwide, including New Town developments in Africa such as Tatu City in Kenya. Tatu City is a New Town designed for 150,000 (future) inhabitants. It is located 24 km northeast of downtown Nairobi. SOM is responsible for designing Tatu City's central business district. In this interview, we discuss SOM's approach to New Town planning through the example of Tatu City.

Rachel Keeton (RK): What was SOM's role in the planning of Tatu City?
Gareth Edwards (GE): SOM's role as masterplanners at Tatu City has been to revisit an area of Tatu City called the CBD, initially designed by a local planner. It is understood that masterplanning is part of an ongoing process and at SOM we bring thinking that embraces and works with the local landscape and natural environment coupled with international best placemaking principles to create liveable communities that often challenge the status the quo or 'business as usual'.

RK: How does SOM's plan for Tatu City's CBD take into account the 80 percent of people who are part of the informal economy in Kenya?
GE: Tatu City and the CBD in particular will be completely open to the public and local businesses. There will be no gates restricting visitors, so people wishing to use the open spaces, amenities, etcetera, can do so and we hope they do as this is what makes a city real and vibrant.

RK: But if we're really talking about the informal economy, like small kiosks and boda-bodas (local motorcycle transportation), is there a place where that comes into Tatu City?
GE: At the moment we have a concept masterplan that addresses the high-level physical framework including the basic street and open space networks, land use, density distribution, and building typologies. Addressing the subject of informal economy is something that needs further development and strategic management to find the optimal 'blend'. It is not necessarily a physical design issue, but a socio-economical one requiring a strong partnership between the different parties. It's crucial to acknowledge the variety of forms of the informal economy as it makes the place 'real', and it offers street life, and animation. The trick will be finding the right balance, location and management strategies to ensure they work together with the other components of the city.
It is early days, but I think this is an important layer of the development which will be further influenced by some of these softer issues that really bring the authenticity to the city in a way that's palatable.

RK: It's complicated to try and combine privileged groups with groups that have traditionally been marginalised in a meaningful way. Let's talk about that in terms of housing in Tatu City. How does that materialise?
GE: This is a very good question. A city or town's vitality and vibrancy comes from its mix of different cultures and socio-economic groups. As masterplanners we strive to create neighbourhoods and communities within our plans that include a variety of different housing offers for different socio-economic groups. When you mix things up at a smaller scale, preconceptions can melt away and people become more integrated. The client [Rendeavour] has committed to a wide variety of affordable housing and building local public schools to improve access to education.

RK: We do see a lot of private New Towns since the 1990s becoming pockets of urban services and amenities and then encircling them you have informal communities without any infrastructure. But people from both communities move between the planned and unplanned areas, and there are social and economic exchanges happening all the time.
GE: Yes, this is evident when one drives around Nairobi.

RK: But spatially, they remain totally distinct.
GE: Yes, unfortunately this is true. This is why affordable housing and new forms of employment must be integrated within developments and New Towns. We understand that there are challenges with this, but to get past this 'us and them' mentality we must be designing towns that are inclusive for all. This is the basic premise of Tatu City overall.

RK: And is that a discussion that you have had with the client?
GE: Yes, absolutely.

RK: West of Tatu City is an informal settlement: Roturu.
GE: This has formed part of the project's contextual understanding and we are extending this contextual thinking to the north, east and south.

RK: Because right now there is a wall between them.
GE: Yes, we are against gated communities anywhere. This was formed at a different moment in time and hopefully as this city grows and the areas around become developed, it will become clear that the developments will work better if they are linked together, permeable and share the natural landscape. As a rule, we try to align streets, open spaces, land uses and development plots so that when dividing walls do eventually come down they can connect seamlessly.

RK: But your responsibility as SOM is limited in the sense that you've been contracted to work on the CBD. How do you do that without being able to influence the design of the rest of the city?
GE: This is a good question. We are now being asked to extend our remit to take on a wider strategy for the interrelation of the entire city. With every project we must understand the broader context, and if possible, try to influence its emerging design to ensure adequate access, complementary adjacencies and densities, walkable routes, and other issues. In the case of Tatu City, this means looking at the edges of the CBD to see how this higher density urban development blends and merges with some of the lower density neighbourhoods.

RK: There are potentially creative ways to integrate very low income housing in the CBD that could still be financially interesting from the macro level. Or is that a false assumption?
GE: It may be challenging to have high quality very low income housing in the CBD due to the land values in such an urban quarter. There are examples where this has been tried with high rise buildings, but in such a context as Tatu I think something akin to a 'sites and services' model could be more interesting, but it's not 100% clear where this would go.

RK: Planning for the demographic that would traditionally be forced to build in unserviced areas can work quite well and also help to control development by anticipating this kind of growth rather than reacting to it later. I've heard the term 'controlled environment' as an aspiration from a few people here at Tatu City, and 'sites and services' is one way to get ahead of unplanned growth, if you know it's going to happen anyway.
GE: The CBD is a mixed-use private endeavor and if we want positive transformative change, we need this investment which does come with its caveats. It's about creating a partnership to allow variety and a mix of typologies.

RK: Have you been to the adjacent communities?
GE: We have toured the site on numerous occasions, and have visited surrounding areas.

RK: Rendeavour has done some street lighting, and other initiatives in those areas, but some men were saying to our researchers: 'if you don't let us in to Tatu City, we'll just rob you.' And the kids in Rotoru think that Tatu City is only for the very rich, or 'if you're a maid'.
GE: It is great that you have engaged these communities as it really does offer valuable insight on how this city is currently being perceived. As masterplanners we hope that this will become a true city that has a place for everyone. We believe that one of the first steps to making this happen is to not have gates at the city's perimeter – like so many other developments here.

Affordable, Available, Accessible and Acceptable Housing in African New Towns

Alonso Ayala, Maartje van Eerd and Ellen Geurts

In this essay, we focus on the perpetual global challenge of access to adequate housing. Notwithstanding many efforts to address this challenge, access to adequate housing continues to be problematic particularly in urban areas of the Global South.[1] It is therefore critical that the development of New Towns in Africa includes access to adequate housing since existing ones have not managed to entirely overcome this challenge. The provision of adequate housing for the urban poor is often overlooked leading to informal, inadequate and poorly-located settlements forming and consolidating at the edge of New Towns.[2] The resulting informal urbanisation provides the only housing alternative for many low-paid workers who have been attracted by the economic opportunities these New Towns offer.

Expanding on the planning principles already explained for New Towns in previous chapters, we aim to introduce and illustrate four principles that elaborate specifically on the concept of housing. We call these housing principles the 'four A's' and they are: affordability, availability, accessibility and acceptability.[3] From our experience, understanding the interrelationship of these housing principles can contribute to the realization of adequate housing for all in the Global South.

Additionally, we visualise the housing market as a ladder, with steps on that ladder representing different housing options. The four housing principles are applied to check whether an adequate ladder has been developed to realise adequate housing. The application of the 'four A's' in relationship to the housing market ladder, as well as the case studies presented in this essay, provide a starting point to answer the question:

1 McKinsey Global Institute (2014) 'A blueprint for addressing the global affordable housing challenge'. McKinsey Global Institute (MGI). Available online: www.mckinsey.com/global-themes/urbanization/tackling-the-worlds-affordable-housing-challenge. See also: UN-Habitat (2016) World Cities Report 2016. Urbanization and Development – Emerging Futures. United Nations Human Settlement Programme. Available online: unhabitat.org/books/world-cities-report/

2 Croese, S., Cirolia, L. and Graham, N. (2016) 'Towards Habitat III: Confronting the disjuncture between global policy and local practice on Africa's 'challenge of slums" in Habitat International Vol. 53 pp 237-242. DOI: 10.1016/j.habitatint.2015.11.037 See also: UN-Habitat (2016) World Cities Report 2016. Urbanization and Development – Emerging Futures. United Nations Human Settlement Programme. Available online: unhabitat.org/books/world-cities-report/.

3 The concept of the 4A's has been developed by the housing experts of the Institute for Housing and Urban Development Studies (IHS) housing team based on the experience of working on affordable housing both in practice and in academics. The term 'adequate' housing in terms of housing rights is broader, however most conventional housing theory limits housing to affordability, accessibility and availability, omitting what we feel is a vital principle, namely that of acceptability.

'How can New Towns make housing accessible for all?' As we will illustrate, this is a challenge that cannot be addressed with one fixed solution; it requires careful consideration of numerous factors.

Principles of adequate housing

The United Nations Human Rights Office's definition of adequacy in housing focuses on seven elements: Legal security of tenure, availability of services, materials, facilities and infrastructure, affordability, habitability, accessibility, location and cultural adequacy.[4] Based on our collective experience of work in cities of the Global South through the Institute for Housing and Urban Development Studies (IHS) at Erasmus University Rotterdam, we have translated the elements underlying the meaning of housing adequacy into the above-mentioned 4 A's. Good urban planning principles embedded in New Town development should ensure that the four housing principles of affordability, availability, accessibility and acceptability apply to the whole housing sector in order to secure adequate housing for all. These housing principles are explained below.

Affordability of housing is widely accepted as a key challenge to overcome as housing (-related) costs are the most expensive once-off and on-going expenditures to households across the globe.[5] Affordability of housing is dependent on the relation between housing costs and household income. The affordability threshold is considered to be approximately 30 per cent of the monthly household income.[6] The type and form of income is critical as eligibility for bank loans is often conditional on secure, regular and formal income. Affordability also needs to be considered over time: very few households can afford a one-off purchase of a house. Thus, the monthly payments should be affordable, encompassing not only loan repayments (e.g., mortgage or subsidies), but also management and maintenance costs for the housing. Housing given for 'free' may thus result in long-term costs for their owners, whereas the market value of such housing may be limited.[7]

Research conducted by the McKinsey Global Institute (MGI) in 2014 shows that over 30 million urban households in the world live in substandard housing or are financially stretched by housing costs. This figure is expected to increase to 440 million urban households by 2025. A large part of these households live in slums in developing countries: some 200 million as of 2014. MGI defines affordable housing by three parameters: affordability threshold, standard unit and income threshold. However, affordability goes beyond these three parameters. It also includes dimensions of tenure and the (non-)functioning of markets and subsidies (investments, finance available, land, etc). When housing affordability is projected as a ladder, it becomes clear that most housing markets lack certain steps on the ladder making the distance too large for many households to move between steps.

Availability of housing goes beyond just making houses available. It refers to the existing or newly-built housing that is adequate for the target group,

4 Committee on Economic, Social and Cultural Rights, 'General Comment n°4 on the elements of the Right to Adequate Housing'.

5 McKinsey Global Institute (2014) Op.cit.

6 Based on a widely accepted definition the costs for adequate should not exceed more than 30% of a monthly household income. The MGI report (2014) on affordable housing also adopts the 30% benchmark for affordable housing. US government uses the 30% as an official indicator to measure affordability. Although there are many discussions on-going about this arbitrary 30% benchmark, it remains to be a widely accepted definition of defining affordability in terms of percentage of income spent on housing. Income to expenditure rations is not the only way to measure affordability. Other common forms are the residual income approach or the incremental finance option. (Smets et.al., 2014; MGI, 2014).

7 Ayala, A., Rabe, P and E. Geurts (2014) 'Best Practices for Roma Integration Regional Report on Housing Legalization, Settlement Upgrading and Social Housing for Roma in the Western Balkans'. OSCE's Office for Democratic Institutions and Human Rights (ODIHR). Available online: www.osce.org/odihr/115737?download=true.

both in terms of the locations where housing is needed and in terms of affordability. Therefore, availability is not restricted to the supply of houses in specific locations but may also include the supply of housing finance. From the housing ladder perspective, this means ensuring that sufficient and necessary steps are provided allowing for both downward and upward movement.

Accessibility to adequate housing means ensuring that access can be granted to each and every step of the ladder. In some cases, certain steps on the housing ladder are provided through 'protected' systems, allowing for instance only specific income or target groups to access housing on these steps. Examples of this include the Hukou system in China, whereby only residents with a Hukou can access housing. The Roma populations in Europe are also affected by this system as their inability to register in municipalities prevents them from accessing housing.

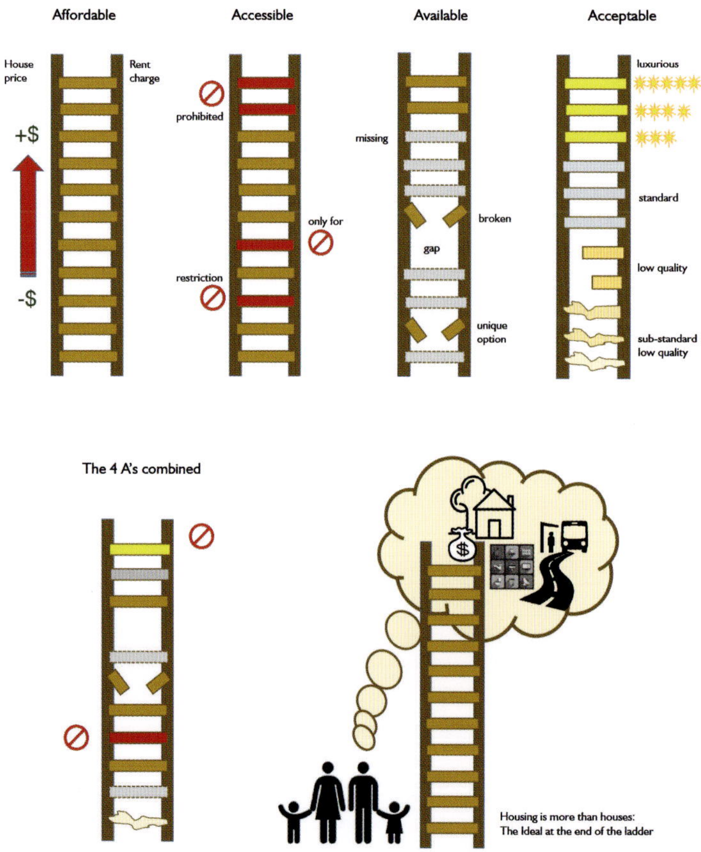

The housing ladder

The three housing principles outlined above lead primarily to broad-based and sustainable housing outcomes. However, these housing principles can be interpreted in a technocratic way and therefore we see a need to introduce a fourth principle: **Acceptability**. This principle aims at insuring the overall quality of the housing package coupled with an understanding of housing needs from a socio-demographic and cultural perspective.
A perfect equilibrium of these four housing principles that provides the golden solution does not exist. Each local housing market needs its own interconnecting ladder with accessible steps which are in turn recognised (accepted) as steps. Therefore, in the housing ladder there is a need for sufficient available steps, with adequate distance between the steps to allow for up- and downward mobility, with no barriers to access and a perception that indeed each step is of a quality that is acceptable. Where markets fail to provide this type of ladder, public interventions are needed (i.e. government policies, regulations and subsidies).

Exclusion of certain households from these steps on the ladder may lead to households resorting to informal solutions or overcrowding on lower steps of the ladder, pushing others even further down the ladder. Many cities (including New Towns) tend to explicitly prevent access to housing for lower-income groups.

Learning practices

This section reflects on a few learning practices vis-a-vis the challenge of developing 'New Towns that make housing accessible for all'. We used the term 'learning practices' rather than 'best practices' because there is much to gain from a spectrum of experiences that range from unsuccessful to successful practices. It is also noteworthy that meaningful 'best practices' regarding the adequate housing challenge in New Tows are difficult to find.

Three learning practices have been chosen to illustrate the four A housing principles.
The first one is the case of Cosmo City in Johannesburg, which, although not quite a New Town[8] does share many characteristics of New Towns. It also illustrates an example where the four A's have been relatively well-realised as supported by the South African inclusionary housing policy. The efforts that have been made can be seen as lessons for New Towns in the development of diverse and inclusive housing approaches.
Secondly, we present the case of Abuja, which was developed as a New Town in Nigeria. Whereas housing was part of the urban plan for Abuja, it has failed to become an inclusive city where adequate housing is accessible for all. As a result, the informal market has stepped in and the proliferation of informal settlements around Abuja is a clear outcome of this. Lastly, we refer to the transformation process of government-built housing as an illustration of how formal housing developments, which do not reflect the housing needs of beneficiaries, adapt to real needs through an incremental process where residents themselves develop and transform their housing conditions over time. Therefore, incremental development of housing is considered a viable option to achieve adequate housing over time, as it allows for the 4 housing principles to at least be met over time for a large part of the poorer households of a society. Acknowledgement of incremental housing processes upfront, and allowing explicitly for a transformation process can therefore seriously enhance housing outcomes over time.

Integrated housing development in Cosmo City, Johannesburg

Cosmo City is a mixed-use, integrated housing development of approximately 12,500 units which is located northwest of the City of Johannesburg. The area has been developed as a collaboration between the Province of Gauteng and the City of Johannesburg.[9] Until the 1990s this was predominantly an area with large farms with some small-scale informal settlements which started to expand as urbanisation proceeded

8 Cosmo City was not developed as a new city but rather as an extension to the City of Johannesburg.

9 PDG (2011) 'Urban LandMark Land Release Assessment Tool: Cosmo City Case Study Report'. July 2011. Commissioned by Urban Landmark. Available online: www.urbanlandmark.org/downloads/lram_cosmo_cs_2011.pdf.

rapidly under the democratic government. Most formal urban planning for low-income households in the Gauteng province focussed on expansion north of Tshwane, south of Johannesburg, and east of Ekurhuleni; pushing low-income households to the boundaries of the province. The decision to develop Cosmo City as an integrated housing development between Tshwane and Johannesburg and in close proximity to some of the wealthiest neighbourhoods of Johannesburg was a bold statement by the Province and the City to realise an inclusionary housing policy. Cosmo City has subsequently been promoted as the best-located affordable housing in the northwest part of Johannesburg by the City of Johannesburg.

Cosmo City is characterised by proximity to jobs, industries, existing transport routes, and urban services. Cosmo City provides us with an example of an integrated housing development where both public and private sector collaborated in its realisation and it is regarded as a Public-Private Partnership (PPP) in inclusive housing development. Cosmo City includes a broad range of housing options, ranging from Reconstruction and Development Programme (RDP) housing (fully-subsidised units for households earning below 3,500 ZAR per month), to finance-linked units (government credit-linked subsidy for households earning below 15,000 ZAR per month for mortgage finance), as well as fully bonded housing, where households are expected to access mortgages without government support. In addition to home-ownership options, the project also includes institutional rental housing, which is managed by a Social Housing Institution and rented out to households earning below 7,500 ZAR per month. Being an integrated housing development, the plan for Cosmo City also includes schools, churches, clinics, crèches, parks, recreational sites, commercial and retail plots as well as an industrial park and an environmental area. Some 75,000 people are expected to live in Cosmo City, where construction has been ongoing since 2005.

Housing typologies in Cosmo City (clockwise from top left) - subsidy housing; credit-linked first phase; bonded housing; credit-linked second phase. (Source: 'Urban LandMark Land Release Assessment Tool: Cosmo City Case Study Report')

Cosmo City is an example of where government interventions in the housing market supplement the vital steps on the housing ladder that are so often lacking. Through the PPP, subsidies enable the market to make units (steps on the housing ladder) available, allow for relatively small increments between the steps ensuring that different affordability levels are met, and has also provided a broader range of options in terms of tenure by stimulating both rental, outright ownership and credit-linked home ownership. The PPP structure that was developed for this project was a unique combination based on a Land Availability Agreement that was signed between a developer and two layers of government, whereby the work was further outsourced to contractors. Government did heavily subsidise this project and although cross-subsidisation was done between the different housing outcomes, the State still made a net loss.[10]

Hlanganani Gardens rental units at Cosmo City. (Source: 'Urban LandMark Land Release Assessment Tool: Cosmo City Case Study Report')

10 PDG (2011) 'Urban LandMark Land Release Assessment Tool: Cosmo City Case Study Report'. July 2011. Commissioned by Urban Landmark. Available online: www.urbanlandmark.org/downloads/lram_cosmo_cs_2011.pdf

The South African inclusionary housing policy does acknowledge the realisation of a balanced housing ladder as a State priority. This example of Cosmo City shows that inclusive housing that is accessible for all, can only be realised when housing is regarded a public asset that requires State support. The South African context is however also quite specific as the level of income inequality is amongst the highest in the world.[11] Secondly, South African housing developments in general continue to separate households based on race and class. Although the first aspect is certainly changing in the democratic South Africa, segregation across classes remains prevalent.[12] In many urban areas, the costs for land are by far the single largest costs to realise (affordable) housing; by developing a large-scale project such as Cosmo City whereby the State takes control over the land, the costs could be significantly reduced and cross-subsidies could be achieved. The success of Cosmo City was therefore wholly dependent on the land model chosen – whereby Government remained in charge.[13]

New Towns are not for the poor: forced evictions in Abuja, Nigeria

The development of the New Town Abuja started with the establishment of the Federal Capital Development Authority in 1976. The official transfer of the Federal Capital of Nigeria from Lagos to Abuja took place in 1991. In that year, the population of the city was put at 378,671[14], but since 1991 the city has continued to grow enormously due to a massive influx of people in search of work and opportunities. While unofficial estimates of the total population, including the informal settlements, vary from 3 to 7 million, the official figure according to the National Population Commission's Report of 2006 (latest census) is 1.4 million with a growth rate of 9.3%.

Abuja consists of the Federal Capital City (FCC) at the centre, surrounded by the Federal Capital Territory (FCT). The Abuja Master Plan was prepared in 1979 on the philosophy of equal access and equal citizenship. From its initial conception, the Federal Government adopted a policy of moving out all the original inhabitants of the FCC and to resettle them outside the territory so that the problem of an 'indigenous' local population claiming to be original owners of parts of the territory would not arise. As there were many more villages in the territory of Abuja than had originally been foreseen, it turned out to be too expensive for the Government to resettle everyone. Therefore, it was decided that others would be resettled when development would reach these villages.

The 'indigenous' villages that were not resettled have expanded over the past 30 years as 'indigenous' people allocated land or rented housing to 'non-indigenous' who moved to Abuja for employment. This included, amongst others, many government staff who moved from Lagos to Abuja but were unable to access affordable formal housing. This resulted in the formation of extensive informal, unplanned and unauthorised settlements within the area designated for the Capital City.[15]

11 OECD (2018) Income inequality. DOI: 10.1787/459aa7f1-en. See also the Atlas on page 79.

12 Onatu, G.O. (2010) 'Mixed-income housing development strategy: Perspective on Cosmo City, Johannesburg, South Africa'. International Journal of Housing Markets and Analysis. Vol. 3. Issue: 3, pp. 203-215. DOI: 10.1108/17538271011063870

13 Ibid.

14 Akor, G.K. (2010) 'Options for leverage for the urban poor in Abuja, Nigeria: mobilising support schemes for human settlement needs.' Institute for Housing and Urban Development Studies ICHUD paper, Rotterdam, Netherlands. P. 9.

15 COHRE (2006) Housing rights fact sheet Nigeria. Centre on Housing Rights and Evictions, Geneva, Switzerland.

'Myth of the Abuja Master Plan', The Centre on Housing Rights and Evictions (COHRE) and the Social and Economic Rights Action Center (SERAC), 2008

16 COHRE (2008) The Myth of the Abuja Master Plan. Nigeria, forced evictions as urban planning in Abuja; Mission Report. Social and Economic Rights Action Center, Nigeria & Centre on Housing Rights and Evictions, Geneva, Switzerland. P. 8.
17 COHRE (2008). Op. cit. P. 11.
18 COHRE (2006). Op. cit.
19 Eerd, M. van (2008) 'Access of the poor to housing, land and basic services in Abuja, Nigeria'. IHS Cordaid process mapping report.

Since 2003 the Federal Capital Development Authority (FCDA) has targeted over 49 informal settlements in Abuja for demolition, arguing that land was zoned for other purposes under the Master Plan and, in some cases, had already been allocated to private developers. The FCDA policy provides full resettlement to 'indigenous', but not to 'non-indigenous'. Because FCDA has not yet been able to complete resettlement sites for 'indigenous', it has refrained from evicting them. Evictions of 'non-indigenous' commenced as early as 2003 with the most contentious demolitions beginning late in 2005. Despite the formal recognition of the 'indigenous' in the FCDA policy document both groups remain under threat of eviction. Since 2003, there have been 500 to 800 thousand victims of forced evictions in Abuja.[16] After a lot of pressure from civil society and publicity given to the scale and harshness of the evictions and demolitions, in late 2005 FCT Minister Nasir Ahmad el-Rufai began discussions about evictions with a 'human face'.[17] Consequently, FCDA has attempted to enumerate 'non-indigenous' before demolitions and has offered those affected access to land in relocation sites that are currently under construction.[18]

Generally, when FCDA wants to evict communities, consultations with local chiefs are made, but the affected communities are minimally involved. This is normally followed by an announcement in both print and electronic media of the proposed plan. This is complemented by announcements made within the community using the public-address system. The affected communities are classified into 'indigenous' and 'non-indigenous'. After enumeration 'indigenous' are resettled while 'non-indigenous' are relocated. The 'non-indigenous' are relocated based on the owner of the building and not necessarily the tenant who is forcefully removed. However, government has stopped giving even the landlords alternative plots of land as a matter of policy. New sites generally have very poor infrastructure and services, if any at all.[19]

In 2010 'non-indigenous' were required to pay 21,000 NGN (approximately 170 USD) as a standard processing fee for land allocated to them, and 12,000 NGN as a survey fee. The 'indigenous' communities, who are officially relocated by government, do not have to pay any charges per square meter of land. They receive free prototype drawings of two or three bedroom appartments. They would further be required to build a home based on certain planning standards within two years or lose their rights to the relocation plot, although so far nobody has been penalised for the inability to develop within that period.

Site selection and design of buildings are predetermined by government officials particularly for the resettled communities. Eviction notices are given at least three months ahead, but the implementation in practice may take a year or two. This extended period creates doubt within communities scheduled for demolition and thus life may continue as before, particularly in situations where government has provided some basic infrastructure and services. Then when they are finally forced to resettle within a period of a few days they are taken by surprise, leading to enormous stress and loss of many assets.

Incremental housing or one-size-fits-all housing solutions? Transformations of government-built housing in Africa.

The main goal of a housing policy should be to meet the real needs of people.[20] When this basic premise is not clearly understood, this usually translates into the provision of a one-size-fits-all solution which is more preoccupied with producing large quantities of houses at lower cost rather than quality houses, let alone culture- and need-specific housing solutions.[21]

In many countries in Africa the provision of government-built housing within a top-down structure has resulted in the widespread practice of housing transformation. In general terms the housing transformation process is defined as the adaptive regeneration of the neighbourhood. This regeneration refers both to the dwelling unit and the neighbourhood layout provided by the housing project. The process is incremental and reflects the changes done to the house unit over time. When the incidence of such a process takes place among a considerable number of dwellings within a neighbourhood, it impacts its urban form, land-use characteristics, and site layout, thus provoking transformation beyond the dwelling. The process is bound to the changing housing needs of households as they go through various lifecycles. In principle, it is triggered by the fixed housing solution which does not reflect the housing needs of households, and completely ignores the incremental housing process that typically characterises the way low income families increase accessibility and affordability of housing.[22]

The unmet needs of the occupiers of these housing projects are addressed through a process of housing transformation with the goal of changing space requirements to create additional habitable and non-habitable space to accommodate household members better. The process also engages in changing the original lay-out of the dwelling to redistribute old and new spaces, in changing the land use (for instance, by adapting or adding space for income generation activities such as Home-Based Enterprises), and rental space. And lastly, in order to provide culturally specific changes by adding dwelling and neighbourhood attributes that reflect the needs of a specific way of living thus increasing acceptability of the housing outcome (e.g. verandas, kitchens or cooking spaces, religious and communal spaces, recreational spaces, etc.).[23]

In its analysis of the housing transformation process of government-built housing of three African countries (Ghana, Zimbabwe and Egypt), the seminal work Extending Themselves: User Initiated Transformations of Government-built Housing in Developing Countries by Graham Tipple (2000) shows that there are several contributory factors determining

20 Shlomo, A. (2000) Housing Policy Matters. Oxford University Press Inc., New York.

21 Ayala, A. (2002) Master Thesis: The Transformation Process of Socialized Housing Projects. The case of Kapayapaan Ville Housing Project in Calamba, Laguna Province, The Philippines. MSc in Regional Development Planning, University of Dortmund, Germany and University of the Philippines.

22 Ayala, A. (2002). Op. cit. And: Tipple, G. (2000) Extending Themselves: User Initiated Transformations of Government-built Housing in Developing Countries. Liverpool: Liverpool University Press. See also: Turner, J. (1976) Housing by People: Towards Autonomy in Building Environments, Ideas in progress. London: Marion Boyars.

23 Ayala, A. (2002). Op. cit., Tipple, G. (2000). Op. cit.

Graham Tipple, 'Extending Themselves: User Initiated Transformations of Government-built Housing in Developing Countries', 2000

the decisions of low income households to engage in such processes. These factors are the need for additional space in relationship to the changes of the household structure and size, which in turn are influenced by the life cycle of a family; economic reasons (e.g creation of some kind of business and rental space), home ownership, and land tenure, the constraint posed by the original design of the dwelling and the relaxed attitude of the local authorities and the community itself regarding the process, which takes place without issuing any building permit or under any regulatory framework. In his research, Alonso Ayala (2002) looks beyond the transformation process of the dwelling and explores the impact such a process has in changing the original neighbourhood layout in its built form (i.e. transformed dwellings), and land uses, from pure residential to mixed uses, commercial uses, educational facilities, health related services, religious buildings and sport venues.[24] This research and others (e.g. Aduwo et al, 2017 in Nigeria) provides a deeper understanding of what constitutes adequate housing for low income households in their particular context.[25]

Conclusion

This essay has shed light on four important housing principles that pertain to the realisation of adequate housing policies. The examples also show that the realisation of adequate housing policies is complex and requires great efforts from governments, in collaboration with the private sector. This applies to New Towns as well as other housing developments.

Access to adequate housing as a human right is at the forefront of the current housing paradigm. The enablement paradigm that dominated the past two decades has created a legacy of enabling the market to work for the poor. Experience has shown, however, that a stronger pro-poor approach is required from governments to realise that markets also work and include the poor. The allegory of the housing ladder shows that the market often fails to provide sufficient steps, adequate steps, choice and appropriate distance between steps. With the realisation of housing as a human right, a more pro-active approach needs to be taken to realise housing justice. This returns housing to its former role as a public asset, rather than an individual commodity, as was so strongly promoted under the enablement paradigm. We advocate for careful consideration of affordability, availability, accessibility and acceptability when planning New Towns as a way to ensure access to adequate housing for the poor.

24 Ayala, A. (2002) Master Thesis: The Transformation Process of Socialized Housing Projects. The case of Kapayapaan Ville Housing Project in Calamba, Laguna Province, The Philippines. MSc in Regional Development Planning. Dortmund: University of Dortmund and University of the Philippines.

25 Aduwo, Egidario and Eziyi O. Ibem (2017) 'Housing transformation in Government Constructed Residential Estates in Lagos, Nigeria'. International Journal of Humanities and Social Science Invention. Vol. 6, Issue 8, August 2017. Available online: www.ijhssi.org.

Selected Bibliography

To Build a City in Africa - Introduction

- Angelopulo, G. (2015) 2015 MasterCard African Cities Growth Index. Crosscurrents of Growth, MasterCard.
- Bafana, B. (2016) 'Africa's Cities of the Future. Proper planning key to sustainable cities', Africa Renewal. April 2016. Pp. 4-5.
- Bigon, L. (2015) French Colonial Dakar: the morphogenesis of an African regional capital. Manchester: Manchester University Press.
- Blaikie, P. (1995) 'Changing environments or changing views? A political ecology for developing countries.' Geography, 80 (3): 203-14.
- C. Marcinkowski (n.d.) 'Africa's Speculative Urban Future', urbanNEXT. Available at: https://urbannext.net/africas-speculative-urban-future/
- Curtis, M. (2016) 'Britain's New African Empire', Huffington Post. Available at: www.huffingtonpost.co.uk/mark-curtis/britain-africa-development_b_11191728.html?guccounter=1
- Ellah, N. (2013) 'Perspectives on the Architecture of Africa's Underprivileged Urban Dwellers'. In: Pieterse, E. and Simone, A. (eds.), Rogue Urbanism: Emergent African Cities. Sunnyside: Jacana Media, Ltd.
- Freund, W. (2007). The African City: A History. Cambridge: Cambridge University Press.
- Ghana National Spatial Development Framework (2015-2035), Government of Ghana, February 2015.
- Gotsch, P. (2010) 'AlphaVille-Tamboré: a NeoTown Between Planning and Self-Organisation', in: Provoost, M. (ed.) New Towns for the 21st Century. The Planned vs. the Unplanned City. Amsterdam: SUN/INTI. Pp. 58-71.
- Heine. B. (ed.), (2000), African Languages: An Introduction. Cambridge: Cambridge University Press.
- Keeton, R. (2011) Rising in the East. Contemporary New Towns in Asia. Amsterdam: SUN/INTI.
- Ligtvoet, W., et al. (2018) The Geography of Future Water Challenges. The Hague: PBL Netherlands Environmental Assessment Agency.
- Marcinkowski, C. (n.d.) 'Africa's Speculative Urban Future', urbanNEXT. Available at: https://urbannext.net/africas-speculative-urban-future/
- Melber, H. (ed.), (2016) The Rise of Africa's Middle Class. Myths, Realities and Critical Engagements. London: Zed Books.
- Murray, M. (2015) 'City Doubles': Re-Urbanism in Africa. In: Miraftab, F., Wilson, D., and Salo, K. (Eds.) Cities and Inequalities in a Global and Neoliberal World. New York: Routledge.
- Murray, M. (2015) 'Waterfall City (Johannesburg): Privatized Urbanism in Extremis', Environment & Planning, Vol 47(3): 503-520.
- Myers, G. (2016) Urban Environments in Africa: A Critical Analysis of Environmental Politics. Bristol: Policy Press.
- Parnell, S. and Pieterse, E. (eds.), (2014) Africa's Urban Revolution. London/New York: Zed Books.
- Pieterse, E. (2015) 'Africa's Urban Imperatives', in: Provoost, M. (ed.), Cape Town: Densification as a Cure for a Segregated City. Rotterdam: NAi010.
- Provoost, M. and Vanstiphout, W, 'Introduction', in: Keeton, R. (2011) Rising in the East. Contemporary New Towns in Asia. Amsterdam: SUN/INTI.
- Provoost, M. (ed.) (2015), Cape Town: Densification as a Cure for a Segregated City. Rotterdam: NAi010.
- Provoost, M. (2016) 'The New Urban Agenda: The Perspective of New Towns', www.newtowninstitute.org/spip.php?article1161.
- Provoost, M and Keeton, R., (forthcoming) 'New Towns in Africa' in: Peiser, R. and Forsyth, A. (eds), Towards 21st Century New Towns: Past, Present, Prospects. Philadelphia: University of Pennsylvania Press.
- Racelma, K. (2012) 'Towards African Cities without Slums', www.un.org/africarenewal/magazine/april-2012/towards-african-cities-without-slums.
- Rakodi, C. (2006) 'Relationships of power and place: the social construction of African cities', Geoforum, 37 (3): 312 – 17.
- Redvers, L. (2012) 'Angola's Chinese Built Ghost Town', BBC News. 3 July 2012. Available at: www.bbc.com/news/world-africa-18646243.
- Scott, J.C. (1998) Seeing like a State. How Certain Schemes to Improve the Human Condition Have Failed. New York: Yale University Press.
- Sheppard, E., Gidwani, V., Goldman, M., Leitner, H., Roy, A., and Maringanti, A. (2015) 'Introduction: Urban revolutions in the age of global urbanism', Urban Studies, Vol 52(11): 1947-1961.
- Roy, A. and Ong, A. (eds.) (2011) Worlding Cities: Asian Experiments and the Art of Being Global. Malden: Wiley-Blackwell.
- Silva, C.N. (ed.), (2015) Urban Planning in Sub-Saharan Africa: Colonial and Post-Colonial Planning Cultures. New York: Routledge.

- Thomas, N. and Nigam, S. (2018) 'Twentieth-Century Climate Change over Africa: Seasonal Hydroclimate Trends and Sahara Desert Expansion,' Journal of Climate, Vol 31 (19): 3349–3370
- UN-Habitat (2014) The State of African Cities 2014, Re-imagining Sustainable Urban Transitions. Nairobi: UN-Habitat.
- United Nations (2014) World Urbanization Prospects. The 2014 Revision. New York: the UN Department of Economic and Social Affairs.
- Van Blerk, H. (2018) 'Africa's Lions: Who are Africa's rising middle class?', Johannesburg: IPSOS. Available at: www.ipsos.com/sites/default/files/2018-04/african_lions.pdf.
- Van Noorloos, F. (2017) 'Africa's new cities: The contested future of urbanization', Urban Studies, Vol 55(6): 1223-1241.
- Wall, R.S., Maseland, J., Rochelle, K. and Spaliviero, M. (2018) The State of African Cities 2018. The Geography of African Investment. Nairobi: UN-Habitat and Erasmus University Rotterdam.
- Watson, V. (2013) 'African urban fantasies: dreams or nightmares?' Environment and Urbanization, Vol 26(1): 215-231.
- Worldbank (2015) Stocktaking of the Housing Sector in Sub-Saharan Africa. Challenges and Opportunities.

Debunking Myths about African Urbanisation

- AfDB (2010), The Bank Group's Urban Development Strategy: Transforming Africa's Cities and Towns into Engines of Economic Growth and Social Development. Tunis: African Development Bank.
- AUC/OECD (2018) Africa's Development Dynamics 2018: Growth, Jobs and Inequalities. Paris: OECD Publishing.
- Centre for Affordable Housing Finance in Africa (2017) Housing Finance in Africa. A review of some of Africa's housing finance markets. Yearbook 2017. Johannesburg: CAHF.
- Kharas, H. (2017) The Unprecedented Expansion of the Global Middle Class. An Update. Global Economy & Development Working Paper, No. 100. Washington DC: Brookings Institute.
- OECD, AfDB and UNDP (2016) African Economic Outlook 2016. Sustainable Cities and Structural Transformation. Paris: OECD.
- Parnell, S., Pieterse, E. and Haysom, G. (2018) 'African Dreams: locating urban infrastructure in the 2030 sustainable developmental agenda'. Area Development & Policy.
- Pieterse, E. (2018) 'The Politics of Governing African Urban Spaces'. In: Ammann, C. and Förster, T. (eds.) African Cities and the Development Conundrum. International Development Policy Series, No. 10. Geneva: Graduate Institute Publications and Boston: Brill-Nijhoff.
- Simone, A. and Pieterse, E. (2017) New Urban Worlds. Inhabiting Dissonant Times. Cambridge: Polity.
- UN-Habitat (2014) State of African Cities Report 2014. Re-imagining sustainable urban transitions. Nairobi: UN-Habitat.
- UNECA [United Nations Economic Commission for Africa] (2015) Economic Report on Africa 2015: Industrializing Through Trade. Addis Ababa: UNECA.
- Van Blerk, H. (2018) 'African Lions. Who are Africa's rising middle class?' Ipsos Views 15.
- Vidal, J. (2018) 'The 100 million city: Is 21st century urbanisation out of control?' The Guardian, March 19.

Tema, Ghana

- Acquah, W.K. (2001) Urban Development Problems of Ghana. The Case of Tema. Lund: Lund University.
- Amarteifio, G.W., Butcher, D.A.P., and Whitham, D. (1966) Tema Manhean, a Study of Resettlement. Accra: Ghana Universities Press.
- Asabere, P. (2007) 'The Demise of Rent-controlled Public Housing Programmes of Ghana: The Story of the Tema Development Corporation'. Urban Studies, No 44.
- Auria, V. d' (2010) 'From Tropical Transitions to Ekistic Experimentation: Doxiadis Associates in Tema, Ghana'. Positions No 1.
- Doxiadis, C.A. (1968) Ekistics. An Introduction to the Science of Human Settlements. London: Hutchinson.
- Ghana National Spatial Development Framework (2015-2035), (2015) Accra: Ministry of Land and Natural Resources, Ministry of Environment, Science, Technology and Innovation, Town and Country Planning Department, National Development Planning Commission.
- Gill, M.S., (2005) Immortal Heroes of the World. New Delhi: Sarup Book Publishers.
- Harris, R. (1988) 'Silence of the Experts, Aided Self-help Housing 1939-1954'. Habitat International 22(2): 165-189.
- Kirchherr, E.C. (1968) 'Tema 1951-1962: The Evolution of a Planned City in West Africa'. Urban Studies 5(2): 207-217.
- Lyssens, M. (2011-2012) Dwelling Transformations in Community 4, Tema, Ghana, Master thesis KU Leuven.
- Ministry of Local Government and Rural Government (2012) National Urban Policy Framework. Accra: Ministry of Local Government and Rural Government.

- 'Toward an African Transport Plan' (1964) *DA Monthly Bulletin* No 63. February 1964.
- Vallin, H. (1966) 'Nkrumah's Downfall'. *International Socialist Review* 27 (3): 115-120.

Mitchell's Plain: The Translation of a British Urban Planning Model to South Africa's Apartheid New Town

- Behrends, A., Park, S.J. and Rottenburg, R. (2014) 'Travelling models: Introducing an analytical concept to globalisation studies'. In: Behrends, A., Park, S.J. and Rottenburg, R. (eds.), *Travelling models in African conflict management: translating technologies of social ordering*, Leiden and Boston: Brill.
- Brand, J. (1979) 'Building a New Town'. Cape Town: City Engineer's Department.
- City Engineer's Department (1985) 'The history of Mitchells Plain'. Cape Town: City Engineer's Department.
- Deacon, J. (1979) 'Mitchells Plain: An investment in the people'. (Brochure) Pretoria: Information Service of South Africa.
- DeBruin, S. (n.d.), 'People barrier'. The Plainsman, Cape Town.
- Dewar, D., Watson V., Bassios, A., Dewar, N. (1990) 'The structure and form of metropolitan Cape Town: Its origins, influences and performance'. *Urban Problems Research Unit Working Paper* 45. Cape Town: University of Cape Town.
- Dillane, J. B. (1966). 'Reports from general practice number 4: General practice in the new towns of Britain'. *The Journal of the College of General Practitioners* 11(4).
- Jacobs, J. M. (2012) 'Urban geographies I: Still thinking cities relationally'. *Progress in Human Geography* 36(3): 412-422.
- King, A. D. (1980) 'Exporting planning: the colonial and neo-colonial experience'. In Cherry, G. E. (ed.), *Shaping an Urban World 2*. London: Mansell.
- Leao Rego, R. (2010) 'Travelling ideas: British Town & Country Planning Models and the transformation of Brazilian tropical hinterlands'. Paper presented to the 14th IPHS Conference, 12-15 July, Istanbul, Turkey.
- Levine, B. M (1983) 'British New Town Planning: A Wave of the Future or a Ripple across the Atlantic'. *Journal of Legislation* 10(1): Article 12.
- Mabin, D. (1977) 'The development of Mitchells Plain'. Paper presented at the Conference of Institute of Housing Management, September 1977, Durban.
- Madell, C. (2016) 'A historical account of the impact of land use planning in the western cape – elusive spatial and economic integration and inclusiveness'. In: Western Cape Government (ed.) *Land use planning law reform in the western cape: the road to transformation*. Cape Town: Western Cape Government.
- Merlin, P. (1980) 'The new town movement in Europe'. *The Annals of the American Academy of Political and Social Science* 451(1): 76-85.
- Monstadt, J. and Schramm, S. (2017) 'Toward the Networked City? Translating Technological Ideals and Planning Models in Water and Sanitation Systems in Dar es Salaam'. *International Journal of Urban and Regional Research* 41(1): 104-125.
- Morris, S.S. (1972) 'Good Hope: a first report on the development of Mitchell's Plain'. Cape Town: City Engineer's Department.
- Peck, J. and Theodore, N. (2010) 'Mobilizing policy: Models, methods, and mutations'. *Geoforum* 41(2): 169-174.
- Provoost, M. (2014) 'Exporting New Towns. The Welfare City in Africa'. In: Swenarton, M., Avermaete, T. and van den Heuvel, D. (eds.), *Architecture and the Welfare State*. London: Routledge.
- Provoost, M. (2015) 'The Openheid State. From closed to open society in Cape Town'. In: M. Provoost (ed.), *Cape Town Densification as a cure for a segregated city*. Rotterdam: Nai010.
- Robinson, J. (2006) *Ordinary cities: between modernity and development*. London: Routledge.
- Rottenburg, R. (2009) *Far-fetched facts: a parable of development aid*. Cambridge: MIT Press.
- Spuy van de, A. (1977) 'Mitchells Plain Town Centre Outline Repost'. Cape Town: City Engineer's Department.
- Ward, S. (2010) 'Transnational Planners in a Postcolonial World'. In: Healey, P. and R. Upton (eds.) (2010) *Crossing borders: international exchange and planning practices*. London and New York: Routledge.
- Town and Country Planning Association (2014) 'New Towns and Garden Cities – Lessons for Tomorrow'. *Stage I: An Introduction to the UK's New Towns and Garden Cities*. London: TCPA.
- Watson, V. (1993) 'Regeneration of the Apartheid city'. Paper presented to the Vision of Cape Town conference, 7-8 October, Cape Town.

10th of Ramadan, Egypt

- Abdel-Kader, N. and Ettouney, S. (September 2013) Rethinking New Communities Development – with Reference to Egypt's 40 Years Experience. Paper presented at the 39th World Congress on Housing Science, Milan.
- Arab Republic of Egypt Ministry of Housing and Reconstruction (September 1974) Terms of Reference for the Industrial Area and Associated City Master Plan Study. Cairo: Arab Republic of Egypt Ministry of Housing and Reconstruction.
- Atimtay, A. and Sikdar, S., Eds. (2011) Security of Industrial Water Supply and Management. Dordrecht: Springer.
- COPA and SWECO (1977) Tenth of Ramadan, New Industrial City Conceptual Planning Report.
- Egyptian Ministry of Water Resources and Irrigation (February 2014) Water Scarcity in Egypt. Cairo.
- El-Sawy, K., et al (2016) 'Detection of Land Use and Land Cover Changes for New Cairo Area, Using Remote Sensing and GIS', International Journal of Science and Research (IJSR), Vol 5 (2).
- El-Sayed, M.H., et. al. (2012) 'Hydro-geochemistry and Pollution Problems in 10th of Ramadan City, East El-Delta,Egypt'. In: Journal of Applied Sciences Research, 8(4). Pp. 1959 – 1972.
- Florin, Bénédicte. 'Urban Policies in Cairo: From Speeches on New Cities to the Adjustment Practices of Ordinary City Dwellers'. In: Abouhani, A. and Simone, A. (2005) Urban Africa: Changing Contours of Survival in the City. Dakar: Codesria Books.
- Golia, M. (2004) Cairo: City of Sand. London: Reaktion Books.
- GOPP (2017) Issues and Challenges for a New Urban Agenda. Cairo: GOPP.
- Möller, J. (1998) 'Working and living in 10th of Ramadan City: The Perspective of Workers in Small Industries'. In: Travailleurs et industrie à l'heure des réformes économiques. No. 33: 67-80.
- Plumer, B. (2013) 'The US gives Egypt $1.5 billion a year in aid. Here's what it does.' In: The Washington Post, 9 July 2013.
- Sadat, A. (April 1974) The October Working Paper. Cairo: Ministry of Information, State Information Service.
- Sims, D. (2012) Understanding Cairo: The Logic of a City Out of Control. Cairo: The American University in Cairo Press.
- Sims, D. (2014) Egypt's Desert Dreams: Development or Disaster? Cairo: The American University in Cairo Press.
- Soliman, A. M. (2014) 'Pathways Towards Self-Help Housing Innovations in Egypt'. In: Bredenoord, Jan; Van Lindert, Paul and Smets, Peer, Eds. Affordable Housing in the Urban Global South: Seeking Sustainable Solutions. New York: Routledge.
- Stewart, D. (1996). 'Cities in the Desert: The Egyptian New-Town Program'. Annals of the Association of American Geographers, 86(3): 459-480.
- Stroud, S. and Ibrahim, B. (2011) Youth Activism and Public Space in Egypt. Cairo: The American University in Cairo.
- SWECO (1982) Growth Plan 1982 Draft Final Report.
- Volait, M. (September 2006) 'Mediating and domesticating modernity in Egypt: uncovering some forgotten pages'. in: Docomomo Journal, special issue Modern architecture in the Middle East, #35: 30-35.
- World Food Programme (May 2013) 'The Status of Poverty and Food Security in Egypt: Analysis and Policy Recommendations' (preliminary report).

Sheikh Zayed City, Egypt

- Abouelmagd, D., Kesteloot, C., and Corijn, E. (2013) 'Housing Projects for Low-income Groups and Modes of Economic Integration: A Comparative Study in Greater Cairo.' Tijdschrift voor Economische en Sociale Geografie 104(4):
- Al-Aees, S. (2016) 'Social housing unit owners demonstrate in front of NUCA for once again failing to respond to demands'. Daily News Egypt. 24 October 2016.
- Almatarneh, R.T. (2013), 'Choices and changes in the housing market and community preferences: Reasons for the emergence of gated communities in Egypt: A case study of the Greater Cairo Region, Egypt'. Ain Shams Engineering Journal 4(3): 563-583.
- Egypt Today staff. (2018) 'Egypt to construct 20 fourth-generation New Towns'. Egypt Today. 10 September 2018.
- El-Laithy, H., Lokshin, M., and Banjeri, A. (2003) 'Poverty and Economic Growth in Egypt: 1995-2000'. World Bank Policy Research Working Paper 3068.
- El-Sayed, A., Arvidsson, R. and Kulhánek, O. (1998) 'The 1992 Cairo earthquake: A case study of a small destructive event'. Journal of Seismology 2(4): 293-302.
- Fahmi, W., and Sutton, K. (2008) 'Greater Cairo's housing crisis: Contested spaces from inner city areas to new communities'. Cities 25 (5): 277-297.
- Fahmi, W.S. (2008) 'The Right to the City: Stakeholder Perspectives of Greater Cairo Metropolitan Communities'. In: Jenks, M., Kozak, D., and Takkanon, P., World Cities and Urban Form: Fragmented, Polycentric, Sustainable? Abingdon: Routledge.
- Hegazym I.R., and Moustafa, W.S. (2013) 'Toward revitalization of New Towns in Egypt case study: Sixth of October. International Journal of Sustainable Built Environment 2 (1): 10 – 18.

- Ibrahim, F.N. and Ibrahim, B. (2003) Egypt: An Economic Geography. New York: I.B. Tauris.
- Beinin, J. (2009) 'Workers' Protest in Egypt: Neo-liberalism and Class Struggle in 21st Century'. Social Movement Studies 8(4): 449-454.
- Joya, A. (2017) 'Neoliberalism, the State and Economic Policy Outcomes in the Post-Arab Uprisings: The Case of Egypt'. Mediterranean Politics 22(3): 339-361.
- Kuppinger, P. (2004) 'Exclusive Greenery: new gated communities in Cairo.' City & Society 16(2): 35-61.
- Sabea, H. (2014). 'Still Waiting: Labor, Revolution, and the Struggle for Social Justice in Egypt'. International Labor and Working-Class History. 86: 178-182.
- Shawkat, Y. (2014) 'Mubarak's Promise. Social justice and the National Housing Programme: affordable homes or political gain?', Égypte/Monde arabe, Troisième série: Ville et révolution en Égypte: 203-233.
- The World Bank (2008) 'Arab Republic of Egypt Urban Sector Update'. Washington DC: The World Bank.
- Wahba, S. (2007) 'Arab Republic of Egypt: Analysis of Housing Supply Mechanisms, Final Note'. Report Number: 41180.

Kilamba, Angola

- African Planning Association and UN-Habitat (2013) The State of Planning in Africa: An Overview. Nairobi: UN-Habitat.
- AFDB/OECD (2008) African Economic Outlook 2007/2008. Paris: OECD Publishing.
- Buire, C. (2014) 'The Dream and the Ordinary: An Ethnographic Investigation of Suburbanization in Luanda'. African Studies Vol 73, Iss 2. Pp. 290-312.
- Cain, A. (2010) 'Research and practice as advocacy tools to infuence Angola's land policies'. In: Environment & Urbanization Vol 22(2): 505–522.
- Cain, A. (2013) 'Luanda's Post-War Land Markets: Reducing Poverty by Promoting Inclusion'. In: Urban Forum 24:11–31.
- Cain, A. (2014) 'African urban fantasies: past lessons and emerging realities'. In: Environment & Urbanization. International Institute for Environment and Development (IIED). I Vol 26(1): 1–7.
- Cain, A. (2015) Climate Change and Land Markets in Coastal Cities of Angola. Washington DC: The World Bank.
- Congress Internationaux d'Architecture moderne (CIAM), La Charte d'Athenes or The Athens Charter, 1933. Trans J. Tyrwhitt. Paris: The Library of the Graduate School of Design, Harvard University, 1946.
- Croese, S. (2012) 'One Million Houses? Chinese Engagement in Angola's National Reconstruction'. In: Power, M. and Alves, A.C. (Eds.) China & Angola, a Marriage of Convenience? Cape Town: Pambazuka Press.
- Croese, S. (2017) 'State-led Housing Delivery as an Instrument of Developmental Patrimonlialism: The Case of Post-war Angola'. African Affairs Vol 116, Iss 462. Pp. 80-100.
- Curien, R. (2014) 'Chinese Urban Planning', China Perspectives No. 2014/3.
- Da Rosa, K. (2011) 'Fazer da cidade de Luanda uma das mais belas do mundo'. Sonangol Noticias 24:24–27.
- Direccao dos Servicos de Estatistica (1971) Populacao de Angola. Recenseada em 1970, segundo os distritos e os concelhos ou circunscricoes: Apuramento provisorio. Luanda: Direccao dos Servicos de Estatistica.
- Duanfang Lu (2006) Remaking Chinese Urban Form: Modernity, Scarcity and Space, 1949 – 2005. New York: Routledge.
- Eric Ross, 'The Grid Plan in the History of Senegalese Urban Design', in: Carlos Nunes Silva, Ed. Urban Planning in Sub-Saharan Africa: Colonial and Post-Colonial Planning Cultures. New York: Routledge, 2015.
- INE (2016). Censo 2014: Recenseamento Geral da População e Habitação: Resultados Definitivos. Luanda: Instituto Nacional de Estatística.
- INE (2010) Inquerito Integrado sobre o Bem Estar da Populacao 2008-2009: Principais Resultados Definitivos. Luanda: Instituto Nacional de Estatística.
- Lacina, B. and Gleditsch, N.P. (2005) 'Monitoring trends in global combat: A new dataset of battle deaths'. European Journal of Population 21(2–3): 145–166.
- Miller, J.C. (1988) Way of Death: Merchant Capitalism and the Angolan Slave Trade, 1730-1830. Madison: University of Wisconsin Press.
- Salinger, J., Sivakumar, M.V.K., and Motha, R.P. (Eds) (2005) Increasing Climate Variability and Change: Reducing the Vulnerability of Agriculture and Forestry. Dordrecht: Springer Netherlands.
- Silva, C.N. (Ed.), Urban Planning in Sub-Saharan Africa: Colonial and Post-Colonial Planning Cultures. New York: Routledge, 2015.
- Steenkamp, A.C. (2008) Space, power and the body - the civil and uncivil as represented in the Voortrekker Monument and the Native Township Model. Delft: TU Delft.
- The Economist (1975) 'Flight from Angola'. The Economist: 16 August 1975.
- Viegas, S.L. (2012) 'Urbanization in Luanda: Geopolitical Framework. A socio-territorial analysis'. Sao Paulo: 15th International Planning History Society Conference.

- Wright, D.A., Sandsbraten, K., and Osvoll, O. (2010) 'Assessing Renewable Water Resources and Water Use in Angola'. In: Beheim, E. (Ed) Integrated Watershed Management: Perspectives and Problems. Dordrecht: Springer Netherlands.

BuraNEST, Ethiopia

- Bewket, W. and Conway, D. (2007) 'A note on the temporal and spatial variability of rainfall in the drought-prone Amhara region of Ethiopia'. International Journal of Climatology 27: 1467–1477.
- Gardner, T. '"Addis has run out of space": Ethiopia's radical redesign'. The Guardian. 4 December 2017.
- Hunnes D.E. (2012) 'Understanding Rural-to-Urban Migration in Ethiopia: Driving Factors, Analytical Frameworks, and Recommendations'. Journal of Global Health Perspectives. Edition 1.
- Oswald, F. (2012) 'NESTOWN: New Ethiopian Sustainable Town; Notes on Urban Transformation and its Architecture in Ethiopia'. In: Cherenet, Z. and Sewnet, H., Eds. Building Ethiopia: Sustainability and Innovation in Architecture and Design. Addis Ababa: EiABC.
- Oswald, F. (2015) 'Looking Back on a Radical Idea: the BuraNEST Cooperative Rural New Town, Amhara, Ethiopia'. Architectural Digest 85(4): 114-119.
- Oswald, F., Giorgis, F. and Stahli, B. (2016) Amhara Model Town. Bern/Addis Ababa: NESTown Group.
- Sosina, B. and Stein, H. (2014) 'Are Rural Youth in Ethiopia Abandoning Agriculture?' World Development. 64: 259-272.
- Taher, M.T. and Ibrahim, A. (2014) 'Transformation of Slum and Squatter Settlements: A Way of Sustainable Living in Context of twenty-first Century Cities'. American Journal of Civil Engineering and Architecture 2(2): 70-76.

New Towns, old places. Four lessons from Konza Tech City

- Bigon, L. (2012). A History of Urban Planning and Infectious Diseases: Colonial Senegal in the Early Twentieth Century. Urban Studies Research. Article ID: 589758.
- Cirolia, L.R. (2014) 'Escaping the Challenges of the City: A Critique of Cape Town's Proposed Satellite Town'. Urban Forum 25: 295-312.
- Datta, A. (2015) 'New urban utopias of postcolonial India: "Entrepreneurial urbanization" in Dholera smart city, Gujarat'. Dialogues in Human Geography 5(1): 3-22.
- De Boeck, F. (2011) 'Inhabiting ocular ground: Kinshasa's future in the light of Congo's spectral urban politics'. Cultural Anthropology 26(2): 263-286.
- Goldman, M. (2011) 'Speculative urbanism and the making of the next world city'. International Journal of Urban and Regional Research 35(3): 555-581.
- Grant, R. (2015) 'Sustainable African Urban Futures. Stocktaking and Critical Reflection on Proposed Urban Projects'. American Behavioral Scientist 59(3): 294-310.
- Johari, A. (2015) 'Kenya's Konza Techno City: Utopian Vision Meets Social Reality', Independent Study Project (ISP) Collection. Paper 2024.
- Moser, S. (2015) 'New cities: Old wine in new bottles?' Dialogues in Human Geography 5(1): 31-35.
- Murray, M.J. (2015) 'Waterfall City (Johannesburg): Privatized Urbanism in Extremis'. Environment & Planning 47(3): 503-520.
- Mwau, B. (2013) 'The planned hatches the 'unplanned''. Living the City: Urban Africa.
- Roy, A. (2005) 'Urban Informality: Toward an Epistemology of Planning'. Journal of the American Planning Association 71(2): 147-158.
- Steel, G., van Noorloos, F., and Klaufus, C. (2017) 'The urban land debate in the global South: New avenues for research'. Geoforum 83: 133–141.
- Van Noorloos, F., and Kloosterboer, M. (2018) 'Africa's new cities: The contested future of urbanisation'. Urban Studies 55(6): 1223-1241.
- Van Noorloos, F., Klaufus, C. and Steel, G. (2018). 'Critical Commentary: Land in urban debates: Unpacking the grab-development dichotomy'. Urban Studies, e-pub ahead of print, doi 10.1177/0042098018789019.
- Van Noorloos, F., Avianto, D. & Opiyo, R. (2019, forthcoming) New master-planned cities and local land rights: the case of Konza Techno City, Kenya. Built Environment, accepted.
- Wapenaar, M. (2015) 'Formal Planning & Informal Settlement. The case of Konza Technology City'. MSc thesis. Amsterdam: Universiteit van Amsterdam.
- Watson, V. (2013) 'African urban fantasies: dreams or nightmares?' Environment and Urbanization 26(1): 215-231.
- Zoomers, A., van Noorloos, F., Otsuki, K., Steel, G., and van Westen, G. (2017) 'The rush for land in an urbanizing world - from land grabbing towards developing safe, resilient and sustainable cities and landscapes'. World Development 92: 242-252.

Affordable, Available, Accessible and Acceptable Housing in African New Towns

- Aduwo, Egidario and Eziyi O. Ibem (2017) 'Housing Transformation in Government Constructed Residential Estates in Lagos, Nigeria'. *International Journal of Humanities and Social Science Invention* 6(8).
- Akor, G.K. (2010) 'Options for leverage for the urban poor in Abuja, Nigeria: Mobilising support schemes for human settlement needs'. *Institute for Housing and Urban Development Studies ICHUD paper*. Rotterdam: IHS.
- Ayala, A. (2002) 'Master Thesis: The Transformation Process of Socialized Housing Projects. The case of Kapayapaan Ville Housing Project in Calamba, Laguna Province, The Philippines'. MSc in Regional Development Planning. Dortmund: University of Dortmund and University of the Philippines.
- Ayala, A., Rabe, P., and Geurts, E. (2014) *Best Practices for Roma Integration Regional Report on Housing Legalization, Settlement Upgrading and Social Housing for Roma in the Western Balkans*. Warsaw: OSCE's Office for Democratic Institutions and Human Rights (ODIHR).
- Bredenoord, J., Van Lindert, P., and Smets, P. (2014) *Affordable Housing in the Urban Global South. Seeking Sustainable Solutions*. London and New York: Earthscan, Routledge.
- Chilongo, M. (2015) 'Investment theme: Access to Housing'. Bertha Centre for Social Innovation and Entrepreneurship. Cape Town: University of Cape Town.
- Committee on Economic, Social and Cultural Rights (n.d.) 'General Comment n°4 on the Elements of the Right to Adequate Housing'. UN Committee in Economic, Social and Cultural Rights.
- COHRE (2008) 'The Myth of the Abuja Master Plan'. Nigeria, forced evictions as urban planning in Abuja; Mission Report. Lagos: Social and Economic Rights Action Center, and Geneva: Centre on Housing Rights and Evictions.
- COHRE (2006) 'Housing rights fact sheet Nigeria'. Geneva: Centre on Housing Rights and Evictions.
- Croese, S., Cirolia, L., and Graham, N. (2016) 'Towards Habitat III: Confronting the disjuncture between global policy and local practice on Africa's "challenge of slums". *Habitat International* 53: 237-242.
- McKinsey Global Institute (2014) 'A blueprint for addressing the global affordable housing challenge'. McKinsey Global Institute (MGI).
- Onatu, G.O. (2010) 'Mixed-income housing development strategy: Perspective on Cosmo City, Johannesburg, South Africa'. *International Journal of Housing Markets and Analysis* 3(3): 203-215.
- PDG (2011) 'Urban LandMarkt Land Release Assessment Tool: Cosmo City Case Study Report'. July 2011. Commissioned by Urban Landmarkt.
- Salama, R. (1998) 'Understanding Public Housing Transformation in Egypt'. *Open House International* 23(1): 32-40.
- Smets, P, Bredenoord, J., and van Lindert, P. (2014) 'Chapter 1 Introduction'. In: Bredenoord, J., P. van Lindert, and Smets, P. (eds.). *Affordable Housing in the Urban Global South Seeking Sustainable Solutions*. London: Routledge. Pp: 1-14.
- Shlomo, A. (2000) *Housing Policy Matters*. New York: Oxford University Press Inc.
- Tipple, G. (2000) *Extending Themselves: User Initiated Transformations of Government-built Housing in Developing Countries*. Liverpool: Liverpool University Press.
- Turner, J. (1976) *Housing by People: Towards Autonomy in Building Environments, Ideas in Progress*. London: Marion Boyars.
- UN-Habitat (2016) *World Cities Report 2016. Urbanization and Development – Emerging Futures*. United Nations Human Settlement Programme.
- Van Eerd, M. (2008) 'Access of the poor to housing, land and basic services in Abuja, Nigeria'. Cordaid process mapping report. Rotterdam: IHS.

Contributors

Diky Avianto
Diky Avianto is an international development specialist with a background in human geography.

Alonso Ayala
Alonso Ayala is an architect and development planner specialised on the fields of regional development planning, human settlement planning and urban and housing research in emerging economies. He has worked at the Institute for Housing and Urban Development Studies (IHS) since 2008.

Zegeye Cherenet
Zegeye Cherenet Mamo is an architect and assistant professor of architecture at the Ethiopian Institute of Architecture Building Construction & City Development (EiABC).

Gareth Edwards
Gareth Edwards is an associate urban designer and planner. At SOM he has worked on projects of a variety of scales and programmes worldwide, including New Town developments in Africa such as Tatu City in Kenya.

Maartje van Eerd
Maartje van Eerd is an Assistant Professor of Urban Housing Equity and Social Justice at the Institute for Housing and Urban Development Studies (IHS).

Anne Sophie Erdl
Anne Sophie Erdl is an urban geographer interested in the mobility of urban planning models and policies.

Ellen Geurts
Ellen Geurts is a housing specialist who has worked as consultant, lecturer, trainer and researcher. She was a staff member at the Institute for Housing and Urban Development Studies (IHS) from 2007-2018.

Fasil Giorghis
Fasil Giorghis is an architect and Chair of Conservation of Urban & Architectural Heritage at the Ethiopian Institute of Architecture Building Construction & City Development (EiABC).

Rachel Keeton
Rachel Keeton is an architect and urbanist specialised in New Towns and a PhD candidate at TU Delft researching adaptive planning in African cities. She is the author of Rising in the East: Contemporary New Towns in Asia (2011).

Israel Marques
Joaquim Israel Baltazar de Oliveira Marques served as the first appointed mayor of Kilamba, Angola from 2011-2017.

Preston Mendenhall
Preston Mendenhall is the Head of Corporate Affairs for Rendeavour, currently Africa's largest urban land developer.

Femke van Noorloos
Femke van Noorloos is assistant professor of International Development Studies at Utrecht University. She is a social science researcher with a broad interest in international development.

Michelle Provoost
Michelle Provoost is an architectural historian, researcher and writer specialised in 20th Century modernist architecture and urban planning. She is founding partner of Crimson Architectural Historians and the Independent School for the City, and director of the International New Town Institute.

David Sims
Economist and urban planner David Sims has been based in Cairo since 1974. He is the author of both Understanding Cairo: The Logic of a City out of Control (2010) and Egypt's Desert Dreams: Development or Disaster? (2015).

Anteneh Tesfaye Tola
Anteneh Tesfaye Tola is an architect and academic focused on questions of social inclusivity and new methodologies.

Acknowledgements

This book represents the considerable efforts of many people. Some, like the authors, interviewers and interviewees, find their names in earlier pages. But many others have not been mentioned and deserve recognition. The fieldwork for this book was supported by an extensive UN-Habitat network, especially Laura Petrella, Rogier van den Berg, Jose Chong, Thomaz Ramalho, Bassem Fahmy, Anas Aladdin, and Abena Ntori. In Ghana, Joe Abbey and Emmanuel Adjeteh were invaluable. In Angola, we would like to thank TJ Zhai, Allan Cain, Manuel Zangui, Adriano de Silvo, António Gameiro, Ma Baowen, Israel Marques, and António Teixeira Flor for their time and expertise. In Egypt, Dr. Hany Ayad, Dr. Ebtihal Ahmed, Nazih Hallouda, Wiebe Ruitenberg, David Sims, and René Boer contributed valuable insights. In Ethiopia, we are grateful to Bizuayehu Jembere, Franz Oswald, Fasil Giorgis, Mastewal Chane, Ato Kefyalew Hailu, Ato Tsegaye Biadglign, and the residents of Bura kebele for their willingness to share the story of the BuraNEST project. INTI interns Megan Bentzin, Grazia Tona, Isabel Potworowski, and Gayatri Mujumdar worked tirelessly on the database of New Towns. Gilles Provoost meticulously drew the original set of maps for the Atlas, while Francesco D'Alessio contributed to the regional maps for case studies. We would also like to thank Han Meyer, Steffen Nijhuis, and Wouter Vanstiphout for sharing their expert opinions on earlier drafts of the Manual, and the participants of Principles Workshop at TU Delft in 2017 who collaboratively reviewed and revised the principles that inform the Manual.

Many others contributed to the contents of this book through street interviews, expert group meetings, and in countless other ways. We are grateful to you all. And finally, we would like to thank Ewout Dorman for designing the layout of this book and the Atlas, and for his unflagging patience with two editors who constantly brought new requirements to the table.

Kilamba (2008), Angola. (Photo: R. Keeton, 2016)

Sheikh Zayed (1995), Egypt. (Photo: R. Keeton, 2016)

KPLC 2100

Dandora, sites and services, Kenya. (Photo: M. Provoost, 2014)

ايرس
للسياحة

10th of Ramadan (1976), Egypt. (Photo: R. Keeton, 2016)

Tema (1960), Ghana. (Photo: M. Provoost, 2007)

Atlantis (1972), South Africa. (Photo: M. Provoost, 2014)

Tema (1960), Ghana. (Photo: M. Provoost, 2007)